On Becoming God

John D. Caputo, ***series editor***

Perspectives in
Continental
Philosophy

BEN MORGAN

On Becoming God

Late Medieval Mysticism and the Modern Western Self

Fordham University Press
New York ▪ 2013

Fordham University Press also publishes its books in a variety of electronic formats. Some content that appears in print may not be available in electronic books.

Library of Congress Cataloging-in-Publication Data

Morgan, Ben.
On becoming God : late medieval mysticism and the modern Western self / Ben Morgan. — 1st ed.
p. cm.
Includes bibliographical references (p.) and index.
ISBN 978-0-8232-3992-4 (cloth : alk. paper)
1. Self (Philosophy)—History. 2. Mysticism—History—Middle Ages, 600–1500. 3. Self. 4. Psychoanalysis and philosophy. I. Title.
BD450.M598 2013
126.09—dc23

2012019759

Printed in the United States of America

15 14 13 5 4 3 2 1

First edition

for Katja

Contents

Acknowledgments

The initial idea and the first draft of this book was conceived, researched, and written up in collaboration with Katja Lehmann, who continued to comment on and guide its subsequent incarnations. The book in its final form is dedicated to her, without whom the whole project would not have been possible. The writing-up and revising process has been enabled by the generous support of a number of institutions. The DAAD funded a very productive research visit to the Sonderforschungsbereich Literatur und Anthropologie in Konstanz in 1999, which greatly assisted the initial orientation of the project. Gabriele Rahaman of the Leo Baeck Institute in London assisted me in tracking down a copy of Bertha Pappenheim's *In der Trödelbude*. The completion of the first draft was made possible by a grant from the AHRB. I am also grateful to the Master and Fellows of Emmanuel College, Cambridge, and the Provost and Fellows of Worcester College, Oxford, for their support of my leaves of absence, as well as to the Modern and Medieval Languages Faculty in Oxford, which funded a further sabbatical. Arne Grøn, Niklaus Largier, and Willemien Otten read the manuscript in its entirety. Drafts of chapters, summaries, and proposals were read and commented on by Pamela Sue Anderson, Peter and Christa Bürger, Claire Carlisle, Terence Cave, Georgia Christinidis, Michael Eskin, Jeffrey Hamburger, Tom Kuhn, Nigel Palmer, Alex Rehding, Ritchie Robertson, Ulinka Rublack, Manfred Weinberg, Tim Whitmarsh, and Charlotte Woodford as well as by various anonymous reviewers. I am grateful to all of them for their criticisms and suggestions. Finally, I would like to thank the people at Fordham University Press who helped the book through the final stages: in particular Nicholas Frankovich for his careful copy editing; and, last but not least, Helen Tartar for backing the book.

Earlier versions of material included in the book has been published as "Developing the Modern Concept of the Self: The Trial of Meister Eckhart," *Telos*, no. 116 (Summer 1999), 56–80; and "The Spiritual Autobiographies of Visionary Nuns and Their Dominican Confessors in Early Fourteenth-Century Germany," in *Autobiography by Women in German*, ed. Mererid Puw Davies, Beth Linklater, and Gisela Shaw (Bern: Peter Lang, 2000), 35–51. The material has been substantially modified since its first publication. Thanks are also due to the MHRA and Maney Publishing for permission to reprint a revised version of material originally published as "Abandoning Selfhood with Medieval Mystics," in *Pre-Histories and Afterlives: Studies in Critical Method*, ed. Anna Holland and Richard Scholar (London: Legenda, 2009), 29–44.

We commonly do not remember that it is, after all, always the first person who is speaking.

—Henry D. Thoreau,
***Walden* (1854)**

Introduction

A text that has become known as the *Sister Catherine* treatise, written in Strasbourg in the first part of the fourteenth century, tells of a woman who, toward the end of a journey that has been both spiritual and physical, awakens from a meditative trance to declare that she has "become God."[1] To a reader in the twenty-first century, a woman becoming God in fourteenth-century Strasbourg might appear to be little more than an intellectual curiosity, and this skeptical attitude is not likely to be altered by a closer inspection of the text in which the narrative appears, for it becomes clear that the status of the woman and her declaration is hard to determine. She is called Catherine because one manuscript introduces the treatise with the heading "This is Sister Catherine, Meister Eckhart's daughter from Strasbourg."[2] But we don't know if such a woman existed, or whether the text was not instead written as a mystical manual: pedagogic inspiration rather than the report of something that actually happened.[3] In other words, the text might not be about a real person or report a real experience. Despite these difficulties, the text presents a problem for the modern reader that neither skepticism nor philological caution can completely solve. If we assume it was written in good faith (and we have no reason to assume that it wasn't), then it is the document of a culture in which people related to certain experiences and aspirations using the idea of "becoming God." But what would that mean?

This book offers one possible interpretation. But in order to write it, I have had to revise the preconceptions, both about personal identity and about the usefulness of a religious vocabulary, with which, as someone who understood himself in a commonsense way as a secular individual, I first approached the subject. The shape of the book reflects the labor of revision. A good deal of the argument takes the form either of clearing the ground to engage with the texts that emerged from the self-divinizing culture of the early fourteenth century or, having done so, of thinking through the implications for writing cultural history. There were in particular three changes of viewpoint, which it is difficult to rank or prioritize, but which transformed my everyday assumptions about selfhood, suggesting a different way of describing what we are doing when we cultivate our identity. The first was the acknowledgment that—*pace* a good deal of the philosophical tradition that includes Descartes, Rousseau, and Fichte but also Levinas—we're not alone. The human animal is born dependent. So individuals who have reached the stage of reflecting on their own personal identity will have been cared for and nurtured as a child and will have developed their particular sense of who they are only against the background of an enabling coexistence. To use the phenomenological vocabulary of the sociologist Alfred Schütz: "As long as man is born of woman, intersubjectivity and the we-relationship will be the foundation of all other categories of human existence. The possibility of reflection or self, discovery of the ego, capacity for performing any epochē [i.e., the ability to exchange one's normal views of things for a defamiliarized one], and the possibility of all communication and of establishing a communicative surrounding world as well, are founded on the primal experience of the we-relationship."[4] This suggests that the sense of individual identity we eventually develop should be viewed as an alteration of an initial state of being together not as the thing that comes first; the *cogito* is not a starting point. In the course of the argument, it should become clear that the modern, Cartesian version of individual identity is less a point of origin than a collection of habits that are used to regulate human togetherness—just like any other form of identity.

The second change affected the way I think about the aspects of human experience that get grouped together under the terms *sexual difference*, *sex*, and *gender*. Regardless of where we draw the dividing line between nature and culture (if we think it is useful to try to draw one at all),[5] we can't conceive of our identity as a man or a woman without thinking also of the sex that we're not. Not only are we men and women for and with other people, we're always men in relation to women (as well as to other men), and women in relation to men (as well as to other women). Simone de Beauvoir made this point when, using a Heideggerian term to which I'll return later, she insisted that "it is not as individuals that men are primarily to be defined; men and women have never opposed each other in single combat; the couple is a primordial form of *Mitsein* [Being-with]."[6] To understand the relations between the sexes as a form of *Mitsein* or necessary coexistence means describing how the woman is not only shaped by patriarchal norms but actively contributes to the couple's shared coping; that is to say, it means noticing the power she shares with the man, even though this sharing has occurred very often without the man acknowledging it. If we follow this thought up, we find that the result is a different sort of feminist undertaking from that of, say, Irigaray; one that does not define the positive aspects of female identity independently of male identity but approaches them only in and through the terms of the historical collaboration of the sexes. As Iris Marion Young has insisted, women's activities "are at least as fundamentally world-making and meaning-giving" as those of men.[7] We can learn to see their overlooked activities as part of the shared basis of human culture. Male and female identities then appear as, among other things, a changing—and changeable—symbiosis for regulating the intensities of togetherness.[8] Prudence Allen has used the term *gender complementarity* to describe philosophical theories that acknowledge the cooperation of the sexes and the position I have ended up at is related to hers, only, as we shall see, I emphasize the shared activities of men and women "doing" their genders with each other rather than explicit theoretical constructions of male and female collaboration, with a result that I see a more or less deficient symbiosis in all periods of human culture rather than the teleological model of an "evolution to higher levels of consciousness of gender identity" gradually expressed in philosophical texts favored by Allen.[9]

The third change of view was in respect of religious habits and a religious vocabulary, but it parallels the second in the way it entails accepting as our starting point what has historically generally been the case. We may not want women to be more responsible for togetherness than men, but historically they often have been and we can change the situation only if we first of all acknowledge its dimensions. Similarly, we may not want to use the word *God* when we describe who we are or what we care about, but historically, religious habits have been a way of taking the individual outside him- or herself and of giving expression to a sense of agency beyond his or her control. To acknowledge an agency beyond the control of the individual reinforces the displacement of an individualized identity already apparent in the first two changes of view (the emphasis on a coexistence that precedes individual identity and the historical incompleteness of male and female identities when viewed on their own).

At the same time, the effects of the word *God* are not only displacing, nor, to forestall possible objections to the idea of a "return" to God, should the idea be identified solely with the violence committed in "his" name. The legacy of the term is much richer, and its effect on secular culture much deeper, than a focus on a narrowly institutional version of religion allows us to see. If, as Wittgenstein suggested, the meaning of a word is its use, then *God* has too many uses to be abandoned without unnecessarily limiting the tools at our disposal for understanding ourselves and the creative unfolding of our lives. In particular, the sense of acceptance of something moving through us is hard to invoke with another term, or when it's invoked with words like *the collective unconscious*, *society*, or *fate*, we are positioned differently and don't have the same options open to us—in prayer, meditation, or other habits—for cultivating a welcoming relation to this aspect of human life. The problem of critiques of religious ideas in the tradition of Freud's *The Future of an Illusion* (1927), such as those of Richard Dawkins and Daniel Dennett, is that they disregard the wider culture underpinning a religious life and focus on a very narrow selection of religious beliefs, such as the belief in a personal God.[10]

When Dennett gives his own description of a spirituality of "letting your self go" and insists it need have nothing to do with the supernatural, I'm not sure he is right.[11] It probably depends who you're talking to. To someone like myself, who has grown up in a still residually religious culture, the religious vocabulary Dennett questions is an inseparable part of the sense of self-surrender, it's one of the tools by which I can be taken outside myself. Other ways of talking about it don't work as well, because I haven't grown up with and in them and so haven't learned the way of life that will make them effective. Nor do I think this is an arbitrary attachment. I doubt whether individuals are in a position to choose which tradition they belong to, as if a cultural tradition were something to be taken up or abandoned at will, like a new set of clothing. The tradition I have grown up in has made me what I am and has furnished me with all the tools I have for relating to others and myself. If I want to go beyond it, this will be a slow process and will be achieved only by drawing on the variety of habits and attachments that have made me what I am. I can't jump over my own shadow.

The three changes of view guide the argument of the book, but they also have implications for what the book aims to do. The central chapters investigate the milieu and sense of personal identity that formed the background to the woman in the *Sister Catherine* treatise "becoming God." They then show the sort of circumstances that produce a change from this way of life to a more self-policing, circumspect, apparently individualized and hence "modern" form of identity. The point of this prehistory of modern forms of selfhood is not to restore through self-knowledge the very sense of control or agency that it questions. Rather it draws attention to the sexed and religious habits through which we've come to our sense of our own identity. Stanley Cavell suggests that the generation of philosophers that included Heidegger and Wittgenstein realized, in their attempts to transform their relationship with a damaging philosophical tradition, that "history will not go away, except through our perfect acknowledgment of it."[12] However, it's not clear that perfect acknowledgment will make history go away either, or help us escape the habits that we have inherited and that we identify with as our "identity." Nevertheless, by acknowledging what we do when we do our identity, we might be able to arrive at a fairer and more fulfilling way of living with our inherited imperfections.

This first part of the book will show why the three changes of view seemed necessary, first by presenting the difficulties confronting Lacan, Irigaray and, more recently, the American cultural historian and philosopher of religion Amy Hollywood when they interpret mystical texts in the tradition of the *Sister Catherine* treatise. Their difficulties arise because they don't revise their assumptions about the self. This isn't an isolated fault of interpretations of mysticism, however. It reflects a wider pattern in critical theory since the Second World War. Theorists who imagine alternatives to current forms of identity very often do so in the terms of the very system they want to escape, casting this limitation as necessary and the alternative identity or experience they aspire to as consequently ineffable. Having shown the wider pattern of which the readings of mystical texts are a part, I set out my alternative assumptions in more detail. Returning to Heidegger's idea of *Mitsein* ("Being with") to see if it can be rescued from the abstraction to which it is abandoned in *Being and Time*, I draw on the work of Beauvoir and Judith Butler, both of whom explore the relationship between human coexistence and sexual difference, but I also look at recent work in neuroscience that explores the physiological equivalents of the connection Heidegger posits at an ontological level. Finally, I discuss how the changed assumptions about selfhood alter the way a history of human identity is approached. The perfect method for revising the history of modern Western forms of identity would combine Foucault's attention to the habits and social practices that give us our identities with phenomenology, which, unlike Foucault's work, does not pretend to be able to stand outside lived experience to catalogue its components but is instead always and fruitfully working from inside it. Foucault turned away from phenomenology in the 1950s,[13] so to develop a method for approaching the history of selfhood we need to learn from the successes and failures of his work, and from other recent attempts to tell the story of the modern self: those of Charles Taylor and Jerrold Seigel in the English-speaking tradition, and of Peter and Christa Bürger in the German. At the same time, it should be emphasized that my method isn't just a theoretical construction, but it developed as I let myself be surprised by the medieval texts, not forcing the mystics to tell me about a self-possessed modern agent if they were speaking about something not altogether different, though nevertheless importantly distinct.[14]

The second part of the book presents the medieval material in more detail. The vernacular sermons and treatises of the fourteenth-century Dominican Meister Eckhart exemplify a way of doing identity that is comparable to later, modern forms of identity insofar as it focuses on a personalized individual development and emphasizes habits of self-examination. At the same time, it differs from modern self-understanding in a number of ways: Individuals are not separated from God, do not take themselves to be the sole agent of their action, and do not identify with the habits of self-inspection—as a later Kantian subject might—but rather with a project of self-overcoming that parallels Sister Catherine's becoming God. Having presented this alternative model of identity and highlighted some of the ways it disappoints the expectations of a modern reader, I go on, in the next chapter, to present the behavioral context, shaped by the flourishing of the *vita apostolica* in many urban centers in the Rhineland and elsewhere in Europe, from which Eckhart's preaching emerged and to which it is a response. In this context, we can see substantial numbers of people responding to a sense of calling, but, at the same time, there also appears in many cases to have been a division of spiritual labor, with men living their calling vicariously through the experiences of a visionary woman. Having presented some of the forms this psychological and spiritual symbiosis could take, I trace a change of climate that occurred in the wake of the condemnation of Eckhart's teachings as heretical in the later 1320s. As people become more circumspect in the way they pursue their calling, so they also cultivate habits and turns of phrase for relating to themselves that strikingly prefigure modern techniques of the self. At the same time, the relations between the sexes are also remodeled by the rise of a spiritually self-monitoring form of identity.

The point of my exploration of fourteenth-century habits of identity is not to reconstruct the origins of modern selfhood, in part because returning to a putative "beginning" of the Western self is to take it too seriously as a way of life and to obscure its connections with other ways that cultures have found of doing their identity. Instead of a beginning, I return to the fourteenth century to present ways of living that are productively different from more-recent habits, and to draw attention to the sort of circumstances that transform these forms of behavior into habits more like our own. The third part of the book is then devoted to developing the sort of psychological vocabulary that is required to integrate into a modern self-understanding the view of identity that emerges from the exploration of the medieval period. To do this, I turn to the beginnings of modern psychology in the late nineteenth and early twentieth century. I start with the striking parallel between the relationship between confessor and visionary woman in the late medieval period and that between doctor and woman hysteric toward the end of the nineteenth century. The parallel emphasizes the degree to which psychoanalysis was part of a longer tradition of collective attempts to structure and come to terms with the longing for connection evident in the medieval texts. At the same time, the parallel also demonstrates the degree to which psychoanalysis, as Freud and Breuer developed it, must be seen as a strategy for controlling rather than fostering the longing to "become God." The last chapter of the book attempts to step back from Freud to gain a defamiliarizing perspective on the psychological vocabulary of the Viennese fin-de-siècle by analyzing the first exploration, in writing, of a slip of the tongue: Lucian's second-century "A Slip of the Tongue in Greeting [*Huper tou en tē prosagoreusei ptaismatos*]." Returning to Lucian allows me to set out the wider project of which Freud's attention to the "psychopathology of everyday life" is a part, and so start formulating an everyday language for talking about the habits through which our gendered identities are reproduced and our longing for connection, which in the anonymous Strasbourg text was called the desire to "become God," is acknowledged, or lived vicariously or kept at bay.

PART I

Clearing the Ground

1

Some Recent Versions of Mysticism

There are different ways of being disaffected, and many ways of remedying the situation when we are. Mysticism appeared as a remedy to intellectuals in the twentieth century who were disaffected with their identity and wanted something radically different.[1] It was rare that they wanted to be mystics—Jung perhaps comes closest to this.[2] Rather, they could use mysticism, as Derrida did, to say that they knew they wanted something but it wasn't quite that.[3] Alternatively, they could draw more positively on the mystical tradition. Heidegger borrowed his concept of detachment, or *Gelassenheit*, from German mysticism of the fourteenth century.[4] But even without such explicit borrowings, the list could be extended to include Musil, Fromm, Bataille, Bachmann, Lacan, Irigaray and many more.[5] In particular, interest has concentrated in two areas, psychoanalysis and feminism, where thinkers are concerned with transformations at the level of personal identity.[6]

Both psychoanalytic and feminist readings have been criticized for instrumentalizing mysticism and reading it as a symptom for something other than itself—in the case of psychoanalysis, as the mother, father, sex, or aggression "in disguise";[7] in the case of feminism, as a strategy for social empowerment.[8] The three thinkers I would like to look at, Lacan, Irigaray, and Amy Hollywood, all on the face of it turn to mystical texts for their own sake, as the products of a different way of living in the world. Yet, though they don't read mystical texts as symptoms, their versions of mysticism can be shown to be limited by the very unmystical assumptions about identity with which they approach the texts. This suggests that the three thinkers identify more with the disaffected identity they criticize than with the mystical texts to which they turn for an alternative.

Psychoanalysts were interested in mysticism long before Freud's famous exchange with Romain Rolland in the late 1920s about the "oceanic feeling" that Rolland believed to be the impulse behind religion.[9] The Swiss pastor and analyst Oskar Pfister published a discussion of the spiritual autobiography of the fourteenth-century Dominican nun Margaretha Ebner in 1911 treating the nun's experiences as hysterical and interpreting their supposed sweetness as a misplaced eroticism.[10] More sympathetically, in his *Psychological Types*, published in 1921, Jung praised the acuity of Meister Eckhart and in particular the way he understood God to be a dynamic psychological state rather than something outside the individual.[11] These two examples illustrate how psychoanalysis has treated mystics as either patients or allies: neurotics whose symptoms can be unpacked, or proto-analysts whose psychological insights can be translated into their analytic equivalent. In both cases, the assumptions with which the text is approached are confirmed by the encounter: Pfister finds an unacknowledged sexuality, Jung the psychological dynamics of which religion is the more or less indirect expression. In contrast, Lacan's encounter with mysticism, in "Encore," the seminar series held in 1972–73, promises to do more than just confirm his preconceptions. He turns to mysticism because it seems to challenge his ideas about the prevailing structure of social identities, offering an alternative model that could take him beyond his own theory of identity.

For Lacan, the mystical experiences of St. Teresa of Avila, St. John of the Cross, or Hadewijch show how both men and women can reject the illusions of a coherent and self-contained identity associated with the phallus and situate their identity "on the side of the not-whole."[12] They can acknowledge their essential incompleteness, stand outside an imposed coherence, and experience a profound release. Lacan's term for this release is *jouissance*, and he asks: "Doesn't this jouissance one experiences and yet knows nothing about put us on the path of ex-sistence?"[13] Mystical experience presents Lacan with a way of being outside oneself or of a dominant form of subjectivity ("ex-sistence"). This nonidentical identity is not confined by knowledge or consciousness. Indeed, the ecstatic mystic does not know, or does not need to know, whether she knows God: "The essential testimony of the mystics consists in saying that they experience it, but know nothing about it."[14] A mystic simply melts voluptuously, as, for Lacan, St. Teresa appears to melt in Bernini's famous statue.

Despite—or perhaps because of—Lacan's evident fascination with mystical release, however, this alternative form of identity remains just an image. For even though he criticizes as illusory the wholeness that he associates with the phallus, it turns out that it is an illusion that constitutes identity and is, as such, inescapable. The ecstatic mystic, whether man or woman, may situate his or her identity beyond the phallus and on the side of femininity, but he or she will always be defined in relation to phallus: "When any speaking being whatsoever situates itself under the banner 'women,' it is on the basis of the following—that it grounds itself a being not-whole in situating itself in the phallic function."[15] There is a fine line between realistically accepting a limit and glorifying it by claiming it can never change, and Lacan's treatment of phallic illusion tends toward glorification. As Malcolm Bowie has pointed out, Lacan not only reproduces the old binary opposition between a system-building, male subjectivity and woman, who is its other or negation, he also makes it immutable and imbues it with a mythical grandeur.[16] This is the effect of Lacan's slogan that woman does not exist.[17] Though his declarations about woman's essential nonexistence are ironic, he allows for no alternative to the position that he ironizes, in effect cajoling his audience into accepting it. Nevertheless, he occasionally seems to undermine this position, saying that men and women alike can occupy the nonplace of femininity, or that femininity does not merely complement masculinity but supplements and exceeds it.[18] But while that might seem to loosen the link between forms of identity and biological sex, it does not change the basic structure of defining everything in relation to the phallus. Despite his claims that his texts belong in the tradition of mystic writers, Lacan seems ultimately too committed to the structure of the old, illusory identity to make mystical release his starting point for a critique of male identity rather than vice versa.[19] Mystical experience, though challenging the terms in which rational male identity is constituted, remains defined by it; the underlying assumptions are briefly shaken but do not stir.

There are no doubt biographical or psychological reasons why Lacan was so attached to the coherent male identity while at the same time being so fascinated by what he thought of as the "not-all" of woman.[20] There are also theoretical reasons arising from his tendency to formulate his position in a way that obscures rather than illuminates the contribution of shared human activity to the phenomena he discusses. Arguing in this vein, Stanley Cavell has suggested that the problem lies in how the Lacanian idea of the phallus reifies sexual difference, treating it not as a lived negotiation but as "a question of some fixed way women know that men do not know, and vice versa."[21] Building on Cavell's critique, Toril Moi argues that a further flaw lies in Lacan's picture of language, a picture that does not approach language as a complex form of human practice but instead focuses unduly on the question of representation: words giving an image of the world. This reduces language to a series of noun labels and encourages Lacan to use spatial metaphors that make language appear to have an "inside" and an inaccessible "outside," where Lacan situates femininity or the jouissance of mystics.[22] Taken together, Cavell and Moi suggest that Lacan reifies the shared activities through which men and women relate to each other and that he props this reification up with an unhelpful, spatial model of language.

A further theoretical problem, which similarly has consequences for the account he gives of human interaction, is Lacan's commitment to a visual model of how identity is formed. His position is formulated in his famous paper "The Mirror Stage as Formative of the Function of the I," which was first delivered in 1936, given again in 1949, and then included in the *Écrits* in 1966. If infants come to a sense of who they are by identifying with an image in the mirror, they will believe that they are as self-contained as the infant's body appears to be and, moreover, that they are constituted independently of other human beings. Both these assumptions are questionable, but the consequence, for Lacan, is not to go back and rethink how the individual acquires a sense of self but instead to argue that identity is founded on misrecognition, or *méconnaissance*.[23] Our subjectivity is, for him, constitutively flawed, yet we cannot escape it; we remain trapped inside "the armour of an alienating identity, which will mark with its rigid structure the subject's entire mental development."[24] To acquire an identity is to be deluded.

Elisabeth Roudinesco has praised Lacan's essay as "a genuinely tragic vision of man."[25] But if the assumptions underlying Lacan's argument are made explicit, it becomes clear that, while his vision is certainly tragic, it is debatable whether the delusion he postulates is constitutive of human identity or instead the product of his own particular approach. Lacan's is not the only way of conceptualizing the formation of identity. Neither of his two main sources for the mirror-stage argument—a discussion from the early 1930s of how infants develop a sense of their own body by the psychologist Henri Wallon, and Alexandre Kojève's reading of Hegel's master–slave dialectic—has the element of necessary and irresolvable misrecognition that characterizes Lacan.[26] Similarly, the British psychoanalyst Donald Winnicott worked with very different presuppositions when he rethought the mirror stage in his paper "The Mirror Role of Mother and Family in Child Development," published in 1967. It takes only a very brief summary of Winnicott's contrasting approach to show that

Lacan's tragic presuppositions are not the indispensable tools for understanding identity that he suggests they are.[27]

Winnicott's version of the mirror stage avoids the drama of *méconnaissance* and qualifies the visual aspects by reintroducing an element of physical and emotional contact.[28] For the British psychoanalyst, infants come to a sense of self through a form of emotional mirroring, finding the echo and confirmation of their emotional reactions in the face of the adult looking after them.[29] Children who get enough mirroring will, in Winnicott's view, achieve a stable sense of themselves and of objects and people around them. If the carer is not able to respond to the child's reactions, or to give back to the baby what it gives out, then the identity that develops will not be so stable. Where Lacan envisages a scenario in which all identity is inherently and unavoidably based on misrecognition, Winnicott insists on an element of human interaction and suggests that the different forms this interaction can take cause an individual's sense of self to be more or less functional. More important, he insists that identity is formed through an emotional exchange with others, avoiding the false choice, faced by the Lacanian subject, between illusory wholeness in isolation from others on the one hand, and, on the other, the nonexistence associated with femininity or mystical experience. Winnicott's emphasis on an emotional exchange finds an echo in more-recent psychological and psychoanalytic literature, be it in the developmental psychologist Colwyn Trevarthen's video and film studies of the mutual mirroring of infant and mother or in the suggestion by Peter Hobson, whose work draws on both the psychoanalytic and experimental traditions, that it is through "emotional connectedness that a baby discovers what *kind* of a thing a person is."[30] Lacan's account of identity formation takes little or no account of the primordial relatedness of the human infant or of the nurturing effects of this relatedness on the child's development.

Lacan's position is thus unnecessarily tragic, because he omits from his account of how the subject is formed a sustaining emotional interaction with others. This omission makes his theory binary, or black and white, producing the false alternatives of a deludedly unified identity or no identity at all. Moreover, the two poles of this choice are stereotypically gendered: the emotionally isolated rational subject confronting the woman who melts beyond reason.[31] If Lacan had been more willing to challenge gendered habits of thought, it's possible that he would not have been so quick to accept a specific, emotionally removed way of relating to oneself and others as if it were the universal norm for subjectivity but might have been more interested, as Winnicott was, in understanding how the interactions of early infancy contribute to the development of a spectrum of different forms of adult identity. This in turn would have suggested an approach to mystical experience that didn't construe it simply as the negation of a deluded, unified identity.

Feminist appropriations of mystical texts such as those of Irigaray differ from Lacan in that they wish to move beyond the false opposition between having a male/phallic identity and having no identity at all. Irigaray's diagnosis of the problem is that women find it difficult to achieve an identity of their own because they grow up in a culture that does not acknowledge a feminine divinity and that therefore reduces female identity to being the appendage of male identity grounded in a male God. Her early work *Speculum* criticized the philosophical tradition for conferring a bogus legitimacy on the assumptions that deny women an independent identity. The male subject of philosophy from Plato to Freud was shown to construct the woman as his negative image, attributing to her all the characteristics he needs to avoiding exhibiting in order to be consistent, conscious, and certain of himself. "Woman remains this nothing at all, or this all at nothing, in which each (male) one seeks to find the means to replenish the resemblance to self (as) to same."[32] However, as well as drawing attention to the assumptions underpinning the male canon, Irigaray had the positive goal of helping women to escape its constraints. This could partly be achieved by a parody of masculine discourse, which shows up its absurdities to the point that, to use Irigaray's metaphor, another music can become audible.[33] For Ann-Marie Priest, this strategy of turning a limited language against itself brings Irigaray close to the tradition of apophatic mysticism, which articulates God through a series of negations just as the early texts of Irigaray articulate woman indirectly through the limiting language of patriarchy.[34] But Irigaray does not confine herself to such indirect invocations of an ineffable other, but also makes a positive attempt to help women find their voice independently of male discourse. As Irigaray describes her project, looking back in the 1990s: "I attempted to define the objective alterity of myself for myself as belonging to the female gender. I carried out an inversion of the femininity imposed upon me in order to try to define the female corresponding to my gender: the in-and-for-itself of my female nature [. . .]. I wanted to begin to define what a woman is, thus myself as a woman—and not only *a* woman but as freely belonging to the female gender or generic."[35]

For Irigaray, this means sketching a "spirituality in the feminine,"[36] a step that she explains in her lecture "Divine Women," first delivered in 1984, showing how for her a critique of patriarchy and an engagement with the mystical tradition are inseparable.[37] She explicitly appropriates the idea of becoming God, elevating it to something like a categorical imperative by arguing that "the only task, the only obligation laid upon us is: to become divine men and women, to become perfectly."[38] In her view, every identity needs a flexible ideal, or what she calls a "horizon of accomplishment," that structures and gives energy to its development.[39] Following Feuerbach, she suggests that God, or the positive image associated with divinity, fulfills this function. "Divinity is what we need to become free, autonomous, sovereign. No human subjectivity, no human society has ever been established without the help of the divine."[40] Historically, divinity in the West has been defined in male terms—in Christian theology, as Father, Son, and Holy Spirit. Women have not had their own horizon of accomplishment within which to grow but have rather had male images imposed on them, preventing them from developing what Irigaray calls "the perspective in which *their* flesh can be transfigured."[41] To change this structure, Irigaray invokes the idea of the "*female* made God," which allows women to stop being defined by their social function in relation to men—as virgin, wife, mother—and to develop an identity of their own.[42]

Irigaray's theory is in many ways closer than Lacan's to the medieval texts from which they both draw inspiration. She wants women to become God rather than to limit themselves to being the ineffable but ultimately dependent negation of masculine identity. By presenting positive forms of identity, her theory moves beyond Lacan's tragically and unnecessarily isolated subject. However, as she reappropriates the idea of divinity for a female subjectivity, Irigaray changes the model of freedom underpinning it. When she became God, the woman from the Strasbourg text gave up all forms of psychological attachment, even the attachment to herself and her desire to be with God.[43] This self-abandonment has parallels in other texts from the same period. Meister Eckhart, who preached in Strasbourg in the early fourteenth century as well as in Cologne and Paris, suggested that the individual should leave behind habit, convention, ritual, and emotional attachment, to be always at God's disposal wherever or whatever that may entail. He prized the freedom "to wait on God in the here and now, and to follow Him alone in the light wherein He would show you what to do and what not to do, every moment freely and new, as if you had nothing else and neither would nor could do otherwise."[44] Marguerite Porete, a French beguine burned in Paris in 1310, similarly suggested that attachments to particular customs, places, and rituals should be relinquished in favor of a freedom to be found "in all places through union with the divine will."[45] Irigaray's model of freedom has little to do with this state of unattached receptivity. Her conception of divinity promotes an individual's self-affirmation, implicit in the idea of a "horizon of accomplishment," rather than self-abandonment. It allows the female subject to become herself rather than go beyond herself: "As long as woman lacks a divine made in her image she cannot establish subjectivity or achieve a goal of her own."[46]

Irigaray's preference for self-affirmation over self-abandonment as a model of identity differentiates her approach from that of Eckhart, Porete, or the Strasbourg text. That need not in itself be a flaw, especially in a situation in which self-affirmation is a useful thing to promote. Nevertheless, it does stop Irigaray's theory from helping to read mystical texts on their own terms, despite the apparent similarities between her texts and those of the mystics. Mary L. Keller has made a similar argument about Irigaray's work in relation to non-European cultures: Irigaray's commitment to modern Western ideals of agency and autonomy prevents her theory from illuminating cultures, be they non-Western or premodern, which do not share her assumptions.[47] Moreover, Irigaray's version of becoming God also has an internal tension that is not fully resolved. Her conception of divinity contains a gender imbalance: Becoming God is positive in her argument only when women do it. The male subject is not positively empowered by God in the way that the woman subject is by the archetypal force of the female divinity. Instead, the male God helps men to maintain order and control, but the form of identity established in the process is not fulfilling, so the male subject longs for the divinity of woman "even as he rapes it."[48] It is not clear why the male divinity could not pull man beyond a limited view of himself and his body as the female divinity helps women to transcend a limited identity.

In fact, Penelope Deutscher suggests that this more balanced model is what Irigaray foresees for the future, when men equally change their relationship to divinity, and men and women alike relinquish unhealthy projections to enjoy "an open-ended process of becoming."[49] This is certainly the logical continuation of Irigaray's model, but Irigaray's own argument does not explicitly endorse it. The relationship between male and female divinities remains unclear, leading Pamela Sue Anderson to wonder whether Irigaray even imagines male and female divinities competing to exclude the other form of identity.[50] The answer is doubtless no, but Irigaray nevertheless lets the male subject be defined and limited by a particular, narrow self-image that the patriarchal subject has had of itself—rational, systematic, above bodily impulse, etc.—while she mobilizes the strength of excluded impulses to affirm the female subject. This introduces between the two sexes an unbridgeable gap that, for Patrice Haynes, imports an unexpected element of alienation into Irigaray's theory. Irigaray overcomes the distance between humans and nature and between humans and God only to replace it with the remoteness of one sex from another.[51]

Lacan views mystics from the perspective of a stable identity he criticizes but will not relinquish. For him, mystics negate a rigid version of subjectivity without in any way changing it. For Irigaray, meanwhile, the idea of becoming God offers an alternative form of sovereignty or self-possession. Both Lacan and Irigaray use mystical texts to further their particular agendas. While it may be impossible to entirely avoid this, Amy Hollywood comes closer to letting mystical texts be understood on their own terms, since she engages not only with the texts themselves but also with the discursive uses to which they have been put. She critically reviews the ways in which mystical experience has been an inspiration for a tradition of francophone thought that includes Bataille, Lacan, Beauvoir, and Irigaray, and she attempts more consistently to mobilize the power of the mystical tradition for a rethinking of identity than do either of the thinkers discussed so far, working both with and beyond francophone critical theory. However, as we will see, although she distances herself from the francophone tradition, she works with assumptions comparable to those of Lacan and Irigaray. This puts all three critics in a similar position: They turn to mysticism as an alternative way of thinking about identity (as opposed to Pfister and Jung, who find their preconceptions confirmed in the mystical texts they read), but, at the same time, they limit their engagement with many aspects of the mystical texts that could actually assist their critique, in particular with the sense of connectedness—to the world, to others, to God—articulated in the texts and the self-displacement and loss of agency that this sense of connectedness entails.

Hollywood criticizes both Lacan and Irigaray and focuses in particular on their assumptions about gender. Lacan, for Hollywood, explains male power, even though he does not contest it. Her reading is, therefore, basically sympathetic to his project and emphasizes the places where he separates his idea of the "not all" from biological sex: "You do not have to be literally castrated to occupy the side of the 'not all.' "[52] However, although Lacan constantly suggests that a different kind of symbolic order might be possible that is not "governed by the phallus," Hollywood observes that he nevertheless cannot take the step toward this alternative. "As long as Lacan continues to use the language of castration, lack, and paternity to name the gap in the subject, he continues to privilege masculinity and to uphold the very fantasy his work set out to subvert."[53] If Lacan remains ultimately indebted to a gendered framework, so too, in Hollywood's view, does Irigaray. Hollywood criticizes her because she makes sexual difference an absolute, rather than, say, treating it as the sliding scale divided into more-rigid categories by the process of socialization that we find in other feminist texts of the 1980s and 1990s.[54] She also questions Irigaray's implicit assumption that symbols are so fixed in meaning that women can identify only with specifically feminine symbols of divinity.[55] In her view, the attachment to a rigid, binary gender divide prevents Irigaray from exploring a more interesting aspect of her thought—namely, the question of how the subject can relinquish the attachment to a set of beliefs or a project and come to terms with the loss of security that this entails. In Hollywood's view, this loss need not be thought of as tragic or even catastrophic; rather, it could describe men and women alike in their relationship to divinity. However, Irigaray does not follow through this line of argument, because she thinks of loss as primarily phallic lack and therefore wants to conceive of a woman's body without loss, rather than asking how women "might symbolize and so mediate their own losses."[56]

Hollywood agrees with Irigaray's premise that the body must be included in any attempt to rethink forms of identity, but does not believe that this necessarily results in a rigid binary division between the sexes. Rather, she suggests that we turn to "the body in its complexity and multiplicity" to free us from false images of gender or an identity protected against loss.[57] If a form of loss or trauma can be acknowledged without being directly equated with castration, then the body need no longer be falsely idealized in the way it is in Irigaray's celebrations of the feminine. The illusory stability of particular forms of subjectivity could then be challenged without being explained entirely in terms of gender or of biological sex. Hollywood's criticism of Lacan and Irigaray thus suggests an alternative reading of the mystical texts that reproduces the relinquishing of preconceived ideas enacted in the mystical texts themselves. Her sympathetic appropriation of Bataille, however, illustrates some of the limitations of her counter-project. For it shows that, although she criticizes the rigidly gendered conception of subjectivity that she finds in Lacan and Irigaray, she, like Lacan and, as we will see, Bataille, continues to understand the subject as essentially isolated.

Bataille wrote a number of "atheological" discussions of religious and sexual ecstasy.[58] In his view, human beings are isolated and their fundamental experience is one of being separate from the world, a state he calls "discontinuity." To achieve continuity or communication is to destroy the very form of our identity, and is therefore potentially life-threatening. However, this experience does not have to be so intense as to physically destroy the subject. In Bataille's account, mystical experience, or "inner experience," is precisely the moment when an individual's securities are shattered and for a moment he catches a glimpse of the world and other people as they are beyond the individual's controlling projects and assumptions.[59] If it sometimes seems as though, for him, only extremes of violence can bring about this change, Hollywood suggests that a shattering in or by a text produces enough upheaval to help individuals peer beyond the confines of discontinuity and witness something beyond.[60] She glosses this invocation of a "beyond" using the Lacanian idea of the real, or, as she explains, "that in history which is unassimilable to its meaning-giving and salvific narratives."[61]

Hollywood questions Bataille's account of mystical experience because he, again, genders the trauma, equating the structures that need to be escaped with the penis or phallus, and making women serve as emblems of an experience beyond phallic illusions.[62] However, even if this unnecessary gendering were omitted, there is another problem affecting both Bataille and Hollywood's own approach. Bataille works with a dubious idea of an isolated subject who communicates only by breaking beyond the confines of identity, an idea that Hollywood effectively reproduces, suggesting that communication will occur only in the elusive and always paradoxical world of deconstructive writing.[63] But this view of communication as explosive would not be necessary if the underlying assumptions about identity were rethought. As we have seen, Winnicott offers a different account in which identity is constituted through communication and affected by its absence. It is, from the beginning, a way of relating to others. This means that communication itself need not be seen as inevitably explosive. Where it is, as in Bataille's concept of self-laceration, it is legitimate to ask what has happened to make communication occur only in this form. Bataille's approach may then appear as, for instance, the product of a particular history, expressing the experience of a generation of male subjects unable to cope with emotion without overdramatizing it and making it inaccessible to the individual by defining it as inherently destructive of his or her identity.

Like Lacan and Irigaray, Hollywood looks to mysticism because it suggests a way of standing outside existing habits of identity and of changing how we relate to them. Her approach is very attuned to the manner in which gendered assumptions can obstruct a productive appropriation of mystical texts. At the same time, she retains the idea that the subject is isolated and cannot change without a dramatic lapse into nonsense. Like Lacan, she regards the subject as either trapped in structures of meaning or as precariously in a state of dissolution, a dichotomy that casts mysticism as always inaccessible, as an experience that we might taste occasionally but that ultimately serves only to remind us of the limitations of our everyday identity. There are, nevertheless, elements of Hollywood's argument that point in different directions, such as her discussion of Beauvoir, whose subject, although autonomous, is also situated, and able to relate to others, without being destroyed by the very idea of human interaction.[64] But Hollywood does not elaborate on Beauvoir's position. One reason for this is that, in Beauvoir's argument, mysticism features only as an inadequate, individualistic solution to problems that need collective resolution. The woman mystic, like the narcissist and the woman in love, is "trying to achieve individual salvation by solitary effort."[65] Indeed, Beauvoir believes mysticism to be essentially a failure in relating to the world and others: "Either woman puts herself into relation with an unreality; her double, or God; or she creates an unreal relation to a real being. In both cases she lacks any grasp on the world; she does not escape her subjectivity; her liberty remains frustrated."[66] Mystics therefore occupy a very different place in her argument from the one they are granted by the other authors Hollywood discusses. Rather than exemplifying an alternative, intensified form of experience, they are an—albeit understandable—failure.

Hollywood's discussion of Beauvoir opens up the possibility of combining the self-abandonment of mysticism with a view of subjectivity as situated and relational, but neither Beauvoir herself nor Hollywood pursue this line of thought further. Beauvoir treats mysticism as a flight from real relations, while Hollywood does not develop a relational model of identity because she takes death to be the most important relationship for the subject's self-understanding, turning to an isolated and isolating confrontation with finitude in a way that, as we shall see, is comparable to the way taken by Heidegger in *Being and Time*. In her view, in our encounter with our own body, we both come to terms with mortality and try to protect ourselves from it.[67] We no doubt also relate to other people and to the world, but this is not the most important aspect of our identity. Hollywood, therefore, like Lacan, Irigaray, and Bataille in their different ways, views the subject as essentially self-contained. Her subject does not believe herself to be invincible, but she nevertheless experiences herself most intensely when she is confronted with her own isolation and impotence.

Lacan, Irigaray, and Hollywood turn to the texts of medieval mystics as an alternative to constricting, modern forms of identity, but none of them radically questions the terms in which identity is conceived. They all retain some elements of the autonomous, self-contained, and sovereign subject: Lacan, the sense of unity and control; Irigaray, a version of sovereignty and autonomy; Hollywood, the subject's isolation. They are all tied, to a greater or lesser degree, to the model they question. For Irigaray and Hollywood, this also means that, despite their sensitivity to issues of gender, they reproduce aspects of a subjectivity—its insistence on sovereignty, its isolation—otherwise associated with the patriarchal assumptions they both reject in

Lacan. This suggests that, rather than the category of gender helping to rethink subjectivity, it is necessary to rethink subjectivity in order to get a clearer analysis of gender. Another way of putting this is to say that whatever it is we believe we're doing with our identity, gender will be one of the ways we do it, but it won't itself be seen as the goal or the thing that we think we're pursuing, unless, that is, we wish to argue that the point of a human life is to be a man, or a woman, rather than a human being. However deep we think the habits and/or biology of a gendered identity go, a discussion of gender needs to be part of a wider argument about what a human life is, rather than being itself the overall framework for discussion.

The question of gender will be dealt with in more detail in chapter 3. To return to the critique of Irigaray and Hollywood: The ideas of sovereignty or isolation that shape the two philosophers' readings of mysticism are, of course, not bad concepts that we should never be allowed to use. Rather, they prevent the two thinkers from doing what they appear to want to do, from drawing on the resources of the mystical texts to help redescribe how we maintain (or don't maintain) our current, patriarchal identities. The concepts are not intrinsically useless but they are too tied up with a particular description of identity to promote self-knowledge in the context in which Irigaray and Hollywood employ them. A comparable problem can be found in a number of attempts by postwar critical theorists to imagine an alternative way of living in the world. The figure of thought that recurs again and again in the texts of critical theorists is that of an empty epiphany: an experience beyond the confines of current identity that is longed for but simultaneously made inaccessible because the theoretical preconceptions to which it offers an alternative define it as impossible. The empty epiphany manifests itself in different ways in the texts of different theorists. In the next chapter, I'm going to look at a version of postmodernity (Lyotard), a version of psychoanalytic criticism (Žižek), a version of poststructuralism (Derrida), and the work of the Frankfurt School (Adorno). To look at only these four critics is perhaps arbitrary, and, if space allowed, the list could be extended—Paul de Man would be an obvious further example. But the important point is the recurring theme that emerges despite the diversity of positions. It suggests that for all their differences, the four men share some deeply held convictions, convictions indeed that are held deeply enough not to feature in their analyses, despite the fact that all four are theorists who attend to hidden depths and enabling or disabling preconditions. What follows is a sketch of a pattern of thought common to postmodernists as much as to modernists, suggesting that other ways need to be found of grouping theorists together than categorization by historical mini-epochs.

2

Empty Epiphanies in Modernist and Postmodernist Theory

This chapter presents, in a very brief form, a critique of an underlying structure in modernist and postmodernist theory in order to suggest the wider implications of an approach that, as it appeared in the last chapter, could potentially be construed as part of a parochial debate in mysticism studies. The readings of the four theorists that I offer are very brief because the challenge I'm presenting to the positions of Lyotard, Žižek, Derrida, and Adorno—namely, the argument that the self-consciously paradoxical positions that they adopt are necessary only because of the particular, questionable, and historically locatable model of identity to which they remain committed—is so fundamental that it makes a more extended reading difficult to sustain. That's not to say that nothing the four theorists have to say is worth reading. But it does mean that, for someone who doesn't happen to identify with the model of identity they identify with, and so doesn't recognize his or her own world in the world of limited choices represented in the philosophical arguments, the enjoyment of individual insights will always be alloyed by the worry that the general direction of the texts is open to question. A more extended reading, which would be a book in its own right, would need to take the form of contextualizing argument, which attempted sympathetically to reconstruct what made the commitment to the form of identity the four thinkers identify with seem the right thing, indeed what made it seem to be an admirable form of philosophical asceticism. At the same time, Derrida and Adorno in particular make arguments that, shorn of the thinkers' questionable attachment to the rhetoric of ineffability, are inspiring and productive: in particular Derrida's painstaking close reading of Heidegger in his first "Geschlecht" essay, and Adorno's inspired attempt, with Horkheimer, to rethink the canon of Western culture from the point of view of the intense experience of connection to which they gave the name *mimesis* in *Dialectic of Enlightenment.*[1] The point of this chapter is not to rule out further engagement with their work but rather to set out as clearly as possible the structure that often proves an obstacle to continuing the lines of thought their work opens up.

Lyotard's essay "The Sublime and the Avant-Garde" (1984) illustrates the pattern of the empty epiphany in a pure form.[2] It discusses a form of fulfilled experience, which, it suggests, can be induced by various works of art from the modernist canon and in particular by the abstract canvases of Barnett Newman. Lyotard describes the experience as a moment of pure presence, or pure "now," that escapes categorization. "Newman's *now* which is no more than *now* is a stranger to consciousness and cannot be constituted by it. Rather, it is what dismantles consciousness, what deposes consciousness, it is what consciousness cannot formulate, and even what consciousness forgets in order to constitute itself."[3] In Lyotard's view, nothing can be said about this experience beyond the question "*Is it happening?*"[4] When the individual momentarily steps beyond his familiar habits of thought, it is to face an ineffable emptiness: "*now* like the feeling that nothing might happen: the nothingness now."[5] The idea allows Lyotard to maintain the hope of a new form of experience, but only by separating it entirely from the consciousness to which it is the indescribable alternative and emptying it of all content.

Jerome Carroll has pointed out that Lyotard's model of the sublime leaves out the context and shared conventions that meaningful experience generally relies on, suggesting that the experience may in fact be less isolated from nonsublime experience than Lyotard makes out.[6] As we saw in the last chapter with the critique of Lacan, this suggests that there are alternatives to the false choice between a constraining identity and its absolute negation. Nevertheless, Lyotard regards the isolated emptiness of the experience of the sublime as a logical necessity, and, to a certain extent, he is right. *If* our very conscious identity is thought to be the product of a delusion, then we ourselves can, by definition, never take the step beyond delusion, and the shared context and conventions of an experience will only be extensions of the delusion rather than the means by which we creatively transcend our current limitations. Of course, that's a very big *if*, and it begs the question as to whether it is necessary to conceive of identity in so constricting a fashion: Would it not be more productive to change the underlying assumptions rather than hanker after an elusive and necessarily empty moment of sublimity? Žižek, Derrida, and Adorno can be read as responding to this question in different ways. Žižek's strategy is to insist even more than Lyotard on the deluded nature of human consciousness, while Derrida and Adorno are not only interested in ways of overcoming the delusion but also step back to ask to whom human identity is likely to seem constitutively deluded in this manner, opening the way for a shift of paradigm to one in which human beings need no longer be trapped in hankering for an empty illumination.

Žižek's position shares and makes explicit the assumptions that fix Lyotard's subject in the position of expecting the constitutively unexpected. In Žižek's Lacanian model, misrecognition is so fundamental to the human condition that the very distinction between alienation and insight becomes meaningless. In Žižek's view, it is ideological to imagine that ideology could end, and equally wrong to use the term *alienation*, because it suggests a nonalienated state.[7] We are deluded not so much because we misperceive reality—an idea that retains the possibility of correcting the misperception—but rather because the behavior through which reality itself is constituted is deluded. Practice is constitutively misguided even more than knowledge is.[8] Our day-to-day behavior creates an ideological reality that we believe to be legitimate precisely *because* it does not match our desires and is experienced as a traumatizing imposition from outside. Yet, despite the inherently frustrating nature of our experience, we are not able to mobilize our desire against the structures we create. There remains a lack at the center of our reality. For this reason, a Marxian critique of society, which hopes to uncover the real social relations behind the objectified surface, must, for Žižek, be replaced by a bleaker vision following Freud and Lacan. "In Marxism a fetish conceals the positive network of social relations, whereas in Freud a fetish conceals the lack ('castration') around which the symbolic network is articulated."[9] How this ineluctable lack arises is not so much explained as asserted to be an inescapable fact of life. As we've already seen in the last chapter, in the contrast between Lacan and Winnicott, if fallible but "good enough" human interaction is included in the argument, the outlook need not necessarily be so bleak. But Žižek prefers to ontologize lack and misperception, to make it a necessary and permanent feature of human life. Nevertheless, there is an alternative in his argument, something like a moment of authenticity, but it turns out to be a deus ex machina. It is what Žižek calls a genuinely ethical act, which breaks all the rules that could govern behavior, creating an entirely new framework for itself.[10] However, it can never be prepared for or predicted, just as Lyotard's moment of sublimity can never be foreseen by the language it disrupts. It can only ever be described retrospectively, and when it does come, it comes, as Žižek himself freely admits, as an act of grace.

Lyotard's "now" and Žižek's ethical act are both caught in the same tragicomical position of gesturing toward something that the theorists simultaneously assert will always elude their conceptual grasp. In her critique of Žižek, Judith Butler has pointed out the paradox into which such theorists maneuver themselves when they declare that there is something that language will never be able to articulate: "To freeze the real as the impossible 'outside' to discourse is to institute a permanently unsatisfiable desire for an ever elusive referent: the sublime object of ideology."[11] This sublime object is in fact merely the by-product of their presupposition that there is a central human truth that eludes communication. For Claudia Breger, such a position is not only paradoxical but brings with it disturbing assumptions about forms of social organization. The flip side of the empty longing for the incommunicable is an unexpected affirmation of a form of tyranny. Žižek's arguments make the "the rigid and immobile character of signification" seem epistemologically and ontologically inevitable and so legitimate authoritarianism, by stitching it into the very fabric of the world.[12] To answer these queries, Žižek uses a figure of thought that he explicitly draws from Meister Eckhart. Looking at his response will give us a clearer sense of the argumentative mechanics that help to keep postmodern epiphanies empty, as well as further illustrating the differences in underlying assumptions that separate contemporary debates from the fourteenth-century mystical milieu in which people related to aspects of their lives through talk of "becoming God" and activities associated with such talk.

Žižek rejects the claim that he hypostatizes the Real in a realm beyond language, in a two-step argument that seems at first to do just what he's accused of, but then he inverts the move. The first step draws on a phenomenological critique of virtual reality by Hubert Dreyfus. Dreyfus discusses the way virtual realities can be lived at a distance that protects us from involvement. We can start over or leave a virtual game at any moment. In nonvirtual reality, we cannot leave behind the commitments of our preunderstanding, or our physical immersion in our environment, or what Dreyfus sums up as "our animal-shaped, emotional, intuitive, situated, vulnerable, embodied selves."[13] Žižek defines his own version of reality in contradistinction to this phenomenological version of the situated human self. The Žižekian Real is not "the prereflexive reality of our immediate immersion in our life world but, precisely, that which gets lost, that which the subject has to renounce in order to become immersed in his/her lifeworld—and, consequently, that which then returns in the guise of spectral apparitions."[14] So the Real, for Žižek, means those disruptive but ungraspable elements that destabilize the world of our everyday coping and that remind us that our social identity was forged at the price of exclusion. This position sounds quite like the structure Butler criticizes: a disruptive but ultimately inaccessible "outside" to our social identities. But then Žižek introduces a twist into the argument by suggesting that the disruptive real is only an effect of appearances, produced by their difference from themselves: "The real is the appearance as appearance: it not only appears within appearances, but it is also *nothing but* its own appearance. It is only a certain *grimace* of reality, a certain impeccable, unfathomable, ultimately illusory feature that accounts for the absolute difference within the identity."[15] This passage is hard to understand, because it depends for its formulation on the distinction between reality and appearance that it claims to be discarding. Nevertheless, it makes an aspect of Žižek's method clear. Answering the argument that he places an ineffable something outside language and socialized identities, he gets rid of the distinction between inside and outside altogether and suggests that the outside is just an effect of the inside, repeating the structure of overcoming oppositions that we saw in *The Sublime Object of Ideology* when he generalized delusion to the point that the opposition "delusion versus insight" became meaningless. This methodological step (the idea of not being alienated is a form of alienation; reality is just an effect of appearance), for Žižek, is comparable to Meister Eckhart's argument when he moves from the idea that God created man (= the Real is outside and beyond human life) to the claim the God is born in the human soul (= the Real is an effect of human life).[16]

Eckhart makes such an argument in one of his most well-known as well as most radical texts, a sermon on the text *Beati pauperes spiritu* (Blessed are the poor in spirit). For Eckhart, the idea that God is born with me and through me is part of a series of arguments by which he strips away his listeners' attachment to their desire to do God's will, know God, or have a place for God in their heart. Each of these desires can lead to the formation of habits and fixed ways of relating to the world that put up barriers between the individual and the experience of God living through them. The idea of God being born through me is part of Eckhart's attempt to break down habitual attachments to the point that the difference between God and me disappears, indeed, so that the very idea of God no longer features in the argument: "Thus we say that a person should have reached such a state of poverty that he neither is nor possesses a place wherein God might work. For when people maintain such a place, they maintain separation. For that reason I pray to God that he might deliver me from God."[17] The sermon thus stages a process of conceptual and practical self-transformation that culminates in a way of relating to the world and to ourselves comparable to the one that the Strasbourg text referred to as "becoming God." Žižek's argument is similar insofar as it is also a monist argument. Just as for Eckhart, we should try to move beyond the distinction between God and myself, so in Žižek we should move beyond the reality/appearance distinction. Nevertheless, the tenor and goal of the arguments are very different. Žižek's argument is about accepting entrapment. He explains this as a giving up of the very idea of an outside or beyond, a renunciation he equates with the "difficult" step to atheism.[18] But neither the idea of atheism nor the inside/outside dichotomy with which he explains it are really the issue. Eckhart's sermon is committed to an idea of development and a form of self-transcendence that Žižek rules out through his flattening of the oppositions between alienation/nonalienation and appearance/reality.

It's not clear what Žižek gains by broadening the idea of misrecognition so much that every action appears to be based in fantasy, and reality is only an effect of the nonidentity of appearances. Certainly, it puts his own argument in a self-contradictory position, since, to be intelligible, his position depends on the reader's sense of an action that, by contrast, is not grounded in fantasy, and on a reality that isn't appearance. Indeed, rhetorically Žižek often appeals to a very straightforward version of what we all unproblematically know, over and beyond his epistemological doubts.[19] Perhaps his model of subjects who are constituted so that they can never even know that they don't know themselves should not be taken literally, as a description of human identity, but rather as a self-conscious exaggeration in the tradition of Horkheimer and Adorno, who paradoxically declared in *Dialectic of Enlightenment* that only exaggeration was true.[20] A reading of this sort casts Žižek as an extreme ironist and raises questions as to whom such an exaggeration would be useful and why. But to answer them would mean changing the terms of the conversation and leaving the Žižekian paradoxes behind, because it would be working from the assumption that people can articulate and acknowledge their motivations rather than be permanently at one remove from them.

The question of whom the empty epiphany arguments would be useful to, and why, is raised more explicitly in Derrida's work. As it appears in his texts, the epiphany has a slightly different structure from the one we've seen in Lyotard and Žižek. Derrida suggests that, rather than our longing for a sublime something that will outstrip our current framework, or for the ethical act to interrupt our necessary misrecognition, our categorical frameworks are always already outstripped and interrupted. All experience is a breaking of categories. At the same time, it turns out that we can never get to this disruptive experience itself, never experience it directly, because we're caught inside the structures it makes possible. Instead, we can only gesture toward it, in a way comparable to Lyotard's asking whether the sublime "it" is happening without being able to say whether it is. Thus the Derridean neologism *différance*, combining the senses of difference and deferral, points to something "beyond" philosophical systems, something that we necessarily cannot name, even though it is the very thing that makes not just philosophical systems but experience possible in the first place. " 'There is no name for it': a proposition to be read in its *platitude*. This unnameable is not an ineffable Being which no name could approach: God, for example. This unnameable is the play which makes possible nominal effects, the relatively unitary and atomic structures that are called names, the chains of substitutions in which, for example, the nominal effect *différance* is still *enmeshed*, carried off, reinscribed, just as a false entry or a false exit is still part of the game, a function of the system."[21]

For Derrida, this constant deferral equally shapes how individuals relate to themselves, which can also only be in the form of "*différance*, that is to say alterity, or trace."[22] However, even as he points toward the elusive nonground of all thought and experience, Derrida refuses finally to permit access to it or even to name it. The very idea of naming something beyond metaphysical systems is as deluded as the metaphysics it wishes to escape, so rather than give it a label, we should confine ourselves to the description of its necessity. We should acknowledge that it is there, while putting ourselves permanently at one remove from it. It will forever be the trace that we talk about indirectly, by crossing it out or coining neologisms. It will never be something we directly encounter or directly engage with, although it shadows our every word and gesture. In Lyotard's sublime and Žižek's act, the epiphany was a punctual moment we could not describe. For Derrida, it is the inaccessible accompaniment to every action, everywhere and nowhere, leaving the world radically transformed but, simultaneously, completely untouched.

In an interesting twist in the work of the 1990s, Derrida suggests that this distancing may be not a philosophical necessity but rather a byproduct of our own apprehensiveness. He draws on the story of the man who recognizes the Messiah when he encounters him but nevertheless asks him, "When will you come?" as a way of putting off the acknowledgment that the moment that filled him with both longing and foreboding is upon him.[23] The story is particularly useful because it fits so closely

Lyotard's model of the sublime, which limits itself to a question ("Is it happening?") that similarly could be read as a strategy for not engaging with, or putting at a distance, something that the questioner is actually already involved in. If the Messiah is already here and we can recognize him, then deferral is no longer necessary but the product of a psychological disposition. Rather than giving a structural account of our inability to bear what Derrida calls "the opening of experience,"[24] we would then need to look at the dispositions, habits, and attachments that limit the encounter. Deconstruction would move from invocations of an impossible justice, or of an encounter with another person who will necessarily remain unknowable to us, to a study of the involvements we are already committed to and of the contact that it is too late to take back but that we often but not always shy away from.

This is not quite the direction Derrida's thought took. He remained instead committed to ideals—of justice, of the gift, of democracy—that we would necessarily fall short of. Our Joycean affirmation of life will always be haunted by a mechanical repetition of itself and so will always be hollowed out from the inside; never quite the affirmation we wanted.[25] So it's not even that, as Beckett put it, we can try again, fail again but fail better, and so introduce an element of change or development into our failure.[26] But rather that we will always and necessarily be at a distance from the affirmation for which we nevertheless are yearning. Thus, if, as John Caputo has insisted, "deconstruction is a passion for transgression, a passion for trespassing the horizons of possibility,"[27] it is also a form of self-censorship that forbids the transgressor from fulfilling his or her potential or ever realizing his or her desire to break out of the patterns that he or she simultaneously wishes so passionately to transgress.

Just as Carroll questioned the logic of Lyotard's empty sublimity from a hermeneutic point of view, and Butler pointed out the paradox that Žižek chooses to inhabit, so there have been critiques of Derrida's idea of an impossible pure presence undermined by *différance*. The experience of life, or what Dan Zahavi calls the "field of lived presence," will necessarily be a complex phenomenon that bundles together the passage of time and our immediate awareness of ourselves. But Derrida artificially takes this bundle apart to produce self-presence plus the traces that mediate and disrupt it.[28] Derrida's texts are haunted by versions of an unrealistically pure identity that both set his arguments in motion and ensure that they remain caught in inescapable but unnecessary paradoxes.[29] As with the critique of Lacan in the previous chapter, such logical challenges make it clear that alternatives are conceivable and that Derrida's commitment to the picture of a necessary hollowing out of experience precedes and underpins his arguments rather than being their product. Derrida's position seems a little less intractable than Lacan's, since he himself stands back from the commitment to an evacuated experience to ask who—when they are, as it were, already faced with the Messiah—might choose to take such a position and why. But he doesn't follow the line of argument through.

Adorno similarly points toward a possible psychological explanation for the empty epiphany structure even as he reproduces it. Like the other theorists, Adorno suggests that individuals aspire to something unattainable, and he uses a variety of concepts to name this: truth, reconciliation, nonidentity, redemption. The individual can, at best, hope to experience it negatively, through its absence, or as a form of folly. "Being the fool is the form in which truth afflicts people who refuse to abandon it amid the untruth."[30] At the same time, *Negative Dialectics* contains a fascinating passage that briefly approaches the problem from a different angle. Some individuals, Adorno suggests, are at one remove from the truth, not because that is the necessary structure of experience in Western societies but because of their attitude or psychological type. "People who are highly intellectual, or who are artists, have often noted the sense of not being quite there or not being fully involved; as if they were not themselves but a kind of spectator."[31] Adorno throws this in as an essayistic observation that he does not follow up. However, it suggests that the figure of the empty epiphany can be interpreted as an expression of a form of subjectivity characteristic of individuals who have learned to be at a permanent distance from their emotional life; or, to put it another way, the empty epiphany can be read as the symptom of a particular way of relating to desires rather than as a confirmation that the desires themselves will never be fulfilled.

The arguments of Lyotard, Žižek, Derrida, and Adorno show that the assumptions underpinning the readings of mystical texts criticized in the previous chapter have a wider currency. Just as Lacan, Irigaray, and Hollywood remained too attached to the ideas of isolation and sovereignty to approach identity from an angle that called these terms into question, so Lyotard, Žižek, Derrida, and Adorno can't stop casting an alternative form of identity as the unreachable "other" of current patterns of thought; they can't take it instead as the starting point of their deliberations. This means the alternative is not described in ways that allow it to be recognizable as an experience that someone could have. In the everyday language game of saying a particularly intense experience was "indescribable," it's not the word alone that helps us understand what our interlocutor is saying. The account of the event that has prepared for the declaration of its being indescribable, our own past experience of circumstances that fitted the "it was indescribable" language game, as well as our tuning in to the palpable elation of our interlocutor give us a pretty good sense of the intensity of feeling that he or she is trying to convey.

If we don't understand, the problem is not likely to be that we've reached the limits of logic and language but rather that we've come across an obstacle at the level of the pragmatics of the conversation; a certain holding back of commitment by the speaker or listener—or indeed both—that prevents a proper sharing of the experience. Similarly, the fact that the descriptions of modernist epiphanies remain abstract need not be thought to suggest that we're running up against the very limits of conceptuality. Instead, Derrida's anecdote about encountering the Messiah and Adorno's aside about intellectual distance both raise the possibility of contextualizing and transcending the intellectual habits that produce the empty epiphany as a recurring figure of thought. It suggests that the empty epiphany is not the necessary form of authentic experience but the product of social and psychological determinants that can be described and even challenged. Breaking out of the structure then becomes a question of problematizing a particular form of identity—in this case, twentieth-century, predominantly male, and not very open to change—rather than of rethinking the very structure of experience itself.

This change of perspective brings with it a number of presuppositions. The first is that identity shouldn't be assumed to be uniform—*all* delusion, or *all différance*. It needs instead to be approached as a fragmentary collection of more of less useful habits that have accrued over time, some of which can be turned against others in a gradual process of self-transformation rather than in a single epiphanic moment. This is the sort of model of identity Dewey set out in *Nature and Human Conduct*, one that gives up the quest for transcending convention and accepts that "a convention can be reorganized and made mobile only by using some other custom for giving leverage to an impulse."[32] Habits must be played off against habits. The second presupposition is that identities are historically variable. There is not a single form of human identity, not even a single form of modern identity, but an array of different identities. To describe them historically, however, and grasp the contingent nature of modern identity by situating it in relation to existing or past alternatives, it is necessary to have thought through the assumptions with which the alternatives are approached.

Some remarks that Hollywood makes in *Sensible Ecstasy* can clarify this point, because they give an example of the way contemporary assumptions are projected onto the past and thereby mask the difference between modern and premodern forms of behavior. In an argument similar to the one I'll make later in this book, Hollywood suggests that mystical texts can help us revise the history of modern forms of identity. In the texts of Beatrice of Nazareth and other women mystics from the late thirteenth and early fourteenth century, Hollywood observes a turn away from external bodily signs of God's grace toward interiority, which she interprets as the beginning of a form of self-cultivation otherwise associated "with men and with the early modern period."[33] In Hollywood's view, Beatrice achieves "the autonomy of the internal self" and should be included in an account of the development of the rich inner life we associate with modern forms of identity.[34] That is indubitably true, and accounts such as those of Charles Taylor in *Sources of the Self* or of Jerrold Seigel in *The Idea of the Self* are scandalously short of texts by women.[35] Nevertheless, Hollywood's claim needs to be put in context. The cultivation of an inner life started long before the early modern period. To give examples from two different historiographic traditions: Colin Morris, in his account of *The Discovery of the Individual*, traced "the growth of a keen self-awareness" and various habits and ideas later associated with modern selfhood back to the cultural flowering of the twelfth century (the dates of his study are 1050–1200).[36] Foucault also saw the beginnings of modern techniques of the self in the medieval period, and in particular in the introduction of compulsory confession and of the first inquisitorial procedures after the fourth Lateran Council in 1215.[37] To understand what is special about the interiority cultivated by the mystics of the thirteenth and fourteenth centuries requires a wider study of the different sorts of interiorities that people cultivated in the period. This is a step that Hollywood does not take. Instead, she employs a modern critical idiom to make sense of mystical interiority: "By understanding how bodily and meditative practices enable human beings to deal with loss and construct an interiorized subjectivity, psychoanalysis can help us understand how Beatrice's emphasis on interiority both emerges from and resists the kinds of meditative and bodily practices discussed in the vita."[38] As well as reproducing the structure, remarked on by Sudhir Kakar, of reading mystical texts as a sign of something else (in this case, overcoming loss) rather than of becoming God, this approach is problematic because it reads the past as a foreshadowing of the present, and as a consequence it masks the very different habits that constituted a mystic's identity in the thirteenth and fourteenth centuries.[39] Beatrice, for Hollywood, becomes a precursor figure for the modern assumptions that are brought to bear on her texts. The ways in which her texts deviate from these assumptions are not articulated, with the result that Hollywood's history of identity merely backdates the development of modern structures rather than recognizing the existence of qualitative differences between modern and medieval cultivation of inner life or reconstructing the unfamiliar activities through which this particular kind of medieval interiority was fostered.

To avoid reproducing this structure in my own argument, I need to change the assumptions with which both mystical texts and the wider history of forms of identity are approached. If the Cartesian assumption that the human subject is isolated and imprisoned in forms of identity he or she cannot escape has not been helpful, maybe it's worth starting from an alternative viewpoint, such as that to be found in the phenomenological tradition of Husserl, Heidegger, and Merleau-Ponty—namely, the view that human beings are inherently open to each other and to the world around them and that the form in which this openness is experienced changes over time.[40] Certainly, this has seemed to be the more useful hypothesis as I grappled with the strangeness of the medieval material. But clearly I have no special faculty for reading mystical texts or thinking about questions of identity that wasn't available to other critics and philosophers discussed. So the approach developed here is ultimately a reflection of my habits and interests. The assumptions with which we approach either mystical texts or the history of selfhood are never an accurate representation of how the subject is "in reality." A theory of identity is, rather, a tool for shaping our way of relating to the world and to ourselves.[41] Instead of asking how accurate such a theory is, therefore, we should want to know what interests or what way of life it serves. Fichte took a similar stance when he suggested that choosing a starting point for philosophy—in his case, consciousness or things in the world; subject or object—was primarily not a question of logic but of attitude. "The sort of philosophy one chooses will thus depend on the sort of person one is."[42] The assumptions that inform the texts of Lacan, Irigaray, and Hollywood as well as those of Lyotard, Žižek, Derrida, and Adorno suggest a world in which change is not possible because individuals are too marked by the structures they wish to escape. This is a habit of thought that in some circumstances may be useful. It encourages a form of humility, since it suggests that the individual is shaped by powers he or she does not fully control. It consoles too, since it absolves the individual of responsibility, saying that if change does not happen this is because the structure does not permit it. But the same assumptions could also be an excuse for cynicism, or for a resignation that justifies its inactivity by appealing to powers that the individual cannot possibly master, when it is conceivable that contingent, less-dramatic factors, such as the inability of a man of a particular generation to cry or talk about disappointment, create the conviction that the whole world is out of joint and the subject is necessarily and permanently exiled from fulfillment. The assumptions shared by Lacan, Irigaray, Hollywood, Lyotard,

Žižek, Derrida, and Adorno help to reconcile the individual with a particular sort of loneliness and emptiness.

My alternative approach, drawing on the phenomenological tradition, does not attempt to reconcile the individual with a necessary isolation but instead offers an account of the ways in which the human potential for communication and fulfillment has been lived to a greater or lesser degree in different historical contexts. As I'll go on to show in the next chapter, Heidegger's work is particularly useful for this project, because he does not take an isolated subject as his starting point, he does not separate the discussion of forms of identity from a consideration of the everyday habits through which we put our lives together, and he includes a consideration of the emotional or affective underpinning of our interaction with the world and other people—that is to say, the "what-it-feels-like" of our shared existence. Despite these promising beginnings, however, his account remains abstract, and, in particular, makes almost no reference to the sex of the identity he's theorizing about. This indifference comes back to haunt him, since his theory returns to the familiar male image of the isolated subject that it wished explicitly to leave behind. To avoid this unwanted return of the lone male hero, I turn to Beauvoir and Butler to explore how the interdependence of humans, which Beauvoir follows Heidegger in calling *Mitsein* and which Butler terms "primary impressionability," can be made the basis of a theory that acknowledges the importance of sexual difference and does not fall back on the image of an isolated subject. Heidegger, Beauvoir, and Butler help to establish the alternative working assumptions that will guide my account of the prehistory of modern forms of identity, the methodology for which will be set out in chapter 4.

3

The Gender of Human Togetherness

Heidegger's sketch for a model of human identity that does not focus unduly on the isolated individual can be found in a brief passage in *Being and Time* that Hubert Dreyfus has suggested is the center of the book's argument and that sympathetic readers of Heidegger have frequently returned to as a way of revitalizing the Heideggerian project of conceptualizing human togetherness.[1] The first stages of the arguments in *Being and Time* defend the idea that human life will always take place in a world, and that it makes no sense to separate what we take to be important about human life, such as consciousness, reflective thought, or agency, from an engagement with our environment. We are creatures who exist by undertaking projects in surroundings that we are part of, and we can't distill an essence of the human that would be separate from these mundane interactions. Having presented the sense of a world without which it is impossible to imagine human life, Heidegger moves on to discuss our relationship with other people. In his view, it is just as absurd to imagine a human life that is not led with and in relation to others as it is to abstract it from its environment. This element of necessary relatedness Heidegger designates with the German words *Mitdasein* and *Mitsein*, arguing that "Dasein in itself is essentially Being-with."[2] One consequence of this argument, for Heidegger, is that isolation or loneliness, even of the most profound sort, can no longer be taken to be the defining attribute of a form of identity. It will always only be a symptom, or a particular, distorted way of relating to, and being with, others. "Being-with is an existential characteristic of

Dasein even when factically no Other is present-at-hand. Even Dasein's Being-alone is Being-with in the world."[3] Human life, in Heidegger's view, just is the process of being open to the world and to fellow human beings. While the Heideggerian individual may experience a sense of isolation, he or she is always available to a world and to others who are in turn available to him or her. Though habit and socially sanctioned forgetfulness may often mask it, this mutual availability can be recovered and intentionally attended to.

Some readers otherwise sympathetic to Heidegger's project have not been able to understand what he could mean by a fundamental connectedness, or *Mitsein*, and looking briefly at their doubts can help us understand what Heidegger isn't saying, so as to get a better grasp of where his focus lies. During the 1940s, both Sartre and Levinas develop critiques of Heidegger's position. For Sartre, the level on which human beings interact with other people is more superficial than the one on which they relate to themselves. Being with other people, in his view, might entail solidarity, of the sort to be found in a rowing crew, but this is not something that could resolve the problem of how isolated individuals escape their isolation and avoid objectifying the others they interact with: "The relation of the Mit-Sein can be of absolutely no use to us in resolving the psychological, concrete problem of recognition of the Other."[4] Levinas is similarly critical of what he takes to be Heidegger's position, even as, in the notebooks he wrote in a German prisoner-of-war camp in the 1940s, he considers various approaches to the way identity is opened up from the inside. He explores the route of taking Jewishness and the related fact of persecution as an ontological category—that is to say, of grounding human identity in a situation that precedes.[5] He also reflects on the idea of participation to be found in early twentieth-century anthropology, which overcomes the distinction between subject and object but which for him seems too much like a fusion that side-steps the problem of how two people can relate to each other without losing their distinct identities.[6] The position that he settles on, and that he elaborates in the lectures delivered in 1946–47 under the title "Time and the Other," returns to ideas he had already articulated in 1937, criticizing Heidegger for treating human solitude as if it could be considered a form of involvement in the world or, in Heideggerian terminology, *In-der-Welt-sein*.[7] For Levinas, in contrast to Heidegger, there must already be someone before anyone can be involved; we must preexist our entanglement with the world. If it is anthropologically true that we are always in relation to others, it is not ontologically true because human individuals are separated by the very fact of their being: "Through sight, touch, sympathy, cooperative work, we are with others.

All these relationships are transitive: I touch an object, I see the other. But I *am* not the other. I am all alone [Mais je ne suis pas l'Autre. Je suis tout seul]. It is thus the being in me, the fact that I exist, my *existing*, that constitutes the absolutely intransitive element, something without intentionality or relationship."[8] For both of these critics of Heidegger writing in the 1940s, therefore, individuals are primarily imprisoned inside their own consciousness: "Identity is not an inoffensive relationship with itself, but an enchainment to itself."[9]

One of the places in *Being and Time* that illustrates most clearly how Heidegger differs both from the positions of Sartre and Levinas and from the views they attribute to him is the discussion of mood. Where a mood might be taken to be a private event that says little about the world, Heidegger approaches the question very differently. He observes that humans are always in a mood of sorts—a good mood, a bad mood, or an indifferent one—and that we never meet the world independently of a mood. The world is rather disclosed to us through our mood, or, to put it more accurately, mood is the medium of our relationship with the world and as such cannot be said to come either from inside us or from outside us.[10] Individuals whose emotional lives are conceived in this way can never be isolated. They will always be in a mood, and that mood will fill the room whether they like it or not. Such at least is the consequence Heidegger draws from his arguments when he returns to the topic of moods in the lectures "The Fundamental Concepts of Metaphysics," which he delivered in the winter semester of 1929–30. Here he explicitly discusses the way the mood of people who are sad or energetic shapes the way we relate to them. We meet them in their mood—that is, as Heidegger puts it, the "how" of our being together with them (*das Wie unseres Miteinander-Daseins*) rather than being a private event inside their mind.[11] Heidegger admits that we often don't reflect on or acknowledge our state of mind.[12] Nevertheless, moods are public, and public interaction occurs through the medium of moods, albeit often in the form of the pumped-up sensations of mass culture.[13] Indeed, Heidegger connects our mood and our shared existence by saying our relations with others—*Mitdasein*—are disclosed in what he terms a shared mood, or *Mitbefindlichkeit*.[14]

The image of the isolated individuals used by Sartre and Levinas doesn't engage with this level of human interaction: the shared affective states that are the medium and precondition of our encounters with each other. Rather than acknowledging the shared moods of everyday encounters, the two French philosophers abstract from everyday experience to make the special case of an individual-sitting-by-himself-in-a-room-and-trying-to-imagine-relationships the model for human interaction. For

Dan Zahavi, their criticisms of Heidegger are a useful reminder that other people remain necessarily strange and cannot be reduced to our understanding of them or to our current projects.[15] Nevertheless, the balance of shared experience and radical alterity that Zahavi hopes to strike with his account of intersubjectivity underemphasizes the departure that Heidegger, in his texts of the 1920s, is making from the self-understanding of the isolated individual. In Heidegger's argument, the shared mood comes first: It is where we meet each other, and it is the basis on which we come to our own sense of ourselves.[16] In other words, there's something going on in which we are already involved that is also the medium through which we come to a sense of each other and of ourselves. This emotional involvement is the background against which both my identity and the strangeness of other people can be experienced.

An appeal to the enabling background behind my identity and my difference from others may seem an overly abstract way of talking about human togetherness, so it is perhaps helpful to look briefly at some of the ways in which recent research in the cognitive sciences can be seen to underpin the idea, give it more empirical definition, and reestablish contact with our everyday experience. Since the accidental discovery in the 1990s by a research group at the University of Parma of what came to be called "mirror neurons" in monkey brains, empirical research into the way humans and other animals understand and interact with each other has been given a new neurological underpinning.[17] Mirror neurons fire in our brains not only when we perform meaningful actions ourselves but also when we observe them in others.[18] Following the initial discovery of mirror responses in monkeys to the experimenters' grasping movements, research has demonstrated them in humans in relation to smells, touch, the affective component of pain, language, facial expressions, emotional reactions, and communicative hand gestures as well as to simpler forms of movement, and it continues to find mirror responses in different areas of human interaction.[19] The findings have given new impetus to existing debates about how we know other people's minds, but they also potentially transform our understanding of human togetherness, moving beyond the choice that has existed since the 1990s between the Theory Theory position (that we know other people by developing a theory about their inner states) and the Simulation Theory position (that we know other people's minds by representing their experiences to ourselves with our own mind).[20]

The discovery of mirror neurons seems on first sight to have isolated the neural substrate for simulations. Vittorio Gallese, who worked in the research group in Parma that initially observed the neurons, thus argues that we understand other people's actions because our mirror neurons allow us to recreate for ourselves the experience that we see the other person going through. Someone experiences something, and we go through a weaker simulation of their experience in response and as a consequence can understand their reactions as reactions like ours: "By means of a shared neural state realized in two different bodies, the 'objectual other' becomes 'another self.' "[21] Nevertheless, Simulation Theory has been criticized from a number of different directions. It has been pointed out that even though it would appear to acknowledge a new degree of human togetherness, it remains fundamentally a Cartesian position that presupposes an isolated subject with privileged access to his own thoughts simulating the behavior of others.[22] Other critics have pointed out that it's not at all clear what the simulation is simulating. Adults and children alike describe the movements of geometric shapes for which they could not possibly be mirroring motor actions as if they were social, intentional actions like caressing or catching.[23] Similarly, mirror neurons have been found firing when human subjects observe the purposive actions of robots, which, once again, can't be said to have a state of mind for the humans to simulate.[24] Shaun Gallagher has challenged the very idea of simulating what is happening "inside" other people. What we directly see will normally be enough for us to understand and empathize with behavior we observe in familiar contexts, because what we directly see is already the product of intelligent subpersonal neuronal processes that make the world and people's responses meaningfully available to us. Mirror-neuron responses are part of the process of direct perception of people's behavior rather than an extra addition: "We do not ordinarily need to go further than what is already the rich and complex comprehension that we gain through the perception of a situated agent—that is, of an agent who is situated in an environment which also tells us something about what that person is doing and thinking."[25] Simulation theory is thus criticized for reaffirming a model that isolates the subject, for being muddled about what exactly is being simulated, and for supposing that everyday behavior has an emotional "inside" to which we need to be given special access by separate neuron responses.

The differences between Simulation Theory and its rivals, Theory Theory and Direct-Perception Theory, can be overemphasized. There is an element to be found in all three positions that looks promising for my argument precisely because it points beyond the image of an atomistic-subject-seeing-other-people-do-things, which all three positions share.[26] To put it another way: If we look again, we will see that all three positions contain a potentially productive tension, positing an isolated individual as the starting point but also moving beyond this atomistic presupposition.[27]

In addition to the mirror-neuron representation of a motor action, the original formulations of Pellegrino and Gallese contain a further element. In their first publication, in 1992, Pellegrino et al. noted that mirror neurons "can retrieve movements . . . on the basis of the meaning of the observed actions."[28] What they mean by *meaning* is quite broad, since it is something the monkeys who were the objects of the experiment share with the experimenters. They seem to mean something like the purposeful activity that both parties are involved in or, as Iacoboni would put it, that is in the behavioral repertoire of both the monkeys and the human experimenters.[29] The monkey saw the experimenter reaching for a piece of fruit and understood the significance of the reaching. Monkey and experimenter are alike involved in significant activity—in "getting things done"—and it is against the background of this shared significance that mirror neurons respond. Gallese's later publications take the idea of interaction on the basis of a common goal and develop it through his notion of a "shared manifold," which he conceives "as a multidimensional, 'we-centric' shared space" that can be "characterized at the phenomenological, functional and subpersonal level."[30] To a reader not used to the mathematical sense of manifold as a sort of space, the tropes that Gallese uses (the manifold, the shared space) are not easy to follow. Nevertheless, the point of his argument is that both parties are involved in and can both respond to something that is larger than both of them and that indeed is the precondition of their meeting as separate people.

This larger, shared involvement is presupposed by all the positions in the debate. For the Theory theorist Peter Carruthers, it features in the form of the innate but nevertheless shared background assumptions that make our simulations of other people's behavior possible in the first place; for instance, it's the know-how that allows us to tell the difference between predicting and intending without having to think that associated with each action is a feeling that we would simulate inside ourselves in order to figure out if the person we're talking to is doing one rather than the other.[31] Recent empirical work on mirror neurons confirms this idea of a guiding framework. One experiment by Valeria Gazzola has already been mentioned: Subjects responded in the same way with mirror neurons to two different films—one of a robot performing an action, the other of a human performing the same action. This leads Gazzola to suggest that "the goal of an action might be more important for mirror activations than the way in which the action is performed."[32] She reaches a similar conclusion in an experiment with subjects born without hands who, seeing purposive hand movements, respond by activating the mirror neurons associated with the foot movements they would perform to achieve the same effect. Once again it is the goal that is important rather than the specific action.[33] Both Carruthers's arguments and the evidence collected by Gazzola thus suggest there is something that we're involved in before we respond by mirroring actions or attitudes. Other experiments confirm this point: If we're already hungry, our mirror-neuron responses to the sight of someone grasping food will be stronger than if we're not.[34] If we are a man and we observe what we take to be a deserved punishment, our mirror responses to the pain of the person punished will be weaker than if we think the punishment is undeserved.[35] If Simulation and Theory Theory presupposed a shared context in which people's responses are immediately available to us, so too do Shaun Gallagher's arguments for direct perception. So it seems that wherever we may position ourselves in the debates about theories and simulations of other people's responses, we will need to presuppose a prior involvement that is the precondition of our wondering in the first place.

The question might arise whether this prior involvement is a theory or a simulation, but it can be neither, since it is the background against which a theory or simulation of another person's actions and attitudes emerges in the first place—indeed, it is the background against which our very idea of ourselves emerges. We learn simultaneously to be with people and to become ourselves by joining in the stream of human behavior that existed before we appeared. For many, this behavioral background doesn't feature in their argument. Instead, a world of fundamentally separated individuals is presupposed, rather like the world to be found in the writings of Sartre and Levinas from the 1940s.[36] Heidegger's approach is productive precisely because it questions this atomistic view of human identity. I initially turned to the mirror-neuron literature to make the Heideggerian idea of being-with more concrete. But if the discussions in the field of neuroscience suggest which physiological substrates may be generating the ineluctable relatedness of human beings, Heidegger's position at the same time illuminates the neuroscience debates. Before there are individuals to have theories about or simulate each other, there is shared human activity in a world. Heidegger's use of the word *Dasein* rather than *individual*, *subject*, or other terms from the philosophical tradition registers just this fact.[37]

For Heidegger, there is a stream of purposive, shared behavior that we find ourselves thrown into and with which we need to come to terms. It is against this stream of shared behavior that we develop a sense of our own identity and that of others, and it is as part of this stream that we resonate with our fellow human beings, or with the robots and geometrical shapes doing recognizably purposeful things; it is as part of this stream that we develop theories about other people's behavior or put ourselves in their shoes. We are meaningfully together before we are meaninglessly apart.

A position such as Heidegger's thus helps us to move beyond the presuppositions that, as well as limiting the debates about mirror neurons I've just been reviewing, we have seen both constraining readings of mystical texts and condemning postwar theorists to celebrating an epiphany that they declare to be incapable of elaboration. Heidegger's idea of being-with unites a sense of connection with an awareness of the meaningful activity through which we live out the connection. The arguments of *Being and Time* also show a theoretical awareness of the social, psychological, and linguistic forms that structure the relations between individuals and keep them at a distance from each other and from themselves. Nevertheless, Heidegger's model of being-with remains incomplete for reasons that have been pointed out by a number of critics: He argues that humans are necessarily social but paradoxically focuses on individual *Dasein*,[38] thus neglecting the communicative or empathetic aspects of human life implied by his claim that the individual is inherently entwined with others.[39] This is arguably due to the fact that he does not clearly differentiate between the enabling aspects of relations with others and the detrimental pressures of conformism. He therefore focuses more on the individual escaping the pressures of social norms than on the nurturing interdependence between human beings.[40] The upshot of these limitations is that Heidegger's account of *Mitdasein* remains very abstract. It does not bridge the gap between the fundamental layer at which the individual is necessarily open to others and the individual's everyday experiences of the constraints of social conformity, which Heidegger describes so feelingly in the initial presentation of *das Man* (the "One" or the "They").[41] Indeed, Tina Chanter has argued that, as his argument develops, Heidegger replaces the idea of our necessary togetherness with the image of an isolated, authentic individual struggling resolutely to affirm himself against conformity, betraying the promise of his own starting point. She proposes Levinas as the source for an alternative model.[42] But, as we have seen, the Levinas of the 1940s queries the very possibility of a fundamental connection, so turning to these texts would be effectively changing the topic of conversation away from primary connectedness to the problems of isolation. His later texts emphasize the rupture at the heart of individual identity more strongly than does *Time and the Other*, suggesting that my identity is, as he terms it, always already "thrown out of its saddle" and "ransomed" by the encounter with other people.[43] Nevertheless, his model depends on the notion of a primary self-possession at odds with Heidegger's account of a shared project. That is to say, in Levinas's model, we must first be in the saddle if we are to be thrown out of it. Heidegger's approach, in contrast, draws attention to the shared activity that is already underway as we more or less successfully construct an identity for ourselves. To find the tools for taking this idea further than it's allowed to develop in Heidegger, we will need to turn to sources other than Levinas for inspiration.

A first port of call is Beauvoir's *The Second Sex*, which explicitly uses the German word *Mitsein*. The term was part of philosophical discussion in France during the 1940s and was associated with attempts to give what was perceived as the individualistic approach of *Being and Time* a more social and political aspect.[44] Beauvoir's treatment of the term is interesting in this context because, while she employs it occasionally in the less emphatic, social sense that it acquired in 1940s Paris, she also uses the term, as Heidegger did, to describe a level of fundamental human connection that questions the model of isolated subjects that underpins the work that Sartre and Levinas were undertaking around the same time. When she uses the term unemphatically, she means something like human solidarity, or the arena of public activity from which women are excluded.[45] When she uses the term more emphatically, it is to describe the fundamental level at which human interaction is affected by sexual difference.[46] Coexistence is shaped by sexual difference on both levels on which Beauvoir's argument operates: the "facts" of biology and social roles. Beauvoir takes it as a biological fact that men and women have different roles in sexual reproduction: to that extent the couple, as we've already seen, can be called "a primordial form of *Mitsein* [Being-with]," since neither could reproduce and raise children without the other.[47] Beauvoir is quick to point out that the particular form the division of labor takes is not fixed, and that there is no simple connection between biological givens and the way societies deal with them, but that there is nevertheless a division and that it's not one that could be abolished. In her view, sexual difference has a different status from differences of class or race. An individual could imagine eradicating members of another social group or race, but it is inconceivable that the other sex could be exterminated (we might now add: without significant advances in genetic technology). The conflicts that arise because the current division of labor is so iniquitous should not be allowed to mask the interdependence beneath the conflict: "The division of the sexes is a biological fact, not an event in human history. It is against the background of an original *Mitsein* that the conflict has emerged, and the conflict has not broken it. The couple is a fundamental unity with its two halves riveted together, and the cleavage of society along the line of sex is impossible."[48]

If *Mitsein*, for Beauvoir, refers to the level of biological givens, it also names the underlying structures of our social interaction. Beauvoir uses the term *situation* to explain how the two levels relate to each other. For French existentialists the word has a meaning roughly equivalent to Heidegger's "Being-in-the-world." Just as, for Heidegger, we should not imagine subjects independent of the world in which they cope and come to a sense of themselves, so, for Beauvoir or Sartre, we cannot imagine a human being who isn't situated. Heidegger's term *world* gives the impression of a single indivisible entity. Beauvoir's use of *situation*, in contrast, allows her to argue that we are in more than one situation at once and that one of those situations is our body.[49] If a situation shapes us, we also shape it. While a division of labor between the sexes is given, what humans make of this division will depend on how we treat it in a particular social context. *Mitsein*, when Beauvoir uses the word in this context, means the technological, economic, and social structure that characterizes human existence in a particular epoch or culture. It is the shared life that explains the communalities of language and symbols much better than does the psychoanalytic concept of the unconscious.[50] Indeed, the term is Beauvoir's equivalent of *the unconscious*. We share symbols and we share a language because we share a way of life with our peers, not because an abstract force independent of our activity shapes the way we think.

Beauvoir thus adds to Heidegger's argument in two ways. She suggests, first, that the experience of connection will be shaped by the data of biology, and, second, that social forms of connection will also be colored by a society's interpretation of sexual difference. Aspects of this argument don't sound very Heideggerian. Heidegger warns us not to treat the data collected in science as though they showed us the world more objectively than did other forms of activity. The scientist experimenting will also be living in the shared everyday world of human activity, and for Heidegger this shared world has epistemological priority over the specialized and narrow view to be gained through the specialist activity of scientific experiment. Newton could formulate his laws of motion only because he lived in a shared world created by human activity.[51] Beauvoir would not disagree, but she wants the account of the shared world to acknowledge that the environment it discloses contains aspects that humans may deny or work to counteract but that will all the same determine the shape of their world. However, if Beauvoir adds to Heidegger the issue of gender, the question of how its biological and social aspects interact needs further clarification. Beauvoir's discussions of *Mitsein* feature adults: the couple. But the adult couple is less instructive about the border between biological and social aspects of our shared activity than is the process of socialization undergone in childhood. Thinking about how the child might experience its connection with the adult couple will allow the balance between nature and culture to be set out in more detail. To begin to develop this thought further, I will take Winnicott as my starting point. Not only does his down-to-earth approach help to curtail mystifications of isolation of the sort that we have seen in Lacan, Lyotard, Derrida, and Žižek, but also his vocabulary shows surprising affinities with that of Heidegger, thus facilitating the combination of approaches. However, when it comes to clarifying how gender roles might feature in the child's development, I'll move beyond Winnicott's framework to look at the work of Butler.

In *Playing and Reality*, Winnicott distinguishes between two different states in the psychological development of an infant, one that he termed *male* and the other *female*, insisting that, as long as they enjoy "good enough" parenting, infants of either sex will experience both.[52] The male state is one in which the infant relates to the world as a set of distinct objects, separate from him or her, in relation to which he or she can have drives and desires.[53] Psychoanalysis has traditionally devoted much attention to this type of interaction with the world, to desires, their objects, and their frustrations. Winnicott, however, maintains "that there are significant mechanisms for object-relating that are not drive-determined."[54] These are expressed in the female state. The female state is one of apparent completeness in which the baby is not even aware of being separate from the mother's breast, let alone from a wider world. For Winnicott, it is an expression of a fundamental sense of security or relatedness that "has to be thought of primarily in terms of holding and handling" rather than merely of the temporary satisfaction of the infant's desires.[55] By physically and emotionally cradling the infant, the person mothering the child allows him or her to experience a sense of total envelopment. In Winnicott's view, the only adequate term to describe this state is that of mere "being," since even to call it "being-at-one" with the world suggests a degree of separation, between me and the not-me I am at one with, which the child has yet to experience.[56]

At the beginning of life, therefore, children are with their parents and will experience what Winnicott calls mere being, since they are not yet aware of the difference between themselves and their environment. The first experience of being(-with) could thus be said to be one of shared impulses and energies, of an apparently uninhibited connectedness. However, social influences, particularly in the form of gendered patterns of behavior, will be structuring this togetherness from the very beginning, something Winnicott implicitly acknowledges in his division between "male" and "female" states. The people looking after the baby will exhibit the gendered habits of their culture to a greater or lesser degree. The baby will learn about the world and itself through these habits. It's possible, for instance, that because Mommy is breastfeeding, a way of being with other people that involves comfort and physical closeness is associated with her. Daddy, on the other hand, may show the child objects and entertain it in other ways that emphasize aspects of the physical environment. As a result, the sense of objects in a world that took shape through playing with Daddy will have been filtered by his particular way of being in the world and his ability or inability to be emotionally connected to the child. The examples are brief and stereotypical, but the point is to illustrate how the very sense of a world with objects and other people, and the range of responses to the environment available to the child, will be learned with adults who themselves are already gendered. Developmental psychology has studied the degree to which infants gain a sense of the world through their interactions with people. They do not relate directly to the world but learn to share attention and do things with the adults looking after them, or with other children, and through that shared attention and joint activity they come to inhabit a world.[57] The grown-ups sharing the activities with them will already have adopted the habits by which, as a man or a woman, they relate to the world and others, so the activities through which the infant gains a sense of the world will always come with a certain gender inflection.

This gendering of the very experience of a shared world would seem to be the experiential background to Judith Butler's argument that gender determines sex. Ever since the publication of *Gender Trouble* in 1990, she has argued that we should not take the biological body as an incontrovertible given. The form in which we experience our bodies, as gendered in a particular way, ethnically defined, and so forth, is culturally determined. In nature there are no male-versus-female or black-versus-white bodies from which social categories take their cue, but rather the continuous spectrum of differently shaped and colored bodies is divided up and given shape by cultural norms and expectations. "There is no gender identity behind the expressions of gender; that identity is performatively constituted by the very 'expressions' that are said to be its results."[58] As well as learning about the world and other people, therefore, the child will learn about its own body through gendered habits. Indeed, it will acquire a body, which is its own and is distinct from those of others to which it nevertheless relates both intellectually and instinctively through these gendered habits. So, to vary Beauvoir's famous phrase, one is not born a body, one becomes one.

Butler's approach promises to clarify how the natural and the cultural aspects of *Mitsein* relate to each other, because it encourages us not to take our bodies as a given but to be aware of their social shaping. However, the disadvantage of her position is that it has no space for the perspective of the human being who is acquiring a body and an identity. Not only biology and sex but lived experience are effaced in her argument by the social codes that produce gender, leaving the codes with no material to work with and no one to do the working. That makes her texts difficult to read. If we look back at the quotation about performative identity, we see that she is using a passive construction ("identity is constituted") and a form of personification ("expressions" are doing the constituting, not the people enunciating them) as well as employing a spatial figure (the preposition "behind") but only negatively, so she invites us to think spatially (one thing behind another) but negates this image without replacing it with another: "There is no gender identity behind the expressions of gender; that identity is performatively constituted by the very 'expressions' that are said to be its results."

Butler embraces these difficulties because she wants to be able to criticize social codes without seeming to appeal to a position outside society from which to assess them. In her argument, the expectations that make bodies socially recognizable, and socially valued or socially despised, are open to infinite renegotiation. Prevailing discourses can be contested and modified, producing new identities that themselves are contestable, and so on.[59] This raises the question of whether what drives the renegotiation is an image of the human body, undistorted by social norms, that discourse could, in principle, adequately represent. Butler, however, insists that this idea is a specter that is produced by the process of socialization itself and that gets projected back as a fantasy into a time before socialization, a time to which we could never have access.[60] In her account, there is no theoretical need for such an image, even though some thinkers—for example, Jürgen Habermas—may insist that renegotiation is possible only if the norms governing that critique can be set out.[61] According to Butler, critique is possible without uncritically fixing the norms in advance of the process of criticism.[62] We can remodel ourselves, and renegotiate the terms of our social formation, from within but, at the same time, *against* the terms of social identity. Indeed, for Butler, virtue is precisely this process of forming oneself against the terms of socialization and making space for new, and as yet uncategorized, forms of identity.[63]

The notion that the norms governing our behavior are varied and flexible enough for some to be turned against others in the gradual process of our self-transformation seems plausible, especially if an individual's identity is not thought of as uniform but rather as a collection of different aspects that can be turned productively against each other. But it's not clear why Butler needs the complexities of a discursively formed identity with nothing beyond discourse to make this point. As Toril Moi has pointed out, her argument is haunted by the specter of an oddly uniform and stable body that she must continuously exclude, allowing a unified subject to control her argument, albeit in the negative form of the prediscursive subject to be denied.[64] In fact, the unified prediscursive subject does not only feature as a specter to be avoided, it is also implicit in the positive formulations of Butler's own position. This becomes apparent in some of the texts that she wrote after *Gender Trouble* and *Bodies That Matter*, moving away from her earlier, optimistic focus on the malleability of social norms.

In the earlier texts, Butler insisted that we can infinitely renegotiate prevailing norms, suggesting that we can learn to speak about ideas, desires, forms of behavior, or ways of life that seemed previously to fall outside socially acceptable language. In *The Psychic Life of Power*, however, she sets a limit to the linguistic contestations, arguing that subjectivity itself entails a "founding ambivalence," which condemns individuals to being permanently at odds with themselves.[65] When thinking about gender roles, Butler is fundamentally upbeat, but, having made the quasi-Heideggerian point that we cannot separate ourselves from the shared conventions of human interaction, she adds that this interaction will always be damaging, giving her theory a tragic twist, which does not seem justified by her starting point.[66] In Butler's view, the individual's autonomy is permanently compromised because it is founded on terms he or she did not choose and on an act of renunciation that will never properly be remembered or redressed. We become ourselves through a process that subjects us to social regulation and that leaves an underlying feeling of melancholy, which we cannot overcome because it makes us what we are. However, we are so entwined with social structures that it is misleading to speak of "internalizing" authority, because this would suggest that we could imagine ourselves independent of it or even "externalize" it and free ourselves. Instead, Butler argues that "the boundary that divides the outside from the inside is in the process of being installed precisely through the regulation of the subject."[67] We become ourselves only through a relationship with power that simultaneously places us at one remove from ourselves.

It is not clear why Butler conceives of the relationship of mutual dependence between individuals in such negative terms. If we are, as Heidegger suggests, always and necessarily with other people, then that social relatedness must fulfill what we are as much as constrain us. Indeed, it couldn't be otherwise, unless human life is being measured by a superhuman standard. It makes no sense to say that the way we are could *never* be fulfilling, for otherwise we could have no concept of fulfillment. Butler's treatment of what she terms "primary impressionability" clarifies the presuppositions about human interaction that underlie her downbeat assessment. Primary impressionability describes a human being's openness to others, through which he or she arrives at a sense of identity. As Butler puts it, the term refers to "a way of being constituted by an Other which precedes the formation of the sphere of the mine itself."[68] This notion that we are constituted "by" another, as opposed to, for instance, "with" others, as in Heidegger's *Mitdasein*, or coexistence, betrays in the very formulation of the idea the direction in which Butler's thoughts are going. In her account, we become subjects by being recognized as such. However, this process of recognition relies on preexisting norms and language, which means that recognition will always divide us from ourselves. Like Lacan and Žižek, Butler is claiming that identity will always be the product of misrecognition. However, for Butler, the problem is not just that the norms that give me an identity are not mine. The dispossession occurs at the level of primary impressionability, before I have a socially encoded identity, and so affects any identity I might acquire. The Other who confers recognition on me is somehow always already having an effect on me, which Butler assumes to be violent: "I am wounded, and I find that the wound itself testifies to the fact that I am impressionable, given over to the Other in ways that I cannot fully predict or control."[69]

Butler does not explain why human interaction will always be violent; she simply assumes that it will be. This parti pris for the bleak is particularly evident in the way she uses Winnicott. In her account of primary impressionability, she briefly mentions the idea of holding, which Winnicott, in almost Heideggerian terms, says denotes "not only the actual physical holding of the infant, but also the total environmental provision prior to the concept of *living with*."[70] For Winnicott, an environment that is "good enough"—it does not have to be perfect—gives an infant a sense of security and warmth and helps it develop trust in the world and a sense of identity. However, Butler uses the term very differently: To her, "holding" entails being caught in a web of social relations and a language that has been imposed.[71] The contrast with Winnicott shows what Butler leaves out of her account. She omits any positive aspects of human interaction, such as the sense of safety that may result from the infant being held "well enough," and as a consequence gives the impression that no socialization could possibly be "good enough." But if no socialization is "good enough" there must linger, behind her account of human development, the idea of a self that can exist better in isolation and have a sense of its identity independently of others. Otherwise, she could not conceptualize our first relationships with others as exclusively hurtful. Butler's arguments are structured by the assumption of a unified self she does not make explicit, but that predetermines her conclusions in a way that doesn't fit the apparently reforming impulses of her texts.[72]

Like the anxiety, betrayed by Bataille and Hollywood, that communication with others will destroy the individual's identity, the presupposition that a sovereign and undamaged subject exists before all interaction is a fantasy image. Whereas the former could be read as an indirect expression of how dangerous emotional interaction feels to a particular type of subject, the image underlying Butler's work could be interpreted as an expression of disappointment resulting from experiences of rejection. Two moves need to be made to stop rejection from then being treated one-sidedly as the sole foundation for a theory of human interaction. The first is to make certain that the argument always includes—or does not exclude—the possibility of connectedness. This is not an easy idea to formulate because, while it is easy to understand how two separate things may become connected, it is difficult to imagine the connection of two things that have never been separated. Nor should it be thought that this sort of connection needs a single label, a new noun to denote it. The experience itself doesn't happen in language, and is a form of activity: a particular way of being aware as two or more people tune into each other. This awareness is also a form of vulnerability, and people get hurt. But the "wounding," as Butler calls it, doesn't happen because a separate Other will always wound me. There is initially no Other, and I get hurt because the connection is limited in some way; because it gets interrupted, or because the person I'm dealing with is ashamed or overly cautious. I (or we both) get hurt when the situation is not able to unfold as it would do of its own accord. Winnicott suggests that experiences have an internal rhythm. A baby given a spoon to play with by its mother will develop an interest in it, make it part of himself, use it and finish with it.[73] He suggests this is because a baby is from the start "not just a body, he [*sic*] is a person."[74]

To use either the term *body* or *person* is perhaps premature: Babies are learning to be bodies and people. If Winnicott insists on the term *person* nevertheless, he is emphasizing the sense of respect a person is due and acknowledging a certain purposiveness in his or her action; not a conscious plan, but an unfolding that we can adapt to more or less willingly. Following Winnicott, contact could also be said to have its own rhythm, which will be respected to a greater or lesser degree by the people involved. To understand this conceptually—rather than intuitively: We probably most of us have a sense of how to share things and of when an experience is finished—requires a particular concept of agency, one that is likely to be expressed in tropes of personification or verbs that suggest we're adapting to something rather than controlling it. The situation, as the subject of the verb, unfolds, and we see how it pans out. We're involved in it, but by tuning in or "going with the flow." To avoid the image, evident in Butler's texts, of a prediscursive unity damaged by interaction with others, we need something like this sense of people meeting in a situation and letting things happen: shared growth.

The second alteration necessary to Butler's approach to prevent wounding being treated as the template of all human interaction is a change in the way constraints and negations are conceptualized. Butler is still Hegelian enough to work with oppositions, at least at an implicit level—for instance, "recognition that adequately acknowledges what I am" versus "wounding that damages me."[75] But these are patterns of thought that ultimately return us to the image of a separate subject or thing confronting other subjects or things, and so they produce various phantom problems—how will these two separate entities relate to each other? do justice to each other? ever know or understand each other? etc.—because we have decreed through our presuppositions that the two are separate from the start and so, in effect, incommunicado.

The alternative is to do without oppositions, so rather than having a choice between recognition and misrecognition, there are different types of recognition, some of which refuse to acknowledge the contact with the other person, others of which establish a framework in which the contact can flourish and develop. We are always already in contact with each other, and our behavior handles the contact in a variety of ways, some more satisfactory than others. This is a conceptual tool used by Heidegger, for whom, as we have seen, loneliness is a deficient modus of togetherness.[76] Individual formulations, such as this one, can sound comic. But they draw attention to the world that must already be in place before we can be lonely, trying to describe as fully as possible the behavior and the context that "being lonely" involves. This will always involve thinking about what happens to human babies, so perhaps one of the attractions of theories that don't do this is that that they don't ask us to remember a dependence that was frequently associated with disappointment, but instead let us imagine that we arrive in the world, like Oskar Mazerath in Günter Grass's *The Tin Drum*, as a homunculus fully in control of our mental and physical faculties, listening from an ironic distance to the confusions of our parents and the self-destructive fluttering of a moth against a light bulb.

If the deep structures of Butler's thought are Hegelian, so too are Beauvoir's, for all her interest in Heidegger's concept of coexistence. In her diary from the early war years, she explicitly reflects on the philosophical choice, as she sees it, to be made between Heidegger and Hegel. Indeed, the entry for January 21, 1941, opens with the question *Hegel ou Heidegger?*[77] In *The Second Sex* she combines the two, suggesting that a Hegelian sense of the conflict between subjects (or between consciousnesses) is needed to complement too rosy a view of *Mitsein* as solidarity and friendliness,[78] but at the same time arguing that the conflict doesn't break or call into question the coexistence.[79] However, despite this apparent even-handedness, and, indeed, despite ironic criticism of his rationalist passion, Hegel has the upper hand. She describes in a Hegelian vocabulary both the iniquities of women's situation and the positive alternative of reciprocal acknowledgment.[80] That's because she assumes, in existential fashion, that the fundamental human situation is one of loneliness rather than *Mitsein*. The family house offers the girl only a false protection against what Beauvoir calls "her abandonment in the wide world."[81] In this bleak environment, liberty is experienced only as a form of anxiety from which, even as children, we flee into forms of alienation.[82]

To suggest that Beauvoir, like Butler, has a deep commitment to Hegelian modes of thought is not to suggest that Hegelian dialectics must be straightforwardly abandoned in favor of Heideggerian patterns of thought. We don't need to choose between the Hegelian and the Heideggerian models. Dialectical oppositions, or Heidegger's suspension of oppositions in a single more fundamental term, should both be treated as, as it were, rhetorical figures: ways of organizing the material that will be more or less useful in different situations. We can't stand outside the situation to verify which fits better. We can only adapt to it as it unfolds and use something like linguistic tact to assess which form of words will be the more useful at any particular time.

We now have a working hypothesis and some rhetorical tools for rethinking the question of personal identity. The working hypothesis is the idea of a fundamental connectedness that precedes the formation of the habits we identify with as our identity. Our connection with others, but also with the world, will, from the very start, be shaped by patterns of gendered behavior, because we can't avoid being born into a world where a person's sex affects how he or she behaves. By the time we're big enough to know about it, the damage is already done, and we can only assess its extent. Our gendered behavior will determine how we deal with our own body and how we relate to the bodies of other people. At the same time, these patterns of behavior are coping with the situation of a body with a particular constellation of sexed attributes, or what Melissa Hines has called "a complex mosaic of male and female characteristics."[83] So while our view of what is defining about our sex or biology will be skewed by our expectations, and while there may be things we habitually are unable to notice, nevertheless, the physiological factors will continue to play a role. In order to change our habits, we do not need to imagine a "natural" body that social expectations could be altered to fit (the static idea of a "fit" is itself a social expectation), nor do we need to derive critical potential only from social norms without any reference to bodily behavior. The whole debate about norms, which has arisen in particular over the work of Foucault, is addressing the wrong issue. Whether it is Habermas and Charles Taylor claiming that Foucault secretly presupposes an ideal of "the body and its pleasure" against which he can measure the structures he criticizes, or Judith Butler saying, on the contrary, that Foucault does without fixing norms in advance, attention is drawn away from what we're actually doing.[84] Norms for bodily behavior are always more than norms. They are part of the practices through which we shape our connection with other people and set our distance from the world. They are part of the way we experience connection, albeit sometimes in the deficient mode of not noticing it. To that extent, we're always doing more than the norms, or always using the norms to do something very particular (manage connection in the way we do), so we don't need alternative norms, but rather we need to describe as fully as possible what we're doing. Once we've noticed as much as we can, we can have a conversation about whether or not what we're doing is what we really want.

Heidegger occasionally says something similar in the way he presents his idea of the One or the They, *das Man*—that is to say, of the shared conventional habits of everyday interaction. Most of the time we're not really being ourselves, we're being what we're expected to be. This is not wrong, in fact it's inevitable, and Heidegger argues that shared assumptions and habits will be a feature of any society (in his jargon, he calls the One an "Existential").[85] These shared habits are necessarily part of the way we relate to others; they are the necessary form of *Mitsein*. If we want to be ourselves more authentically, we don't need to escape the arena of shared interpretations; in fact, we can't.[86] We need instead to modify the shared conventions.[87] This modification takes the form of noticing what we've being doing all along. So the problem is not what norm can we reach to legitimate our critique but rather how can we notice what it is we're already doing. Heidegger's answers, as we've already seen, return us to an image of the isolated individual. He also, as Beauvoir does too, claims that anxiety and dislocation are a more fundamental way of being in the world than trust and a sense of at-home-ness, the latter being a modification of the former.[88] But the image of the isolated hero that underpins these comments again only distracts attention from the way our sense of who we are and what we want is inseparable from our connection with other people. So we need a clearer account—clearer than Heidegger's, Beauvoir's, or Butler's—of how we come to notice what we've been doing all along.

The difficulty is not primarily epistemological or theoretical but psychological. It is not that the behavior is unavailable for inspection; it's more that we don't like to look at it, or we don't think it's worth looking at, because it's too trivial or too obvious, or because it shows our involvement in processes it would be easier not to have to acknowledge. The inability to acknowledge what we're doing is astutely portrayed in a story that Kafka wrote near the end of his life. "A Little Woman" was written while Kafka was living with Dora Diamant in Berlin during the winter of 1923–24.[89] It records a male narrator's difficulties with a woman who is distressed and angered by his every action and indeed by his very existence. Her suffering is all the more puzzling because, as the narrator insists, "No relationship exists between us that would force her to suffer on my account" (322). He once suggested to her that she should try to forget him, but the idea provoked such an outburst that he resolved never to mention it again (323). Instead he makes small attempts to reform himself, even though he does not altogether believe that the woman is in pain—he suspects she may suffer solely in order to cast him in a bad light (324). But his efforts are to no avail. It is not individual aspects of his conduct that cause the problem but the mere fact of his existing, or having ever existed—not even suicide would be a solution (328). A friend suggested that he solve the problem by travelling, but the narrator feels the need to stay in order to contain the situation (329). Though he insists he is guiltless, he nevertheless lives with the nagging sense that the woman could one day provoke a crisis, or that an outsider might feel moved to call him to account. On a rational level, he is certain that this moment of decision will never occur and that, even if it did, he has nothing to fear beyond the unpleasantness of being called on to justify himself. Yet for all his intellectual grasp of the situation, his body cannot give up the sense of impending doom (332). Given the situation, his conclusions are surprisingly sanguine. "However I look at things, therefore, it always emerges, and that remains my position, that, even if I am, as it were, only just keeping this little trifle hidden behind my hand, I will nevertheless be able peacefully to continue my life as it is, undisturbed by the world, for a very long time, despite all the raging of the woman" (333).

The story portrays an exhausting but nevertheless unbreakable relationship. It has tended to be read in ways that focus on the perspective of the male narrator: as a portrait of Kafka's landlady in Berlin, as a Gnostic miniature of suffering allayed, or as an allegory of feminized Jewish identity.[90] These are all interpretations that look at how the man copes with the monstrous woman, or at how the woman is in fact a symbol for male identity. But what if, as Elisabeth Bronfen asks, in a similar vein, of the femme fatale, "rather than treating her as a fetish, projection, or symptom, one were to treat her instead as the subject of her narrative?"[91] There is no reason to privilege the man's voice over the woman's. When both views are taken into account, the story then appears as the tale of a psychological symbiosis. The male narrator, whose rationality has been officially acknowledged by society (the text mentions a diploma, 332), finds himself unable to grasp what binds him to a woman or to understand her account of their relationship. At the same time, he betrays the strength of the unintelligible bond through his own behavior: He cannot leave her alone and devotes the greater portion of his energy to containing the threat that, to his imagination, she potentially poses. Indeed, it could be concluded that he acknowledges her power and wants something from her, but this want exceeds both his rational and his imaginative grasp of the situation. The text offers no explanation of the bond that exists between the man and the woman, nor does it sketch a resolution.[92]

The story records a situation in which neither party can articulate what it is that binds them together. At the same time, the story describes more than it explains, such as the fact that their routine seems to involve the woman's being outside the house whenever he leaves in the morning (328) and that on at least one occasion she has been in the same room as him, raging and sinking into an armchair (330). The narrator also draws attention to his nervousness, even though he explicitly denies it has anything other than physiological causes, being the product of his exhaustion (332). The narrator's actions are thus not entirely determined by or confined to behavior that fits his self-image. Something, however, prevents him from making the connection between what he actually does and what he acknowledges to himself that he does. Is it his investment in the socially recognized diploma to the certificate of which he thinks the woman's raging can add only a curlicue (332)? Is it the fact that he doesn't seem to have a body? Until his exhaustion registers itself at the end of the text, he seems to be only a collection of respectable opinions, whereas aspects of the woman's physical appearance and demeanor are repeatedly drawn to our attention. Is it a reluctance to acknowledge his loneliness? The woman has friends and family who worry about her (324), whereas his daily life seems to be solitary, apart from the conversation he reports with the friend who advises him to travel for a while (329). Is his situation also contributed to by the fact that the woman, in her wrath, herself omits to say what it is, other than everything he does, that she's angry about? Both sides of the couple sustain the failure of communication, not because she's his Other but because neither can say why it is that they need each other.

To resolve a situation such as this needs a form of honesty, rather than theoretical somersaults, and a willingness on behalf of both parties to see how they contribute. The norms and expectations governing their behavior will already be part of the situation. They don't need to be added from the outside, and there can be no point adding new injunctions if they're not actually the ones determining people's responses. One possible obstacle to the process of acknowledging what we do might be the feeling that it is impossible to say the things that need to be said (as Lyotard, Derrida, Žižek, and Adorno all appear to have thought they couldn't describe what they wanted). But this feeling of inarticulacy needn't be generalized into a fact about language as such. It's more likely that the feeling arises because we haven't yet found the right words or the right person to confide in. In this situation, Stanley Cavell suggested, we are grateful to poetry.[93] But that's a comment that puts him firmly among the generation of modernists, like Adorno, who looked to a particular version of art to say the things their habits didn't otherwise allow them to articulate. There's no reason to confine to art the ability to revivify our vocabulary. There are other ways of reminding ourselves of the things that it is possible to say. Psychoanalysis is an obvious contender, with techniques like free association. But just as the hopes associated with art are indissociable from the habits of a particular generation—that is to say, from a particular form of identity—so psychoanalysis can reinforce some of the habits we might in fact need to modify if we are to notice and articulate things we can't currently see. We've already seen this in the way that Lacan's, Irigaray's, and Hollywood's readings of mystical texts were limited by unexamined assumptions about identity. I'll return to psychoanalysis in the last section of the book, once it is easier to do so without shoring up bad habits. In the meantime, we can learn to see the contours of our own behavior more clearly by comparison, either with the assumptions and customs of others cultures or with the habits of the cultures of which we ourselves are the inheritors.[94] In the argument that follows, I plan to take the historical approach, because that better fits my training as a cultural critic. But I wouldn't claim that, where the aim is to surprise ourselves into noticing more about our own behavior, a historical rather than an intercultural approach need be thought to have methodological priority. Either might be effective, depending on the circumstances. But whichever approach we choose would be effective, not because identity is inevitably imbued with the past, or because identity is inevitably shaped by the cultures it excludes, but to the degree that it supplied ways of describing human activity that enriched and expanded our view of what we do when we do our identity.[95] It would be effective because of the way it combined with our current habits and facilitated their modification or development. In neither case are we guaranteed success. We can look to the past or to alien cultures merely to confirm what we already know about ourselves. If someone doesn't want to learn, there's little to be done to force him or her. I don't, therefore, need a theoretical justification for my turning to the past as a way of surprising myself, but I do need to be as clear as possible about the tools with which I'm approaching the material, since they will shape the image of identity that I formulate and, as a consequence, my chances of noticing something new, as we've seen in the cases of Lacan, Irigaray, and Hollywood. Before moving on to the historical material, we thus need to review some better- and some less-well-known approaches to the history of modern Western forms of identity, starting with the later work of Michel Foucault—to review them in order to understand which tools will help us most in elaborating a fuller, defamiliarizing description of what we do when we do our identity.

4

Histories of Modern Selfhood

When Foucault turned to his investigation of sexuality in Athens of the fourth century BC and Rome of the first and second centuries AD, it was precisely to write a history of forms of selfhood that did not confirm what he already knew. "The object was to learn to what extent the effort to think one's own history can free thought from what it silently thinks, and so enable it to think differently."[1] He called this process getting free of oneself, or "the knower's straying afield from himself."[2] In a sense this is what his work had been trying to do ever since the 1960s. Having abandoned a phenomenological approach, Foucault was interested in understanding what gave experience its particular form in any era. He was always concerned to stand outside the category of the human subject and analyze how we came to have a sense of the human in the first place, asking what made the category come into being, and what alternatives it excluded.

An investigation into the framework structuring our experience would seem to be a good way of drawing attention to the otherwise unremarkable habits through which our contact with the world and with other people is given its shape and texture. However, in the works of the 1960s and 1970s, Foucault's take on human activity is too abstract to give a clear picture of the concrete behavior through which we constitute our own identity, and it's not until the works of the 1980s that this question can be more directly addressed. In the 1960s and 1970s, Foucault seems to suppose that, because he is analyzing what made the very category of humanity arise, the agent of this process will not be human beings but rather "an anonymous and polymorphous will to knowledge, capable of regular transformations and caught up in an identifiable play of dependence."[3] Foucault's job, as the historian of knowledge, is then to wryly record the transformations of the will to knowledge. In the course of the 1970s, his approach to human activity becomes less abstract and his work is more obviously populated with people rather than discursive effects. *Discipline and Punish* moves away from the constitution of academic disciplines to trace the way particular forms of behavior were inculcated by prisons, factories, schools, and military training, producing the docile body necessary for the smooth functioning of an industrial society: "a working body that is concentrated, diligent, adjusted to the time of production, supplying exactly the force required."[4] The book isn't very interested in recording from the inside what it feels like to be a disciplined body; as Sonia Kruks has observed, "Foucault's disciplinary subjects do not appear to feel fear, frustration, anxiety or unhappiness."[5] Nevertheless, it acknowledges that disciplinary processes will also produce an inner life, that they are a "technology of the soul" as much as a bodily regime.[6] However, the activity that drives social developments is still described very abstractly. Foucault suggests that in the eighteenth and nineteenth centuries the "production apparatus" changed and demanded a new "physics of power."[7] The production apparatus is a more concrete motor of social change than the anonymous and polymorphous will to knowledge—in fact, it sounds quite close to a Marxist idea of the mode of production, except that there's no class behind the production apparatus and no class constituted by it. At the same time, the underlying structure of Foucault's argument is similar to that of his earlier work insofar as an anonymous apparatus shapes people rather than people being shaped by the human activity that they encounter and participate in as they are socialized.[8]

The first volume of the *History of Sexuality* addresses this problem by rethinking power. When Foucault extends his history of the normalized docile body to look at the question of sexuality, he decides that bodies aren't so docile after all. The practices that normalize them also make them agents, subjects who act as much as subjects who are subjected.[9] But he still doesn't leave much of a space for describing human activity. Everything that occurs in the life of a subject is now simultaneously forming a docile identity and shaping a potential site of resistance. But the balance between docility and resistance is unclear. If agency is to be found wherever the abstract structure is, then normalization and resistance become indistinguishable and we're back where we started. We need specific actions producing specific effects in particular contexts, and we also need a sense of growth or cumulative effects if resistance is to be more than the punctual, tactical interventions—leaving no lasting mark on the situation—that Michel de Certeau adds to Foucault's arguments in *The Practice of Everyday Life*.[10]

To solve this problem, Foucault looked first to the idea of "governmentality"—that is to say, the discourses and practices through which control is exercised and a normal population is generated. Power becomes less abstract where there are discourses assessing how it should be deployed. The processes of power can be questioned and shaped, and Foucault, in this phase, gets interested in liberalism not as a doctrine or form of politics but as a "critical reflection on governmental practice."[11] Power can interrogate how it deploys itself. Nevertheless, human activity is still hard to spot behind the personifications of power and discourse, and it's still not quite clear what purposes a normal population serves other than those of an anonymous apparatus. Finally, in the late 1970s, Foucault shifts focus from government to self-government.[12] The stage is then set for his history of what he called "practices of the self," through which he'll document not just the wider codes shaping human experience but the way these codes are internalized and used by individuals as they make themselves the ethical subjects of their own behavior.[13]

By the 1980s, therefore, Foucault's investigations of the framework of experience acknowledge that the behavior and background assumptions we otherwise take for granted are the product of human activity rather than being shaped by a quasi-metaphysical principle such as the will to knowledge or the disciplinary apparatus. Human activity can return to the scene, because Foucault has found a way of describing even self-consciousness as a form of activity, so there is no risk of experience seeming to have an immediacy that makes it independent of social structures. Self-knowledge, viewed from this perspective, is not the product of privileged moments of introspection but is the result of different forms of self-testing, such as testing what deprivations one can withstand.[14] It need no longer be viewed in isolation but, as Foucault explains in the summary of his lectures for the academic year 1979/80, can be placed "in the much broader interrogation that serves as its explicit or implicit context: What should one do with oneself? What work should be carried out on the self? How should one 'govern oneself' by performing actions in which one is oneself the objective of those actions, the domain in which they are brought to bear, the instrument they employ, and the subject that acts?"[15]

The vocabulary of Foucault's later work has the methodological appeal of talking about the varieties of self-activity without assuming either that a technique of the self necessarily requires a stable agent to be in place for the activity to happen or that self-reflexive introspection must be given a special status. Foucault is not troubled by assumptions about agency and self-consciousness that can otherwise limit discussions of identity—the assumption, that is, that individual agency and self-awareness, the very things that need to be analyzed, are not only given in advance but have some special normative status that forbids us to call them into question. But if this is the advantage of his approach, it is also one of the disadvantages. One of the reasons Foucault can treat his vocabulary of techniques of the self so lightly is that the identity he is studying—that of the free man in Athens and in Rome—is one that his primary texts do not question. They do not interrogate what it is to be a citizen subject; they ask only how to do it more stylishly. An approach of this kind could be said to be descriptively true; that's to say, in a society there will be existing models for behavior that we adapt to and take over. We don't invent our identity from scratch; identity is rather a preexisting current of activity that we join in with. In that sense, it's not really our identity at all, which is one of the reasons Heidegger uses the impersonal term *Dasein*. Agency (behaving as an individual who is more or less stable and who takes responsibility for their actions) and self-consciousness (being someone who cultivates and values moments of introspection) are socially approved models of behavior available in some cultures, not the abstract key to identity in all cultures.

In Foucault's argument, we become agents of our own lives in the way we relate to this existing stream of activity and give it our particular mark, elaborating and stylizing our activity in what he terms the exercise of our power and practice of our liberty.[16] We don't, however, question the underlying assumptions. We don't, for instance, ask about the habits that keep the free man apart from the women in his household, from his slaves, or from non-Athenians. It's not clear whether Foucault thinks we should. His arguments are hard to pin down, because his general technique or guiding trope is that of irony. He never conceals that he is writing only about free men and that the behavior described is not always great for women or slaves. Indeed, he states explicitly that he's describing an "ethics of men made for men."[17] Nevertheless, the text contains elements that go beyond the distancing documentation of the exploitative practices of Greek and Roman patriarchs. Alongside the irony is another element that it is hard not to call autobiographical. As it is presented in the introduction to the second volume, philosophy appears to be a way for the "I" who is present from the very first sentence of the book to get free of himself. The book is an autobiographical essay in the sense of being an experiment on himself by the philosopher: "an exercise of oneself in the activity of thought."[18] Irony serves this self-overcoming by allowing Foucault to escape a moralizing, introspective discourse about personal identity that he seems to find limiting and to focus instead on the self-fashioning of the free man of classical antiquity.[19] But for all his ironic highlighting of the virility of these techniques of the self, Foucault does not question the self-controlling isolation of the free man. He may note that, in first- and second-century Rome, it was "a generally accepted principle that one could not attend to oneself without the help of another."[20] But he nevertheless seems to identify too strongly with the self-mastery and self-stylization of the self-contained free man to challenge these traits methodologically. Indeed, in one of his last interviews, he uses a Socratic exhortation to be self-controlled as his closing slogan: "Make freedom your foundation, through mastery of yourself."[21] As a result, when he reads the prescriptive manuals for sexual activity that are his main sources, he does not stand back to ask either what the behavior they promote excludes or what it depends on. He confines himself to the texts, and does not reconstruct the way of life of which they were only a partial reproduction. He does not use other sources or, indeed, a close reading of the texts themselves to uncover the emotional and behavioral preconditions, not only for the man but also for his household, of the ideal of virile self-mastery.

Foucault thus develops a vocabulary for talking about activities that constitute identity, but he is not concerned to explore the shared basis of these activities. Instead, he writes a history of different sorts of self-control, questioning the idea of an inner secret to identity but not the model of an isolated individual. This should perhaps come as no surprise to the reader of his early work, since the ideal of a detached stoic self-mastery reproduces in another guise the distanced, ironic perspective that was the hallmark of his earlier texts. To break out of this pattern, it would be necessary to look not just at techniques of the self but at the techniques of coexistence, through which individuals delimit their identity—that is, to make visible the wider context of shared activity of which the techniques of self-mastery are a part.

The shared activity from which our habits of selfhood arise features more prominently in Charles Taylor's *Sources of the Self* because of his focus on what he calls "moral frameworks."[22] The premise of his history of modern forms of identity is that we can't not be morally involved. Moral ideas aren't something we add on to a world that in itself is essentially neutral; they are part of the very process by which we develop a sense of the world in the first place. Presenting what he calls a "phenomenological account of identity,"[23] Taylor argues that we always live in a situation that matters to us in some way and in which we're elaborating our projects in conversation with others. This line of argument draws on a tradition that does not separate the person knowing or engaging with the world from the things he or she studies but rather, like Heidegger, develops a position beyond the Cartesian subject–object division. In line with this tradition, Taylor also adds that our world will always be shared with other people, it's not a fiction we make up independently.[24]

The shared habits have evolved historically, and it's a major part of Taylor's argument that this historical evolution has in the West not produced an easily unifiable collection of attachments but rather ways of doing things that are in conflict with each other without being able to explain each other away.[25] No single habit can trump or absorb all the others, so the modern identity is inescapably involved in activities that pull in different directions. The bulk of Taylor's book is devoted to sketching the different habits that have developed since the Reformation to claim our allegiance. These are, among other things, the habit of valuing, and defining ourselves by, what we do in our everyday life that Taylor traces back to the Reformation; an aspiration to think things through for ourselves, without reference to tradition or authority, and an associated ideal of individual autonomy, developments that Taylor brings together under the title of "self-responsible freedom" and traces back to the seventeenth century and in particular the philosophies of Descartes and Locke; and, finally, the belief that nature both outside us and within us can guide and ground us, even where we lack a shared vocabulary for affirming it and must rely on the imagination of poets, be they Romantic or modernist, to find the right words. Taylor's objection to the criticisms of modern forms of identity, such as those leveled by Derrida and Foucault, is that they do not acknowledge that they themselves, both in their theory and in their day-to-day lives, draw on the habits that in their writings they claim to be able to do without. In the form of their texts, they celebrate the deconstructing or self-fashioning power of subjectivity even as they dispel the myth of human agency in their content.[26] Moreover, Taylor doubts that they have given up ideas of agency, responsibility, or fulfillment in their everyday lives, and so they are in their day-to-day existences "living by variants of what they deny."[27] Taylor aims instead to make visible the range of habits we draw on in our everyday lives and to argue that we can't pick and choose; we are implicated in the whole "package."[28] The developments that he traces in the seventeenth and eighteenth century, from the formulation of Cartesian philosophy through to the Romantic rejection of disengaged reason, established a multifaceted framework that still shapes our habits whether we acknowledge it or not. We will be in a much better position to engage with this inheritance if we do acknowledge it.

Taylor's account draws attention to shared activity and asks us to acknowledge the habits that we're actually involved in. At the same time, the vocabulary he uses to describe this behavior is no less abstract than that we have seen in Heidegger and Butler. He frequently uses the metaphor of a space when discussing the shared framework, talking about a "moral space," a "space of questions," a "space of moral issues."[29] But it's not clear where or how such a space exists. The metaphor occludes the human activity that Taylor wishes simultaneously to draw attention to, by separating activity from belief and focusing more on the latter. This is partly a product, as Taylor freely admits, of his primary focus on philosophical and literary texts.[30] Taylor counters this with more general accounts of the wider culture that gave the formulations of philosophers and writers their appeal.[31] Moreover, the breadth of his study, and his determination to include and do justice to "the language in which I actually live my life," combine to give a portrait of modern assumptions that rings very true.[32] But there are a number of points in the text that show it is not just a lack of space, or Taylor's modest reluctance to attempt causal explanations for the developments he's tracing, that take the focus away from activity. He seems to think that human beings are ultimately motivated by concepts, rather than thinking that concepts are the tools with which they come to terms with, shape, and articulate impulses that are played out primarily through the interactions of which language is only a part. Taylor treats language as the defining horizon of our activity, rather than seeing language as one of the things we do, but not something to which all other things are reducible.[33]

A case in point is his brief summary of research into the acquisition of language by children. He draws on the work of Jerome Bruner, who investigated games and activities between carer and infant, and the forms of what developmental psychologists call joint attention, out of which language use first arises. Taylor calls these activities a "proto-variant" of language.[34] But Bruner's own emphasis is slightly different. Rather than calling the activities a form of language, he suggests we are involved in activities—that is to say, in human culture—and that language is a way of dealing with these activities: "It is the requirement of using culture as a necessary form of coping that forces man to master language. Language is the means for interpreting and regulating the culture."[35]

This opens up a line of argument that Taylor doesn't pursue in *Sources of the Self* but that doesn't seem entirely at odds with his project. Or is it? What do we lose, if anything, from Taylor's account if we emphasize activity more than language and moral spaces? The argumentative stakes are particularly clear in the passages where Taylor discusses forms of connectedness that go beyond isolated individual identity—in other words, those points of the argument that break with what he calls "disengaged anthropology" and develop instead "anthropologies of situated freedom."[36] Taylor suggests there is a "craving which is ineradicable from human life" to be in contact with the good.[37] In twentieth-century society, one of the forms in which this craving found fulfillment was modernist poetry, and in particular Rilke's *Duino Elegies* (1912–22). These poems, for Taylor, show a writer discovering the vocabulary to articulate his vision of the wider order of which he is part and in which the reader can share through the medium of poetry. Modernist epiphanies become in his account the vehicle through which individuals enjoy a sense of connectedness that is more than the projection of emotions onto the world, a moment of genuine contact, albeit necessarily mediated through the personal experience: "a transaction between ourselves and the world."[38]

But Taylor's formulations of a sense of connection remain incomplete. When he talks about a craving, that seems concrete enough, but the abrupt shift of register from "craving" to the philosophical "contact with the good" disappoints any expectation we might have had of a description of particular habits or actions associated with the craving. A craving for ice cream is obviously not the sort of thing Taylor is writing about, but a craving for human contact, or recognition—that is to say, a craving that can color interaction with others—is. This latter kind of longing is lived out in various ways that Taylor could have engaged with in more detail. One such activity might indeed be poetry as it was used in the early part of the twentieth century. The problem here is how the poet's experience of contact, achieved in the process of writing and publishing, relates to that of the reader. Taylor claims: "The great epiphanic work actually can put us in contact with the sources it taps. It can *realize* the contact."[39] Yet this is something he asserts but doesn't demonstrate. He doesn't show how in the early twentieth century the private experience of reading comes to substitute for something like religious contemplation. To describe these evolving, shared habits could only reinforce his argument for what he calls "the transcendental embedding of independence in interlocution"—that is to say, for the fact that individuals who think of their identity as being separate from others are in fact always involved with them nevertheless.[40] But Taylor does not describe this interrelation in more detail and so does not make the step from what he termed "anthropologies of situated freedom" to the anthropology of connectedness.

The reason for this seems to be bound up with his model of moral belief. For Taylor, a moral belief is something like a conceptual tool. For example, when Taylor observes that proponents of Enlightenment ideals and their critics behave in ways that do not fit their theories, he writes: "Disengaged rationalists still puzzle through their personal dilemmas with the aid of notions like fulfillment; and anti-moderns will themselves invoke rights, equality, and self-responsible freedom as well as fulfillment in their political and moral life."[41] Moral beliefs are notions we can use to "puzzle through" a dilemma or ideas we can "invoke." They are related to forms of activity (the language games of puzzling through and invocation), but to very specific ones, that follow primarily the model of intellectual debate. A moral belief, for Taylor, is an idea we use to justify our behavior. It might come in the form of an "unstructured intuition" or a fully-fledged metaphysical theory, but it is still primarily a concept. But a concept is more than an idea in somebody's head. It is part of a way of doing something. For this reason, a thinker like Bourdieu refuses to separate belief from learned bodily habits. "Practical belief is not a 'state of mind,' still less a kind of arbitrary adherence to a set of instituted dogmas and doctrines ('beliefs'), but rather a state of the body."[42] For Bourdieu, belief arises from a bodily familiarity with our environment and others, from "the pre-verbal taking-for-granted of the world that flows from practical sense."[43] It needn't be confined to what people know, or think they know. Its index is what they do.[44]

Bourdieu's approach has its limitations. It views habits from the vantage point of the skeptical outsider and is not at all interested in the feeling or the "what it is like" of experience as it unfolds. This means that as well as being indifferent to the dynamism of our involvement with our lives, Bourdieu claims to know that belief is always premised on forms of misrecognition, without making clear where he is standing that he can know that.[45] But we don't need to follow Bourdieu in adopting this ideal, disengaged perspective. Even without standing outside belief, we can understand that it is grounded in social practice, that it's part of shared activities and attachments, of the habits and ways of doing things that I've come to identify with and that give me my sense of a world.

That Taylor is reluctant to adopt this view of belief suggests the degree to which he himself identifies with the habits that, as his own account argues, have since the end of the eighteenth century given modern individuals their special sense of inner depths.[46] Rather than seeing inner depths as something we learn to have with other people, in the same way that the child's sense of his or her mind and the minds of other people arises from the joint activities the child learns about with carers, Taylor prefers to imagine concepts that people hold in their minds and that help them to order their equally interior moral intuitions in a metaphorical space that needs no mediation through actual behavior, like talking, sitting and thinking, or being part of and investing emotion in a particular group. But in so doing, he reifies the metaphors of "interiorization" and "internalization" that we frequently use to talk about psychological development and treats the mind as if it really were a place.[47] As Jeremy Carpendale, Charlie Lewis, Noah Susswein, and Joanna Lunn have recently argued, drawing on their empirical research into the way children first develop a sense of their own and other people's minds, mind itself should be seen as activity between people: "Beliefs and desires are not things and the mind is not a place. Human activity exists in the world and 'mind' and 'mental processes' are ways of conceptualizing aspects of human activity in the world."[48] While Taylor is right to insist that an account of the modern self needs to register and engage with our attachment to our inner lives, that needn't blind us to the wider context of activity of which these ideas are a part.

But can we describe our activities and still care about things? Won't the enumeration of our habits remove us, as it does Foucault or Bourdieu, from the phenomenological stream that gives our life its tenor and its meaning and so cause us to lose the sense of involvement and honesty that makes Taylor's account so appealing?[49] For Meister Eckhart, as we'll see, there needn't be a conflict; reflecting on our activities is what allows us to give up our psychological attachments and so come closer to the habits of self-surrender he associates with being with God.[50] The description and the involvement complement each other. A defamiliarizing history of modern habits of identity needn't be faced with the stark choice between tossing aside "the whole tradition of Augustinian inwardness" and being constrained by metaphors of inner moral space but can draw on both Taylor and Foucault. As we've seen, Taylor has a clearer sense of joint activity than does Foucault. Taylor acknowledges that we cannot help but be involved—we're part of a stream of human striving that's already started when we join it; and for this reason we can't magically exempt ourselves from being involved with habits we may not approve of or may wish we had overcome (like valuing self-responsible freedom, our daily life, and a sense of inner nature). But if we're going to have a defamiliarizing history that helps us acknowledge what we're already involved in, then it's going to need to find ways of being more specific about our habitual commitments than Taylor's spatial metaphors allow him to be, combining something like a Foucaultian vocabulary of techniques of the self with a Taylorian acknowledgment of their situatedness and our attachment to them; the perfect marriage of irony and involvement.[51]

There is an important aspect of modern identity to which neither Foucault nor Taylor devote much attention, the question of an individual's sex.[52] A man or a woman need not be defined entirely by his or her biological sex. To do so is a habit that intensified in the latter part of the nineteenth century and that has been extended, albeit with different intentions, by more-recent approaches, which treat gender as the defining aspect of experience.[53] Nevertheless, the individual's sense of being a man or a woman, and his or her desire to be a good man or woman for and with other people, will be an important part of his or her identity and needs to be added to Taylor's list of the inherited features of modern identity that we must learn to acknowledge: our particular, modern ways of being men and women together.

But how do male and female identities relate to each other? To answer this question entails clarifying an aspect of Taylor's account that has puzzled critics: the relation between the different parts of the "package" of modern identity and the relation of this package to patterns of behavior that don't fit into it. Quentin Skinner has suggested that Taylor identifies so strongly with the modern self that he does not register the alternatives that its habits often violently excluded.[54] Alasdair MacIntyre has similarly pointed out that Taylor's account does not allow for the way in which even the writers he values, like the modernists Pound, Eliot, and Joyce, may not fit as neatly into the narrative of the modern package as he hopes.[55] Taylor chooses the term *package* precisely to avoid the implication that its different aspects will fit easily together. At the same time, he doesn't want to decide in advance either that its constituent parts or that the habits of other cultures will be necessarily incommensurable with it.[56] This approach allows him to articulate some of the conflicts, in particular those between habits of instrumental reasoning and the desire for self-expression, that he believes characterize modern forms of identity.

There are conflicts, however, that this plural model of identity still cannot register. It cannot include habits that don't fit the dominant pattern—for instance, the self-understanding of those (mystics, for instance) who have no aspiration to be a self, or of those who from inside the habits of modern identity appear not to qualify for the title of having a self (women, for instance, or people from other cultures). I agree with Taylor that it's better not to fetishize alterity, but there needs to be a way of acknowledging exclusions nevertheless. One footnote in the text explicitly addresses these problems, acknowledging spiritual traditions such as Buddhism, that don't take it as axiomatic "that a self is what we ought to want to have or to be."[57] Taylor, here, considers ways of moving beyond the inner moral space of individuals to a "conception of the human good as something realized *between* people rather than simply within them," offering as an example theories of the complementarity of the sexes.[58] This suggests that it is possible to conceive of a version of Taylor's argument that included both habits that were not cultivated to generate a sense of self and the idea that one form of identity might exclude and/or depend on others—for instance, in the way that aspects of male identity have excluded while simultaneously being dependent on female identity.

To develop this argument further requires once again that we focus on activity and study what our habits of identity cause us to do with, and to, other people. Approached in this way, the incommensurablilty of cultures and forms of identity is not a descriptive fact about the world before which we mournfully capitulate but a problem in human relations that we have to deal with in real time. Caught up in their own habits, people use and hurt each other, and the hurt can't be undone. But people can nevertheless try to establish contact with each other by acknowledging what they're doing and what they've done.[59] As we have seen, Beauvoir and Irigaray have powerfully described the way male identity casts female identity as its Other. But in their texts it finally remains unclear how male and female identities jointly contribute to this structure, since both theorists assume a model of isolated subjectivity rather than giving an account of the shared habits by which men and women structure and distort their being-together. This problem is more explicitly addressed in Peter Bürger's account of male and female modern identities, which draws on research, published by his wife, Christa Bürger, into female forms of identity that do not conform to patriarchal norms.[60] However, while theirs is the first extended history of modern subjectivity to deal with the identities of men and women side by side, it remains problematic because the vocabulary they develop for describing the interaction fixes male and female identities as necessarily and constitutively distinct.

Like Taylor, Peter Bürger insists that modern forms of identity have different facets, which he describes using the metaphor of a field. He suggests that ideas about selfhood do not develop after the seventeenth century, that instead philosophers rework positions established by Montaigne, Descartes, and Pascal. Montaigne explores a form of bodily, fragmented experience; Descartes unifies the individual's sense of self at the cost of separating it irrevocably from the body; Pascal circles around the combination of anxiety and *ennui* that the Cartesian subject experiences if for any reason it gives up its attempts to control its environment and emotional life. The unified consciousness of Descartes cannot, in Bürger's argument, be separated from the fragmented, bodily material on which it works or from the anxiety that tracks it like a shadow.[61] Similarly, the rationalism of Voltaire cannot be separated from the fanaticism of Robespierre, and Valéry's attempt to escape from the body into consciousness must be read alongside Bataille's desire to escape from consciousness into a bodily ecstasy.[62] The field of subjectivity, for male subjects, is inescapable. The elements of bodily fragmentation, self-control, and anxiety are always there to determine all possibilities for action.

If the "field" of subjectivity is apparently inescapable for men, it has an outside nevertheless. Drawing explicitly on material from his wife's book, Bürger also discusses female writers whose self-portrayal does not fit the triangular constellation established by Montaigne, Descartes, and Pascal. In the seventeenth century, Mme. de Sévigné's idolatrous relationship with her daughter suggests a form of identity that combines passion and dialogue in a manner unknown in the male masters. Similarly, the mystic Mme. Guyon abandons the constrictions of the nascent self to find an identity beyond selfhood, an identity that needs neither regimentation nor structure but has found in the ecstatic union with God a ground beyond self-grounding.[63] In the eighteenth century, the novelist Isabelle de Charrière, preferring interaction with others over a constant, isolated battle with ennui, counters the melancholic self-obsession of Benjamin Constant with the simple advice that he leave himself behind a little.[64]

In the closing pages of his argument, Bürger then finally turns to the question of how the female experiments relate to the field of male subjectivity.[65] He suggests that there's a time in the seventeenth century, before the structures of male subjectivity are entirely fixed, when it was still possible for women like Mme. de Sévigné and Mme. Guyon to develop identities centered on interaction rather than on an isolated self-consciousness. But from the eighteenth century onward, women are allocated the position of being the negation of a male subjectivity, the negation of knowledge and experience.[66] It is not, he claims, possible to speak of this nonexperience from within the field of subjectivity, because everything I say will turn into a purposive act. Nevertheless, he holds out the hope of a form of life-affirming renunciation, which allows the inkling of another form of life to shimmer forth from the ineffable suffering of the woman nonsubject.[67]

Bürger's argument acknowledges an interrelationship between the identities of men and women, but his account of this interdependence is limited in two ways: by the metaphor of the field and by the habits of thought associated with Hegelian dialectics. Bürger's presentation of his "field" remains as abstract as Taylor's "space of moral issues." Like Taylor's space, it takes the place of a more complete scrutiny of the shared dispositions that prevent people from relating to each other and to themselves. If Bataille could not escape the reflexivity of his experience even in ecstasy, as he records in *L'expérience intérieure*,[68] this says something about his inability to let go in the moment, rather than being an incontrovertible truth about identity. Thinkers in other periods have not been so wedded to reflexive self-awareness. For a medieval thinker such as Meister Eckhart, as we shall see, self-reflexivity was experienced neither as an inescapable prison nor as the measure of human action.[69] For Bürger, in contrast, Bataille's problem demonstrates a logical limit. This is in part because he takes the self-descriptions of male writers at face value and does not reconstruct the forms of interaction and connectedness they were actually involved in while they propounded their theories of inevitable isolation. But even where in the closing pages he does note an interdependence between male and female identities, the dialectical model confronts men and women with the false choice between being permanently marginalized and being absorbed into male identity in a synthesis that cannot acknowledge its outside. The rhetorical invocation of change with which the book ends is empty insofar as, even if one accepts the book's bleak vision, Bürger's preferred conceptual tools make it difficult to imagine any real human behavior that could lead beyond the impasse.

A further symptom of the way the book removes itself from the practicalities of human interaction is its idealization of the texts by women that feature in the argument. As Ruth El Saffar has argued in her discussion of Spanish women mystics of the sixteenth and seventeenth centuries, such texts must be read on at least two levels. If they suggest alternatives to patriarchal models of behavior, they simultaneously bear the scars of acculturation in a male-dominated society.[70] But Bürger reads the women's texts without any interest in such scars. He pays little attention to the psychological and social constraints dictating the limits of the women's experience, depriving a Sévigné of the potential for psychological growth, or a Guyon of a spirituality that was not violently abusive of her body. Christa Bürger's study had already prepared the way for this idealization. Bürger wishes to record the way in which different women attempted to break out of the structures imposed on them by male discourses, casting off the isolated modern subject's obsession with plans for the future and self-control, and relishing instead moments in the present and in communication with others. She suggests that the texts she analyzes embody "another form of thought, which must exist because we need it, and for which I [Christa Bürger] . . . can provisionally propose only the term *immanence*."[71] The method she chooses for her analysis is self-consciously nonintrusive. She does not stand outside the texts to judge them but attempts instead to support their opposition to the restrictive patriarchal norms of isolation and control. To a large degree, she lets the energy of the texts speak for themselves, quoting extensively from the writings of the women whose letters, diaries, and fictional texts she explores: Mme. Sévigné, Mme. Guyon, Isabelle de Charrière, an anonymous correspondent of

Rousseau's, Maria von Herbert, Colette Peignol, and an East German pastor, Christa S. This method prevents the texts from being judged by male standards to which they never wished to conform. On the other hand, it does the women a disservice because it masks the wider context and does not consider how their reactions could themselves have been different. For instance, Bürger records how Isabelle de Charrière created a character who, rather than sustain the masculine attitude of standing outside the moment to structure and control it, either relished it then and there or, where it could not be enjoyed, withdrew from it to imagine an alternative.[72] One course of action that was not open to this figure was for her to intervene actively in the situation to adapt it to her needs and make space for development. Where Christa Bürger values her surrender to the moment, this surrender seems itself to be scarred by the situation to which it is a reaction, and as such it is not something to be unqualifiedly endorsed. By depriving herself of a vocabulary beyond that of the women she studies, Christa Bürger limits her critique of the Cartesian tradition to a repeated invocation of a moment of replete presence cut off from interaction. She can articulate neither the ways in which this moment of presence might be an inadequate substitute for psychological growth nor the ways in which it is a form of involvement with people and the environment, a more or less deficient way of being with others and in the world.

A history of modern forms of identity needs to find a vocabulary that does not mask the shared activity from which a sense of self arises. This activity does not only constitute an identity, it also delimits it; it sets it off against others, compartmentalizing or delegating aspects that the individual does not want to experience more directly. But this compartmentalization will never be an abstract act. It will always involve people doing things to themselves and to others, regulating their intercourse and limiting their openness. Foucault offers a useful vocabulary but not the awareness of interaction. Taylor writes very clearly of our involvement and of the unresolved conflicts of which we are the heirs, but at the same time he remains too attached to a particular model of inner life to be very interested in uncovering its preconditions. The Bürgers challenge us to consider what lies beyond the self-understanding of the individual modern self but, like Taylor, also remain attached to the habits of thought of the tradition they investigate: to conceptual metaphors and a dialectical framework.

Can such attachment be avoided? Taylor's argument might suggest that it can't, and Heidegger would similarly insist that we are unable to choose the habits of thought and interaction into which we're thrown. We cannot start from scratch. In my own case, I can certainly see how both the rhetoric and the conceptual tools I use for my own argument fit into Taylor's overall sketch of modern developments: My appeal that we learn honestly to acknowledge what we actually do with each other in our day-to-day lives attempts a "retrieval of lived experience" of the kind that Taylor suggests was so important to the modernist epiphanies of figures from Pound to Heidegger. It also continues in the tradition of self-acceptance that he traces from Hume to Wittgenstein and Rilke.[73] So my approach is not only partial, it is indebted to the tradition it aspires to analyze. But that will always be the case. My criticism of Foucault, Taylor, and the Bürgers, or indeed of Lacan, Irigaray, and Hollywood, is not of their debt to a tradition but rather of the job for which they're using the tradition. I would agree with Taylor that we can't simply drop the array of concepts associated with modern identity, and the related habits, as if we didn't identify with them and use them in our day-to-day lives. Nor should we want to. The habits of modern identity, be they thinking for oneself, valuing one's everyday life, the freedom to act for oneself without interference from authority, or the habit of respecting and feeling a part of nature, are in themselves just tools; one could even say they are part of human technology. The tools are being used to manage our relationship with the world and with others and can be used to produce different effects; they can foster different sorts of life. My disagreement with Foucault, Taylor, and the Bürgers is that their arguments shore up a story of human loneliness by finding tools to explain it, justify it, and give it dignity.

Another recent history of modern selfhood, Jerrold Seigel's *The Idea of the Self*, ostensibly avoids this glamorization of loneliness by explicitly giving more space to social interaction in the account it gives of personal identity. Indeed, the criticism that Seigel levels at Foucault is that he cannot properly integrate the social aspects of identity into his theory. Not willing to acknowledge what Seigel calls the multidimensionality of the self, he is not able to balance the apparently autonomous, self-fashioning aspects of identity with its being embedded in and hence constrained by social relations. This for Seigel explains the way Foucault's position can lurch from, on the one hand, the total determination by discursive forces in the work up to *Discipline and Punish* to, on the other hand, the apparently untrammelled self-creation of the later work. Foucault's two phases have in common the inability to conceive of a multidimensional identity negotiating the claims of embodiment, interaction with others, and conscious reflection. In neither can he countenance a mean between "extreme subjection and radical liberation."[74] Seigel's alternative is a messier model of selfhood in which consciousness, embodiment, and our social interactions are always played off against each other and in which what we call our self is the unfinished and unfinishable project of holding meaningfully together the different facets of our identity: "a self-in-formation."[75]

This view of selfhood is appealing because it integrates different facets and also includes an awareness that our identity is what we do as much as what we say or believe. To that extent, Seigel might seem to offer tools for a history of the activities through which human togetherness has been lived and managed. But it turns out that his theory is much less pluralistic than it initially seemed to be, and that what he contributes to the methodology of writing the history of modern forms of identity is instead a reminder of how easily a history interested in shared activities can loose touch with the phenomenological stream that will be part of any identity: my tacit awareness that my awareness is in some sense mine, as are the activities in which I find myself involved. Thinking about how the "mineness" of identity can be included in the defamiliarizing account of the practices and habits that underpin it will be the last stage in my methodological reflections, before we move on in the following section of the book to look at a particular episode in the history of Western notions of individual identity.

Seigel draws the inspiration for his pluralistic approach to modern identity from a tradition of thinkers writing in the relatively liberal and commercially prospering climate of Britain post-1688: Locke, Mandeville, Hume, and Adam Smith. All of these thinkers "recognized, if only implicitly, that the self was a compound of bodily, relational, and reflective elements."[76] He contrasts this tradition with thinking about the self in France and Germany, in which the social climate produced different emphases: in France, a tendency to separate identity from the incursions of a dictatorial social sphere and thus to overvalue the reflective aspects of identity at the expense of the body and social relations; in Germany, a tendency to model nature and the state on the self's self-development, an approach that can lead the individual to mistake his own projects for the projects of history and so make him want to impose his will on all around. For Seigel, Heidegger's support for National Socialism disastrously illustrates this risk.[77]

Seigel's situated, pluralistic approach to the self is appealing because it involves considering what philosophers did as much as what they said, viewing theoretical ideas in the wider context of the activity through which identity is created and reproduced. Thus, in Seigel's account, Descartes's focus on reflective consciousness is seen to depend on the doubtful, bodily subjectivity he wants to exclude in the *cogito*. Moreover, the way he presents his ideal of a self-constituting reason is shown to be self-contradictory, since it is addressed to his audience as a lesson to their powers of reasoning that, according to his theory, their reason would not need if it were properly self-constituting.[78] In a similar vein, Seigel points out that Diderot's correspondence, particularly the confessional letters he wrote to Sophie Volland in the 1760s, cultivates an interest in the psychological events that form a human being in a way that contradicts his insistence in his theoretical texts that we are simply what nature made us before education or experience.[79] In both cases, personal identity is made messier, and the dependence on shared bodily activities made clearer. The list could be extended to include other thinkers Seigel discusses. What emerges in the process is his picture of the "modern problematic of the self."[80] In a situation in which the individual no longer finds a place in a preestablished hierarchical order but is responsible for putting his or her own life meaningfully together, thinkers have negotiated in different ways the demands of the facets of identity that Seigel groups together under his three headings of reflectivity, embodiment, and social interaction. Whether they acknowledged it or not, each thinker was having to balance these different elements, and Seigel's account shows the compromise they reached in their life as much as in their writings, as well as giving a sketch of the cultural context in which each particular version of a modern identity made sense.

Despite this apparent interest in activity and cultural context, however, it turns out that Seigel's argument is weighted in favor of one particular aspect of his multidimensional self in a way that compromises its plurality and weakens the link to historical context. The element that Seigel privileges is reflectivity. He situates his arguments in the tradition that runs from Fichte and Sartre to Dieter Henrich and Manfred Frank in Continental thought and Sydney Shoemaker in Anglo-American thought, arguing that, if we are to understand how any sort of self-aware thought functions, it must be granted that individuals have a prereflexive familiarity with their own consciousness. If they did not recognize their thoughts as their own without any need for further reflection, mediation, or an outer standard, then self-knowledge would be caught in an infinite regress, as each new level of introspection failed to help individuals recognize their own thoughts as their own.[81] To argue that our thoughts are immediately available to us as our own is not in itself controversial. Dan Zahavi has pointed out that many thinkers in the phenomenological tradition, Husserl and Heidegger included, have made a similar presupposition.[82] But there are two related problems in the way Seigel uses the idea. The first is the slippage from prereflexive self-awareness to other versions of reflective activity that allows Seigel to make reflectivity the privileged term among the different aspects of identity. It might seem that this problem could be dealt with by using the idea of prereflexive self-awareness more circumspectly. But more-differentiated formulations of the idea, such as those of Manfred Frank or Dan Zahavi, suggest that the second, more fundamental issue is an overly narrow conception of what is unproblematically given. I am never given to myself as a form of pure self-awareness. I'm available to myself doing something in a particular situation: a body unfolding in a world with other people. Heidegger's term in his early writings for this dynamic predicament was "factical life" (*das faktische Leben*): the something happening into which we find we've been thrown and that makes us always already involved with a world and with others.[83] Seigel, as we will see, is unwilling to think through the ways in which our reflexive awareness is always qualified and situated. Having briefly shown how Seigel's claims for prereflexive self-awareness become increasingly less modest, I'll finish off by giving an account of the dynamic situatedness and "with-ness" of our prereflexive self-awareness, so as to clarify the focus of the historical approach that the rest of the book will be sketching.

Seigel's initial comments on the way we are immediately given to ourselves insist that this self-awareness must remain connected to other aspects of identity.[84] But while he approvingly cites Zahavi's phenomenological arguments linking our immediate awareness to the experience of being a body that is spatially and temporally situated, the connection that Seigel is most keen to establish is that between the prereflexive self-awareness and reflective consciousness: thinking about ourselves and knowing that we're doing so.[85] This is because it turns out that reflectivity is responsible for holding the three dimensions of identity together.[86] For Seigel, thinking about ourselves by itself brings the different elements of life together, rather than our experiences of being a body involved with the world and others also being part of the process of understanding ourselves as ourselves.[87] By the end of the chapter on Locke, this reflectivity has become a sort of moral agency, a form of accountability for oneself that groups together the different aspects of life as a moral project for which we acknowledge responsibility.[88] It's not clear what form this agency could take if it's not doing things with people in the world. For reflectivity really to have the special privilege Seigel wants to accord it, it would have to be some purely mental event that leaves no outward trace on the world. Nevertheless, in his view, to try to escape this moral agency is self-deluding. A philosopher such as Heidegger may hope to escape a model of subjectivity centered on reflectivity, but there will inevitably be a reflective core tying together the different moments of experience and recognizing these moments as belonging to its own life. Behind Heidegger's *Dasein* there will always be "something very much like the 'unity of apperception' that Kant posited as the presupposition of experience."[89] It turns out, therefore, that, despite Seigel's criticism of theories of identity that claim a special authenticity or genuineness and that hope therefore to disqualify other ways of negotiating between life's elements, he has his own version of what he calls "the only genuine mode of selfhood."[90] This is one in which reflectivity acknowledges other elements but is nevertheless still responsible for binding them together. Past thinkers are effectively ranked according to how close they come to Seigel's position. The philosophers Seigel favors are helped to acknowledge the appropriate combination of plurality and reflectivity even if they did not directly express any such acknowledgment. (Formulations such as "Although Nagel does not put it this way . . ." or "Hume did not quite say so, but . . ." ring like a refrain through the argument.)[91] Those whom Seigel disapproves of are excoriated for their attachment to a unidimensional model of selfhood regardless of the fact that Seigel's position is itself a form of unidimensionality in disguise.

For all its flaws, Seigel's position nevertheless represents an important challenge. It poses the question of how an historical and contextualizing account of modern identity can be squared with the apparently unchanging obviousness with which a human being is given to him- or herself. Is there some way of understanding this givenness as itself historical so as to overcome what seems to be an otherwise unbridgeable opposition between historical narratives and an anthropological constant? In his Marburg lectures "Fundamental Problems of Phenomenology," delivered in the summer of 1927, the year *Being and Time* was published, Heidegger in his brief comments on the way human *Dasein* is disclosed to itself gives an indication of how the gap might be bridged. He starts his discussion with the fact that what he calls the self is always "disclosed" or "uncovered" with whatever situation *Dasein* finds itself in. (The German terms he uses are *Mitenthülltsein des Selbst* and *Miterschlossenheit des Selbst*.)[92] Like Seigel, Heidegger suggests that we are available to ourselves before any reflection or introspection has started.[93] But Heidegger then moves to the question of how this immediate self-disclosedness shows up in the world, and the answer is that it is through our involvement and activity. We never come across the self-awareness on its own. Using a phenomenological vocabulary, Heidegger reminds us that our awareness is always intentional; it's always *of* something in a particular situation. It is not possible to separate our intuitive, prereflective awareness of ourselves from the bigger package of being delivered up to and involved in the world, caring about things that matter to us in some way. Involvement and prereflexive awareness go together.[94]

If we are inescapably involved in the world, then the step from intuitive self-awareness to historical context is no longer so difficult to imagine. Pre-reflexive self-awareness is not something at odds with history. It is the form of our historical involvement. We are historical through and through because our access to our lives will always be a situated one, self-reflection will always be something we acquire through our unfolding engagement with our predicament. Our being-given-to-ourselves will always also take the form a "being-with-," since a human life is unthinkable without others. That is not to say that self-awareness is in some way reducible to relations with others, for these relations themselves cannot be imagined without the givenness, without the fact of availability. Rather than privileging one or another element, we need to include the whole hyphenated compound in our deliberations: being-delivered-up-to-the-world-and-others-and-available-to-oneself-in-life's-unfolding.

Although it may sound paradoxical, this in effect means that there is no such thing as prereflexive awareness, or at least not as an isolatable phenomenon. While research has shown that infants have a sense of themselves from the moment they are born, and probably even in the womb, this self-awareness arises in movement and in response to others. It is part of a compound, or to put things more technically: The infant's "mirror neurons" respond to the purposive actions of others, allowing him or her to "be with" other people's activity in an immediate way while understanding them in relation to his or her own potential for movement: "My visual experience of the other person communicates in a code that is related to the self. What I see of others' motor behavior is reflected and played out in terms of my own possibilities. . . . Body schemas, working systematically with proprioceptive awareness, constitute a proprioceptive self that is *always already* coupled with the other."[95] This compound of me-and-the-people-around-me will always be historical; my self-awareness will be situated and responding to shared purposive action: doing things for reasons in a world that is disclosed and coped with through our activity. The party has always started before we show up or, to be more precise, before we are born into it, and it's at the party that we get to know ourselves.

But if our intuitive self-awareness is only part of a compound, where or how are we to start our arguments, given that we can't say everything all at once? There is always a risk that the element of the compound that we chose as our beginning will be given an undue privilege, as is the case with Seigel's emphasis on reflectivity. This problem can be solved artificially by an analysis that attempts to isolate the most fundamental aspect or, as Manfred Frank terms it, the "base element."[96] The base element in his argument is an anonymous familiarity with ourselves (*anonyme Vertrautheit*), the givenness to ourselves that precedes and enables self-awareness and self-knowledge.[97] But the very term he uses betrays something of the background he is unnecessarily excluding. In German, *vertraut* is used to articulate forms of know-how and intimacy, similar to the English *familiar*. The term covers being familiar with a person or an object, familiarizing ourselves with rules or operating instructions, having someone as our confidant.[98] What Frank means by the term "anonymous familiarity" we understand by modeling the abstraction on exactly the sorts of activities and interactions through which our disclosedness to ourselves is ordinarily experienced. Frank's term is in effect piggybacking on a phenomenological background that it does not acknowledge. Significantly enough, when Frank discusses the passages in Heidegger's lectures on "Fundamental Problems in Phenomenology" that deal with our availability to ourselves, it is precisely the involvedness of the experience that he omits, presenting Heidegger as a theorist of self-reflectivity manqué, rather than a phenomenologist who uncovered the wider background of what we normally take for granted.[99]

So where should we start? The answer is that we can start anywhere, but it will make a difference where we start, and the choice of starting point has probably already been made before we begin. We can start anywhere, since any bit of the compound will bring the other elements with it: being-delivered-up-to-the-world-and-others-and-available-to-oneself-in-life's-unfolding. At the same time, we will always already have started. There'll be something we're looking for and a vocabulary we have inherited to start looking. The strength of Taylor's position is his insistence that we are already inheritors of, as he called it, a "package" of habits and assumptions, of ways of behaving that we identify with and that make us what we are. Starting, from this point of view, means beginning to make explicit our attachments and in particular making explicit how we manage the conflicting habits that we're committed to. If we have a special loyalty to the habits of thought associated with the Cartesian or Lockean tradition, then it's as well to acknowledge that rather than to treat these habits as if they were the inevitable structure of identity.[100] If we resist the temptation to ontologize habits and misconstrue them as the structure of subjectivity itself, and if we also give up the hope of a foundation or starting point for the argument, it is likely that we will be more interested in the sorts of ways people have ordinarily related to themselves, turning away from the texts of philosophers that in particular dominate Seigel's account of modern identity, but also those of Taylor and the Bürgers, to look at what people said and did who weren't philosophers. Where we do use canonical texts, it won't be because we believe that they are able to speak for, as Seigel puts it, "their less articulate contemporaries."[101] Rather, it is because they further the project that I'm already engaged in, and help me make something explicit about its unfolding. It's not the canonical authors themselves that are ever important but the project, the shared unfolding.

The argument that follows begins with Meister Eckhart and the mystical milieu of the late medieval Rhineland. The reason for choosing Eckhart is the particular sense of both familiarity and strangeness that his texts provoke in a twenty-first-century reader. The sense of familiarity arises because he addresses listeners whom he assumes to be involved in a personal, introspective project of spiritual growth. The strangeness comes from his apparent unconcern about questions of autonomy and agency, and from his final lack of attachment to the habits of self-monitoring that have become an almost inescapable fate for individuals born into modern Western societies; part of the "package" of modernity. His texts and the milieu in which they were written thus offer us the opportunity to assess our shared activities to see what habits we have inherited and whether we relate to them in the deficient mode of not acknowledging them, and, if so, what we want to do about it. In addition, since Eckhart's writings are in conversation with the radical forms of spirituality adopted by many women who were his contemporaries, they aid a reflection on the role that gender plays in the management of human togetherness. Yet, if Eckhart offers a fruitful starting point, he is not the only place to start, nor is his milieu the cradle of modern identity. Other starting points are thinkable—in the third part of the book it is the second-century texts of Lucian that provide the combination of familiarity and strangeness necessary to surprise us into a revised idea of the project in which Freud was involved. Our choice will depend on the particular issues we want to clarify or explore. The particular respect in which Eckhart's texts are indispensable to my argument is the clarity with which they present human life as caught up in an unfolding process that precedes it and makes it possible and that we can realign ourselves with, sharing in the project that, in the *Sister Catherine* treatise, was formulated as the longing to become God.

PART II

A Brief Prehistory of the Modern Western Self

5

Meister Eckhart's Anthropology

In the closing years of the thirteenth century, Meister Eckhart was prior of the Dominican friary in Erfurt, a flourishing town in Thuringia in eastern Germany.[1] One of his responsibilities was to lead evening sessions, or *collationes*, for the instruction of novices, during which the interpretation of scripture and more general questions of monastic and spiritual life would be discussed under the guidance of a senior cleric.[2] A record of these talks survives in the text *Die rede der underscheidunge* (Talks of instruction, 1294–98). The practical orientation of the text makes it a useful indicator of habits and assumptions that prevailed in the particular milieu in which Eckhart was active.[3] At the same time, it offers a succinct introduction to some of his key concerns.

Taking Leave of Selfhood

Eckhart's project is summed up in a sentence toward the beginning of the text. "Examine yourself and wherever you find yourself, take leave of yourself—that is the best way of all."[4] For a modern reader, there are likely to be a number of obstacles to understanding this exhortation to self-examination and self-abandonment, all of which are the product of assumptions about identity unfamiliar to Eckhart and his audience. A key modern assumption is that a thought or action needs someone—a subject—to be attributed to. Kant, for instance, argued that in order for something to be experienced, there must be a thinking subject to lay claim to it. "The *I think* must be capable of accompanying all my representations, for otherwise something would be represented in me which could not be thought; in other words, the representation would be either impossible, or at least it would be nothing to me."[5] Despite years of critique (be it Nietzsche's insistence that a deed needs no doer, or Foucault's dismissal, in *The Order of Things*, of philosophers "who refuse to think without immediately thinking it is man who is thinking"), this assumption is still deeply ingrained.[6] As we saw in the last chapter, thinkers in both the continental and analytic traditions maintain that if we are to recognize and know ourselves reflexively, we must have a core of immediate, intuitive, prereflexive familiarity with ourselves.[7] Similarly, Anthony Cohen, from an anthropological point of view, defends the "unique essence formed by the individual's personal experience, genetic history, intellectual development and inclinations" that prevents human actions from being the mere reflex of social or linguistic codes.[8] Common to these two disparate examples is the assumption of a barely articulated layer of self without which human creativity, autonomy, and rational self-awareness are inconceivable.

Eckhart did not presuppose such a layer. He appeals to personal experience, and indeed to a sense of individuality. But neither of these is indivisibly linked to a sense of self or to the patterns of self-monitoring and self-control with which later subjects learn to identify. Even events in the individual's inner life do not need to be attributed to a subject; thoughts themselves do not need an "I think." If we do not think or act for ourselves, there is always God to think or act for us: "Intend only [God], and have no thought as to whether it is you or God who performs these things in you."[9] There is experience, but it is not necessary for Eckhart to allocate it to a subject.

This difference in approach is recorded in the language used to discuss identity in the thirteenth and fourteenth centuries and, more particularly, in Eckhart's way of engaging with it.[10] Middle High German at the turn of the fourteenth century did not have an equivalent to the modern word *self*. It had reflexive verbs, possessives, pronouns, and adverbial forms, all of which included forms of the word *selb*, but it did not have a noun like the modern *das Selbst*, which appeared for the first time in a German dictionary in 1702, modeled on the English *self*.[11] The closest Middle High German came was the word *selbheit* and its related forms, which, as it was employed in the mystical texts that coined it, had two main meanings. It could be used to describe an attribute of God—"the highest unity and self-identity or his essence" over and above the divisions of the Trinity (*dú hôhste glihheit und selbsheit des wesens*).[12] At the same time it could be used to describe something more like human willfulness or self-love—not my "self" but my "selfness" or self-orientation. This self-orientation is exactly what the mystical literature encouraged its readers to leave behind. Heinrich Seuse (1295/97–1366), a Dominican friar who knew Eckhart probably from the time when the latter was preaching in Strasbourg or Cologne (1313–ca.1325), describes the spiritual process as the "losing of one's self-orientation [*dú verlornheit sin selbsheit*]."[13] The Eckhartian tract "Von der edelkeit der sêle" (On the nobility of the soul) similarly suggests that the individual must forget his self-centeredness. "[The spirit] is most free where it forgets its self-orientation and flows with everything that it is into the groundless abyss of its origin."[14] There is a historical link between this form of language and the modern vocabulary of selfhood, as we will see later in the argument. However, there is also a fundamental difference between the two. The word *sëlpheit* refers to something that can be relinquished and with which the individual does not identify, whereas the self, in modern usage, is ever present as the silent tag that marks experiences as my own.

Interestingly enough, forms of *selbheit* are found in texts arising from the milieu in which Eckhart wrote, but they are not found in the sermons and treatises most reliably attributed to Eckhart himself. This could be an accident of transmission. But if it were true that Eckhart eschewed the word available to his followers, that would be an important indicator of his spiritual and psychological program. Where Seuse or the Eckhartian author of "On the Nobility of the Soul" used the idea of "selfness," Eckhart tends to prefer alternative formulations, the common factor among which is their dynamism. In the "Talks of Instruction," he speaks of "a pure leaving behind of what is yours [*ein lûter ûzgân des dînen*]" and of giving up or examining "what is one's own [*sich sîn selbes* [*verzîen*]]."[15] When in a sermon he summarizes his own preaching practice, he says "that one should disencumber oneself of oneself and all things [*daz der mensche ledic werde sîn selbes und aller dinge*]."[16] These formulations emphasize activity (the movement of *ûzgân*) where the formulations of his followers were more abstract, speaking of loss or forgetfulness. The difference suggests that what his followers saw more passively and more abstractly as "forgetting" or "losing" "self-orientation," Eckhart grasped as something more concrete and more active.

A comparison with the Latin model for the "Talks of Instruction" confirms this impression. At a number of points, Eckhart's text reads as a translation into the vernacular of the epistle on regular observance, "De vita regulari," written ca.1255 by the former master general of the Dominican order, Humbert of Romans (ca.1200–1277).[17] The Latin term used by Humbert to describe what should be left behind is *spiritus proprius*: "And indeed, if by this means we have been emptied of self-spiritedness, we will justly be filled by the divine spirit [*Et vere, si per hunc modum evacuati fuerimus spiritu proprio, replebimur non immerito tunc divino*]."[18] Eckhart renders this as: "Wherever a person through obedience leaves what is his and empties himself of his own, God must of necessity go into him."[19] The Latin uses passive constructions and an abstract noun (*evacuati fuerimus spiritu proprio*). Eckhart speaks of obedience, but at the same time he suggests that the individual actively contributes to the process, by changing how he or she relates to himself, thereby making way for God. Eckhart's reworking of the passage makes the individual an active participant in the process of remodeling. This activity is not the sign that there is an inescapable "self" participating in the process of self-abandonment. It shows rather that Eckhart situates the spiritual transformation at the level of activities and practices—the leaving behind of habits and assumptions.

This more concrete approach explains the critical attention that the "Talks" and many of the later sermons devote to ascetic rituals. The surviving autobiographies and convent histories from the late thirteenth and early fourteenth centuries vividly document the culture of self-castigation to which Eckhart was responding. The *Vita* of Heinrich Seuse records how, as a young man, he deprived himself of fruit and meat, drank almost no water, wore a crucifix spiked with nails underneath his habit, and carved the letters of Christ's name into his flesh.[20] Similarly, the autobiographies and histories from convents in the region in which Eckhart was active as visitor and confessor describe some of the violent ascetic regimes adopted by nuns. The spiritual autobiography of Christine Ebner (1277–1356) tells of self-flagellation with nettles, switches, and thorns and of her cutting a cross into her chest because she was ashamed after confession.[21] In the case of religious women, such ascetic attention to one's own body has been given a positive interpretation and read as an attempt by women to establish an element of control over "religious superiors and confessors, God in his majesty, and the boundaries of one's own 'self.' "[22] Eckhart is frequently critical of such practices, but not because they challenge his authority, or, as other critics have suggested, because he wants to impose a rational order on the emotional and bodily excess of which the self-castigation is a symptom.[23] He is critical of them where they replace the breaking down of an attachment to "what is one's own" with what is in effect a further form of attachment—namely, a preestablished pattern considered to have an authority and legitimacy in its own right. Eckhart questions ascetic regimes where they become forms of self-justifying habitual inflexibility hindering rather than furthering the process of development toward God. "If any external work hampers you in this, be it fasting, keeping vigil, reading, or whatever else, you should freely let it go without worrying that you might thereby be neglecting your penance. For God does not notice the nature of the works but only the love and devotion and the spirit that is in them."[24]

Eckhart's alternative is an individualized program that engages with the specific attachments of each person. "Christ fasted for forty days. You should follow him in this by considering what you are most inclined or ready to do, and then you should give yourself up in that, while observing yourself closely. It is often better for you to go freely without that than to deny yourself all food. And sometimes it is more difficult for you to refrain from uttering a particular word than to refrain from speaking altogether."[25] In a way that might appear contradictory, Eckhart's version of self-abandonment encourages an attitude that is explicitly individualized and that lays a greater emphasis on inner life than do the texts of some of his close contemporaries, such as those of Seuse or the Dominican nun Margaretha Ebner (1291–1351). Seuse's *Vita* and Ebner's autobiographical *Offenbarungen* (Revelations) suggest two things about the type of identity that flourished in this milieu. The first is that conscious control could in certain circumstances be easily relinquished. Both authors describe moments when they go into the choir in the church of their respective Dominican convents and are taken into a state of rapture brought on by the spiritual importance of the choir itself.[26] This form of identity is like that of the crowd subjects described by Freud in *Group Psychology and the Analysis of the Ego* (1921) insofar as the conscious, controlling level of individual identity can be swept away.[27] However, for the medieval mystics, it is not the suggestive power of the group that causes the self-loss but rather the aura of the ecclesiastical space. This leads to the second feature of the identity type. The individual in Margarethe Ebner's or Heinrich Seuse's texts gives up control but at the price of becoming attached to particular spaces or particular rituals that generate the sense of rapture. Intensity is experienced through a process of externalization or projection. Eckhart questions such externalization, encouraging practices that strengthen the individual and prevent his or her spiritual experiences from being dependent on outside objects or rituals. At the same time, the product of this attention to oneself is not a modern "self" but a new set of habits that produce a different relationship to oneself, to external practices and to God.

Eckhart describes these new habits by saying, "We must learn to maintain an inner emptiness."[28] To explain what he means by this, he differentiates between the level of conscious thought (thinking about, remembering God) and a more permanent restructuring of an individual's psyche.

> This real possession of God is to be found in the heart, in an inner motion of the spirit toward him and striving for him, and not just in thinking about him always and in the same way. For that would be beyond the capacity of our nature and would be very difficult to achieve and would not even be the best thing to do. We should not content ourselves with a thought-about God, for, when the thought comes to an end, so too shall God. Rather we should have an essential God who is beyond the thoughts of all people and all creatures.[29]

One acquires this "essential" God through a program of conscious effort, self-observation, and repeated exercises. But the end product should not be a new consciousness. Instead, Otto Langer has suggested using Bourdieu's term *habitus* to describe the product of spiritual exercises repeated over and over until they become automatic.[30] Eckhart compares the acquisition of such a self-relationship, or what could be called a new "technique of the spirit," to learning to write. The scribe first consciously imitates a pattern, but later he writes freely and automatically.[31] The habit of inner detachment is similarly an acquired *technē*.[32] However, the impulses thus trained are, for Eckhart, almost physiological. If learning to write provides a model for the process of spiritual training, a raging thirst and the feeling of loving something describe the result.[33] Once we have successfully acquired the habitus, the relationship to God will accompany the individual everywhere, as do thirst and passionate longing.

Eckhart presents his model of identity as a set of practices by which we train ourselves in self-abandonment. Before we look at the model in more detail, it's worth noting the ways in which it differs from the habits and assumptions associated with the modern "package" of identity. The first is that Eckhart sees no ultimate division between the individual and God. Since he has a behavioral or psychological grasp of what separates humans from God, he can equally establish a behavioral or psychological program for overcoming this distance.[34] This is not ultimately a theological point. On the contrary, in texts by Thomas Aquinas or Luther, doctrinal debates about the incommensurability of the human and the divine are themselves behavioral imperatives. To insist that God and humanity will always operate on different levels is to forbid or exclude patterns of behavior that foster a different attitude to the experience that in Eckhart's era is described theologically as being "in God."[35] An anthropological view, such as that taken by I. M. Lewis in his discussion of shamanism and its equivalents, suggests that every society is negotiating the relationship with the spirits, albeit with different behavioral tools and a different vocabulary.[36] In their own different vocabulary, Horkheimer and Adorno similarly suggested that the management of the sense of connectedness was one of the main aims of the practices of modern rationality.[37] Eckhart promotes "techniques of the self" that foster a sense of permanent connection to, or openness for, God. The behavior he criticizes focuses on certain privileged sites and techniques as ways of engaging with the spirits, externalizing and reifying the relationship and creating boundaries. Eckhart in contrast personalizes it. The individual is encouraged to examine him- or herself and observes and alters his or her own behavior.

This brings us to the second difference from modern assumptions: the way Eckhart's text appeals to the individual's inner life without privileging terms such as consciousness or self-control or without encouraging an identification with the behavioral apparatus of self-observation. The appeal to a relationship with God is alien to many modern critics who are wary of reading Eckhart's, or other, mystical texts as evidence of particular experiences.[38] However, if the experiential level is excluded, it becomes impossible to describe how Eckhart's focus on the individual's inner life differs from modern habits of self-cultivation. It also means excluding a fundamental layer of human experience, however it is described: be it as the relationship with God or with the spirits or, in more secular vocabularies, with the heart or the unconscious. It means excluding the sense of connectedness and the dynamism of our necessary involvement. To explore in more detail how Eckhart combines a cultivation of individualizing "techniques of the self" with a relationship with God, I want to look at two of the later sermons. In Sermon 2, Eckhart further develops his critique of ascetic practices; in Sermon 77 he meditates explicitly on questions of identity. Like the "Talks of Instruction," the orientation of the sermons is practical, so once again they help to establish a sense of the behavior that underpinned Eckhart's theory of self-abandonment.

Painting God's Portrait

Sermon 2 was used as evidence against Eckhart in the heresy proceedings launched in 1325. He disputed that the surviving text was an accurate record of what he preached, without distancing himself from the ideas themselves, leading scholars to conclude that he was challenging the accuracy of individual formulations recorded in the trial documents, rather than denying the argument of the sermon as a whole.[39] The text that has survived apparently contains two sermons stitched together, with Eckhart's critique of ascetic practices to be found in the framing, outer sermon. To understand his argument, it helps to be aware of the particular way in which he is using the Middle High German word *eigenschaft* in the text. In the late thirteenth and early fourteenth centuries, the word had a number of meanings over above the modern sense of "attribute" or "characteristic." It could mean "property" or "possession" (cognate with the modern German *Eigentum*). It could also mean legal agreements or legal documentation related to the transfer of property—that is, evidence of possession.[40] It was also used in mystical and religious texts to describe a possessive attitude, in relation not only to worldly goods but also to one's own habits. In the "Buch von den zwei Mannen" (Book of two men, ca. 1352), attributed to the patrician layman from Strasbourg, Rulman Merswin, the author, counsels his reader: "You must thus free yourself of all the works you have taken on for yourself, which you own or practice possessively [so mvͦst dv aller diner selbes ane genomener eiginer werke . . . lidig werden, die du . . . mit eiginschaft gevͤbet vnd besessen hest]."[41] Eckhart uses the term in the sense that is taken up by Merswin a generation later. With it, he refers to a certain possessiveness or rigidity in relation to one's own rules and habits. It is the closest his terminology comes to the *selbesheit* used by his followers, but it is etymologically closer to the *spiritus proprius* of Humbert of Romans, since it emphasizes property and possession rather than the more abstract "self-orientation."

The possessiveness in question in Sermon 2 is the attachment to prayers, fasting, vigils, and other ascetic rituals, which Eckhart likens to a form of marriage, contrasting it with the virgin's unencumbered state:

> Married folk bring forth little more than one fruit in a year. But it is other wedded folk that I have in mind now: all those who are bound with attachment to prayer, fasting, vigils, and all kinds of outward discipline and mortification. *All* attachment to any work that involves the loss of freedom to wait on God in the here and now, and to follow Him alone in the light wherein he would show you what to do and what not to do, every moment freely and anew, as if you had nothing else and neither would nor could do otherwise—*any* such attachment or set practice which repeatedly denies you this freedom, I call a *year*; for your soul will bear no fruit till it has done this work to which you are possessively attached, and you too will have no trust in God or in yourself before you have done the work you embraced with attachment, for otherwise you will have no peace.[42]

This passage contrasts possessiveness with a freedom grounded in self-trust and trust in God. The individual who exhibits *eigenschaft* clings to external forms of prayer and penance and has peace only when these rituals are performed. The freer individual waits for God's bidding. The contrast is interesting for a prehistory of the self because it formulates a critique similar to what we have seen being formulated by Eckhart's followers, but using the word *eigenschaft* rather than the term *selbheit*, that is to say, using a word more distant from modern terminology of selfhood. Eckhart's use of the word *eigenschaft* shows that the focus of the critique is not "self" or "self-orientation" but rather an attitude of anxious dependence on forms, which could be internal or external. Eckhart in effect treats, all on the same level, types of prayer, ways of sitting, ways of thinking, ways of dealing with dreams and visions. The line of division is not between inner and outer or between individual and Church, but rather it is an internal one between *eigenschaft*/attachment and *vrîheit*/freedom.

Consistent with this internalizing approach, Eckhart appeals to the personal experience of trusting oneself. His freedom is individually experienced. A number of commentators have observed how the mystical milieu in Germany in the thirteenth and fourteenth centuries produced forms of selfhood not that different from our own. For Georg Misch and Siegfried Ringler, the autobiographical texts of fourteenth-century visionaries such as Margaretha Ebner, Christine Ebner, Adelheid Langmann, Heinrich Seuse, and Friedrich Sunder are early stirrings of a modern self. They are evidence of a culture in which an inner life was actively cultivated and written and talked about in ways not dissimilar to the habits of self-cultivation we now take for granted.[43] Eckhart's appeal to personal experience confirms such a reading. At the same time, his texts show how this appeal to a sense of individuality differs from modern practices of selfhood. Individual experience is appealed to as only one step in the development that leads beyond the individual to God. Private experience is depersonalized in the course of Eckhart's arguments. Once again, we are dealing with experience that is not attached to a self-monitoring or self-possessing form of subjectivity. This will qualify the "mineness" of the experience, leaving us with a thought that to the modern mind seems almost inconceivable: that an experience could be personal but not characterized by "mineness."

This is particularly clear in Sermon 77, which features an extended meditation on questions of identity. The occasion for Eckhart's argument is the difference between Old and New Testament versions of the same promise: "Behold I am going to send my angel [*Ecce ego mittam angelum meum*]" (Mal. 3:1). When the phrase is repeated in the Gospel (Luke 7:27), the Latin text omits the word *ego*: "Behold, I send my messenger [*Ecce mitto angelum meum*]." This prompts Eckhart to explain when God says "I" and for what reasons. He says "I" to represent his permanence and unity. On the other hand, he omits the word *I* because neither he nor the soul can be named, and because to use the word (for God to say "I") would be to suggest a difference between God and the soul, whereas they are one and the same. Some critics have read this and similar discussions in Eckhart of God's "subjectivity" as the beginnings of a modern, abstractable, and self-constituting self of the sort which finds fullest expression in the philosophy of Johann Gottlieb Fichte.[44] This claim is based partly on misreadings that ignore the differences between medieval and modern usage and treat as if they were nouns the adverbial phrases and pronouns that Eckhart uses to talk about identity.[45] But equally important, the approach looks only at arguments and not at the practices or way of life of which they are a part. It does not try to reconstruct the activities through which identities were formed in Eckhart's milieu.

The text actually contains a direct reference to one such activity. Toward the end of the sermon, Eckhart uses portraiture as an illustrative example. He explains that we are made in God's image, in the same way that someone who wanted to make a portrait of Conrad would not represent a generic person, or Henry, but would try, to the best of his talent and ability, to capture the likeness of Conrad. We are the image of God, as Conrad's portrait is the image of Conrad:

> We should be like angels, and so we would be an image of God, for God made us in his own image. An artist who wants to make an image of a man does not copy Conrad or Henry. For if he made an image like Conrad or Henry, he would not be portraying man, he would be portraying Conrad or Henry. But if he made a picture of Conrad it would not be like Henry: for, if he had the skill and the ability, he would portray Conrad perfectly himself, exactly as he was. Now God has perfect skill and ability, and therefore he has made you just like him, an image of himself.[46]

The example is informative on a number of levels. The first is what it tells us about practices of the self in the fourteenth century. There may be no abstract noun equivalent to the modern *self*, but there are practices of portraiture to which Eckhart can refer unproblematically. The capturing of physiognomic likenesses was not much attempted in the West between the seventh and the late thirteenth centuries. From the late thirteenth century it sporadically returned.[47] Boniface VIII, who was pope between 1294 and 1303, commissioned no less than eleven stone likenesses of himself, which appear to have been produced following a painted or drawn model. After a brief hiatus, Charles V of France around 1370 commissioned sculpted likenesses of himself and his wife that he seems to have judged so successful that he had the sculpted portraits duplicated. The practice was not instantly popular or uncontroversial. The images of Boniface were thought to encourage idolatry. On the other hand, the contemporary chronicler Ottokar of Steirmark questioned the very idea of portraiture. The rhyming history of Austria that he wrote around 1310 records how Rudolf of Habsburg (d. 1291) had carved for his tomb a portrait of himself that caught the likeness of a man like no image before it.[48] The sculpture recorded all the marks left on the Emperor's face by ageing. But this caused problems for the mason, who found that he had constantly to update the portrait, whenever a new wrinkle was noticed on Rudolf's brow.[49] The anecdote suggests that Ottokar viewed the renascent art of portraiture as a futile undertaking, which attempts to catch in stone an object that is continuously changing. Like the mason in Ottokar's chronicle, other craftsmen of the era aimed similarly to individualize their sculptures. But their attention focused on costume, coats of arms, genealogy, and family relationships rather than on physiognomic likeness.[50] "In an era of few likenesses, one identified people, as well as their portraits, by their costumes, attributes, or arms."[51] The face itself was held to be too unstable a phenomenon to be worthy of reproduction.

Eckhart's sermon contains the same double movement as does Ottokar's chronicle. It invokes the idea of the perfect portrait, only to call it in question. Around 1300, it seems, people were aware of the possibility of capturing their facial distinctiveness in stone or in paint. At the same time, the identification with this image could be called into question, since people apparently did not define themselves by their facial features to the same degree as did later generations. Eckhart's appeal to individuality thus culminates in a rhetorical gesturing beyond the limits of human portraiture and language to an identity with God that neither words nor pictures can express. Ironically, when Eckhart reaches this point in his sermon, he interrupts himself to speak in the first person. "More I do not know and cannot tell, so my sermon must end here. But I once thought on my way. . . ."[52] The sermon describes the perfect individual likeness, turns this idea inside out to suggest the individual's identity with God, and then speaks apparently autobiographically of a personal limitation and a personal meditation. Eckhart speaks from a position of personal involvement and personal limitedness while at the same being catapulted beyond any sense of individual identity by the perfection of God's portraiture: humility and connectedness all at once.

Perhaps one way of describing this particular version of self-fashioning is to say that it is one in which emotions and the inner life are valued, though not as a means of self-definition but rather as part of the process of spiritual transformation. A small devotional picture from Cologne in the 1320s (the period when Eckhart himself was active in the city) shows angels weeping at the sight of Christ on the cross. Emotional reactions and human suffering are worthy of representation. (Christ started visibly to suffer on the cross in the mid-thirteenth century. Prior to that he was represented upright and triumphant over death).[53] At the same time, the figures are not facially individualized. There are none of the physiognomic markers being used by sculptors of the period to give carved faces plasticity and life, even where they are not attempting a direct individual likeness.[54] The emotion is not attached to a particular identity. In Eckhart's rereading of the New Testament story of Martha and Mary, he criticizes Mary for indulging in the pleasure of being close to Christ, when Martha is able to combine a closeness to God with detachment and activity. "We suspect that she, dear Mary, sat there a little more for her own happiness than for spiritual profit."[55] Emotion itself is not a problem for Eckhart. "Our Lord Jesus Christ was often 'moved,' and so were his saints, but they were not flung from the path of virtue."[56] In the same vein, his own sermons are full of evocations of the joy of being close to God, such as his description of a colt frolicking on the meadow. Emotional intensity itself is not questioned, only the identification with emotions as an end in themselves or as a confirmation of identity. Emotions that are not clung to or identified with are part of the onward thrust of our involvement with God and of God's involvement with us.

Conclusions: Eckhart's Anthropology

The vocabulary of selfhood from the early fourteenth century is subtly different from the language of today, suggesting that practices of the self were different too. The self is not treated as a center or inescapable point of reference at either a grammatical or a practical level. One Middle High German translation of the passage from Galatians 2:20, in which St. Paul describes his decentering by Christ reads, "I live now not I, Christ lives in me [Jch leb ieczunt ich nicht, Cristus lebt jn mir]."[57] Paul's Greek is emphatic and rhetorically balanced, but not agrammatical: "ζῶ δὲ οὐκέτι ἐγώ, ζῇ δὲ ἐν ἐμοὶ Χριστός [Zō de ouketi egō, zēi de en emoi Christos]." Modern English translations are smooth: "and I no longer live, but Christ lives in me"; Luther's German, clarificatory: "Ich lebe aber, doch nun nicht ich, sondern Christus lebet in mir."[58] In contrast, the ungrammatical "I live not I" of the Middle High German text highlights the effort made and the degree of flexibility available in the vernacular for describing a relationship with one's own inner life that did not center on consciousness or self-control. Grammar could be bent to describe a state that negated the "I" as the subject of an individual's actions. Other groups in the fourteenth century undertook a similar grammatical disruption by forbidding themselves to speak of themselves in the first person.[59] At the same time, these linguistic habits arise from a milieu in which inner life and personal spiritual experience were actively cultivated. There was subjective experience, but not subjecthood.

To a degree, we can reconstruct what this looked like on a practical level. This is not because Eckhart himself gives a direct description of how to behave. Rather, the lifestyle of convents governed by the Dominican rule is well enough documented, as are some of the habits of the lay congregation in the flourishing urban economies of cities such as Erfurt, Strasbourg, and Cologne, where Eckhart was most active. During the year and a day of their novitiate, aspiring friars learned to regulate every aspect of their comportment, from where they directed their eyes to how they put on their habit. At the same time, the particular emphasis of Dominican training was learning. When Dominic took over the church of St. Romain in Toulouse, he added a cloister with cells for study. This promotion of education remained a dominant feature of Dominican life. Offenses related to study were written into the order's rule from the very beginning so that mistreating books, sleeping in lectures, reading prohibited texts, behaving disreputably while preaching, or working carelessly as a scribe were counted as faults on a par with eating meat or wearing linen underclothes. The rule promoted scholarly qualities and protected the apparatus of scholarship as much as it fostered humility and obedience, for "the preacher's intellectual formation was as essential as his apostolic character, and the one merited the same legislative care as the other."[60]

Eckhart's pastoral texts respond to this culture of regulation, self-observation, learning, and attention to detail. They work to prevent both the practical and the intellectual apparatus from becoming fixed and unchallenged structures, cut off from personal experience. At the same time, they encourage self-observation and intellectual development. If there is one rhetorical structure that characterizes Eckhart's preaching, it is the habit, as Kurt Ruh has pointed out, of setting up a proposition and then triumphantly going beyond it.[61] The proposition can be a quotation from an established authority, or it can be an argument from a sermon that Eckhart preached himself. What is important in either case is the moment of transcendence, the moment when Eckhart adds: "But now we put it differently," "But I say more," pushing his listeners beyond a conceptual, psychological, or behavioral barrier.

Eckhart's attitude to the nascent practices of capitalist rationality flourishing among his lay congregation is similar to his treatment of regulated life in Dominican convents. The merchants were learning to observe their own behavior no less than were friars, keeping records of income and expenditure, minimizing waste, balancing the books, and, by their success, encouraging others to see the virtue of "the commercial habit of measuring and calculating in monetary terms."[62] Eckhart in his sermons and treatises adopts the language of trade, describing the overcoming of attachment in economic terms. "It is a fair trade and an equal exchange: To the extent that you depart from things, thus far, no more and no less, God enters into you with all that is his, as far as you have stripped yourself of what is yours in all things."[63] At the same time, he is critical of economic rationality. Christ cast the merchants out of the temple, and in his sermon on this episode in the gospel, Eckhart is no less dismissive. "See, those all are merchants who, while avoiding mortal sin and wishing to be virtuous, do good works to the glory of God, such as fasts, vigils, prayers, and the rest, all kinds of good works, but they do them in order that our Lord may give them something in return, or that God may do something they wish for—all these are merchants. That is plain to see, for they want to give one thing in exchange for another and so barter with our Lord."[64] Eckhart values the habits of self-observation and the monitoring and evaluation of behavior. But he has little time for calculating rationality, doing *x* to produce effect *y*, in one's relationship to God. Since the individual does not possess his or her actions, there is no trade to be established. God may observe a balance, filling individuals as they empty themselves. But since the individual acts through God alone, he or she can bring nothing to the transaction.

Eckhart's preaching emerges from the context of the friary and the city. He encourages rationalized, regulated behavior. But he discourages identification with the rules as an end in themselves and criticizes a possessive attitude to one's own actions, however rational. Externally, it seems, the Eckhartian spiritual aspirant appeared very much like his or her fellow friars, nuns, and merchants. Indeed, Eckhart specifically bid his listeners avoid clothes, food, or words that would differentiate them from others.[65] At the same time, his sermons foster a detachment from regulating habits, suggesting that the habits are less important than the spiritual experience they promote. It is difficult to assign the resulting practices of the self to a particular period. The outer trappings of the convent or the medieval city are very different from our own, but in both the rule of the friars and the developing account books of the merchants we find versions of rational behavior that will eventually become the dominant mode. In contrast, Eckhart's spiritual redeployment of these modes of rational behavior is neither medieval nor modern. To say this is not merely to acknowledge that twentieth-century writers like C. G. Jung or Erich Fromm promoted an attitude similar to the one that Eckhart encouraged in his listeners.[66] Rather, Eckhart's spiritual project is not classifiable because it builds on the "modern" potential for autonomy that was the by-product of study, self-observation, and account keeping, but at the same time he retains the relationship with God. Eckhart's model of identity resists schemes of historical periodization because the combination of individual autonomy and freedom before God has never been a dominant form of identity in the West.

So far the argument has focused almost entirely on Eckhart. But his sermons and treatises make sense only to the degree that they articulate an experience that he shared with his congregation, as Eckhart himself explicitly suggested. "If anyone cannot understand this sermon, he need not worry. For as long as a man is not equal to this truth, he *cannot* understand my words, for this is a naked truth that has come direct from the heart of God."[67] This truth from the heart of God and the lifestyle associated with it had a name in the twelfth and thirteenth centuries: the *vita apostolica*, or apostolic life, a life of itinerancy, preaching, and begging, for which individuals abandoned wealth and security in imitation of Christ and his apostles.[68] In its most radical or most successful forms, this lifestyle culminated in the sense of identity with God that found a rhetorically elaborate expression in Eckhart's comments on portraiture. In a more direct language, the woman visionary who is the protagonist of the anonymous Eckhartian tract called the *Sister Catherine* treatise awakes from a trance to announce to her confessor: "Sir, rejoice with me, I am become God!"[69] Bernard McGinn has noted how almost identical formulations occur in mystical texts of the period where there is no evidence of direct transmission, such as between the texts of Eckhart and Hadewijch. He explains the parallel formulations as similar responses "to a widespread yearning to give expression to a new view of how God becomes one with the human person."[70] If the yearning was new in late medieval Europe, it is not the sole preserve of the medieval Christian tradition. A similar sense of connectedness and freedom can be found in other cultures and in other epochs. According to a long-standing Sufi tradition, the mystic al-Hallaj was publicly executed in 922 for his ecstatic declaration that he was the Truth or the Divinity.[71] Shamanistic traditions equally allow individuals to maintain a proximity to the spirits, while the tradition of Japanese Zen promotes practices of self-abandonment of an intellectual sophistication that are similar to those of Eckhart.[72]

It is important to make and explore such comparisons, since they take something of the mystique from mysticism: Comparative anthropology of religion helps to counter critics who can't conceive that the texts such as Eckhart's could refer to relatively everyday experiences to be found in different periods and across a variety of cultures. At the same time, the realization that the habits and attitudes found in Eckhart's texts are not an isolated example but find echoes in other periods and other cultures presents something of a challenge to the self-understanding of a modern Western self. Eckhart's texts are at once very familiar and very alienating: familiar because they discuss forms of personalized spiritual development; alienating because they have little regard for the ideals of individual autonomy and agency, and little sense of self-awareness as an end in itself. By looking now at the wider context from which Eckhart's writing emerged, we can perhaps understand more clearly how it was that the habits he promotes came to be displaced by practices of self-control and self-monitoring that specifically distance the individual from the experiences referred to by him and his contemporaries as "being in" or "becoming" God. We can perhaps explain why the version of the apostolic life that was so successful in thirteenth-century Europe was unable to establish itself more widely as one of the accepted ways of life in the modern era.

6

Becoming God in Fourteenth-Century Europe

One of the peripheral texts in the Meister Eckhart corpus is a legend that, both in its content and in the form in which it has been transmitted, illustrates the social and psychological context from which Meister Eckhart's preaching emerged. In manuscripts in Munich and Wolfenbüttel, it is entitled "Of the good conversation which a good sister had with Meister Eckhart." The Stuttgart manuscript specifically allocates the text to a genre. "This exemplum is called Meister Eckhart's Daughter."[1] The exemplum reads as follows:

> A daughter [of God] came to a Dominican friary and asked for Meister Eckhart. The porter asked, "Who shall I say wants him?" She said, "I do not know." He said, "Why do you not know?" She said, "Because I am neither a young maiden nor a wife, neither a man nor a woman, neither a widow nor a virgin, neither a master nor a maid nor a servant." The porter went to Meister Eckhart. "Come out to the most wonderful creature that I have ever encountered, and let me come with you, and put your head out and say 'Who asks for me?'" This [Meister Eckhart] did. She told him what she had told the porter. He said, "Dear child, your words are quick and true. But tell me more what you mean by them." She said, "Were I a young maiden, I would be in the state of first innocence; were I a wife, I would unceasingly give birth to the eternal word in my soul. Were I a man, I would strongly resist all sins; were I a woman, I would be faithful to my one,

beloved consort. Were I a widow, I would always long for my one love; were I a virgin, I would live in reverent service. [Were I a master, I would have dominion over all divine virtues,][2] were I a maid, I would be humbly subservient to God and all creatures, and were I a servant, I would work hard and serve my master with all my will without gainsaying him. Yet I am none of these, and am just a thing like any other thing and so go on my way." The master went to his brothers [or "his disciples"—the manuscripts give both alternatives],[3] and said, "I have seen the purest person that I have ever seen, or so it seems to me."—This example is called Meister Eckhart's daughter.[4]

A woman, described as a "daughter" and addressed by the cleric as a "child," comes to consult Meister Eckhart, the senior Dominican. We do not know if the legend is based on fact or is purely fictional. It names an historical figure, but at the same time it is rhetorically tightly structured as well as being in one manuscript described as a pedagogical or mystagogical example. However, we do not need to know the exact balance of reporting versus construction. The debate that has developed in academic discussions of German mysticism between two schools—those who insist that the texts record actual experiences and those who instead point up their rhetorical construction—polarizes issues unnecessarily.[5] The empirical truth of the events described in a text of this sort is less important than what the content and the form of the narrative itself reveal about structures and expectations in the period. The text may not be evidence of a particular encounter, but it is on some level evidence of a way of life, which can be understood by sketching in historical background. Once this is done, the specific interest of the legend itself will become clearer, as will the assumptions and behavior of which it is a record.

Background to the Legend (1): The Apostolic Calling

In the broadest terms, the legend may be said to record an aspect of the apostolic life as it was lived across Europe by very many men and women in the twelfth, thirteenth, and fourteenth centuries. From the early twelfth century, individuals began to embrace a life of voluntary poverty and itinerant preaching in imitation of the apostles. This marked a change in expectations. The view that an established order of priestly successors to Peter and the apostles should mediate the individual's relationship with God was replaced by the expectation that this relationship could be personal and individually binding.[6] This personalized striving was often associated with heretical doctrines, but, as Herbert Grundmann argued, the doctrinal differences are only the symptom of a deeper challenge to the Church, as what Grundmann called "newly awakened spiritual needs" prompted a search for new forms of social and religious practice.[7]

The appearance of these new spiritual needs can be accounted for in a number of ways. They can be seen as a paradoxical by-product of Gregorian reforms in the latter part of the eleventh century. Gregory VII and Urban II sought to establish the freedom of the Church from lay control, subordinating the laity to the clergy, stripping kingship of its sacramental character, and establishing the primacy of the pope. However, the reflection on the Christian organization of society that the Gregorian movement encouraged also focused attention on the gospel, with the result that the Gregorian program for restructuring earthly society was "subtly transformed into a summons to reshape men's lives in accordance with the life and commands of Christ."[8] The success of the apostolic movement among laypeople can then partly be explained by the continuing discrepancy between the affluence of the Church and its prelates and the ideals of the gospel.[9] At the same time, the flourishing urban economies, and in particular the rising textile industry in Lombardy, the Rhineland, the Netherlands, Flanders, and northeastern France produced a qualitative change in town life. A new, more anonymous social environment emerged, mediated by money, and apparently contradicting the moral framework that, up to that point, had disapproved of merchants and usury. The developing lay piety can be seen as a reaction to the new environment and the associated anxieties and moral dilemmas. Apostolic poverty both rejected the problematic practices of urban trade and fostered an alternative sense of community as groups attempted to adapt Christian spirituality to the new context.[10] It was also a form of liberation that mirrored in some ways the new social forms that it criticized. The merchant and the apostolic preacher were alike in having abandoned the old feudal ties.[11]

A study of changes in ecclesiastical and urban life can explain some of the factors influencing the rise in lay piety. But as well as adopting this kind of broader social perspective, one needs to consider the experience of the individuals who felt and acted on spiritual needs. The apostolic life was a movement of the heart as much as it was a response to the movement of capital. Indeed, the feeling of inner motivation and the accompanying sense of authority are especially important to an understanding of the movement, since they provoked recurring conflicts with institutionalized forms of power that are in many ways the movement's defining characteristic. The words attributed to Francis of Assisi when Cardinal Hugolino (who later became Gregory IX) attempted to persuade him to adopt the rule of either St. Benedict or St. Augustine for his fledgling order illustrate the terms of the conflict. Erich Auerbach commented on Francis's talent for staging rhetorically unsophisticated but emotionally striking scenes, and this episode is a clear example of this talent.[12] Francis is supposed to have led Cardinal Hugolino silently before his brothers before making an impassioned declaration in which the ecclesiastical authority of Sts. Benedict, Augustine, and Bernard is contrasted with a different type of authority, the vehicle for which is individual forms of calling, witness, and imitation. "My brothers, my brothers, God has called me by the way of simplicity and of humility, and he has pointed out this way as being the true way, both for me and for those who wish to believe me and imitate. So don't talk to me about some rule or other, neither that of St. Benedict, nor of St. Augustine, nor of St. Bernard, nor about any life or way of life other than that which the Lord has mercifully shown and given to me."[13]

In Francis's appeal, an individual responds to a sense of being called on which he learns to model his life ("Deus vocavit me"), rejecting ecclesiastically imposed regulation. It is tempting to read the appeal as evidence of a conflict between individual and social structures, making Francis one in a long line of heroes stretching forward to the individualist strongmen of Hollywood movies. But such a celebration of individual conscience obscures as much as illuminates the conflict. Inner experience and social forms are to be found on both sides of the equation. Francis suggests a model of collective action guided by personal trust and imitation: "God . . . has pointed out this way as being the true way, both for me and for those who wish to believe me and imitate [hanc viam [Deus] ostendit mihi in veritate pro me et pro illis qui volunt mihi credere et me imitari]." He does not question social forms as such. Indeed, as Auerbach observed, he appears to have been keenly aware of the force of public, theatrical enactment of his principles, as when he posed as a beggar to demonstrate that his brothers' table had become too lavish.[14] On the other side of the debate, we find a similar combination of experience and social form. Hugolino feared that "without precise, strict regulation of common life and communal discipline, every *vita religiosa* was in peril of losing its way and sure foundation."[15] The important factor is the element of anxiety. In their anthropologically colored account of the rise of modern rationality, Horkheimer and Adorno suggest that a combination of awe and anxiety generated the social practices that eventually became modern forms of rationality.[16] Debates about the apostolic life in the thirteenth century illustrate in a more concrete form the process that the authors of *Dialectic of Enlightenment* imagined as an anthropological fairytale. In the thirteenth century, we find both the sense of connectedness (what Horkheimer and Adorno termed "mimesis") and the anxious need for order and control.

To gives some further examples: For Mechthild of Magdeburg (ca. 1207–ca. 1282), as for many other visionary writers, the slightest action performed in the love of God is equal to the most sublime moment of contemplation. The important contrast is not between the day-to-day and the sacred but between those actions performed with a sense of closeness to God and those that are not. "Thus I think relieving my most basic need counts as much in God's sight as if I were in the highest state of contemplation that a human can attain. Why? If I do it out of love in order to give honor to God, it is all one and the same. But when I sin, I am not on this path."[17] However, the apparent absence of external regulation could prompt angry reactions. This is clear in the attitudes to beguines (the name given to women who followed the apostolic life but without being bound by a rule) whose way of life was experienced as an affront by some of their contemporaries.[18] The challenge they posed is recorded in their very name. The term *beguine*—like that given to members of similar groups in different parts of Europe, such as *lollards* and *papelards*—is derived from the old French word *béguer*, "to stammer."[19] They are characterized as a group whose mumblings and prayers are not generally comprehensible, who do not exhibit the recognizable, outer signs of an orderly life. Their life often followed a general pattern, but for many the pattern was not regulated enough. Generally, they lived in small groups in houses marked by a white cross on the door and situated near Dominican and Franciscan friaries. They earned their keep in the flourishing economy of the medieval town, exploiting the increasing opportunities that the urban context offered single women in the areas of wage labor (washing, spinning, sewing, domestic service, or care of the sick), and retail (selling feathers, soap, milk, honey or ale).[20]

For some contemporary commentators, such as Nicholas of Bibera, who wrote a satirical account of life in Erfurt in the 1280s, the beguine life was admirable precisely because it was not rigidly codified.[21] But for others it needed regulation, as one can learn from the defensive texts of beguine writers themselves. The first of the poems in strophes by Hadewijch, another thirteenth-century beguine visionary, complains at external attempts to control her relationship with God: "The while they are busy scrutinizing me, / Who shall then love their beloved?"[22] Hadewijch responds to her critics by suggesting that their attempt to establish control is in fact a form of neglect. They too have a relationship with God that they ignore in their disciplinary zeal. This defense shows a contemporary treating *both* the attitude of the beguine *and* that of her critics as ways of responding to the sense of being called. Hadewijch views both her own practice and the practices of her critics as what Heidegger might have called more or less deficient ways of loving God. Official sources were unlikely to admit to this similarity. The bull *Cum de quibusdam mulieribus*, promulgated after the Council of Vienne (1311–12) and proscribing the beguine way of life, complained that the women "promise obedience to no one, . . . and do not make profession of any approved rule."[23] It also explained why this lack of regulation appeared so dangerous. The question of whether laypeople, and in particular women, should be allowed to preach was a topic of fierce debate in the late medieval period.[24] A trace of this debate can be seen in the decree, which tells of beguines "who, as if led by a peculiar insanity, argue and preach on the Holy Trinity and the divine essence."[25] The sense of calling and the preaching that went with it was outlawed as a form of derangement by the disapproving clerics who drafted the decree.

The division between those who responded to the calling and those who sought to impose order on it should not been seen as one between those who had the experience and those who did not. It should be seen as a conflict of attitudes toward a level of experience that in the medieval period was described theologically as a relationship with God. A modern history of selfhood will find it hard to name this level, since there isn't an agreed vocabulary for doing so. A Heideggerian vocabulary of being-in-the-world and being-with-others captures theoretically the sense of involvement and dynamism, but, as we've seen in chapter 3, it remains too abstract. The same could be said for other contenders. The phrase "mimetic impulses" used by Horkheimer and Adorno or similar terms from psychoanalytic theory (Freud's "oceanic feeling," Jung's "collective unconscious") remain specialist terms that do not connect with everyday experience in the same way that the medieval language of God did. In the medieval period, this level of experience had a vocabulary and a set of practices to nurture and control it, but there was no vocabulary of selfhood. In the modern period, the vocabulary of selfhood has flourished, while the language and practices of nonself have tended to decline or to become a specialism. To overcome this limit, it helps to turn to comparative anthropology, which confirms that the experience has an equivalent across cultures and that, if modern Western culture has no shared vocabulary for relating to it, that can itself be read as a set of techniques of the nonself: techniques for keeping "God" at a distance.

Background to the Legend (2): Gendered Visions

Even the briefest comparison with the material discussed in I. M. Lewis's anthropological survey of *Ecstatic Religion* confirms that behavior of the sort observed in the apostolic movements in the twelfth and thirteenth centuries can be found across a variety of different cultures. In a vocabulary and form adapted to the particular social environment in which the experience occurs, God, a spirit, or the power of the cosmos intrudes into the life of an individual. He or she then learns to come to terms with the sense of being called, and, in cultures that tolerate a shaman or its equivalent, to live with and control the powerful force.[26] Lewis notes that it is most often individuals from marginalized or relatively powerless social groups, and particularly women, who experience the visions and visitations and appeal to their authority.[27] In medieval Europe, mystical experience was also gendered. Francis of Assisi, as a male visionary, represented a less frequent occurrence in the thirteenth century than did the visionary woman. Men were more likely to be involved as confessors in the regulation and policing of mystical experience than they were to have firsthand knowledge of divine visitation. As Hadewijch suggested, this practice of control was no less a relation (albeit a negative relation) to divinity than was the relation to divinity experienced by the visionary women. Lewis, in his survey of ecstatic cults, notes that men show a respect for and obedience to the spirits that speak through the women, even where this directly challenges their social position, and he interprets this to be a tacit acknowledgment of the women's contribution and commitment to the society.[28] Male clerics in Western cultures since the medieval period have similarly admired and envied the authority and freedom of the visionary women in their charge. But they have on other occasions treated them with a brutality not found so often in the cultures studied by Lewis, torturing them and burning them at the stake. This contradictory relationship between the regulating authority (usually male) and the individual who answers the visionary calling (usually female) is the next aspect of Eckhart's context that needs to be explored if one is to appreciate the position of his preaching in the development of the modern Western self.

The apostolic movement of the later Middle Ages in many ways conforms to the pattern observed by Lewis. Women played a major role, and a level of spiritual collaboration can be observed between men and visionary women that complicated the prevailing, theological view of women as "cooler, weaker, less intellectually competent, and generally less perfect than men."[29] The predominance of women in the apostolic movement has been explained in a number of ways. One argument was that the Crusades left a surplus of women who could find no husband and so turned instead to a religious life. Herbert Grundmann was already challenging this explanation in the 1930s and arguing that women who became nuns or beguines were rather reacting against the constraints of marriage.[30]

More recently, historians have continued to emphasize the advantages to women of the religious vocation.[31] However, while the convent or beguine house may have offered women a certain freedom to explore their own experience, one should not overlook the opportunities available in other spheres in the period. In Cologne during the fourteenth century, there were women who were grocers, bakers, belt makers, silk makers, yarn makers, gold spinners, lead merchants, pepper traders, linen weavers, importers of iron gloves, and importers of wine.[32] In cities where the family remained the main focus of production, women actively participated in trade and manufacture.[33] The turn to the apostolic life cannot have been motivated only by a desire to escape a constraining social environment. That adherents came from all classes—from the aristocratic women who peopled the convent in Helfta to the lowliest peasant—also suggests that material opportunities were not the primary motivation.[34]

A further aspect of Lewis's argument helps to make these different explanations cohere. He observes that ecstatic religions tend to flourish where there is instability and "acute social disruption and dislocation."[35] The twelfth and thirteenth centuries were indeed a period of social transformation. Expanding trade produced the qualitatively new, anonymous, and more fluid environment of the city. At the same time, intellectual securities were being eroded. The works of Aristotle began to be translated in the twelfth century because they filled a need. With the rise of towns, a new class of intellectual arose, the professional master, who did not simply convey God's wisdom to a wider public but more actively learned about the world and about claims made about the world by pre- and non-Christian thinkers, using the new conceptual tools of logic and dialectic.[36] As early as the 1220s, Arnold of Saxony's *De floribus rerum naturalium* collected the opinions of around eighty Christian and non-Christian authorities on matters of science without including a single biblical quotation, establishing the investigation of nature as a realm apart from the revealed truths of scripture.[37] Albert the Great made this division explicit: "When it comes to nature, we have not to inquire whether and how God the creator in accordance with his perfectly free will uses his creation to produce a miracle and so advertise his power. Rather we should only investigate what is possible in the realm of nature by natural means as a result of natural causes."[38] Miracles were the business of theologians. Philosophers and scientists, on the other hand, were to devote themselves to understanding the laws that govern the natural universe.[39]

The erosion of the old intellectual habits remained incomplete. The separation of the new natural philosophy from theology entailed neither an end to argument by authority nor untrammelled empirical observation. For Albert the Great, it meant a pluralization of authority: Augustine for matters of faith, Galen and Hippocrates for medicine, Aristotle or other experts for natural science.[40] These authorities influenced what was discovered through empirical observation, from the relatively harmless observation of the Galenic properties of cold and humidity in the spinach leaf to more telling pronunciations about the nature of women.[41] Although human dissections were already being performed in Bologna at the end of the thirteenth century, "the benefits of experiment were minimal."[42] Joan Cadden has reconstructed the confusion and diversity of opinion among medieval philosophers attempting to describe women and sexuality with the tools available in Galen, Hippocrates, and Aristotle.[43] In her survey, the new intellectual habitus of the thirteenth century appears as little more than what the imagination needed in order to link together the conflicting theories of texts that were conferred with an auratic authority. Elements that did not fit the established patterns were barely noticed. The identification with authority was stronger than the impulse to observe or learn from experience.

Women took a major role in the apostolic reaction to the new social environment not only because, statistically, they were more likely to migrate from the country to the town as they looked for work and therefore to experience the "deracination" firsthand.[44] They also had less reason to identify with prevailing social, psychological, and intellectual patterns, be they the older feudal ties or the new hierarchies and systems being established in the course of the thirteenth century. The subordination of women was an assumption so ingrained in the customs of the thirteenth century that Thomas Aquinas barely needed to explain its causes.[45] "The woman needs the man not only for purposes of generation, as with other animals, but also for education: For man has the more perfect reason and the greater strength . . . . Woman is naturally subordinate to man as her governor."[46] Indeed, the imbalance appeared so natural to him that he believed it to have structured the relations between men and women even before the Fall.[47] The one area in which Thomas Aquinas conceded that a woman's soul was equal if not superior to a man's was that of prophecy.[48]

The unstable situation not only permitted but also actually demanded a restructuring of forms of identity. Where the identification with authority remained strong, this was likely to consist in a bricolage of accepted wisdom adapted to the new context. Where that identification was not so strong, the loss of social power could be compensated for by an openness to the sense of being called where this sense was felt. "I have wisdom with me here. This shall always guide me to choose the best."[49] Given the systematic devaluing of the feminine at an ideological level, whatever the room for maneuver in day-to-day practice, it is not surprising that women should have broken with external authority to follow the apostolic vocation. We also saw, in chapter 3, that a society that associates femininity with a certain greater openness to the fact of human togetherness is likely to reproduce this gendering of connectedness in the earliest stages of a child's life.[50] It's not possible retrospectively to reconstruct the exact neurological or hormonal mechanisms that, in the thirteenth and fourteenth centuries, interacted with social expectations and shared habits to reproduce this gendering.[51] Nevertheless, it's worth bearing in mind that human bodies too will have played their part, as each individual's "mosaic" of gendered attributes fed into and constrained the experience of human togetherness, and the statistical regularities that emerge as a result of the hormonal influences colored people's expectations and helped to shape the tools available to individuals for coming to terms with their particular bodily inheritance, however near to or far from the statistical norm this may have been.[52]

Returning to the thirteenth century: There was also a degree of official acknowledgement of the women's visionary authority, as Thomas Aquinas's concession on prophecy suggests. Indeed, there were many cases in which male clerics and women visionaries established a form of social and spiritual symbiosis. In the trances and ecstasies of the women, the male clerics experienced vicariously a proximity to divinity that they felt themselves to be incapable of achieving.[53] On the other hand, the relationship with the male cleric offered the woman recognition, status, and institutional protection.[54] These relationships emerged as the growth of the penitential system and of ecclesiastical bureaucracy in the course of the thirteenth century defined and fixed the male clerical role while simultaneously excluding women from certain areas (preaching, cure of souls, consecrating the Eucharist).[55] In reaction to these changes, a counterrole developed for women: that of the visionary whose access to God was more direct precisely because it did not depend on the trappings of ecclesiastical power.[56] In Caroline Bynum's account, the two spheres of action—clerical power and female charisma—could be held in paradoxical tension with one another during the thirteenth century, with the woman's mystical authorization never finally undercutting the institutional legitimacy of the male clerics.[57] As the argument develops, we will see that the relationship was more dynamic and, in certain circumstances, more dangerous for both parties than Bynum suggests.

To sum up: One of the forms that developed out of the apostolic movement was a symbiotic structure in which the woman had closer access to what contemporaries understood to be God but that might also be called mimetic impulses, the collective unconscious, or the sense of connectedness. The male cleric, on the other hand, had a more secure social position.

Such relationships were the positive equivalent to the intrusive control complained of by Hadewijch. Just as she saw the attempt to regulate her relationship with God as itself a negative response to the sense of being called, so the more sympathetic clerics can be seen to be managing their own sense of vocation through the relationship with the visionary woman. This psychological and spiritual interdependence has implications beyond the medieval context. It is an example of techniques of selfhood that cannot be understood in isolation from one another but that rather structure the inner life of each individual through the relationship with the other person. It is a commonplace of psychoanalytic theory that an analysis of the individual cannot be separated from a consideration of social relations.[58] Nevertheless, it is hard to find a historical study of the practices of selfhood that takes this interdependence into account.

Philosophical histories of the self have only very recently started to investigate the relationship between masculine and feminine identities. Where in Charles Taylor's *Sources of the Self* gender seemed to play almost no role in the shaping of the subject's inner life, Christa and Peter Bürger's parallel histories of masculine and feminine identity, as we have seen, explicitly address the issue. The Bürgers, however, still approach masculine and feminine forms of subjectivity as two incommensurable structures, situating women's identities in an impotent space outside what Peter Bürger calls the "field" of modern male subjectivity.[59] The relationship between confessor and visionary woman is particularly fruitful for a history of forms of selfhood, since it helps to introduce both gender and reciprocity into the theoretical debate and prevents feminine subjectivity from being cast as the ungraspable other of masculine self-certainties. It allows an exploration of the contributions that both sides make to a common structure. To demonstrate this in more detail, I want to turn to three examples of the pastoral relation in the fourteenth century. The first is between Margaretha Ebner and Heinrich von Nördlingen. This shows how the relationship functioned when it was intense but orthodox. The legend of Meister Eckhart's daughter, and the sparse records that survive of Eckhart's own pastoral activities, raise some interesting questions about how in practice Eckhart related to the spiritual experience of women. Finally, the anonymous *Sister Catherine* treatise develops the reciprocity of the relationship to its utopian limit.

Projection: Margaretha Ebner and Heinrich von Nördlingen

Margaretha Ebner and Heinrich von Nördlingen had direct connections with other Rhineland mystics. Heinrich is known to have associated with

Johannes Tauler, a pupil of Meister Eckhart's, in Basel, and a letter from Tauler to Margaretha has survived.[60] Heinrich also translated Mechthild von Magdeburg's *The Flowing Light of the Godhead* from the original Low German into the High German in which it has survived. However, their texts—a spiritual autobiography and a letter by Margaretha, fifty-six letters by Heinrich—make no mention of Eckhart. Margaretha started to write her autobiography in 1344 at Heinrich's behest. Heinrich was a secular priest with a particular talent for preaching and pastoral care. Before he was forced into exile by the struggles between Louis of Bavaria and the papacy, he spent his time administering to a circle of devout women in Nördlingen (in the diocese of Augsburg in modern-day Bavaria) as well as to Cistercian and Dominican nunneries in the surrounding area. Margaretha, a Dominican nun from a patrician family, entered the order as a young girl and, following an illness in her twentieth year, had a series of experiences that established her reputation as a visionary.[61] Heinrich bid her write her autobiography in order that he, and the circle of *Gottesfreunde* (friends of God) in Basel with whom he was at the time associated, be not denied the insights with which she had been blessed. Margaretha enjoyed a relationship with God that they too wanted to be able to experience vicariously.[62] But the relationship was not just one-sided. Heinrich also inspired Margaretha, intensifying her experiences each of the eight times he visited her in the course of their nineteen-year friendship. The relationship between the confessor and nun, in other words, seems to have promoted the spiritual life of both participants.[63] At the same time, the strict division of spiritual labor also functioned to regulate the longing of both participants by attaching it to particular places, routines, and rituals and thereby fixing it.

There are two moments in Ebner's autobiography when the relationship that it describes between confessor and nun comes closest to the ideal overcoming of limits to be found in Eckhart's sermons. When Margaretha first encountered Heinrich on October 29, 1332 she was inconsolable over the loss of a friend who had died eight months before. Heinrich bid her "give him" both the body and the soul of her friend, and did so in such a way as to break the fixation that her mourning had become.[64] His suggestion that Margaretha record her experiences was similarly energizing, bringing with it an intensification of visions and dreams and of the feeling of being close to God.[65] In both cases, Heinrich helped Margaretha overcome a psychological barrier—in the first case, the fixation with her dead companion; in the second case, her assumption that her text, if it was to be written at all, should be written by a man.[66] Heinrich encouraged and empowered Margaretha's psychological and spiritual development.

At the same time, Margaretha and Heinrich wittingly or unwittingly limited the intensity. In Margaretha's case the limits were imposed psychosomatically. Her autobiography records again and again how an experience of intensity generated a backlash of physical suffering or behavioral rigidity. The closeness to Heinrich, "God's angel," on his second visit in 1334 was accompanied by a loss of appetite and by positive pleasure at forgoing the food that her body desired.[67] Similarly, Heinrich visited her in 1335 to witness "speakings" (pronouncements and screams over which she had no control) that were accompanied by an aversion to sleep and the sense that food made her sad and heavy.[68] Margaretha was aware of this rhythm herself but interpreted both the intensity and the suffering as signs of God's work. Whenever God was playful with her in her dreams, she wrote, the nocturnal delight generally presaged physical discomfort in her waking life.[69]

This self-understanding can be questioned without going as far as the early psychoanalytic critic Oskar Pfister, who noted the way Margaretha was psychosomatically punished for her ecstatic experiences, but explained both the ecstasy and the punishment in sexual terms.[70] The texts of Hadewijch and Meister Eckhart suggest an alternative, contemporary critique of her behavior. Clinging to tears or to rituals of ascetic self-punishment is neither the sign of God that Margaretha believed it to be nor, as Pfister suggested, a fear of one's own sexuality but rather a displaced form of self-limitation. For Hadewijch, such behavior was an erroneous form of obedience inspired by the individual's fears, hopes, or emotional attractions rather than by a loving surrender to God.[71] For Eckhart, it was the identification with one's own habits that he termed *eigenschaft*.[72] Viewed from this perspective, Margaretha's mysticism appears constantly to have been constrained by the rigid structures that she shared with many of her contemporaries. She assumes that only overt physical suffering can legitimate a women's spiritual experience.[73] She also exhibits the tendency, criticized by Eckhart, of treating "grace" as an ecstatic end in itself rather than as a platform for further action in the world.[74] Finally, she associates mystical experience primarily with specific locales (the choir of the convent)[75] and with specific objects (a sculpture of the infant Jesus).[76] All these habits distanced Margaretha from her experience, as she actively cultivated forms that predetermined the rhythm and order of her life. The cycle of the Church calendar came to fix absolutely the sequence of her spiritual experience, causing her suffering to reach a predictable peak each Good Friday, the day of Christ's crucifixion. Margaretha did not experience Eckhartian freedom but surrendered instead to the routine of the liturgy.

According to the surviving documents, Heinrich helped Margaretha to break out of this repetition only on the two occasions already mentioned; otherwise, he did not want her to change. Instead, he admired the richness of her inner life—symbolized by her relationship with God—the like of which he could not achieve but onto which he could project the wishes he was too weak to fulfill for himself. "I lay on you the greater part of my suffering, for just as you have more love than I, so you are able to bear more than I."[77] He could turn to this embodiment of the spiritual life for reassurance, as when he asked Margaretha to pray for a vision that would tell him what to do when he was about to go into exile, or when he asked her to authenticate a relic he had acquired.[78] The underlying structure of the relationship is captured in the detail of a nightshirt of Margaretha's that Heinrich bid her send him in 1339 and that he still appears to have been wearing eight years later, in 1347.[79] Heinrich needed fixed tokens to act as markers for the intensity that he could not feel himself. These intermediary markers relieved him of acknowledging either his longing or Margaretha's own needs.

The relationship between Margaretha and Heinrich was an ambivalent mixture of activity and control. Its potential intensity was limited by rigid forms of external mediation: the role projected by Heinrich onto Margaretha, and the importance Margaretha attached to physical suffering, states of ecstasy, and sacred places and objects.[80] These forms of external mediation gave it a visible place in ecclesiastical structures (occurring in the choir, during Communion or on Good Friday, etc.), so it was not as threatening as the inaudible and therefore inscrutable murmurings of an unregulated spiritual life. It also allowed Heinrich and other male clerics to comment on, interpret, and legitimate it. At two points in the autobiography, an editor has interpolated Latin comments, drawing parallels between her experience and those of St. Augustine and St. Bernard and giving the technical term *sagitta acuta* for the shooting sensation that she reported feeling in her heart.[81] Writing an autobiography in this case was arguably as much a form of self-regulation as of self-expression. Margaretha perceived the initial act of writing as a transgression of her womanly role[82] and found that the recording of the experiences resuscitated their intensity.[83] Nevertheless, the text itself can be seen as another form of distancing. For Heinrich, it replaced more-direct contact. For Margaretha, who reported her own thoughts and actions uncritically, it offered a blanket affirmation of her experiences and absolved her of the need for the kind of critical self-inspection propagated by Eckhart and Hadewijch. It seems that the act of writing in itself was not sufficient to modify ecclesiastical and behavioral structures. Where individuals responded to their longing for God with the externalizing habits that we observe in Margaretha and Heinrich, the act of writing reinforced containment rather than facilitating change.

The relationship between Margaretha and Heinrich shows the apostolic life in an orthodox form. The confessor and nun meet, as it were, on the same terrain (a shared longing for communion with God). But the symbiosis does not question ecclesiastical structures. The individuals concerned accept a certain predetermined form for their experience. This was not inevitably the case. The traces we have of pastoral practice in Meister Eckhart's milieu suggest that the assumptions that subjected experiences to predetermined forms could be called into question. Before looking at the most extreme example, we can return to the legend of Meister Eckhart's daughter and see what this can tell us about the relation of Eckhart's preaching to the visions of inspired women.

Meister Eckhart's Daughters

The legend shows a world in which the Dominican friary was already established as a place to find counsel and official support if one was a follower of the apostolic life but did not belong to a particular order. It starts with the, as we have now seen, familiar figure of a woman consulting a friar confessor. There are other records of women seeking advice from Meister Eckhart, and the comparison shows what is special about the legend. A document from the convent in Ötenbach tells of an Elisabeth of Beggenhofen who took advice from learned clerics as to how she should behave when God did something with her, and on one occasion it is explicitly mentioned that she consulted Eckhart.[84] Similarly, records from the convent at St. Katherinental tell how Anna Ramswag went secretly to confess to Eckhart, and, although she was initially unwilling to tell other sisters what she spoke to him about, it emerged on her deathbed that she spoke to him of three particular visions.[85]

Both these cases suggest women having particular, intense experiences that they discuss with Eckhart in an attempt to assimilate them. Indeed, of Elisabeth of Beggenhofen we are told that, as a result of Eckhart's advice, she henceforth adopted an attitude of self-abandonment that helped her cope with subsequent unusual events.[86] The woman in the legend, in contrast, does not report visions, speakings, or other bodily manifestations of divine visitation. Indeed, she does not directly report an experience, although she does speak her views in the first person, quoting no further authority. What she represents instead is the attitude of detachment, which, taken to this extreme, complicates the attempt to report experiences, because there is no subject to attribute them to. Given the clear gendering of the figures (female visionary, male cleric) that the legend draws on, it is particularly striking that the bulk of the text consists in a questioning of gendered types: the young maiden, wife, man, woman, widow, virgin, master, maid, and servant. The woman describes her situation with reference to both masculine and feminine roles. Her attitude to the allocation of attributes is not critical. (The male roles represent moral strength and physical hard work; the female roles, innocence, spiritual fertility, faithfulness, reverence, and humility.) Nevertheless, the woman speaking can describe her own state with reference to both masculine and feminine models. This is an attitude to gender divisions that is similar to the one found in Eckhart's sermons.[87] The framework of medieval thought is itself not called into question. But the individual's relation to this framework is treated as flexible. The daughter can move beyond all the listed roles to become an unencumbered thing.

The legend echoes Eckhart's own treatment of women's spirituality. For Grace Jantzen, Eckhart's preaching is "weighted against women," since he denigrates bodily experience even as he accepts conventional gender attributes and associates the body and the senses with femininity. "It is clear, therefore, that the misogyny of Eckhart's teaching is more than metaphor-deep: the metaphors are indicative of a whole view of God, human nature and the spiritual path which keeps women in an inferior position." [88] This critique can be qualified in a number of ways. Since every society is cultivating a relationship of some sort with the human body, there is no particular value in somatized mystical experience except where it loosens social constraints. The underlying methodological point is that the experience and reactions of both parties, confessor and visionary woman, should be approached as an ambivalent mixture of genuine longing and social constraint. As Ruth Anthony El Saffar argues, we need to be able to discern the conflicting impulses recorded in these late medieval texts. On the one hand, the individual will have internalized the hatred of body and sexuality to be found in his or her surroundings and will reproduce it both in reality and in fantasy through various forms of self-punishment. On the other hand, he or she may harbor impulses toward a less policing relationship with embodiment, a relationship that helps to restore to the experience of divinity the attributes otherwise denigrated as female.[89] When they are read in context, Eckhart's texts do not appear as misogynist as Jantzen suggests they are. Not only are his sermons as critical of the intellect as they are of sensual attachments, since concepts themselves, even the very concept of God, divide the individual from divinity.[90] But the particular arguments that Eckhart used should not be separated from the constraining spirituality to which they were in many instances a reaction. The texts emerging from women's houses in the period show an attachment to bodily states and to ritual. As we have seen, Margaretha Ebner's *Revelations* record a series of afflictions—illness, screaming fits, losing the capacity to speak—that closely chart the Church calendar. Her repetitive autobiography suggests the degree to which, during the fourteenth century, the spiritual horizons of a Dominican nun were determined by the rigid pattern of her quotidian routine (the eight hours a day set aside for liturgy and prayer).[91] It also suggests the degree to which she might have shared the paranoid convictions of her contemporaries, as when Margaretha lends divine authority to the fear that the Jews were responsible for the Black Death.[92] Eckhart's preaching worked to break these attachments and widen the horizons of possible experience. To this extent, he was going against the tendency of some of his clerical colleagues, who actively cultivated the connection between women's spiritual experience and bodily states because they found it reassuring to have visible signs of grace and clearly defined gender roles.[93] Eckhart's own preaching opened the way for further psychological and spiritual development, because it broke the identification with particular gender roles and the associated attitudes to the body. The same approach is recorded in the legend. Rather than reporting a bodily visitation and having her confessor fix it as a divine emblem, the woman shows that she has transcended the expected behavior of the confessing female visionary.

There is one role, however, that the woman does not escape, that of being an example. The problem with the legend is not so much that it is antibody but that it is not dynamic. There is neither development nor exchange in the brief sequence. Instead, the attitude with which the woman arrives is fixed as something that the men can admire, effectively keeping her at a distance. The text is very short, so it might seem unjustified to expect a subtle psychological dynamic. However, even in its brevity, it is significant that it focuses only on presenting her miraculous perfection and the reaction of the male clerics. The other two examples of encounters with Eckhart did not do this. Elisabeth of Beggenhofen was helped by the advice alter her behavior. Anna Ramswag discussed with Eckhart experiences that she finally divulged on her deathbed. Both anecdotes contain an element of development. In contrast, the legend shows a figure that remains static rather than dynamic. The tendency to stasis seems to have increased as the story was copied. Eckhart's "brothers" (friars of equal status) changed to "disciples" ("jungern"), and the final line is added, classifying the text as an example.[94] The treatment of the woman in the legend thus remains ambivalent. On the one hand, she is given authority (speaking in the first person) and moves beyond the gender roles with which the tale starts. She is also recognized by the authority figure (Eckhart). On the other hand, she does not have her own story, there is no communication, and she is treated as an object of admiration and demonstration by the master before his male pupils.

It is difficult to ascertain how much this attitude reproduces Eckhart's own practice as confessor and spiritual advisor to visionary women. Many historians have solved this problem by emphazising what they take to be the orthodoxy of his teaching and arguing that he rationalized the potentially heretical spirituality prevalent in the nunneries of the era.[95] Indeed, it has even been suggested that he was the theological authority to whom the bishop of Strasbourg turned when he was persecuting and burning beguines between 1317 and 1319.[96] Aspects of these claims are borne out by the existing records. From 1314, Eckhart, once even called "vicar of the master general," features thrice in documents from the Strasbourg area, where he had some responsibility for affairs in women's communities.[97] He features in this role in a document of November 13, 1316, wherein Eckhart and the prioress of the Dominican convent of St. Mark in Strasbourg allow the endowment of masses in memory of a deceased knight (*Ritter*), Fritzemann von Schaftoltzheim.[98] A further document dated December 10, 1322, from Herveus, the master general of the Dominicans, ratifies disciplinary measures that Eckhart and another vicar, Matthew of Finstingen, imposed on the Dominican convent of Unterlinden bei Kolmar.[99] These documents confirm that Eckhart's duties included contact with women religious, and the document from 1322 shows that he was involved in organization of chaplains and confessors for women's houses. Nevertheless, they do not reveal much about his response to the visionary experiences on a day-to-day basis. The legend and the two surviving records from convent histories show him as an iconic figure to whom women turned for spiritual advice. The sermons show him encouraging development and the abandonment of attachments. But none of the texts tell us how Eckhart dealt with individual cases.

Medieval readers might not have been so concerned with Eckhart's individual intention or approach, even where they were interested in the authority of the writer. Lienhart Peuger (ca.1390–ca.1455), a copyist in Melk, adapted Eckhart's texts to his own purposes, separating his sermons clearly from the text of other authors but nevertheless editing and altering them in accordance with his particular model of pious devotion.[100] There is not enough evidence to decide whether Eckhart was an adjunct of inquisitorial tribunals, or an inspiring, charismatic confessor, or a mixture of the two. But in a sense this is not important, even if it is disappointing. There is another text, not by Eckhart, but arising from the context of his preaching in Strasbourg, that demonstrates something of the dynamic potential of the relationship between confessor and nun. The text, the *Sister Catherine* treatise, shows another way of reacting to and absorbing the apostolic calling. If it does not report actual experiences, it is, through the combined form and content, a record of structures through which experiences were managed and integrated. It can be read as an image of the dynamic potential that the relationship between confessor and visionary woman was held to contain, even if we do not know that such relationships existed in practice.

Becoming God in Fourteenth-Century Europe

Sister Catherine records the spiritual development of a beguine and her confessor.[101] In some manuscripts, it is explicitly suggested that she is Meister Eckhart's spiritual charge, and, indeed, the nineteenth-century Eckhart editor, Franz Pfeiffer, published the text using a manuscript title that made such a connection. "This is Sister Catherine, Meister Eckhart's daughter from Strasbourg [Daz ist swester katrei Meister Eckehartes Tohter von Strâzburc]." But the reference to the Dominican master is no sure indicator of an actual relationship. The text consists in five dialogues between the woman and the cleric. In the first four she seeks him out. In the last, the roles are reversed and he seeks her. The cleric starts with conventional advice, bidding the woman be mindful of the seven gifts of the Holy Spirit and the six works of charity, following the gospel and Thomas Aquinas. But the woman's spiritual needs are not to be catered to in this manner. She is happy neither with mere contemplation of her sins nor with a spiritual journey limited by her confessor. "When I leave all things behind I must also leave you."[102] The cleric tries to persuade her not to leave, but the woman is determined to embark on a journey of apostolic poverty, and in her determination she lays claim to qualities of strength and potential for action that the text highlights as specifically masculine (351/324). Like Eckhart's texts, the dialogues present the journey toward God as a progressive stripping away of the fixed assumptions that might otherwise stop the individual from being ready at any moment to do his bidding.[103] This entails a flexibility about gender roles similar to that found in Eckhart's texts and the legend. But it goes further than Meister Eckhart's sermons in that it also suggests that the confessional relationship can be, if not abandoned, then at least remodeled.

Although his role is modified, the confessor nevertheless plays an important part in the woman's spiritual development.[104] He will eventually become her spiritual charge, listening to her instruction in the long, final section of the text. Before that, however, he demonstrates a theoretical knowledge that helps the woman to advance. She complains that she has for too long listened to the instructions of her confessor and other clerics instead of following God. "I regret with all my heart that I followed human advice for such a long time and that I resisted the advice of the Holy Spirit for so long."[105] The confessor replies that not all the Dominicans and Franciscans in the world could control someone who is moved by the truth. "No one can hinder you but yourself."[106] In this exchange, both parties formulate insights important to the woman's development, helping her to follow her inner promptings. The woman speaks out against a constraining confessional relationship, the man points out that she controls herself. At a later stage, the woman returns from having traveled and is initially not recognized by the cleric. As with the Eckhart figure in the legend, he is so impressed by what he hears from her that he reports back to his brethren. "I have listened to [the confession of] a person and I'm not sure if she is a human being or an angel."[107] However, where the legend stopped at this point, the story in the *Sister Catherine* treatise continues.

The woman still has not reached the state she longs for, and the cleric realizes that the last obstacle that she must overcome is her very desire for God (358/333). This completes her development. She goes briefly into a meditative state, from which she returns to announce, "Rejoice with me, I am become God."[108] The confessor remains a participant in the dialogue even at this point, bidding her wait to see whether the new state is permanent. After three days in something like suspended animation, during which time the cleric prevents the woman from being mistaken for dead and buried, she comes back to herself with the knowledge that the state is permanent indeed (359/334–35). However, her spiritual work is not yet complete. She resists her confessor's request that she now stay where she is, and she continues to travel. Her soul is now permanently with God, but her body must follow Christ's example and be active in the world (359/335). The priest must therefore come to find her when he wants her advice. He does so, and consults her on matters of doctrine. She shares her knowledge on a variety of issues—hell, purgatory, the resurrection and assumption of the body, the erroneous belief that being "with God" in this world entails an absence of all moral constraint. During this final stage of the treatise, the woman talks more than the man, teaching him. The cleric already knows much of what she has to say, but his knowledge is theoretical rather than lived (358/334). This finally changes when he too is drawn into a state of rapture. "The daughter tells him so much about the greatness and power and the providence of God that he loses his senses."[109] However, as we discover at the very close of the text, this is only the beginning of his spiritual journey. The text ends with the woman's brief description of what the confessor has yet to learn before he arrives at the state that she has achieved (383/370).

The text shows a relationship between confessor and visionary woman that is both flexible and reciprocal. The woman pushes beyond the limits of the confessor's control, and the confessor learns from her, becoming himself a visionary at the very end of the narrative. It is possible that no such relationship existed. The editor of the critical edition, Franz-Josef Schweitzer, for one, treats the text as purely fictional.[110] On the other hand, it is also clear that the text was not produced in a vacuum. It is in dialogue with other writers, echoing texts from the area and the period (sermons by Eckhart and Nicholas of Strasbourg, other treatises of mystical import such as "Von der edelkeit der sêle" [On the nobility of the soul]).[111] The beliefs that the woman expounds are also similar to those that can be found in the records of interrogations of beguines and beghards (their male equivalent) from Strasbourg in 1317. Here too we find a privileging of inner impulses no less radical than that of the woman in the treatise. "Man should rather behave according to his inner sense than follow the truth of the gospel as it is preached every day."[112] While there is no evidence that the text is based on a particular confessional relationship, there is also no evidence that such relationships did not exist in the milieu from which the text arose.

Such an encounter appears fictional to a modern reader because the attitudes that it reflects are not only unfamiliar but, to a certain degree, taboo. We're not meant to become God, because God is to be kept habitually at a distance, either by not being believed in or by being conceived of as absolutely other and so necessarily distinct from human experience. John Caputo has qualified this idea, suggesting that God's otherness needn't be treated as otherworldly. It can be an event disrupting the routine of this world: "For the event is not what happens but what is going on *in* what happens that makes it restless with the future. Thus instead of opposing two worlds, or of opposing God and the world as if these were two realms of being, I distinguish between the world and the event by which the world is disturbed, the unconditional claim that solicits the world from within, that interrupts and summons it."[113] In contrast, what is striking in the texts of Eckhart and his contemporaries is the very different temporality. "Becoming God" is not an event in the future, or even the disruption of the present by an open future "absolutely other and new."[114] It is something that has potentially already occurred and with which we come to terms as we continue to live in the world: "I *have become* God." In the medieval texts, God is not banished to another world, or another time zone, but has already happened to us. If this seems unsettling to modern readers, this is probably a behavioral as much as a conceptual problem, resulting not so much from the texts' disregard of any ontological necessity of keeping the human and divine separate but rather from their indifference to or rejection of habits that keep at a permanent distance those parts of experience we engage with when we talk of God.

The *Sister Catherine* treatise exemplifies alternative, non-distancing habits. While it may not be possible to anchor the text in the life of named individuals, or of a named author, it *is* possible to reconstruct the assumptions of the way of life that produced it. The first is that "becoming God" is both desirable and feasible. The progress of the woman and her confessor toward this goal then shows indirectly which conventions and assumptions regulated the relationship with God. The confessional relationship itself is an obstacle as long as it imposes a fixed pattern on the woman's behavior. Preconceptions as to what behavior is fitting for men and for women are also constraining. However, both the ecclesiastical relationship and the gendered behavior patterns can be redeployed to further the individual's development. Another assumption that the woman must overcome is the need to follow a preestablished model of moral behavior. Where she worries that she has never perfectly embodied a virtue and that she has never done as much as she could, the confessor encourages her to relinquish control. "People cannot make amends for even one sin, unless God forgives them out of love."[115] As the conversation develops, it emerges that the following of the model is actually a form of self-orientation that prevents her from doing God's will. Theological concepts can function as a similar obstacle, so the text repeatedly takes up prevailing ideas, like that of hell or the resurrection of the body, and glosses them, saying, "That is right, but it is not as people take it to be."[116] In the discussions of both heaven and hell, the text questions the idea of a radical division between "this" life and "the next." The attitude toward God, be it one of attentiveness or of neglect, that you cultivate in the here and now will be the state in which you remain after death (363/340–41). The text does not repudiate structure as such. Indeed, it is in many ways an orthodox text, defending the doctrine of transubstantiation, keeping ecclesiastical penance, and criticizing the antinomian beliefs otherwise associated with the heresy of the free spirit.[117] However, it uses the gospels, theological concepts, Eckhartian and other speculative ideas, and the existing institutional relationship of confession to discredit behavior and thought patterns that separate the individual from God. The confessor participates in this process no less than the woman does. His authority and position help to break some of her habits, encouraging her finally to abandon the desire for God. At the same time, he is also inspired by her example to experience the development himself rather than make do with theoretical knowledge alone.

The text undermines institutional, behavioral, and conceptual barriers between the individual and the sense of connection to God. Conspicuous by their absence in this process are reports of particular visions. In this respect, the treatise is very close to Eckhart, who equally concentrates on the transformation of attitudes rather than on the reporting of visionary rapture. This is explicable in terms of the text's pedagogic project. It shows the transformation of behavior, and challenges the idea of privileged access to God (for the cleric, for the woman, for the saints, for the dead). It is therefore consistent that it should establish neither a particular model (access to God comes in the form of a particular vision) nor a focus of projection. It does not want us to admire or worship the unnamed woman as an example of extraordinary sainthood. That again would only put a barrier between the individual and the experience of divinization. Yet, if it eschews visions, the text does not eschew social detail. It operates in a recognizable setting, taking the woman as its starting point in a way that, given the context, could be called realist. It also takes up the language associated with this setting (just as Eckhart takes up the vocabulary of economic exchange). In this respect the text is socially critical rather than esoteric. It responds to familiar character types to be found among the adherents of the apostolic life and fosters detachment and spiritual development.

The attitudes of Sister Catherine and her confessor did not become those of the modern self, and it is this, rather than a lack of social grounding in the text itself, that makes them seem "otherworldly." Indeed, the habits and attitudes fostered by the text are arguably ones that modern habits of identity developed expressly to control. Existing accounts of the rise of modern forms of selfhood, as we have seen, can describe some of the habits and social procedures for self-monitoring and self-discipline associated with this identity. But they find it harder to give an account of how and why individuals might feel it urgent to develop these habits. The devil in this respect is not in the detail but in a basic, methodological problem—namely, that the theorists, identifying with the habits whose genesis they want to reconstruct, are not able to perceive the impulses that the habits developed to regulate or exclude. The next chapter will try to break out of this deadlock, to show how, using the example of Eckhart's milieu in the Rhineland of the early fourteenth century, it is possible to reconstruct the kind of context from which habits associated with modern forms of self arise. This is not to say that the self was born in fourteenth-century Germany. But rather to suggest that habits like those of the modern self will emerge from contexts in which, as was the case in the Rhineland of the fourteenth century, the individual is under pressure to regulate the desire to "become God." As we shall see, forms like those of the modern self arise where the individual polices his or her own relationship with divinity.

7

The Makings of the Modern Self

The Church in the fourteenth century did not approve of individuals aspiring to "become God" in this life, even if only momentarily. The orthodox position, following Thomas Aquinas, who was canonized in 1323, was that man could become God's full image only in the afterlife.[1] From this vantage point, the church regulated and controlled the spiritual life of individuals but in a manner that almost inevitably produced conflicts with the adherents of the various apostolic movements, and that provoked an incident very illuminating for the development of modern ideas of selfhood.

The apostolic movements sought to foster a more direct relation to God in this world by remodeling the individual's habits.[2] However, despite the changes in doctrine and daily practice that this entailed, many followers of the apostolic life themselves had no desire to challenge the Church. In the 1170s, Waldo, the founder of the Waldensians, gave up the wealth he had earned as a cloth merchant in Lyons to preach, and he refused to think even one day ahead, living instead from alms of food and clothing. In 1179, he went to Rome to seek papal permission for his preaching. Permission was not granted on the grounds that Waldo, as a layman, was theologically incompetent, but the story illustrates how little he wished to step outside the Church.[3] The Church could tolerate this new form of life only if it adopted a monastic rule, allowed itself to be regulated, and limited its preaching to moral exhortation rather than matters of doctrine. The new religious groupings accepted this ordering insofar as it did not directly interfere with their longing for God. During the thirteenth century an unstable compromise reigned, of which the mendicant orders were themselves a product. Frameworks had been established within which a more intense religious life could legally prosper, but the ecclesiastical institution still felt itself to be in control. By the beginning of the fourteenth century this compromise was breaking down, and it is no coincidence that this is also a period in which the mystical fervor of the apostolic movements intensified. One symptom of this collapse was the proscription of a heresy, the heresy of the free spirit, which, as Robert Lerner has argued, had no adherents before it was created by papal decree after the Council of Vienne in 1311–12.[4] The dispute over the heresy neatly crystallizes the terms of the conflict between the Church and the apostolic movements.

It is hard to ascertain what views the people accused of the heresy actually espoused. They were accused of all sorts of crimes, from preaching in the nude to sexual orgies and infant sacrifice. But it appears that these accusations bear little resemblance to what the people actually did.[5] Records were kept of interrogations, but these records do not directly tell us what people did or said outside the interrogation. Inquisitorial tribunals in the period defined the erroneous doctrines that they were looking for *before* interrogating suspects and then asked if suspects believed tenets *x* or *y*. Documents are likely to be a record of inquisitors' presuppositions as much as of actual beliefs.[6] If it is hard to reconstruct exactly what behavior or what beliefs were singled out as heretical, it is nevertheless possible to deduce two possible grounds of conflict from the hostile sources. The first is that the behavior of the persecuted groupings was visibly different. An inquisitorial report written in Strasbourg in 1317 condemns congregations and conventicles of beguines and beghards that had a particular way of talking, living, and interacting with each other.[7] The second problem was one of attitude. As we have seen in chapter 6, the bull proscribing the beguine life, *De quibusdam mulieribus*, which was drawn up at the Council of Vienne in parallel with the bull defining the heresy of the Free Spirit, portrayed the beguines' sense of calling as a danger. It belittled and dismissed inspiration as a form of derangement.[8] The challenge that the apostolic movements posed to the Church was one not primarily of doctrine so much as of attitude and lifestyle.[9] This conflict flared up with renewed intensity at the beginning of the fourteenth century.

One high-profile casualty of the conflict was Meister Eckhart himself. In the bull *In agro dominico*, published March 27, 1329, seventeen articles from his texts were condemned as heretical and a further eleven as ill sounding.[10] There have been a number of different explanations of his condemnation. Some focus on internal politics in the Dominican order (observant versus less observant strands), others on conflicts between the

Franciscans and the Dominicans. Some suggest that Eckhart's texts were misinterpreted, others that the condemnation was a local affair and that the ban was published only in the diocese of Cologne. Robert Lerner has found a copy of the bull in an inquisitor's manual compiled in Mainz in the late fourteenth century.[11] This suggests that, however much the inquisitors may have misinterpreted Eckhart's teaching, and however much proceedings against Eckhart may have been initiated as the result of rivalries within or between the mendicant orders, the condemnation was neither local nor an accident. The heresy proceedings against Eckhart are a symptom of the clash between the regulating discourse of Church institutions and the behavioral experiments associated with the apostolic movement. To study this example is to see in more detail how the desire to "become God" was institutionally regulated and how individuals came to terms with the disciplinary intrusions of the Church. From the context of this regulation arose habits and practices that prefigure modern techniques of selfhood.

Meister Eckhart on Trial

The first place to look if one wants to understand why Eckhart was condemned is the bull proscribing his teaching: *In agro dominico*. The message this gives is that Eckhart was a thinker who did not respect order, who undermined ecclesiastical hierarchy and threw into turmoil the economy by which the Church attempted to mediate and regulate the individual's relationship with God. The bull condemned statements in which Eckhart declared that the individual could become identical with God or Christ ("Nos transformamur totaliter in Deum et convertimur in eum").[12] It also singled out articles that suggested that we should not wish *not* to have committed sins, that "he who blasphemes God himself praises God,"[13] and that God does not value good works any more than any other kind of action ("God loves souls, not external works").[14] In these statements, all the barriers that the Church erected to establish a distance between man and the divine, and to regulate his behavior on earth, were overturned. Eckhart seemed to the inquisitorial tribunal to advise his listeners to renounce all fixed forms of devotion, to stop distinguishing sinful from virtuous behavior, and to stop drawing too rigid a line between God and his creation. Indeed, the categories and concepts that otherwise so carefully regulated God's distribution are disregarded even to the point of God becoming apparently dependent on the individual.[15]

The bull misread Eckhart's texts. Eckhart did in some instances qualify the value of ecclesiastical rituals. In the "Talks of Instruction," he suggested that if you trod on a stone while seeking God "it would be a more godly act than if you were to receive the body of our Lord while being concerned only for yourself and having a less detached attitude of mind."[16] But, in other passages, he straightforwardly upheld ecclesiastical distinctions: "It is better to pray than to spin, and a church is a worthier place than the street."[17] Taken together, these two statements tell us that Eckhart did not disregard ecclesiastical order, but at the same time he never made order for its own sake his primary term. He respected ecclesiastical rituals, but he valued even more highly the process of turning to God. He placed attitude and experience over structure and established hierarchy: "Intend God alone and seek him only. Then whatever kinds of devotional practice come to you, be content with those."[18]

The bull did not register this qualified attitude to order. This failure was not the fault of individuals who finally assessed Eckhart's teaching at the papal curia in Avignon. The misreading was rather institutionalized in the inquisitorial process—indeed, that was its goal. For it was precisely this kind of qualification or questioning of ecclesiastical structure that inquisitors were seeking to control. It is worth reconstructing the assumptions and practices that underpinned the method of inquisitorial reading in some detail, because it exemplifies the structures of control with which adherents of the apostolic life came into conflict.

When doubt was cast on a text or series of texts, theologians or clerks of the court would copy out those statements that appeared most suspect and submit the extracts to an inquisitorial commission for evaluation. In Eckhart's case it appears to have been the archbishop of Cologne, Henry of Virneburg, acting in collaboration with two friars from Eckhart's own order, Hermann de Summo and Wilhelm von Nidecke, who initiated proceedings sometime between August 1325 and September 1326.[19] The commission would then assess what it took to be the literal meaning of the words. (The phases "prout sonat," "ut sonat," "ut verba sonant" are repeated over and over in the report that a second commission drew up once Eckhart's case had moved from Cologne to Avignon.)[20] They would take heed neither of context nor of authorial intention. Inquisitorial tribunes were concerned only to establish if individual articles read literally could be construed as heretical.[21]

In Joseph Koch's account, the inquisitorial process developed in subtlety in the sixty years from 1270 to Eckhart's condemnation in 1329. The extracted articles were quoted with increasing accuracy, and the verdicts passed on the material became increasingly differentiated, as the business of evaluation became more and more a scholarly exercise, with expert theologians being called on to assess the work of their academic colleagues.[22]

However, Koch's vision of an ever-more scholarly process of investigation obscures the hermeneutic premises on which Eckhart's trial and other inquisitorial procedures were based nevertheless. Inquisitorial procedure is an example both of the burgeoning of argumentative and logical techniques that characterized the thirteenth century and of the (to the later observer, irrational) purposes for which these techniques were actually deployed.

A number of historians have emphasized rational gains that the inquisition represented.[23] The basic form, a legal process *per inquisitionem* that recognized the priority of evidence over that of reputation, was established in the procedures, set out by the Fourth Lateran Council in 1215, for disciplining lax clerics. Innocent III's attempt to reform the Church had been thwarted by the difficulty of putting cases against senior clerics under the old process of *accusatio*. In the old system, the individual who raised the accusation was liable to punishment himself if his case did not succeed. The accused, on the other hand, had only to swear an oath supported by a sufficient number of people of good repute to restore his reputation. Both these factors hindered the removal of bad clerics. Innocent III created the new role of inquisitors who could gather evidence ex officio where there was sufficient public clamor about an individual to warrant further investigation. In the inquisitorial process, the failure of the case no longer entailed punishment for those who raised the complaint, and the investigation stood a better chance of being impartial.[24] The new system was also more transparent in the way it handled its evidence. Statements by reliable witnesses, bound by oath, would be recorded in writing and then submitted to the accused before he was himself called for examination in order that he might be given the opportunity to defend himself. The names of witnesses were also kept public.[25]

This form of inquiry developed from being an internal, disciplinary procedure to one employed for the evaluation of suspected heretics. In the process, some of the rationalizing impulses were carried over from the original context into the newly developing form.[26] Nevertheless, the rationalizing elements were subsidiary to other impulses that in legal terms appear as the influence of Roman law. Following laws in force both before and after the Christianization of the Roman Empire, heresy was defined as a form of lèse-majesté, *crimen laesae maiestatis*. For Roman law, this meant those crimes judged to be against the Roman people or against their security.[27] Two things are important in this definition. The first is the way heresy is equated with a breach of social order, confirming Richard Kieckhefer's view that "whether genuinely heretical or not, religious deviants were seen as a threat to society."[28] The second is the aura that this social order was perceived to radiate. In the period before Christianization, Roman law judged *crimen laesae maiestatis* to be an insult to the gods rather than to the *res publica*, and this same association reappeared in medieval legal thought that treated heresy as an insult to the Christian God's majesty.[29] As a consequence, the practices of investigation and punishment became both more brutal and less transparent than those linked to the initial disciplinary *inquisitio*. In Roman law, slaves and other discredited persons were admitted as witnesses, torture was allowed as a means of obtaining evidence, and those found guilty were ritually burnt, a form of execution otherwise unusual at the time.[30] All these practices were incorporated into the inquisitorial procedure as it developed in the course of the thirteenth century. Torture was permitted by the bull *Ad extirpanda* of 1252; criminals, perjurers and children came to be admissible as witnesses; and those found guilty would be ritually immolated.[31]

The individual inquisitors responsible for developing inquisitorial procedures during the course of the thirteenth century were less interested in rational forms than in the more urgent task of defending an auratic order. Bernard Gui's *Manual of an Inquisitor* gives an inkling of the priorities of the resulting process.[32] The book is the fruit of many years of questioning suspected heretics. It includes descriptions of the major heresies Gui encountered, accounts of the heretics' beliefs and way of life, and questions that one should use to interrogate a suspect but also tips on how to maximize the yield from an interrogation. The most important step, Gui suggests, is the swearing of an oath. In swearing the oath, however, Gui's victims were not merely assenting to tell what they took to be the truth. "They are to use words in the sense intended by the investigator, without any ruse or artifice [*secundum intellectum inquirentis, absque omni dolo et fallacia*]."[33] The defendant had to take an oath to speak the language of the inquisitor. This language, Gui insisted, knows no other criteria of evaluation than the inquisitor's own. If heretics appealed to their own reading of the life of Christ, they were accused of calling evil good and turning darkness into light.[34] If they objected that the statements that the inquisitor demanded of them offend God, the inquisitor was to inform them that the sole determinant of an offense to God "is not their false notion but the judgment of the interrogator."[35] Nor was there any refuge in silence. A heretic who refused to talk on these terms could be excommunicated, starved, incarcerated, chained, or tortured "as the nature of the case and the status of the individual involved may require"[36] and so be persuaded to capitulate. If defendants persisted in their refusal for more than a year after they were first excommunicated, the law viewed them as heretics anyway. A year's silence was equivalent to a confession of heresy.

Victims could at this point be turned over to the secular arm of the law to be burned. The hermeneutic principle behind Gui's interrogations is clear. Heretics gave up their own experience and submitted to the language the inquisitor imposed on them, or they died. The inquisitorial tribunal functioned as a kind of enforced reintegration into the auratic order represented by the Church.

The assumptions that underpinned Gui's control of meaning underpinned the papal commission's interpretation of Eckhart's teaching. When the heretics of Languedoc appealed to their own inner conviction to explain why they held their beliefs, Gui was deaf. He heard either a diabolical inversion of established truths or a challenge to his authority as inquisitor. Eckhart's judges were similarly deaf, indeed they expressed their lack of understanding in exactly the same words as did Gui.[37] The term ignored is in both cases that of inner calling.[38] Just as the sermons and the "Talks of Instruction" made the turning toward God the sole guarantee of practices, rituals, or beliefs, so in the trial Eckhart defended himself by appealing to his godly intention. This was partly tactical. Heresy, as it was defined in the later Middle Ages, was always a question of attitude. Important was not the fact that an individual had made a theological error but the fact that he or she pertinaciously clung to the mistake even after the inquisitor had pointed it out. To counter the accusations of heresy leveled at him by the inquisitorial commission, Eckhart made a declaration in the Dominican church in Cologne that he had "always abhorred all errors in faith and all aberrations in morals." He also said that he would willingly correct and retract any teachings that were found to be erroneous.[39] Yet if the public proclamation was a tactical necessity, the appeal to genuine intention was simultaneously the substance of Eckhart's defense. In the record that survives of his self-explanation before the tribunal in Cologne, Eckhart repeats again and again that his texts will cease to appear erroneous or false once we take account of the spirit of devotion out of which they were written. As soon as we acknowledge this genuine intention, as soon as we attempt "reasonably and devoutly" to reconstruct its meaning, we would, Eckhart believed, perceive the "excellent and useful truths of faith and moral teaching" that his writings contain.[40] Then even the most extreme turns of rhetoric would arouse only "love of virtue and of God."[41] As in his treatises and sermons, so in his defense Eckhart made the inner turning toward God the guarantee of both doctrine and practice.

To the theologians assessing Eckhart's teachings, this sole reliance on the individual's sense of being called by God was not merely heretical. It encouraged others to sin, for it stripped away the ecclesiastical structures that would otherwise regulate their behavior.[42] Where Eckhart's texts presuppose an individual guided by longing for whom doctrine, rhetoric, and ritual are not an end in themselves but tools to further his or her self-overcoming, the inquisitors acknowledged no such inner guidance. Their contrary view of the individual is betrayed by a term that crops up in Eckhart's final condemnation but that can also be found in other similar documents: the legal fiction of "simple folk" (in the words of the bull, the "hearts of the simple," or "corda simplicium").[43] These simple subjects are individuals with no inner life or will of their own, individuals whom specious doctrine will inevitably corrupt. They are individuals with no spiritual experience but also no guiding context or prior behavioral commitments. These blank ciphers are the flipside of the defendant in Gui's interrogations, who has surrendered all interiority in the oath she took to speak the inquisitor's language. Between them, the two images represent the model of identity on which the inquisition was premised and to which it adapted its practices of interpretation and interrogation: individuals ripped out of the context of their own longing and their everyday life and instead framed and controlled by the inquisitor's language and the auratic institution for which he is the emissary. This individual has delegated all experience of God to the institutions and offices that claim to represent him. Eckhart, in contrast, was condemned because his whole pastoral project depended on an individual yet shareable and quotidian experience of divinity.

Eckhart did not believe himself to be a heretic, nor did his congregation. In the wake of his condemnation, individuals were left with the problem of reconciling their own desire for spiritual and intellectual development with the demand for regulation imposed by the Church. How Eckhart solved this dilemma we do not know. He is said by the bull to have recanted his errors before he died, but the exact circumstances both of the final recanting and of his death are unknown. Some groups in similar circumstances reacted by leading a double life and protecting their longing for contact with God beneath a public life of orthodoxy. Such was the response of many German Waldensians to the threat of persecution.[44] But a more interesting case for the history of the modern self is that of Heinrich Seuse (1295/97–1366)—a pupil of Eckhart's—and of a Dominican nun in Seuse's pastoral care, Elsbeth Stagel (ca. 1300–ca. 1360). Stagel and Seuse did not adopt a double life, nor were they satisfied with simply delegating their longing for God to institutionally recognized mediators. Two texts in particular show how they balanced the sense of inner calling with the regulatory demands of the Church, forging in the process a set of new practices of identity. The first is the *Book of Truth* (*Daz Bůchli der Warheit*), which Seuse appears to have written around 1330 as a direct response to the bull condemning Eckhart.[45] The second is the biography of himself that he claims to have written in collaboration with Elsbeth Stagel and that forms an extended preface to the edition of his own works that he prepared in Ulm in the 1360s.[46] Before we see how the relationship between nun and confessor could be redeployed as an instrument of regulated individuation, we need to see how Seuse in his defense of Eckhart prepares the way for modern Western techniques of the self.

Heinrich Seuse Invents a Self

The Book of Truth describes the spiritual and theological education of a young man. At the beginning of the book, the man has an experience in which he is told, "You must know that inner detachment brings man to the highest truth."[47] In the course of the text he then learns to differentiate real detachment from a false, disorderly freedom (*ungeordente friheit*).[48] The book takes the form of a series of dialogues. The young man asks questions and is answered by the Eternal Truth or the Word. In the penultimate section, he himself is allowed to pass on the wisdom he has learned to the figure called the "wild one" (*daz wilde*), who quotes Eckhartian articles banned by the bull and is taught by the young man how better to understand them. In the final section, Eternal Truth instructs the young man once again, telling him what outward form his life should take.

The purpose of the text is to establish a conceptual framework for spiritual experience. Without such a framework, the individual is likely to go astray, as the young man explains to the "wild one."[49] This framework does not replace spiritual longing. (This is an important point for the subsequent development of forms of modern identity.) On the contrary, ample space is given to the sort of ideas and desires discussed in Eckhart's sermons or the *Sister Catherine* treatise. Moreover, the state to which the young man is guided is described as a form of union with God, and the vocabulary used to describe both the state and the progress toward it is, as with Eckhart texts, drawn from theological discussions of Christ's incarnation.[50] Nevertheless, where Eckhart's method is dynamic, using rhetorical and conceptual tools to overcome philosophical and behavioral limits, Seuse's method is constraining. This is registered in the form, which, for all the appearance of dialogue, remains essentially monological. The young man asks, and the Truth gives him an answer. There is none of the scope for exchange apparent in the *Sister Catherine* treatise.[51] The constraining method is also noticeable in the content of the arguments themselves. While union with God is contemplated as a theoretical possibility even in this world, the text repeatedly limits and qualifies the terms in which the union is to be imagined.[52] However much individuals strive to overcome themselves, they will never "be born in the Son and become one Son" in the way Eckhart's sermons suggested but will always remain limited by their own humanity.[53] The union that can be achieved in this life is reserved only for an elect few.[54] It will also be only a taste of what is to come in the next life.[55] Even in moments of rapture, the type of individual imagined in Seuse's text will always be aware of his or her own understanding and will never wholly disappear in the nothingness of God.[56] To this extent, the limits of the experience have always been determined before the dialogue begins.[57]

Seuse wrote the text to defend the doctrine of his teacher, Eckhart, in the immediate aftermath of the latter's condemnation and himself seems to have been disciplined as a result, being removed from his position as lector at the Dominican friary in Constance around 1332.[58] Loris Sturlese emphasizes the courage needed to put his name to the defense of a proscribed author.[59] The danger of the situation has left its mark on the text, which shows how Seuse effectively internalized the hermeneutic and behavioral demands of the inquisitorial tribunal. Eckhart defended his position by appealing to attitude that ensured that his rhetorical and conceptual daring remained educative. In contrast, Seuse establishes an orthodox conceptual framework with which to determine the limits of spiritual experience in advance. This transforms the model of freedom toward which he aspires. Where the Eckhartian individual stands free to do God's bidding, whatever it might be, at any moment, Seuse's adept is free because he or she imposes constraint on him- or herself rather than submitting to external force. "But if he does not have constraints, that is because he himself performs out of detachment what the wider community performs because it is forced to."[60] There is a conflict—between the sense of calling, on the one hand, and, on the other, the ecclesiastical demand that access to God be externalized and institutionally regulated—that Seuse's individual resolves by himself learning the habits of policing.

This self-policing produces structures similar to those of the modern self. As we have seen, in moments of rapture, Seuse's individual is still aware of his or her own rational capacities. The effort of self-monitoring encourages an attitude in which consciousness cannot be escaped. The effort of establishing a conscious conceptual framework also produces something like the vocabulary of modern selfhood. Where Meister Eckhart's texts had no direct equivalent to the modern word *self,* Seuse's text unexpectedly discovers the noun itself: *das sich*.[61] The discovery is superficially prompted by an analysis of the verb "to take leave of oneself," the Middle High German *sich lazsen*.[62] True to the scholastic habit of cutting up a phrase or sentence so as to draw meaning from its individual elements, Seuse offers a series of glosses on both of the words *lazsen* and *sich*. He is trying in effect to define more closely what it is the individual must abandon when he takes leave of himself, to define the "oneself" that differentiates and distances the individual from God. However, the effort of definition forces Seuse to group together and fix as a noun impulses that for Eckhart never have the same abstract coherence or rigidity. It forces him to invent the term "a self of his own"—*ein eigen sich*.[63]

The formulation is perhaps fortuitous, and the difference from equivalent formulations in Eckhart's texts not enormous. One text of Eckhart that approaches this usage is the sermon on the text *Renouamini spiritu* (Sermon 83). The text is a classic statement of negative theology. "What we can know or say of the First Cause reflects ourselves more than it does the First Cause, for this transcends all speech and understanding."[64] However, having argued that the attributes we give to God are always inappropriately human, Eckhart changes tack. He says we should stop talking about God but at the same time adds that we should make all our own attributes God's attributes. For to transform them in this way will mean realizing their inadequacy and so slipping beyond them into the nothingness of divinity.[65] In describing this process, Eckhart uses linguistic forms not unlike Seuse's *ein eigen sich*. He talks of "your yourness" (*dine dinisheit, din din*) and of God's "hisness" (*sine sinesheit, sin sin*). Returning to the theme a little later in the sermon, he adds: "God must become me and I must become God, so entirely one that this 'he' and this 'I' become one 'is.'"[66]

Such turns on phrase are similar to Seuse's insofar as they use possessive adjectives or pronouns as nouns. Yet they remain distinct nevertheless, for the process Eckhart is describing differs fundamentally from that described by *The Book of Truth*. In Eckhart's text, the individual casts off the attributes that fix him or her in familiar habits, in order to be united with God. In this process, monitoring attributes and possessions is only one step that one quickly goes beyond. The terminology used to describe the step is correspondingly improvised. Eckhart plays with any number of varieties of a language of selfhood (*dine dinisheit, din din, ein min, dis 'er', dis 'ich'*). But his aim is always to push beyond it to a mode of being beyond self-orientation. Seuse, in contrast, has set a limit to his desire to be united with God. He knows in advance that his surrender must never be total, and the language he uses to group together the attributes that separate him from God is correspondingly more definite. It is as if the energy that would otherwise have propelled him toward God is rechanneled into the scholastic fixing of the features, such as the enumeration of the five-level self, that keep him in exile.[67] More important than the actual words (*dis 'er' vnd dis 'ich'* versus *ein eigen sich*) is the attitude behind them. Eckhart coins phrases to break habits and push ever closer to God. Seuse coins phrases to fix distinctions and to establish the limits of behavior. It is this attitude of self-fixing, rather than the particular usage that it engenders, that Seuse shares with the later self-monitoring techniques of the modern Western self.

Seuse's text shows us the origins of the modern self, but not because it is the moment where suddenly a new identity appears fully fledged. Rather the text demonstrates the constellation of elements from which, over hundreds of years, the habits of modern selfhood arose. The key element is the longing to "become God": the pursuit of openness of which Eckhart's texts and the *Sister Catherine* treatise were so strong an expression but that was also the starting point for the young man in Seuse's text. It is hard to give a modern gloss to the longing—if that's the right term for it—to the extent that we live in a culture that doesn't attend in the same way to the sense of involvement, dynamism, and being-moved-through that is evident in the texts of Eckhart and his contemporaries. This is not a theological point; if anything, it's a phenomenological one. In Eckhart's texts, or in the *Sister Catherine* treatise, there is an acknowledgment of a dynamic thrownness: being-delivered-up-to-and-involved-with-something-that-moves-through-us. This state of deliverance is the background against which our relation to ourselves and our relations to others emerge. When it is lived in the early fourteenth century as the sense of being called by God, it is individualized and personalized. It encourages introspection and a certain kind of autonomy from received wisdom and institutional behavior.

Eckhart's texts and the *Sister Catherine* treatise criticize all structures onto which individuals, without taking responsibility for them, project their longings. The texts also resist the delegating of spirituality onto auratic people, rites, or regulations. This leads to the second point in the constellation from which something like modern habits of identity emerge: the institutional misreading of the calling to God. To criticize the attachment to people, rituals, institutions, or spaces to which a special power has been attributed was to challenge one of the main sources of emotional security in medieval society (and, indeed, of subsequent societies, including our own). Jacques le Goff has observed how the force of inertia "seems to have absorbed a large part of the mental energy of medieval men."[68] This inertia was due in part to the emotional investment that was encouraged in shared rituals, shared institutions, and shared authorities, as we saw in reactions of theologians to the changing intellectual situation of the thirteenth century.[69] To question these shared investments without offering an alternative external authority as a substitute was to incur the wrath of the collective, as we can see from the way the violence of the Roman legal treatment of the *crimen laesae maiestatis* was integrated into inquisitorial procedure. In the early part of the fourteenth century, the challenge of the apostolic movement provoked a particularly strong response. The burning of Marguerite Porete in 1310, the definition of the heresy of the free spirit 1311–1312, the promulgation of the Clementine decrees in 1315, the persecutions of beguines and beghards in Strasbourg and Cologne, and finally the condemnation of Eckhart himself all indicate a changed atmosphere. Individuals who broke with emotional conventions to follow their sense of being delivered-up-to-and-involved-with-something-that-moved-through-them faced violent reprisals in addition to the obloquy and social isolation of which the texts of Mechthild and Hadewijch occasionally complain.

A safer alternative to the radical program of Eckhart's sermons or the *Sister Catherine* treatise was the path taken by Margaretha Ebner and Heinrich von Nördlingen. Both nun and confessor delegated responsibility for their spiritual longings and submitted them to the sort of external structuring that the ecclesiastical authorities found less threatening. Heinrich let Margaretha act as his spiritual deputy, while Margaretha watched her spiritual life play itself out in the form dictated by liturgy and by the architecture of the convent itself.[70] For Seuse, neither of these paths was acceptable. Eckhart's was too dangerous, and Margaretha's and Heinrich's demanded that one relinquish the elements both of development and of individualization in one's spiritual life. He instead adopted a compromise in which a level of self-determination was preserved by internalizing the mechanisms of control. Emotion in this model is invested in the process of self-monitoring as much as in the rules and rites that one is policing oneself to obey. Self-policing replaces self-abandonment as the individual's ultimate aim. This emotional investment differentiates modern or protomodern forms of selfhood from the individualized forms of identity described in Eckhart's texts and in the *Sister Catherine* treatise as well as from the premodern forms that identified more strongly with external structures.

In individual cases when studying subsequent developments, one will probably find a mixture of the three different tendencies: self-control, self-abandon, and the identification with external forms. Indeed, to give one example, an investigation of the physician–patient relationship in the early phases of psychoanalysis reveals all three.[71] The focus on Eckhart's condemnation and Seuse's reaction does not produce a temporal framework for the history of the self (pre-1330 medieval forms of identity, post-1330 protomodern). Instead, it allows a shift in the guiding assumptions with which the history of forms of identity is approached. Viewed from the perspective of this episode, it becomes possible to see all three tendencies (self-control, self-abandon, and the identification with external forms) as reactions to the same problem. All three are ways of managing the relationship with what, for want of a better word, and in the light of the discourses with which it has most frequently been associated in monotheistic cultural traditions, we had better call "God." Forms similar to modern habits of identity arise as a way of managing and controlling the relationship with God in a manner that preserved a sense of autonomy and dignity for the individual but without enduring the violent reprisals that were the fate of Marguerite Porete and other anonymous beguines and beghards of the early fourteenth century. The new identification with the habits of self-control fundamentally shifts the orientation of the individual's day-to-day practice, away from God, away from external embodiments of authority, and toward his or her own strategies of self-regulation. In a way that Seuse did not intend, these habits come to be valued in and for themselves; they become what we call our self. The new habits also, as we shall now see, had long-lasting consequences for the relations between the two genders.

Gendering the Self: Elsbeth Stagel and Heinrich Seuse

The encounters in Seuse's *Book of Truth* occurred inside the young man "in the silence of his soul [*in der stilli sins gemůtes*]."[72] However, the patterns of behavior that he learned did not only have consequences for his soul. They also had an effect on his relations with other people, and particularly women. This is true of any form of identity. The sense that individuals have of who they are arises through the loose set of practices by which they manage their relatedness to the world: their emotions, their relationship with their body or the space around them, and their interaction with other people.[73] Seuse in the autobiographical text that he wrote during the 1360s left a record of the form that these further practices took in his case. The text tells the story of his, the "servant of truth's," spiritual progress, starting with his first feeling of a special calling at the age of eighteen. It then charts his development through a phase of severe self-castigation to a more measured form of spiritual life, which nevertheless has its own adventures, including an encounter with a murderer in a forest on the banks of the Rhine. The second half of the text introduces another character, the figure of Elsbeth Stagel, who first prompted the "servant" to record his religious development. Her education by Seuse is charted, as a parallel to his. The text closes with a speculative theological discussion between the two, with Stagel appearing to Seuse after her death to "show him how nobly she had merged with the pure godhead."[74]

The text is full of anecdotes and details, but recent research has emphasized that these should not be read as a direct record of prevalent practices. Like many texts of the period, the purpose of the vita is to establish a model rather than accurately to record a set of events, and it makes its points as much by invoking literary topoi as by telling it how it was.[75] With little information to corroborate what Seuse recounts, it is hard to know whether, for instance, the extreme acts of self-torture that he details, are a heuristic exaggeration or an accurate depiction of life for an inspired young Dominican friar in the early fourteenth century. However, if the content of the text is not reliable, it nevertheless can be shown to demonstrate attitudes and behavior through its form, so it is still a very useful source of evidence for a history of emerging patterns of identity. As we will see, the strategies of the text can themselves be read as empirical evidence as much as the anecdotes can. On both levels, the concern of the text is similar: to establish forms of psychological control.

Control is evident in the very manner of the text's composition. As the text recounts, the book started out as a form of intellectual theft (*geischliche dúpstal*) challenging Seuse's pastoral authority. Elsbeth Stagel is supposed to have asked him questions about his spiritual life and then secretly written down his answers.[76] When he discovered the theft, Seuse burnt half the papers. But as he was about to burn the second half, God stopped him, with the result that Stagel's biography was preserved and transformed into an autobiography. There has been a good deal of debate about the authenticity of this story and about the degree to which the existing text should be attributed to Elsbeth Stagel, with current scholarship tending to conclude that the narrative is merely a framing fiction.[77] However, whether the story is taken as a historical record (content) or as a pedagogical device (form), the end result is similar: that of Seuse establishing his power over the text and over the figure of Elsbeth Stagel. Indeed, Seuse explicitly admits that, after Stagel's death, when he could no longer work collaboratively with her on the text, he used her for his own purposes, putting words into her mouth to reinforce the doctrinal message of the text: "Some good instruction using her figure was also added by him [Seuse] after her death."[78]

The text's controlling urge exemplifies the wider project of which Seuse's autobiography was only a part. Toward the end of his life, Seuse presided over a new edition of his texts to prevent the circulation in his name of corrupt or incomplete accounts of his teaching.[79] The autobiography functioned as an extended preface to this edition, showing by example the order to which an individual seeking spiritual development should submit his life.[80] To ensure the orthodoxy of this framing narrative, Seuse submitted first the speculative (and therefore potentially confusing) parts and then the whole text to the Dominican authorities, in the form of the provincial of Teutonia, Bartholomew of Bolsenheim, to be vetted. Bartholomew had approved only the speculative parts when he died. But he returned to Seuse in a vision to give his final verdict and confer his blessing on the project as a whole.[81]

This impressive authorization in itself is not enough to guarantee that later readers will correctly understand the text. To deal with the problem, Elsbeth Stagel is written into the second half of the text as a model reader whose spiritual desires are taken up and corrected by the book. The first impulse that the book controls is the nun's interest in Meister Eckhart. Wishing to read speculative texts of the sort that Eckhart wrote, Stagel comes to Seuse but is told that to read such texts is damaging as long as she has not acquired the necessary interpretative tools. Until that point, she should limit herself to questions that are appropriate to her stage of development.[82] This prohibition, however, is not merely hermeneutic. The point is that she should be so inculcated with Seuse's rules for the management of inner life that a misreading of Eckhart's or Seuse's more speculative moments becomes a behavioral impossibility. Indeed, when, toward the end of the book she is finally allowed to venture onto this territory, it is only because she has now been adequately shaped by Seuse's education. In the imagery of the text itself, Stagel, like "wax softened by the heat of a flame," has been "imprinted" with Seuse's seal, so there is no risk of her misinterpreting.[83]

The wax-and-seal image is a traditional figure, one source for which is the Songs of Songs (8:6: Set me as a seal upon your heart). When Eckhart uses the image, it is to describe the soul's longing to be united with and contained by God. "Concerning this, the soul says in the Book of Love, 'Press me into thee like wax into a seal.'"[84] When Seuse appropriates the image, his teaching is the seal, Stagel's behavior the wax. Doctrine takes the place of God. If Seuse's use of the image contrasts with Eckhart's, the context in which it is used also shows a striking difference from the *Sister Catherine* treatise. The beguine in the treatise comes to her confessor seeking the shortest way to God and is helped to a union with God that eventually inspires the male cleric to follow in her footsteps.[85] In the Seuse text, in contrast, the nun inspired by an Eckhartian text is told to put her longing to one side until she can be shaped by the doctrine of her confessor. This is as close as Seuse gets to "becoming God." His theoretical framework usurps the place of God and remakes the woman aspirant in his image.

Even after her spiritual activities have been reformed, Stagel's role in the speculative conversation is limited to affirming the conceptual divisions expounded by Seuse. In a manner similar to that of *The Book of Truth*, Seuse's text establishes a conceptual framework that must be in place before spiritual experiences may be trusted. It sets out Seuse's preference for conformity over individual reasoning; it warns, in direct contrast to the *Sister Catherine* treatise, that even the mystic cannot cast off human coarseness to become one with God.[86] It also insists that humans will always remain separated from divinity by their *accidentia*, or empirical attributes.[87] Stagel's voice is used to confirm this policing of mystical surrender: "The daughter said, 'Praise to the God of right reason!' "[88]

The changing attitude to spiritual surrender transforms the status of the woman, both in the relationship between confessor and nun and in the text. In the relationship presented in the *Sister Catherine* treatise, or in that between Margaretha Ebner and Heinrich von Nördlingen, it is acknowledged that the woman has access to a form of truth not available to the male cleric. This experience is admired and accorded validity. Stagel's experiences are not accorded validity independently of Seuse's framework. When, excited by Eckhart's texts, she comes to Seuse, she is told that she is untutored and should learn instead to follow the model offered by Seuse, who in contrast to the other two confessors is not willing to be inspired by anyone but himself.

> You seem to be still a young, unpracticed sister. For that reason, it is more useful for you and people like you to know about the beginning of the process, how one should start, and about the lifestyle one should observe. You should also know about the good, saintly models, such as this one, or those of the friends of God who also had a godly beginning. You should know how they first learned to live and suffer with Christ and what they underwent and what forms of inner and outer behavior they adopted. You should also know whether God educated them with sweetness or hardness, and when or how the bad images fell away from them.[89]

Even if one assumes that she was supposed to be younger and less experienced than Margaretha Ebner when this advice was given, the underlying attitude is both more patronizing and more controlling than Heinrich von Nördlingen ever allowed himself to be. Seuse does not look at Stagel's individual case to see what she needs to help her develop. He diverts her attention to the models that she and others like her should learn to imitate. Her role in the relationship is then limited to the affirmation of structures she is offered. Her own sense of being inspired plays no further role.

Stagel did not exist only in Seuse's text. By comparing what we can ascertain of Stagel's life beyond the text with her treatment within it, it is possible to delimit even more precisely how Seuse's attitude and textual practice transformed gender relations. Stagel had a life independent of her confessor's biography in which she herself recorded the stories of her fellow nuns in the convent of Töss near Zurich.[90] Convent books of this sort from the fourteenth century have been celebrated as a form literature written by women for women that gave authentic expression to women's experiences.[91] Following this line of argument, it might seem that Stagel's text could be contrasted with Seuse's to show what it was that he was controlling. This is true to an extent, but the experiences indirectly recorded in the text themselves bear the mark of the patriarchal society in which they occurred.

The evidence of the convent book suggests that Elsbeth Stagel lived in a milieu very similar to the one that produced Margaretha Ebner as well as to the one to which Eckhart's sermons were partially a response. The text records a similar range of visions and reactions, such as that of a nun whom the Virgin Mary offers her breast to suckle at, and that of another who cries uncontrollably for a long period of time after God has given her knowledge of her sinfulness.[92] Like Margaretha Ebner's *Revelations*, the convent book of Töss records a spirituality that is connected to particular spaces, rituals, and objects and lived through strong emotions and bodily intensities. The mystically inclined convents of the late medieval period offered a space in which women could live out their spiritual desires while enjoying a degree of autonomy and social prestige even as they reproduced the misogynist and antisomatic prejudices of society at large.[93] Like Ebner's text, Stagel's book reflects the same ambivalent combination of freedom and social constraint. What is important in relation to Seuse's text is not so much its own articulation of experience but rather the way in which Seuse's reaction differs from the empowering responses of a Hadewijch or an Eckhart to a similar context. Seuse was responding to circumstances similar to those Eckhart was responding to.[94] Eckhart worked rhetorically to undermine his congregation's attachment to particular rituals and experiences and so to free their intuition and creativity. In contrast, Seuse substitutes his model for the women's experience. In addition to the framework of theological distinctions that he imposed on the "wild one" in *The Book of Truth*, he establishes a behavioral pattern modeled on an account of his own development.

To this end, Seuse had to modify the form of autobiography. In his history of the genre, Georg Misch allocated Seuse's text a privileged place among the vitae of the Middle Ages. For the first time since Augustine's *Confessions*, a text presented and interpreted the metaphysical significance of the author's life in a form that followed the sequence of the experiences themselves. In Misch's view, it imposed neither the established form of Christian stories of conversion nor classical models of the natural steps of intellectual development, nor did it remain merely episodic in structure.[95] More-recent critics have discerned models behind Seuse's text. Its account of mystical rapture is similar to St. Paul's, and the text as a whole can be seen to follow a scheme of three stages of spiritual development.[96] Nevertheless, Misch's underlying point is still valid. The main concern of the text is neither literary or pedagogical topoi nor theological distinctions but a particular sort of image, that of a life that shows people how to model their behavior. As Seuse explains in his prologue, the book "uses an illustrative method to recount a spiritual life and shows in an indirect manner the order that a person rightly embarking on the spiritual path should follow for both his outer and inner person according to God's most beloved will."[97] Seuse makes a point that his illustrative method recounts events that "in truth happened this way [*dú in der wahrheit also geschahen*]."[98] A modern reader may see the literary influences more than the realism, making the text seem less than lifelike, but Seuse tells us that he has nevertheless attempted a likeness.

The contrast with Eckhart's rhetorical deployment of the idea of portraiture is instructive. We saw Eckhart invoke the idea of the perfect portrait only the better to subvert it, as the perfect likeness united God with the individual whom he made in his image.[99] Seuse's literary self-portrait does not have an equivalent moment of self-undermining. It is lifelike, though not in order to transcend the very idea of portraiture but rather to encourage a qualitatively new technique of selfhood. The individual life is permitted its own logic and contours, as the sculpted face might be allowed its wrinkles. But it is given individualized form only the better to block undisciplined inner development. Seuse is using the form of autobiography in a way similar to that in which he used the nominalized form of "oneself," *ein eigen sich*, as part of the effort to police inner life: in *The Book of Truth*, his own inner life; in the case of the autobiography, the inner life of others. In this respect, it is not important that the details of the autobiography rework literary topoi. As long as they simultaneously convey the sense that they "in truth happened this way," they will perform the task that Seuse wants them to perform. It is the form of the text (the effect of truthfulness) rather than the content that allows it to play its part in the developing practices of selfhood.

Jeffrey Hamburger has noted an irony in what he terms Seuse's "medieval self-fashioning." Like many medieval writers before him, Seuse describes a model of behavior to which he encourages his readers to conform. Despite its concern for conformity, however, Hamburger notes that the vita is "profoundly original."[100] He is particularly referring to the way Seuse's text deployed drawn images as part of its program to influence and shape its readers. But Seuse's texts are equally original in the way they use language, prefiguring the modern vocabulary of selfhood; in their deployment of the literary self-portrait; and, as Heinrich Stirnimann argued, in the way they deploy the dialogue form, a device little used in German vernacular texts in the Middle Ages (though of course we have seen it used effectively in the *Sister Catherine* treatise).[101] This impulse to innovate is more than an irony. It is the product of the particular way in which Seuse positioned himself in relation to the apostolic life. Seuse had to be so inventive in his use of rhetorical and aesthetic devices because he was developing a new sort of control, appropriate to a milieu in which a highly personalized cultivation of inner life was the norm. Seuse devised strategies that maintained the element of personalization, but now he employed it in the pursuit of self-control. If there is something new about modern forms of selfhood (it is always hard to tell whether the impression of novelty does not arise only because the same questions have not been asked of earlier texts), it is the personal grid that they place between self-awareness and an individual's longing. It is their encouragement of the identification with, and indeed of the love for, habits of self-monitoring and self-control. Seuse's innovative techniques all serve the purpose of encouraging personalized self-vetting in others, establishing the inner framework within which individuals will judge which experiences are permissible. This is of course a form of conformity. But it is one in which the individual, or at least the masculine individual, believes himself to be the authority to whom he submits.

An important further consequence of the new practices of identity exemplified in Seuse's texts is that it becomes impossible to talk about gender roles. The experience that had been the ambivalent privilege of the women visionaries in the other texts is allowed no place in Seuse's model. The sense of inspiration that Stagel, having read Meister Eckhart's texts, brings to her confessor is dismissed as immature, and she is told instead to imitate the model supplied by Seuse. In the other relationships between confessor and nun, it was acknowledged that the women contributed something substantial. Heinrich von Nördlingen admired the enthusiasm and energy released by Margaretha's experience of love because through this he could feel closer to God. Similarly, the confessor in the *Sister Catherine* treatise admired the ardor of the beguine and the development and changes that it wrought on her. Meister Eckhart did not delegate to others the sense of being close to God, but neither did he deny it to his congregation. His sermons depend on a common intention and a common experience. In all three of these cases, experience is gendered, but both sides of the gender division have substance. In the best circumstances, the roles are even allowed to change and develop. In Seuse's texts this is no longer the case. Seuse does not delegate but rather controls spirituality, intuition, and creativity, forcing others to experience on his terms. This means, in effect, investing in the policing structures more than pursuing one's own impulses. As a result, the practices of selfhood that Seuse discovers as he polices spiritual life have the effect of preventing rather than fostering exchange. The subject that he presents to us is literally autistic, willing only to allow his interlocutor to express him- or herself to the extent that he or she conform to the model he expects. Stagel's contributions are limited to mere affirmation: "The daughter said, 'Praise to the God of right reason!'"[102] This noncommunication eliminates gender, despite appearances to the contrary, since it cannot tolerate deviation from its structures of control. Indeed, the elimination of gender difference is visible in the very way Seuse deploys misogynist arguments. Seuse advises Stagel that it would be inappropriate for a woman to imitate the severe self-castigations to which Seuse as a younger man had submitted himself for sixteen years.[103] As well as being barred from mystical surrender until Seuse can be certain she will observe the categorizations of orthodox theology, Stagel is denied even the limited momentum of anorexic self-determination. She is allowed neither self-abandon nor self-fashioning but only self-regimentation—the observation of the rules for the governing of inner and external life propagated by Seuse's autobiography. To enforce this prohibition, Seuse uses a gendered argument about what is or is not appropriate for women. But the aim of the proscription is to neutralize deviant experience and submit everyone to a uniform grid. With Seuse's text, we move into the sphere of miscommunication between the genders, described by Irigaray in *Speculum*.[104] The woman does not have any experience of her own but rather conforms to the framework permitted by the masculine authority. If she does not submit to this regime, she will be either branded as chaotic and evil or physically punished, as we see from two further anecdotes in Seuse's vita. Stagel's education in the second half of the text includes the story of a less happy collaboration between Seuse and a fallen woman in his pastoral care whom he attempted to help. When she did not mend her ways, Seuse abandoned her, prompting her to claim that he fathered her illegitimate child. The text concludes that "she bore a wolf's heart beneath a mild exterior and hid it so well that the brother was not able to discover it for a long time."[105] When the woman fails to meet Seuse's expectations, he labels her with a stereotypical image of evil (the wolf's heart). Similarly, in another episode, a nun will not be persuaded by Seuse to abandon worldly forms of love and to stop being flirtatious with men. He reacts by castigating himself and claims through this act of penance to have successfully called upon God to stop her, since she returns to the convent with a deformed back that puts an end to her flirtation.[106]

In Irigaray's *Speculum*, the false choice between conformity and exclusion is hard to escape. From reading Seuse's texts in the larger context of the apostolic life, it is easier to have a sense of alternatives. The structure of miscommunication is not so fixed, since, to a historically informed reader, the voice of the woman visionary, or, more important, of the experience that she shares with a sympathetic confessor is still audible. The voice has not yet become that of an incomprehensible alterity. The variety of options still accessible in the fourteenth century also helps us see alternatives to the solution that Irigaray's later theory offers for the impasse of *Speculum*—alternatives, that is to the project of cultivating a female divinity as the horizon for the development of an autonomous female identity.[107] Viewed in the context of the fourteenth century, it's clear that Seuse's innovations in the way he and his spiritual charges related to themselves and others must be understood as a way of managing the longing to "become God"—or, in other words, his innovations are a particular way of "doing connectedness." If we want to challenge them, then, it is to the underlying project that we must return, laying bare the communion that modern habits of self relate to by keeping it at a permanent distance. The problem remains, however, of the vocabulary that we should be using for this process of discovery if we are to avoid the infelicity of a phrase like "doing connectedness," which remains abstract despite its apparently colloquial character. The phrase has no place in the day-to-day habits by which I manage my sense of involvement and dynamic connection. It's not part of my normal emotional vocabulary, or the way I respond to dreams; I wouldn't use it to pray or meditate or silently reflect or perform whatever other practice I might have for taking stock, and I wouldn't use it to share with my friends or family an experience of particular intensity. So what words should I be using instead? As we saw in the first chapter in the work of Lacan, Irigaray, and Hollywood, an approach inspired by psychoanalysis has been used to forge a connection between modern or postmodern experience and the power of the mystical tradition, but with the result that the habits of an isolated identity were imposed on the mystical texts that I have argued are the record of very different attitudes and behaviors. Now that we have seen more of these alternative attitudes, rather than view the mystical tradition from the perspective of psychoanalysis, we can do the converse, returning to the language of psychoanalysis to find out what it has to offer for the project of uncovering and acknowledging the commitments of our shared predicament when it is viewed from the perspective of the mystical tradition.

PART III

Alternative Vocabularies

8

Taking Leave of Sigmund Freud

When on December 31, 1900, Freud's patient Ida Bauer ("Dora") broke off her analysis, she left behind not only her physician. She left behind a number of other things that her treatment with Freud—with or without his help—had enabled her to overcome.[1] She abandoned the image of the cherished father, of whose death she dreamt shortly before ending the therapy. She also abandoned her previous image of the family friends, Herr and Frau Zellenka (in Freud's account, Herr and Frau K.), and forced from them confessions that Herr Zellenka had made indecent advances toward her and that Frau Zellenka had betrayed her for the sake of an adulterous affair with her father. In this process of asserting her independence, walking out on Freud was a crowning gesture that broke the rules of gendered, hierarchical behavior, and could be said to have reestablished, in relation to Freud, the dignity that Bauer had lost before her father and before the Zellenkas. Freud himself did not construe Bauer's behavior quite so positively, but he did observe that the dream in which her father died announced that she was ready to leave behind the old constraints and go out into the world.[2]

At many removes, Ida Bauer's walking out on Freud repeats the gesture of the beguine who, in the *Sister Catherine* treatise, walked out on her confessor. "When I leave all things behind I must also leave you [*sol ich alle ding laussen, so muos ich uch och laussen*]."[3] Bauer, too, left behind the attachments of an older identity, and, as we shall see in more detail later, did things that appear to Freud as masculine as the determination and strength of the beguine appeared to her confessor. At the same time, Ida Bauer was by no stretch of the imagination a mystic. She was an educated seventeen-year-old from a prosperous family of assimilated Jews who, during her therapy, referred to religion only indirectly when she briefly mentioned a painting of the Madonna.[4] The relationship between woman patient and analyst resembles that between woman mystic and confessor in structure rather than in the language with which that structure is described. In both we see women breaking out of existing patterns of behavior and finding—in varying degrees—support from a man in a position of institutional power who identifies with her endeavors. The relationship between beguine and confessor offered both participants a chance to develop the feeling of connection that they called "becoming God." The relationship between psychoanalyst and female hysteric offered the woman, if not the man, an official space in which she could transform her relation to the emotions and impulses that Freud called the unconscious.

Paradoxical though it may seem, the vocabulary developed by psychoanalysis will not help us understand this parallel, notwithstanding that, in the Schreber case history, Freud approvingly quotes the Persian mystic poet Rumi or that, toward the end of his life, he wrote a note specifically reflecting on mysticism, calling it "the dark self-perception of the realm beyond the ego, of the id [*Mystik die dunkle Selbstwahrnehmung des Reiches ausserhalb des Ichs, des Es*]."[5] A note such as this may seem to offer the basis for an exploration of the similarities between religious experiences and psychoanalysis. But, as I will argue, the particular emphasis that Freud develops with his terminology of conscious, unconscious, ego, and id obscures the behavior, emotions, and relationships that it would be necessary to reconstruct in order to understand the similarities, or to place psychoanalysis in the longer history of techniques of self-development and self-control. To situate psychoanalysis in this manner, it is more useful to step outside it, return to its historical context, and reconstruct how it emerged from behavioral patterns in late-nineteenth-century Vienna. Describing, as far as is possible, what Freudian therapy involved on this practical and emotional level will clarify its relationship with practices of identity, such as those of the beguine and confessor, that similarly transform the individual's understanding of and relation to his or her longings.

The origins of psychoanalysis are a well-researched area. Henri Ellenberger's *The Discovery of the Unconscious* (1970), in particular, offers a wide-ranging account of the development of what he calls "dynamic psychiatry" from the 1770s to the early twentieth century.[6] Ellenberger traces the continuous efforts to understand and control emotional states that, until that point, had generally been viewed as the territory of the Church. In his argument, a symbolic transition occurs in 1775 when Prince-Elector Max Joseph of Bavaria calls on Franz Anton Mesmer (1734–1815) to scientifically evaluate the exorcisms of Johann Joseph Gassner (1727–79).[7] From that point, an unbroken line can be followed that leads from the experiments of the animal magnetists and Romantics to Freud and Jung. Ellenberger's account is open-minded and sympathetic to the efforts he describes while remaining unsentimental about inflated claims on the part of the practitioners, be they hypnotists or psychoanalysts. This allows him to show the historical development of which psychoanalysis was the culmination, and to draw parallels between ways of dealing with emotional and unconscious life that do not share the same vocabulary but that, at a practical level, are very similar.

One limitation of Ellenberger's approach is his presentation of the mechanisms of change. He reconstructs lines of intellectual influence, for instance, discussing Janet's library of books by early nineteenth-century hypnotists, or Freud and Breuer's acquaintance with the ideas of the Viennese physician Moriz Benedikt. He also sketches a wider social and political context. But he is not concerned much with the development of behavior or with the "techniques of the self" and the habits that shape gender relations in daily life. To supplement Ellenberger's account in this respect, I want to give a sketch of behavior and attitudes in Vienna in the latter part of the nineteenth century. My main sources will be the memoirs of Rosa Mayreder, née Obermayer (1858–1938), and Ulrike Döcker's survey of etiquette manuals in nineteenth-century Germany and Austria.[8] Mayreder, a contemporary of Freud, grew up in central Vienna during the period in which the *Ring* was constructed and later became "one of the sanest interpreters of her generation," writing numerous essays on issues of feminism and sexuality.[9] Her memoirs give an insight into the way behavior patterns were gendered, both confirming and enriching Döcker's account of the expectations formalized in the etiquette manuals. The reason for preferring these texts to existing accounts of fin-de-siècle Vienna is precisely that they allow an imaginative reconstruction of the behavioral rather than the textual or intellectual context of early psychoanalysis. As much as being an elaboration of existing science, as Sulloway suggests, or a reaction to the political stagnation in the Imperial Vienna, as Schorske and McGrath have argued, psychoanalysis was a form of social behavior through which individuals learned to regulate their relationship to themselves and to others.[10] Once it has been recast in this light, its position in the longer development of modern practices of selfhood becomes easier to determine. What also emerges, as we will see, is that psychoanalysis often had surprisingly little to contribute to the transformation of the gendered and self-censoring behavior of modern Western forms of selfhood because its practitioners did not engage with the emotional patterns with which they were actually presented. In its ideal form, psychoanalysis would contribute to the development of a culture of respect, listening, empirical observation, and personal warmth and would build on the "direct and always deeply personal appeals to our common humanity" that Bruno Bettelheim sees as the soul of Freud's writing and of therapeutic practice.[11] If Freud's texts do not quite fit the image that Bettelheim paints, it is not only because, as he argued, they have been insensitively translated into an abstract idiom when they were transferred to the English-speaking world but because Freud himself did not describe the structures he encountered in himself, his patients, and the social environment, but preferred instead to create the fiction of the unconscious as an alien realm the logic of which he would be the first to catalogue. As we shall see, this choice was inseparable from the emotional attitudes that Freud shared with many of his contemporaries and that he brought with him into the consulting room.

Controlling the Emotions in Nineteenth-Century Vienna

When carriages entered Vienna during the 1860s, they had to stop at the Mariahilfer customs line and pay eight Kreuzer to be allowed to take horses into the city. It was also necessary to submit to a customs inspection. The customs official had an iron rod with which he poked into the areas of the coach in which illegal comestibles might be hidden. This could include the crinolines of women travelers, searched through lest these also concealed contraband food.[12] The intrusions of power into the lives of women in nineteenth-century Vienna were not always so crude. However, women's lives were regulated and intruded on in ways that those of their male contemporaries were not, if for no other reason than that the men could more easily vent their frustrated anger and imagination on women. In the period of rapid transformation toward the end of the century, this gender imbalance took on a new inflection.

The Habsburg Empire in the late nineteenth century was in a state of political stagnation, a defensive "fortwursteln" by the emperor Franz Josef and his administration, to which there was no effective parliamentary opposition.[13] At the same time it was a period of momentous social change. The population of Vienna more than doubled in the forty years between 1869 and 1910, and rapid economic modernization post 1870 produced a social climate in which both collective and personal cultural assumptions were called into question.[14] Mayreder reports how, in the 1860s, it was still customary for an individual with sufficient income to cover the road outside his or her apartment with straw when ill. A policeman stood by the straw, ensuring that coaches rode over at walking pace to minimize the disturbance to the invalid.[15] The example shows that rich individuals could shape the social exterior as they wished, supported by state institutions. Etiquette manuals of the period, as we will see, suggest that, toward the end of the century, individuals of this type were replaced by ones with less power to directly influence their environment, and consequently with less of a sense of their own sovereignty. Of course, the etiquette manuals themselves are not necessarily accurate records of how people behaved. But they nevertheless document attitudes, if only indirectly, and as such can be read as an index of behavioral uncertainties caused by the rapid pace of social change.

From the 1780s to the 1840s, etiquette books had been published, most famously Adolph Freiherr von Knigge's *Über den Umgang mit Menschen* in 1788, which gave guidelines but allow individuals to actively negotiate how they should be implemented. If two gentlemen should have the misfortune to arrive at a door simultaneously, it was assumed that they would have the ability to solve this social dilemma themselves, without further guidance. Later in the nineteenth century, this confidence disappeared. The two men were left, as it were, stepping hopelessly back and forward while the writers of etiquette manuals attempted to define an appropriate solution.[16] The sovereignty that was attributed to individuals earlier in the century, allowing them individually to balance the needs of their inner life with the demands and expectations of their peers, was replaced in the latter part of the nineteenth century by a new combination of discipline and obedience.[17] From the 1870s on, a wave of books appeared in which the standards of interaction became increasingly rigid. Each situation or social space (the theater, the sickbed, the family gathering) was given a set of postures, phrases, and clothing that the individual was supposed to conform to. It was no longer sufficient to rely on naturalness and warmheartedness (*Natürlichkeit und Herzlichkeit*) in one's social interactions, instead one needed to master the rules.[18] At the same time, the number of rules was proliferating, producing less and less consensus as to what was appropriate in the standardized situations as different social groups looked for new securities, and new ways of defining themselves.[19]

For the upper middle classes, this meant adding further accomplishments to those of title and wealth, to which they might previously have aspired: "knowledge of art, sartorial confidence, rhetorical skills, the fact of having travelled and musicality."[20] A new set of metropolitan, middle-class values was added to the older, courtly and mercantile ones. At the same time, the individuals aspiring to them changed. Though the etiquette books gave them less space for individual negotiation, they simultaneously demanded from them a more virile bearing. Knigge had suggested that, when in the company of a woman, it befitted a man to show "a touch of feminine gentleness." This could extend even to the point of sharing confidences and allowing himself to show feelings.[21] In contrast, Emil Wallberg, whose *Wie der Wiener ein Gentleman wird* (How the Viennese Man becomes a gentleman) was first published in 1860 and went through numerous editions, explicitly challenged this advice. The gentleman, in his view, should show strength not feminine softness, he should not share feelings or confidences but overcome them. "Much that goes on around him in the world causes a gentleman real pain. Yet he strongly resists any inclination to melancholy. That which hurts him but which he cannot change he locks deep in his heart. To let such wounds occasionally be visible in his dealings with women so as to win their pity and whatever else might be associated with that would be comparable to the approach of a beggar who thrusts an open sore before passers-by so as to force a donation from them, and is beneath the dignity of a gentleman."[22] The gentleman was meant never to show his suffering to the outside world. On the contrary, he must be all the more stoical in his self-control, as the author of another guide, called *Der gute Ton* (The right note), emphasized in 1865 when he defined civility. "Good manners . . . are a fitting and permissible cloak for concealing our unpleasant feelings from others, and the more we have ourselves under control and have made the habits of tactful behavior our own, the more we will be able to protect ourselves from unpleasant phenomena without hurting the feelings of others."[23]

The etiquette manuals suggest a change in what counted as manly behavior in nineteenth-century Vienna. The expanding city produced middle-class men who hoped to keep control by internalizing the rules that they believed to be appropriate to their situation and hiding the emotional cost. No doubt in individual cases there was room for improvization, breaking the rules, or making it up as one went along. But for the present argument the two important aspects of the way men responded to the rapidly changing environment were, on the one hand, the desire to establish and internalize rules, albeit ones that they were not able to generalize, and, on the other, the code of virile silence. Writers in other fields around 1900 noted comparable changes to those traced by the Viennese etiquette manuals. Thomas Mann, in *Buddenbrooks* (1900), portrays a similar generational shift in the patrician classes of Hanseatic northern Germany through the character of Thomas Buddenbrook, the self-controlling merchant who can create the image of the decisive entrepreneur only by the power of intellectual analysis (*Reflexion*). As Thomas explicitly thinks to himself, as he mulls over a difficult business decision, his father and grandfather embodied practical virtues in a less self-conscious, self-controlling way than he.[24] Similarly, Max Weber, in his *Protestant Ethic and the Spirit of Capitalism*, first published in 1905, notes how the spiritual longings that informed business habits and gave them their dynamism in the late seventeenth and eighteenth centuries had by the nineteenth century disappeared to leave only the routine of managing worldly affairs as an "iron cage."[25] In their different idioms, Mann and Weber register a loss of sovereignty and a loss of the ability to inhabit a lifestyle, as opposed to following externally imposed rules, a loss that echoes the change found in Viennese etiquette manuals.

A form of emotional inertia accompanied the change documented in the etiquette manuals. The old objects of admiration and identification (the aristocrat, the systematic philosopher) lost their legitimacy. But the etiquette manuals show men looking for new standards of power to identify with rather than ways of questioning and transforming control. This is especially clear in the treatment of women. Women were objects in relation to which control could be redoubled, as well as figures onto which emotions otherwise not acknowledged could be projected. Gynecology appears retrospectively symptomatic of this combination of control and projection because of the way it mobilized the authority of new scientific observations in the service of old prejudices. Claudia Honneger has studied the change in attitude that occurred around 1850 as modern forms of empirical sciences became more firmly established. The ideal of anthropology as an integrated science of humankind was replaced by different disciplines such as biology, sociology, and psychology that specialized, and forwent grander speculative ambitions. This entailed a change in the treatment of gender. Where the anthropological theories of the first half of the century had attempted to grapple directly with different sexes, the new disciplines silently took the male human to be the subject of their investigations. They relegated "the human being as woman [*der Mensch als Weib*]" to being considered by gynecology alone. However, as well as being the site for the scientific consideration of gender, gynecology retained the speculative ambitions of the earlier theorists. As late as 1913, a gynecologist at the university of Dresden could still take it to be his role to lecture on "the position of women in modern life."[26] To perform this dual role, gynecology developed into a form of psychophysiology.[27] New, empirically based observations about anatomical differences between men and women, such as the understanding of ovulation, were used as an opportunity for male gynecologists to elaborate theories about the essential differences between the sexes, differences that were no more empirical than the theories of medieval theologians. Thus, for the influential founder of cellular pathology, Rudolf Virchow, woman was not ultimately a social being but could be viewed as the mere extension of her own reproductive apparatus. "Everything that we admire and honor as truly feminine about womankind is merely an extension of the ovary."[28]

Gynecology used new anatomical observations as the spurious grounding for old theories about the deficiencies of women. Attributes familiar from existing definitions of womanhood, such as patience, modesty, feeling, were in the latter part of the nineteenth century viewed as feminine "functions" and explained by using a vocabulary supposedly grounded in science.[29] The appeal to science could not in itself ensure that the theory produced a consistent view of woman. As well as being modest, and patient, woman was supposed to be weak-willed, illogical, a willing proponent of her own inferiority, tending to hysterical exaggeration, decorative, charitable, emotionally supportive, but also mysterious and sphinx-like.[30] The contradictions prompted Rosa Mayreder to open her *Critique of Femininity* (*Zur Kritik der Weiblichkeit*, 1905) with an ironic collection of the conflicting claims made about woman by male philosophers.[31] But they also meant that women were subjected, in the name of the new scientific authority, to the pressure of irreconcilable behavioral injunctions.

On an everyday level, the conflicting claims were experienced as various forms of control. Modesty was a kind of posture and bodily poise as much as it was a state of mind. "No one can resist the magical sight of a young girl, inwardly well brought up, who has endowed her outer manner with the attributes [of modesty], with an innocent laugh bubbling from her charming mouth, while the posture of her spine remains at once straight and modest, and only her little head with its lively eyes is looking upward a little."[32] But the discipline to which a middle-class woman submitted in day-to-day life was not only one of posture. Nor indeed was the discipline imposed only on the female sex. Both sexes submitted to a strict and wide-ranging regimen from childhood on. The nursemaid, Hanni, took the Obermayer family children to walk in the Prater every day that the weather was fine enough. The outing consisted in promenading along the Praterallee with the wind behind them. The children were not allowed to stray from the avenue itself, lest they get their feet wet, get lost, or fall into the Danube. On the other hand, the walk brought with it the potential thrill of encountering Archduchess Sophie, the mother of the Kaiser, who promenaded in the Prater with a similar regularity, and who one day even graced the Mayreder party with a direct question.[33] The outing was a form of social display, and hence subject to the rules of display, as much as it was an opportunity for exercise. Indeed, for Daniel Spitzer, whose satirical vignettes of Viennese life were contemporary with Mayreder's childhood, exercise could itself only be an opportunity for social display: "Where should a sportsman go for his walk if not to the Prater?"[34]

The behavior of the Mayreder children was required to adapt to the demands of this social arena: The outdoors were no less a social space than the indoors. During the summer months, when the Obermayer family moved out to Hetzendorf or the Hohe Warte, the children were allowed to play outside only in the garden, so that they would not be exposed to the unpredictable world beyond.[35] These restrictions on movement and play are only the more visible examples of the restrictions on activity, posture, and emotional expression to which children would submit as they were educated and socialized. Of course, the children did not always comply. Mayreder records how her sister refused to recite the life of St. Paul in her catechism classes, while she herself was compliant in the lessons only because she ate all the way through them.[36] The children took liberties where they could. Nevertheless, conformity remained the rule, and found its expression in the routine of asking mother and governess for forgiveness before the children went to confession. In retrospect, this custom appeared to Mayreder as the ritualized denial of her own personality.[37]

The constraints on the young girls limited the freedom of movement, both physical and intellectual, more than those on the boys did. During winter, once the children had outgrown the daily stroll in the Prater, the girls were considered to need only the walk to school and back. Other outdoor activities, such as skating, were thought to be unnecessary or unseemly, leaving the girls confined to the house.[38] The summerhouse on the Hohe Warte was chosen because the boys in the family would still be able to travel back to school every day. It was accepted that this would not be possible for the girls and that they would repeatedly miss the last few weeks of the school year.[39] The girls had access neither to the bodily nor to the intellectual arenas that were open to their brothers. At the same time, their bodies were trained to take appropriately feminine forms. The girls were not allowed outside without hat and gloves lest their face and hands lose their attractive pallor. Gymnastics were not allowed since they were thought to make a girl's hands unflatteringly big and strong. Shoes had to be as narrow as possible. From the age of twelve, the girls wore a corset, which, for festive occasions, would be tied a centimetre tighter than normal to emphasise the narrowness of the waist. Studying was thought to be detrimental to their figure, as well as to cause hair to fall out.[40]

Rosa Mayreder was one of a generation of women who challenged the constraints to which she was supposed to submit. From the age of eighteen she stopped wearing a corset, even though her contemporaries thought this indicated the lack of a sense of shame.[41] As an adult, she also wrote, had a public career, and persuaded her husband to tolerate her platonic love affair with another man.[42] The crumbling of received habits that caused the gentleman subject to codify behavior simultaneously offered women a limited opportunity to recast the mold into which they were supposed to fit. At the same time, the rights to vote, to work, and to be educated were not the only issue. As the description of male behavior suggests, the emotional attitudes of one gender influenced the options available to the other. Women's lives were constrained and defined by what men did or did not allow themselves. On the emotional level, change was harder to secure than on the political, and the roles were less flexible, as Juliet Mitchell has observed of the repeated attempts by women since the turn of the twentieth century to modify behavior. Changes in the rights or status of women have often been followed by a backlash, as behavior returns almost to the point that it started from.[43] Mitchell suggests that to understand this inertia we need some account of the unconscious thought processes by which men and women relate to each other and contribute to the formation of gender roles. The point is made in a psychoanalytic vocabulary but is useful nevertheless, since it draws attention to the habits of emotional mismanagement that bind the sexes together. As well as controlling the movement, intellectual development, and bodily expression of men and women, the patterns of behavior associated with the gentleman subject also distributed emotions. On the one side there was the man who did not allow himself emotional expression and who had no hidden feelings because he had torn them out of himself "root and branch."[44] On the other hand, there was the woman who was the repository of instinctive feeling, exaggeration, sphinx-like seductive powers, and other threatening manifestations of emotional life. Given that the gentleman who claimed to be without socially unacceptable feelings could not have transformed his psychological makeup to remove emotional responses altogether, he must have found a way of relating to his emotional life that did not require him to acknowledge it as his own. At the same time he had also found a way of excluding his feelings from the conversation. Such emotions were called childish, unmanly, irrational, and inappropriate. For a history of the development of psychoanalysis, it is particularly interesting to note that another word used frequently to disqualify emotions was the term *hysterical*, as a story entitled "Nervös: Geschichte einer Ehe" (Nervous: The story of a marriage), published in the magazine *Dokumente der Frauen* in 1902, critically recorded.[45]

In the story, a woman called Marion Nell has been put out of action by back pain and general exhaustion since the birth of her first child. The first doctor diagnoses hysteria, much to the horror of her husband, who starts to withdraw from his wife and look for another woman. Marion attempts to remedy this situation, spurred into action by the advice of a female friend. She seeks the opinion of a second doctor, who confirms that her sufferings are physiological rather than psychological and suggests that she be admitted to his clinic without delay. Marion does not want to stay in a clinic lest her absence from home finally cause her husband to leave her for the other woman, so she contradicts the doctor's proposal. The doctor does not wish to be contradicted, but Marion remains insistent. "But Madam forgot all civility and self-control. Madam left the room with a face like that of a scolded child.—'What a hysterical creature!' Professor Barth murmured as she disappeared. 'The sort of creature that enjoys being weak and just won't let herself be healed.'"[46]

The story records how a woman could be dismissed as hysterical where she forgot the rules of civility and self-control, acted in a childish manner, and contradicted a man in a position of institutional authority. In the text, Marion rebuts the dismissive categorization of the doctor and wins back her husband by angelically bearing her physical ailment.[47] The social or psychological disorder is replaced by a less threatening natural illness. The story criticized the use of the diagnosis of hysteria as a form of social proscription, but in replacing hysteria with an ennobling physical frailty, it did, if anything, a disservice to the women it sought to defend.

The element of truth in the doctor's diagnosis is that hysteria was indeed the terrain on which the emotions and responses otherwise excluded from social interaction found limited recognition. Through their paralyzed limbs, speech disorders, and phobias, the hysterical patients, both men and women, acted out the emotions that neither they, their families, nor the doctors who treated them could allow themselves to express more directly. Hysterical symptoms should be seen to belong to any complete picture of the emotional habits of late-nineteenth-century Vienna. They should be viewed not as exceptions or a separate category but rather as forming part of the general structure through which emotions were managed and distributed. The diagnosis of the doctor in "Nervös" shows how the term functioned to belittle and reject. But not every doctor of the period found it necessary to use the term as a means of excluding experience. Other physicians, such as Breuer and Freud, as we shall see, respected the experience articulated in hysteria—respected it sufficiently to help it find a social place again. At the same time this entailed an admission of dependence, since the male doctor was confronted with the way he, like his hysterical patient, participated in the same set of conventions for managing the emotions. This insight was apparently very often too threatening to be fully articulated, with the result that the emotional roles barely changed. In all but the fewest cases, the gentleman subject continued to dictate both the terms on which emotional life was to be managed and the responsibility for emotions disproportionately distributed.

The Beginnings of the Talking Cure

Breuer and Freud were by no means the first psychologists to let themselves be inspired by their women patients. In the essay "Psychiatry and Its Unknown History" (1961) as well as in *The Discovery of the Unconscious* (1970), Henri Ellenberger observed how breakthroughs in the development of dynamic psychiatry often depended on two things. One was the "creative illness" by means of which psychologists came to understand psychological phenomena through their own experience of neurosis. Robert Burton's description of melancholy in *The Anatomy of Melancholy* (1628), George Cheyne's of hypochondria in *The English Malady* (1733), and Bénédict-Augustin Morel's of emotive delirium in 1866 all drew on the writer's own illnesses.[48] Freud's self-analysis from 1897 to 1900 similarly occurred at a time when he said he was suffering from "neurasthenic" symptoms.[49] Jung came near to psychological collapse as he formulated the insights that provoked the break with Freud.[50] All these writers had experienced the phenomena they analyzed; they did not describe them from a distance. The second recurring pattern observed by Ellenberger was that of intense relationships between a male doctor and, most frequently, a woman patient. Either the patient aided the doctor to arrive at the formulation of new insights or, alternatively, the relationship that he or she developed with the physician closely prefigured the methods adopted by forms of psychotherapy in the twentieth century. A number of the examples that Ellenberger cites have a direct bearing on the relationship between analyst and hysteric that developed from the 1880s. In 1836, Despine, a French general practitioner in Aix-en-Savoie, began treating a bed-ridden eleven-year-old girl. In hypnosis, a character called Angeline emerged who said that Estelle should be given what she wanted and that she would not abuse the situation. In hypnosis, a healthy girl who could walk and eat normally began to appear, whom Despine managed to integrate into Estelle's waking identity, at the same time breaking the sick girl's morbid attachment to her mother.[51] For two years Johann Christoph Blumhardt (1805–80), a German Lutheran pastor, fought the demons that possessed the twenty-eight-year-old Gottliebin Dittus, relying only on fasting, prayer and a good deal of time spent with the sick woman. He was successful, and overcame the possession, and the techniques that he employed appear retrospectively similar to those used by therapists who treat schizophrenia by giving primary attention to their own "countertransference" (the equivalent of Blumhardt's praying and fasting).[52] The first published "case history" in modern psychology was that written by the poet and physician Justinus Kerner (1786–1862) of Fredericke Hauffe (1801–29). Fredericke Hauffe was brought to him in 1827, suffering from convulsions, catalepsy, hemorrhages, and fever, which other doctors had not been able to treat. Kerner, who had been interested in Mesmer's theories and had gone so far as to collect biographical material on him, discovered that hypnotizing his patient helped. For the next three years, Kerner studied and recorded the experiences of the woman, which ranged from conversing in an unknown language to being able to prescribe her own medications for her ailments. After her death, Kerner published a book entitled *Die Seherin von Prevorst* (The visionary of Prevorst), which recorded his clinical observations and experiments.[53]

Ellenberger gives further examples, such as Charcot's relationship with the "prima donna" of hysterics, Blanche Wittmann,[54] or the study made by Theodore Flournoy (1854–1920), professor of psychology in Geneva, of the medium Catherine Muller.[55] The repeated message is that psychological techniques that prefigured psychoanalysis arose from close cooperations between the physician or priest and the patient. Common features were that the man giving the treatment may himself have suffered from experiences similar to those of his patient and that a form of bargaining occurred during which the patient was enabled to articulate what he or she needed to recover. The pattern is also similar to that observed by I. M. Lewis in *Ecstatic Religion*. Once again, men in a position of power take seriously and respond to interventions that disregard the rules of communication otherwise established between men and the socially less powerful.[56] But where the appeal to spirits often remains the exception to the rule and leaves the status quo unchanged, the examples of Despine and Estelle, or of Blumhardt and Gottliebin Dittus, show a new relationship being established, with new forms of interaction and the lasting integration of the troublesome emotions and experiences.

The first case history in psychoanalysis, Breuer's famous treatment of "Anna O." (Bertha Pappenheim) in the early 1880s, looks less extraordinary in the light of these earlier collaborations. Indeed, as Ellenberger remarks, it makes a different kind of sense against the background of treatments that, unlike those of Charcot and other hypnotists of the latter part of the nineteenth century, did not transform hypnosis into an instrument of authoritarian display.[57] One of the most striking things about the case is the close relationship between Breuer and his patient.[58] Breuer started treating Pappenheim in 1880 when she was twenty-one. The daughter of a strict and prosperous Orthodox Jewish family, she had fallen ill nursing her father during the illness that eventually killed him. She was suffering from a variety of symptoms, which continued to develop as Breuer treated her: a nervous cough, listlessness, disturbances of her vision and speech, and the loss of feeling and motor capability in various parts of her body.[59] Breuer admired and respected her, as his brief character sketch at the beginning of the case history shows. "She was markedly intelligent, with an astonishing quick grasp of things and penetrating intuition. She possessed a powerful intellect which would have been capable of digesting solid mental pabulum and which stood in need of it—though without receiving it after she had left school. She had great poetic and imaginative gifts, which were under the control of a sharp and critical common sense."[60] This respect led Breuer to collaborate with Pappenheim to help overcome some of her symptoms rather than merely do to her things drawn from the range of medical interventions available at the time (prescribe medication or diet, massage, hypnotism). One important product of the relationship was a ritual to which Pappenheim gave the English name the "talking cure," whereby Pappenheim and Breuer found that, by speaking about the circumstances that had caused a particular problem, she was able to free herself from it. This discovery was taken by Freud to mark the beginning of psychoanalytic techniques.[61]

The originality and success of Breuer and Pappenheim's method has been much debated. Historians of science have pointed out that similar cases already existed of patients talking about the origins of symptoms, such as those recorded by the Viennese physician Moriz Benedikt, who noted the therapeutic effective of uncovering and articulating a pathogenic secret.[62] Indeed, the idea seems to have been something like common sense at the time. Readers in the 1890s of Fontane's novel *Effi Briest* (1895/96) will have heard the ailing Effi accompanying her final words to her mother with the assertion that to "get something off one's chest [*etwas von der Seele heruntersprechen*] brings a sense of peace."[63]

Just as the idea of a talking cure was not new, its efficacy has also been disputed. Breuer wrote the case up for publication more than ten years after it occurred, drawing on notes he had made in 1882.[64] The discovery of Breuer's original notes, as well as records from the sanatorium in Kreuzlingen to which Pappenheim was admitted shortly after her treatment by Breuer had finished, have led some critics to argue that Breuer exaggerated the success of his interventions when he wrote the case up in the 1890s. In the published case history, Breuer suggested that, having reconstructed the traumatic events at her father's sickbed, which he believed to have induced the symptoms, Pappenheim was able to free herself from the main ailments as well as "from the innumerable disturbances which she had previously exhibited."[65] He conceded: "It was a considerable time before she regained her mental balance entirely."[66] Nevertheless, the cure was presented as being complete. In contrast, the report from the sanatorium at Kreuzlingen paints a less sanguine picture. Pappenheim appears here as a woman to whom large doses of morphine were being administered to enable her to cope with the pain of facial neuralgia and who, in the assessment of the doctor in Kreuzlingen, still exhibited "signs of hysteria [*hysterische Merkmale*]." To some critics, the face pain in particular demonstrates that Breuer was misguided in his approach and underplayed the degree to which Pappenheim's symptoms were of neurological rather than psychological origin.[67] As a consequence, he made too great a claim for the efficacy of the cathartic cure, asserting that changes were effects of the talking when they might equally have been spontaneous remissions.[68] According to Richard Webster, this misjudgment was underpinned by an erroneous view of hysterical symptoms. Rather than following through to their physiological origins, Freud and Breuer, like Charcot, erroneously held that "ideas could lodge in an unconscious portion of the mind where they could actually be transformed into bodily symptoms."[69] To uncover these ideas could then appear to them as a way of freeing the body.

Webster goes too far when he reduces Pappenheim's problems to neurological dysfunction, since the fact that a particular symptom can sometimes have physiological explanations is no guarantee that it necessarily did in Pappenheim's case.[70] More important, his approach ignores the social element of the disorder. He has no sense of what Foucault would have called the techniques—intellectual, social, emotional, somatic—through which an identity is formed and reproduced and through which persons submit themselves to social control. As a result, he pays little attention to the most striking aspects of the relationship between Breuer and Pappenheim, which he instead views as accompanying but not influencing the physiological symptoms as they played out their natural course. Rather than claim that Pappenheim's disorder was purely physical and the relationship an accidental by-product, it is equally plausible to argue that the relationship between Breuer and Pappenheim modified the terms of their social interaction and in so doing helped Pappenheim, even if it did not produce a miracle cure, by lifting the pressure of convention and habit weighing down on the young woman. Many details of the case history suggest this.

The skeptical reading of critics such as Webster and Borch-Jacobsen has recently been challenged by Richard Skues, who revisited the available documents and put them back in the context of medical discourse of the 1880 and 1890s, showing that, when it is read in this light, the case history cannot be said to be misleading. The first stage of his argument is to reconstruct what Breuer believed himself to have done. The answer is that Breuer thought the "taking cure" only to have cleared up residual hysterical symptoms but not to have overcome the underlying hysterical illness, which followed a rhythm of its own, nor to have cleared up other somatic symptoms, the presence of which he was more than willing to acknowledge.[71] One psychological symptom that persisted after the termination of his treatment was Pappenheim's inability to talk German, but that was only for about an hour a day and so was less dramatic than it had previously been. The other symptoms had receded, leaving the facial neuralgia and the concomitant problem of an addiction to pain-relieving drugs, which was the affliction for which Pappenheim, after a brief visit to relatives in June 1882, was admitted to the Kreuzlingen sanatorium.[72] Given this more modest view of what the "talking cure" achieved, Breuer's account can once again be seen to be reliable. What then emerges is a picture of the founding case of psychoanalysis in which the talking is only part of the treatment of a disorder seen to have multiple determinants. In addition, it is clear that the intensity of the form of therapy that Breuer and Pappenheim had developed together brought with it social and emotional difficulties for both doctor and patient. Indeed, it challenged their self-image and sense of socially appropriate behavior, as a brief account of the details of Breuer and Pappenheim's interactions shows.

Breuer remarks that, even before she fell ill, Pappenheim had the habit of withdrawing into what she called her private theater (*Privattheater*).[73] As a highly intelligent and energetic young woman for whom her domestic environment allowed no creative outlet, she would daydream. "While everyone thought she was attending, she was living through fairy tales in her imagination; but she was always on the spot when she was spoken to, so that no on was aware of it."[74] The symptoms that Breuer believes himself and his patient to have cured are often the result of impulses being controlled because Pappenheim restricted her behavior to what she thought was acceptable. She developed a nervous cough, having stifled the desire to go to the neighbors' party and dance rather than nurse her father (*Studien*, 31 / *Studies*, 95). She lost the ability to drink as a result of not expressing to her English lady companion her disgust at the sight of the companion's dog drinking from a glass. "The patient had said nothing, as she had wanted to be polite."[75] The consequence of this self-censorship was a progressive splitting of Pappenheim's personality, one side of which was, according to Breuer, normal if relatively anxious, the other being badly behaved, swearing, throwing things around the room, and refusing to be cooperative (*Studien*, 17 / *Studies*, 76). Breuer and Pappenheim developed a method for keeping the fractious personality at bay while also relieving the disturbances of mobility, vision, and speech that spilt over from the "condition seconde" into her normal life. Pappenheim had the ability to put herself into a hypnotic state, during which Breuer discovered that, when offered words that she had muttered to herself during previous lapses, she began to tell stories that calmed her down. Initially the stories were fairy tales, in the manner of Hans Christian Andersen (*Studien*, 22 / *Studies*, 82). But the routine developed to include the retelling of actual occurrences (*Studien*, 24 / *Studies*, 85), and Pappenheim learned to retell three different types of information. There were the fantasies and the real events that had troubled her since she had last had a session of what she ironically called "chimney sweeping" (*Studien*, 23 / *Studies*, 83). But she also recounted, in reverse chronological order, all the instances in which she had been afflicted by a particular symptom (such as temporary loss of hearing). Once she had retraced the symptom to its origin, it disappeared (*Studien*, 26–29 / *Studies*, 86–89).

Skues's careful reconstruction of the case suggests that Breuer's treatment did not miraculously make all psychological and physiological symptoms vanish. Nevertheless, even a skeptical assessment of the material, such as that of Malcolm Macmillan, acknowledges that symptoms were talked away.[76] It is easy to assume that it was the talking itself that was the crucial element, and certainly the model of cathartic talking influenced the subsequent development of psychoanalysis. Rereading the case history, however, one sees that the talking appears as only one aspect of the relationship between Pappenheim and Breuer, and cannot be separated from other aspects of their interaction. Breuer was the only doctor in whom Pappenheim was willing to confide in this manner, and she spoke to him only after scrutinizing his hands to assure herself of his identity (*Studien*, 23 / *Studies*, 83). Not talking in general but talking specifically to Breuer brought about an amelioration of symptoms. An intense rapport developed between doctor and patient partly because of the enormous amount of time that Breuer devoted to the case; in one phase, he had to close her eyes before she went to sleep in the evening and then he would return in the morning to open them (*Studien*, 29–30 / *Studies*, 92). It has been calculated that they spent over a thousand hours together during the year and a half of the treatment.[77] As well as devoting his time, Breuer responded both sensitively and respectfully to the promptings of his patient, accepting the talking cure as a routine but also varying it to help the recounting of events be accomplished more quickly (*Studien*, 28 / *Studies*, 91). The relationship also did not exclude physical contact (checking Breuer's hands, closing Pappenheim's eyes). The patient was given bodily as much as emotional reassurance of Breuer's reliability. Moreover, Breuer allowed Pappenheim to define the terms of her cure, even to the point of deciding on which date she wished to be cured by and then working hard with her to retrace the origins of her symptoms in time to meet the deadline (*Studien*, 32 / *Studies*, 95). It was not only through speaking but through the establishing of a respectful, collaborative, and personal relationship that Breuer and Pappenheim found a way of overcoming the constraints on the young woman and of giving more space to the side of her that was otherwise censored.

The resulting therapy was both a qualified success and a failure. The successful aspects are those that are most similar to the practices of Kerner, Despine, and Blumhardt: the close rapport, the physician letting himself be guided by the patient's contribution, the humanity of the encounter. Breuer fostered the intellectual activity of his woman patient and allowed her actively to shape the response to her ailment. For this reason Christina von Braun has suggested that the encounter between Breuer and Pappenheim was the last case of genuine psychoanalysis. "A therapy, which consisted in putting consciousness in direct relation to the unconscious—without theories or a doctrinal edifice pushing themselves in between. Through this treatment, Bertha Pappenheim could become what she was—herself."[78] Braun overstates the case. The records from the sanatorium in Kreuzlingen show that Pappenheim was still quite ill when the treatment with Breuer stopped. In addition, the case history itself is not as tolerant as Braun suggests, as a comparison with Despine's treatment of Estelle and other cases summarized by Ellenberger demonstrates. A number of therapists working in the nineteenth century observed that the personalities who emerged during hypnosis or during an illness were livelier and cleverer than the patients were in their normal life. This makes sense insofar as hypnosis or illness removed the learned constraints on behavior that otherwise guided and limited the individual's activities. Indeed, there were some cases in which the supposedly sick personality was seen to be healthier and more normal than the anxious, self-constraining patients were in their normal lives. A therapy like what Despine undertook with Estelle integrated the unconstrained personality with its obedient and self-constraining counterpart. It is obviously impossible without fuller documentation to directly compare these cases with Pappenheim's. Nevertheless, the contrast does highlight a limit to Breuer's treatment. Breuer is keen to emphasize that the truculent character who emerges in Pappenheim's illness was not her true identity and that the talking cure helped her to maintain her proper self. "It was especially noticeable in Anna O. how much the products of her 'bad self,' as she herself called it, affected her moral habit of mind. If these products had not been continually disposed of, we should have been faced by a hysteric of the malicious type—refractory, lazy, disagreeable and ill-natured; but as it was, after the removal of those stimuli her true character, which was the opposite of all these, always reappeared at once."[79] Breuer wished to defend Pappenheim against the accusation that she was a troublemaking hysteric of the sort that the doctor in "Nervös" branded the wife as being when she resisted his diagnosis. Breuer stood up for his patient, but only insofar as she conformed to a standard of behavior that he and his patient shared. Seen against the background of other treatments from the nineteenth century but also against the background of the more-radical encounters from the fourteenth century, the relationship between Breuer and Pappenheim can be seen not to have fostered the woman's development or to have allowed an integration of the behavior that found distorted expression in the illness.

If Breuer did not encourage his patient to step beyond the role of the obedient young woman, he also did not let his own role change. There has been much speculation about the way his treatment of Pappenheim ended, speculation fueled by the interpretations that Freud gave of the case in later years, after he had developed his own theories about the sexual etiology of hysteria. If one puts aside Freud's retrospective extrapolations, it appears that, after Pappenheim had been admitted to the Kreuzlingen sanatorium in the summer of 1882, Breuer declined to continue treatment and that this was because his wife, Mathilde Breuer, asked him to give up the patient who was occupying so much of his time and energy.[80] Rumors at the time circulated of an affair between the two, but Freud's own letter to his fiancée, Martha Bernays, who was also an acquaintance of Bertha Pappenheim, explicitly excludes this interpretation.[81] On Breuer's part there are no statements beyond the comment in a letter written thirty years later that the treatment had been an ordeal ("Ordal").[82] What is clear is that the strain that the treatment of Pappenheim put on himself, his marriage, and his reputation was more than Breuer was willing to tolerate when the request came from Pappenheim's mother that he continue.[83] Breuer did not wish to change from being a respected family doctor to something more like confessor, friend, and beloved advisor of the younger woman.

The evidence of the case history and other documents indicates that neither the patient nor the physician radically transformed their position, their habits, or their relationship with themselves and others. It is clear why this is the case from Breuer's perspective. For all the support he gave her, he finally let Pappenheim stay in the role of the "good" personality and confined himself to playing that of the family physician. But that does not explain Pappenheim's perspective. Pappenheim eventually became an active and respected writer, educational theorist, and social worker, but this career did not begin until the late 1880s, after three more prolonged visits to a sanatorium at Inzensdorf.[84] The relation between this recovery and the empowering or disempowering aspects of the treatment with Breuer remains unclear. Mikkel Borch-Jacobsen insists that the "unexpected recovery" toward the end of the 1880s "owed nothing whatsoever to the 'talking cure.' "[85] But that is because he does not see the relationship between Breuer and Pappenheim as in any way socially empowering. Pappenheim's biographer, Marianne Brentzel, suggests that in particular what opened the path to recovery was the encounter with her cousin, Anna Ettlinger (1841–1934), when she was staying in Karlsruhe late in 1882 immediately after being discharged from the sanatorium in Kreuzlingen. Ettlinger was a woman who had chosen a career as writer and teacher over the marriage her family had planned for her, and she is supposed to have encouraged Pappenheim to write. However: "Anna Ettlinger was significant for Bertha not just because she encouraged her to write. The most important message for Bertha Pappenheim at this point was contained in the independent way Ettlinger managed her life."[86] Pappenheim's progress in the years between 1882 and 1888 when she moved to Frankfurt with her mother is not well documented, so it is difficult to assess how and when she recovered and what role the treatment by Breuer played in the process. However, one of the texts she published after her move to Frankfurt is indirectly instructive. After she had published a short book of fairy tales, *Geschichten für kleine Kinder*, anonymously in 1888, Pappenheim published a longer collection, *In der Trödelbude* (In the secondhand shop) under the name Paul Berthold.[87] The book consists of a framing narrative and nine stories told by objects in the shop. It is not explicitly autobiographical, nor does it discuss psychotherapy in any form. Nevertheless, it is an account of a process of psychological healing that can plausibly be read as showing what Pappenheim felt to be necessary for recovery. These stories have been relatively neglected by historians of psychoanalysis, even though, apart from the brief note written in English while she was in the sanatorium in Kreuzlingen, they are as close as we can come to hearing about Pappenheim's development from her point of view.[88] Reading the text can help to establish how Pappenheim might have modified her treatment to make it more fruitful for herself, as well as showing the constraints with which she was struggling in her attempts to create a workable identity. By helping us to step beyond the myths and the inflated claims both for and against the "talking cure," the text can help to situate and assess the cure and see what opportunity psychoanalysis missed when the male physicians stuck to their roles and stopped following their initial intuitions and the intuitions of their patients.

From the Perspective of Anna O.

In der Trödelbude is a book about remembering. It tells the story of Franz, who owns a junk shop, and of nine of the objects. The appearance of a friend whom Franz has not seen since he was at school prompts him to tell the tale of his unhappy marriage. As a student at the beginning of a promising academic career, he had been faced with the choice of giving up his studies or not being able to marry his childhood sweetheart, Eva. He chose to marry her, putting his energy into her father's book business. Eva had wanted Franz to do this rather than wait until he had become a professor, because, as a beautiful young woman, she longed to live more actively and hoped for distraction and excitement in marriage. But married life continued to bore her, and, when Franz went on a business trip to Vienna, she eloped with Count Konrad. Franz fell ill with the shock of her disappearance, neglected the business, and finally had nothing more than a few old books and maps and the secondhand-goods shop he bought after the collapse of the other business. However, although to his friend the shop seems chaotic and impoverished, to Franz it is a surprising resource, for he can hear the stories that the objects tell:

> "Don't dismiss my junk for being dead and ugly," Franz said and a light smile illuminated his features. "The junk is not as dead as you think. At night, when everything alive is otherwise sleeping, the shop is closed and the doors to my room open, a whispering and muttering goes through the shelves, and some of the objects, which look insignificant and worthless, tell of their different experiences. I listen, and when I hear how much misery there is in the world, how little to be cheerful about, I think that my own misfortune is only a very small part of the general suffering."[89]

Most of the book consists of the stories told by the objects themselves—a piece of lace, a doll, a coffee mill, a birdcage, a good luck charm, a pince-nez, a thimble, a broken streetlamp, and a music box. Two of the stories have happy endings. The piece of lace tells a story that is effectively the inverse of Franz's: The lace that an aristoricratic girl is dressed in for her christening saves her from being struck by lightning. When, years later, she is praying before the lace (which was given to the church as a token of gratitude for the miraculous escape), she finds the teacher's son despairing because his father has just died and he will be forced into an apprenticeship he does not desire. She asks her father to help him study instead, which he does, and, after more years, the two meet by chance in front of the same piece of lace being displayed as part of an exhibition of church artifacts. The result is a happy marriage.

The other happy story is that told by the pince-nez, which is purchased by the strict principal of an educational establishment for young ladies. The pince-nez tells the story of an outing that the mistress organizes on which, with the help of a more boisterous friend Ina, the quiet and serious Emma is able to meet up with and get engaged to the young doctor for whom she has been pining. In contrast with these two stories, the other stories are almost uniformly bleak. The doll is given to a child who unexpectedly dies on the Christmas Eve, the coffee mill is broken when a careless cook stuffs into it a postcard that she has received from an admirer, because she wants to conceal from her mistress that she is not concentrating on her work. The birdcage is lovingly constructed by a music teacher, who puts a beautifully voiced nightingale in it, but the music teacher gets injured, cannot work any longer, and dies of cold and starvation, and so too does the bird. The good-luck charm belongs to a young circus girl who plunges to her death from the high wire; the thimble, to a woman who is exploited by a drunken husband and drowns herself. The streetlamp realizes its uselessness when confronted with a blind person who longs to see the spectacle of the lights across the city. Finally, the music box attempts to rescue something from adversity, telling the story of what happened when the boy who owned it broke it by taking it apart. This childhood disaster prompted the boy to study to become a mechanic so that he could learn to fix the machine, which he did, insofar as was possible, given the damage that as a boy he had done to the machine. The repaired music box then sits in the house of the father and sister of the young man who become poorer and poorer, have no luck in finding work, and finally have the idea that playing the music box and begging might give them a meager income. However, when he tries out the music box, the father inadvertently attracts the attention of his own son, who has returned from his travels to Vienna, with no idea of the state his father and sister are in. So the faulty tones of the repaired music box reunite the family, even though subsequent generations forget the significance of the instrument, abandoning it finally to the secondhand-goods shop.

These stories are interrupted by the arrival in the shop of a young girl who looks exactly likely Eva, the wife who abandoned the shopkeeper. She has come to sell a medallion. It turns out indeed to be Eva's daughter by the count with whom she eloped, who has come to pawn her last remaining treasure, since her mother has died. The medallion is an image of Franz's own mother, which was the only piece of jewelery that he could afford to give Eva at the time of his marriage. Realizing who has walked into his shop, Franz comforts the girl while at the same time beginning finally to overcome the shock of himself being abandoned all those years ago. "The comforting words of explanation, that sounded with a soft voice in the girl's ears, had in their turn a comforting effect on the speaker."[90] He decides to adopt the girl and look after her, and in so doing he recovers from his lethargy and returns to the book business that he had neglected when Eva abandoned him.

The stories do not directly reflect the life of Bertha Pappenheim. Nevertheless, there are aspects of the fictional text that shed light on her case history, her treatment by Breuer, and the process of recovery. Of course, the recovery in the text happens in a fictional world and is not achieved in Pappenheim's name. But if we study how it is achieved in the fiction, we might learn something about Pappenheim's own situation. In the text, there are a number of key devices that underpin the transformation. The first is the male voice—the text is written in the guise of Paul Berthold and centers on a disappointed male character, Franz. Much of the world in which the text moves would, at the time, have been recognized as specifically feminine (lace, dolls, the kitchen, the institution for young ladies, the thimble), but the character whose transformation we watch is that of the shopkeeper himself. When Pappenheim imagined speech, it was from the position of man, even if the domain of experiences discussed was not masculine.

The second important device is that of prosopopoeia (personification), or speaking through the objects. This allows Pappenheim to address indirectly a set of feelings and attitudes that, given the case history and context, it is plausible to assume she herself experienced. She was perhaps better able to engage with the emotions of the situation when she spoke not in her own name but through the objects themselves. The objects return repeatedly to the question of usefulness and their ability or inability to intervene. The first story, told by the lace, has the function of a positive fantasy and is told by an object that seems correspondingly deluded. It inverts the catastrophe of Franz's life. Where Franz had to give up his hopes of studying to marry an impatient Eva, the young school master's son, in the lace's story, is helped to study by the intervention of the aristocratic girl whom he will later marry. There is suffering in the story (the young boy loses both his parents). But the lace is the witness to, or passive participant in, the events that help this position of helplessness be left behind. Corresponding to the positive experiences of the young man is the lace's own pride at being on display in a museum (*Trödelbude*, 25). This is in direct contrast to the doll of the following story, which reports the discomfort of being inspected before being purchased from a toy shop. "It is not a pleasant experience to be viewed from every angle and to have one's looks and value assessed."[91] If the lace's story sets right in fantasy what caused such suffering to the owner of the secondhand shop, the ensuing stories return to feelings of uselessness, and disappointment, which are lent special emphasis by the defenselessness of the inanimate objects.

The objects' stance with respect to the events they narrate is that of passive spectator. Often, they understand events only because of the fragments of conversation they overhear from other participants (*Trödelbude*, 32, 44). They are also unable to offer assistance. As the doll complains: "It is awful to be nothing more than a puppet beside a sickbed and to be unable to help."[92] The birdcage laments in similar terms: "And it was an endless worry for me to see my dear good master standing before me lost in his dark thoughts, without being able to help him."[93] The streetlamp is equally frustrated at its inability to assist the blind woman (*Trödelbude*, 86). The doll and the birdcage are pleased to have made the suffering human briefly happy even if they were unable to change his situation (*Trödelbude*, 34, 44). But the coffee mill is not content with being merely useful. She has her own soul, as she puts it, and wants to be loved (*Trödelbude*, 37–38). But while she is briefly the object of the attentions of another kitchen utensil, she is helpless before the carelessness and self-interest of the cook who stuffs the postcard into her. The doll is similarly defenseless, being thrown to the ground by the dying child and then trampled on by the horrified mother (*Trödelbude*, 34–35).

The device of personification defamiliarizes emotions by attributing them to inanimate objects, but this new context allows the emotions, in particular the feeling of helpless passivity, to become more dynamic. For the use of objects does not make the passivity unchangeable. On the contrary, in the last story, told by the music box, the constellation changes. The box, like the doll or the coffee mill, is broken when the young boy takes it apart. But the boy reacts by taking steps to mend it and learning to become a mechanic. The music box is not fully restored, because individual parts were damaged during the first dismantling. Nevertheless, the damage gives it the distinctive tone that unites the family at the end of the story (*Trödelbude*, 95).

The characters in the last story have acquired a different relationship to the world. In the lace's story, the world is watched over by a benign and wealthy father who can solve problems that seem unsolvable. In the stories told by the doll, the coffee mill, the birdcage, the good-luck charm, the thimble, and the streetlamp, the characters are unable to intervene. The mother cannot combat the child's illness. The cook is at the mercy of her lovers and the mistress of the house and takes her frustration out on the machines. The teacher who made the birdcage is unable to halt the process of pauperization that his accident sets in train. The old man does not intervene to help the child performer. The suffering wife has apparently no way of escaping her drunken husband other than suicide. The blind woman can do nothing to restore her sight. The story told by the music box differs in this respect.[94] The brother, Robert, can study to change the situation, because he connects the choice of study with his ability to shape his environment. His father is also more active than characters from other stories. When his daughter is unable to find work, he decides that he must himself contribute, if only by begging with the music box. This decision, and the ensuing test of the music box, causes Robert to find his father and sister again.

The changed attitude of the objects and characters of the stories finds its extension in the changed attitude of Franz himself in the closing chapter of the book. He too is given the opportunity to intervene and does so, adopting the girl and returning to his former trade. Accompanying this transformation is a further device employed by the book, which is that of reflecting on and questioning the generic conventions governing the stories and the behavior of the characters. Characters and objects alike return repeatedly to the similarity of events to those in a fairy tale. In the opening chapter, Eva reads fairy tales in her father's book shop and tells Franz, when they are still children, that she will marry him only if a prince does not turn up in the meantime (*Trödelbude*, 9). When the Count appears, Eva elopes with him, effectively preferring the promise of a fairy-tale fantasy to a more active engagement with her frustration at life in a provincial town. Franz suffers because Eva does not act to change her situation but instead waits for a fairy-tale prince to fulfill her dreams. The lace's story offers a counter–fairy tale, as it were, to soften the pain of Franz's abandonment. But the inadequacy of the solution is explicitly commented on by one of the objects listening to the story. "When it [the lace] had finished speaking, the old wooden pill case, for whom refinement of the lace was a constant source of irritation, said sarcastically: 'And they lived happily ever after, like a prince and princess in a fairytale.'"[95]

The subsequent stories detail suffering that cannot magically be made good. In the tale of the good-luck charm, fairy tales feature again explicitly. After he has befriended the circus performer, the old man reads fairy tales by Hans Christian Andersen with her (*Trödelbude*, 52). This offers the girl the opportunity of escaping the circus identity imposed on her, but it is not enough to prevent her death. Eva similarly discovers that the fairy tales offer no protection when, as we hear in the final chapter of the book, she is left ill and without her count and returns to her home town to discover that the shop in which she had read the fairy tales no longer exists (*Trödelbude*, 103). A more helpful form of text seems to be romantic fiction, since, in the tale of the pince-nez, Ina is able to use the tricks she has learned while reading about love in theory to realize Emma's romantic desires in practice. The important aspect is the different attitude that the genres foster, passivity in the case of the fairy tale and a mischievous determination in that of romantic fiction. The development toward activity in the course of the text is paralleled by an abandonment of the fairy tale as a point of reference. The final reconciliation of the book differs from that of a fairy tale in that Franz becomes an active agent, protecting the young girl, when the opportunity presents itself, rather than waiting for restitution.

The final device to mention is irony. The process of transformation is accompanied by a wry reflection on storytelling and the expression of emotions. The irony arises as a result of personifying inanimate objects, as the text repeatedly draws attention to the fact that the objects in question are normally incapable of both narrative and feeling. Where the nightingale can respond to the music teacher with song, the birdcage cannot communicate its feelings (*Trödelbude*, 45). Similarly, the streetlamp is happy to be extinguished, since it cannot cry in sympathy for the blind woman. "Streetlamps of course cannot weep."[96] The sensitive and empathetic guitar, in contrast, is able to echo the sigh of the coffee mill (*Trödelbude*, 36). The coffee mill, meanwhile, is driven to tell its story despite the irreparable damage done to it by the cook's carelessness. "But a coffee grinder, which feels the need to get something off its chest, and which has been asked to do so, soon overcomes any such moment of weakness and being at a loss for words, and it started off telling its story with a slightly screechy voice."[97] Irony notwithstanding, the storytelling is both appreciated and efficacious. Franz defends the objects because they whisper their tales to each other at night. Similarly, despite the need to justify themselves before they speak, the objects encourage each other in their storytelling. The narratives are valued because they create a community of sufferers.

In the text, the self-exposure involved in telling one's story is both mocked and appreciated. However, while Pappenheim reflects on the effect of individual tales, the overall composition of the book is not commented on. The developing logic of the sequence is left for readers either to observe or to experience for themselves in the identification with Franz and his changed situation. This raises the question of the purpose of the book as a whole. Amy Colin suggests that the novel is a rejection of the talking cure, which simultaneously offers only a temporary alternative by impersonating a male voice.[98] To see the book as a part of Pappenheim's continuing development makes sense. But its relation to the talking cure is more complex than mere rejection. The novel takes up and modifies aspects of the therapy as Breuer reported it. This is clearest in the treatment of fairy tales. When Breuer and Pappenheim first started "chimney sweeping," it was fairy tales that were recounted (*Studien*, 22 / *Studies*, 82). The stories moved closer to Pappenheim's actual experiences, until the talking cure reached the point of minutely recalling the different occasions on which Pappenheim had suffered a particular symptom. *In der Trödelbude* similarly moves beyond fairy tales. But what changes is not the relation between the story and the life, since the stories continue to be told by inanimate objects. Instead the change is one of attitude. The characters in the stories of the pince-nez and of the music box are able to intervene in and transform their situations. As Pappenheim presents the transformation in the novel, the telling of one's own story is apparently less important than a narrative that empowers. This is understandable as soon as it is recalled that an individual's relation to a narrative is mediated by more than simply saying "I did *x* or *y*," since there is more to an individual's identity than the narrator of their self-image. Recollection and the reexperiencing of emotion remain important in the novel, but development and a change of attitude even more so. The novel lets something—a secondhand shop—grow that does not, at the outset, appear to warrant the title of an identity. It lets a broken man and some objects speak and in so doing recovers a sense of purpose and vitality.

Viewing a process of recovery from Pappenheim's perspective can thus be seen to add two significant elements to what we have already seen of the limitations of the relationship between Breuer and his patient. To recapitulate the limits from Breuer's side: He approached Pappenheim's well-behaved persona as the model of acceptable behavior and did not attempt to understand or integrate the behavior associated with the other, more troublesome side. Second, he did not let his role change as the intensity of the relationship increased. Each of these limitations has its equivalent when the problem is viewed from Pappenheim's perspective. If Breuer had assumptions about acceptable feminine behavior, so too did Pappenheim, since both shared the prejudices of their culture. When she wished to speak and be respected, she spoke with the voice of a man, or of damaged objects, not with the voice of a young woman. Woman, for Pappenheim, was, in effect, not a subject; identity was masculine. However, when she spoke as a man, or through the objects, she was at least able to arrive at a position where she could imagine the young girl being looked after. In an indirect way, the fictional text eventually addresses the needs of a feminine subject, albeit as they appear in the unthreatening form of a young girl. Breuer's own approach did not display even this degree of flexibility. He did not learn to recognize his patient in a role or form that he had not expected. In this sense, once again, the confessor in the *Sister Catherine* treatise shows far more willingness to experiment, as he lets the beguine leave him behind, but equally adapts to the changed woman who returns from her travels.[99]

The second significant aspect of her novel is the change of attitude, from fairy-tale passivity to active intervention. Breuer's therapy stopped before the roles of physician and woman patient were radically altered. The fictional text, in contrast, charts a development. Again, the development is skewed by gender prejudices. The most active characters are the shopkeeper Franz and Robert, the young man who trains to be an engineer. Ina acts too, but only to help Emma fulfill her romantic ambitions and become engaged. In this respect, the position of a beguine in the fourteenth century was easier, for it represented a recognized course of development, albeit one that was difficult for a woman to follow. Pappenheim had no such role. Being a hysteric was not a satisfactory long-term solution, and an alternative was barely imaginable until she had more contact with and encouragement from her cousin Anna Ettlinger. Even the role of social reformer that Pappenheim eventually adopted does not appear to have been completely satisfying. A poem written in 1911 ("Mir ward die Liebe nicht" [Love did not come to me]) records a sense of emptiness and suggests that work and a duty are no substitute for the reciprocity of love.[100]

When it is viewed in conjunction with Pappenheim's novel, Breuer's treatment can be seen to have reached its limits at the point where the physician, and to a lesser degree his patient, were unable to alter existing patterns of socially acceptable behavior. The failure of the case is finally a social failure. At the same time the treatment did point beyond its limitations, especially in those aspects that were most similar to the earlier undogmatic experiments of Blumhardt or Despine: the close rapport, the respect, the willingness to adapt to the new situation. This is not, however, how Breuer and Freud came to understand the therapy that they were developing. Their theoretical statements focus neither on the social determinants of behavior nor on the particular quality of the relationship between doctor and patient but rather on the recollection of emotions associated with a traumatic experience. The "Preliminary Communication" of 1893, in which they first presented cathartic talking, argued that memories from the past cause symptoms where the associated emotions were not "abreacted" at the time. These emotions can be relived and so discharged. "Recollection without affect almost invariably produces no result. The psychical process which originally took place must be repeated as vividly as possible; it must be brought back to its *status nascendi* and then given verbal utterance."[101] Breuer and Freud do not discuss the relationship that makes the reliving of emotional states possible, so they cannot consider whether the relationship itself is as important for the patient's recovery as is the recounting of traumatic events. Borch-Jacobsen has noted that the emphasis on the recall of traumatic events was added to Pappenheim's case when it was revised for publication in the 1890s, to match Breuer and Freud's interest in Charcot's model of hysteria. In the 1880s, Breuer "was nowhere near conceptualizing the stories that his patients told him in terms of 'traumatic memories.'"[102] The revision is an example of how theory obscured the observation of habits and the recording of experience in the development of psychoanalytic techniques. Freud continued this tendency even further than did Breuer. Breuer had been generally open-minded and receptive in his response to Pappenheim but finally unable to question or step beyond the gendered norms of behavior. This allowed Breuer's practice to be more flexible than the theory that it produced. In Freud's case, this element of flexibility was replaced by an approach that was led by theory rather than observation. As we will see in the case of "Dora" / Ida Bauer, Freud responds to the woman he has before him only insofar as her experiences can be made to confirm his speculative constructions. Where Breuer's treatment of Pappenheim engaged to a degree with the situation of his patient, Freud's treatment of Bauer almost totally ignores it, constructing a theoretical account of his patient's experiences, both with her family and in the consulting room, that bears little relation to what can be reconstructed of the events themselves. Freud's techniques continued to engage with patients on a practical level, if not always to therapeutic effect. But the theory that he developed did more to mystify than to illuminate the encounter.

Dora's Cultural Quest

Ida Bauer at age seventeen was sent to Freud by her father.[103] Hers was not an especially dramatic case of hysteria. The physical symptoms from which she was suffering were a nervous cough, loss of her voice, and occasional fainting fits (*Bruchstück*, 24–25). Her father wished Freud to be consulted after Bauer had claimed (in her father's view, falsely) that a friend of the family, Herr Zellenka, had made indecent advances. When her parents did not believe her, she had written a suicide note and insisted that her father stop seeing the woman, Frau Zellenka, who had nursed him while he was ill. In the course of the treatment it transpired that the pass made by Herr Zellenka had indeed occurred and was not the first one. When she was thirteen, he had cornered her and forced a kiss on her, having contrived a situation in which the young girl was alone with him. It was also true that her father was conducting an affair with Frau Zellenka and that both he and Frau Zellenka were willing to disregard Ida for the sake of preserving their relationship. Her father obfuscated when his daughter told him about Herr Zellenka, and Frau Zellenka betrayed the intimacy that she and Ida had previously enjoyed by saying that the allegations were the product of an overactive imagination, fired by reading Mantegazza's *Physiologie der Liebe* (Physiology of love). It turned out that Ida and Frau Zellenka had read the book together, but the shared reading was held against Ida when it suited the older woman.[104] Bauer's problems had first started when she was eight, and she suffered from breathing problems that doctors at the time had taken to be physiological in origin but that might also have had psychological causes. She discussed all these symptoms with Freud but did not complete the therapy, breaking off the sessions prematurely on December 31, 1900.[105]

Freud's record of the case suggests that he engaged with neither the possible physiological nor the emotional determinants of her condition. His theoretical presuppositions and his desire to maintain his ideas about infantile sexuality led him to disregard the possibility of a physical aetiology for some of Bauer's symptoms as well as to overlook many aspects of her family situation. On the physiological side: Bauer had long suffered from a vaginal catarrh (*Bruchstück*, 75). For Freud, this was proof that she masturbated as a child—a suspicion that, for him, was confirmed by Bauer's admission of stomach cramps, which, following Wilhelm Fließ (*Bruchstück*, 78), he believed to be a further indication of masturbation. Fließ's experiments with cocaine had led him to conclude that certain areas of the nose were linked to other areas of the body, because administering cocaine to these nasal reflex zones could relieve pain and other symptoms.

Fließ was unaware that cocaine entered the bloodstream through the nose and assumed it worked only as a local anaesthetic, suggesting esoteric affinities between the nose and the rest of the body. In his theory, he wove together stomach pains, masturbation, and "genital spots" in the nose to construct an erroneous sexual etiology for a variety of complaints.[106] Freud shared his erroneous beliefs about masturbation and imposed them on Bauer rather than investigating her vaginal catarrh further to discover if it was a relevant symptom. Bauer also suffered from a dragging foot after appendicitis. Freud interpreted this symptom as a hysterical staging of her desire to have had a child by Herr Zellenka.[107] Modern research, on the other hand, suggests that pelvic appendicitis could cause a dragging foot.[108] Freud's mistake was not that he could not make a diagnosis unavailable in 1900 but that his approach excluded possible physiological alternatives.

Freud also ignored his patient's emotional situation. On a superficial level, he supported Bauer in her debunking of relations in her family. He listened to her accounts of Herr Zellenka's impositions without denying them, and he also supported her claims about the affair between her father and Frau Zellenka. To that extent, he helped her view the family situation for what it was. This process reached its high point when, in the spring of 1901, Bauer visited the Zellenkas and called them both to account, making Frau Zellenka admit to her affair and Herr Zellenka to his advances (*Bruchstück*, 118–19). Nevertheless, Freud consistently made Bauer herself complicit in what had happened to her. He assumed that she must in fact desire Herr Zellenka and that the failure of the thirteen-year-old to experience sexual excitement when the older man imposed himself on her is abnormal, insisting that he would "unhesitatingly consider every individual for whom the occasion of possible sexual excitement primarily or exclusively calls forth feelings of displeasure to be hysterical."[109] In Freud's view, her symptoms were the product of her inability to admit that she desired Herr Zellenka, of her harboring a homosexual attachment to Frau Zellenka, and of her self-disgust at the damage she had done to her body by masturbating.[110] Where something had been done to Bauer (she has been assaulted by Herr Zellenka, her trust had been betrayed by Frau Zellenka and others, her father had put his own interests before hers), Freud turned the tables to suggest that her desire made her the co-perpetrator.

The problem with Freud's approach was not that it went against Bauer's understanding of her situation to explain how, on a level she was not aware of, her father's and Frau Zellenka's treatment of her should have so upset her.[111] Psychotherapy will often overturn the attitude that has led to the patient becoming ill, and to that it extent will question the patient's view of him- or herself.[112] The problem is rather that, in going beyond Bauer's initial grasp of the situation, Freud ceased to engage with her.[113] This can be seen in his interpretation of the two dreams recorded in the case history.

In the first dream, the house is on fire and Bauer's father stands at her bed. Her mother wants to go back and save her jewelery case, but her father says he does not want his two children (Ida and her brother) to burn for that.[114] In the second dream, Bauer is walking around a town that she does not know. She goes to her lodgings to find a letter that tells her that her father has died. She tries to find the station to go back home. However, she cannot reach it, even though, having entered a thick wood, the station is in sight. In the dream, she is then at home. The maid tells her that her mother and others are already at the cemetery. She goes up to her room and starts peacefully reading in a big book on her table.[115]

Freud used the dreams as evidence of the theory that he set out in *The Interpretation of Dreams*, arguing that they represented the fulfillment of a wish. The first dream, for Freud, uncovered Bauer's fear that she could give into Herr Zellenka. It also represented a maneuver by which Bauer could remember masturbating and desiring her father as a child but still cover over her illicit and unacknowledged desire for Herr Zellenka when she was a teenager.[116] The second dream, for Freud, showed Bauer identifying with the position of a man and imagining that she deflowered a woman. The book that she read was for Freud a lexicon about sex.[117] It is not possible fully to reinterpret the dreams without access to Bauer's own thoughts and feelings about them. Nevertheless, the material recorded in the case history allows one to make a few basic points suggesting directions that Freud did not follow up on but that are closer to the situation of his patient. The two dreams suggest the importance of Bauer's relationship with, and image of, her father. Freud recalls that the first dream recurred during the therapy itself, having first been dreamt after Herr Zellenka made his second pass.[118] Bauer's conversations with Freud confirmed her skeptical view of her father and offered her the space to voice her anger, as well as to place it in the wider context of her experiences as a child. In the first dream, her image of her father is upheld. Just as he had woken her as a child to stop her wetting the bed, so he appears in the dream to save his two children. Bauer's mother would rather save something valuable to her (the jewelery), but the father wants his two children. Ida Bauer remains her father's daughter. By the time of the second dream, she had left this image of her father behind. He is symbolically dead, and she is experiencing a freedom that Freud can understand only as masculine.

The change between the two dreams suggests that the therapy helped Bauer to alter her view of her own childhood and acknowledge that her father had not treated her as she would have wished. Freud himself also helped her inadvertently, by giving her the opportunity to experience the power she had as a young adult to leave the men who did not treat her properly. Freud suggested that, by breaking off the therapy, she was reenacting her past experiences and avenging herself on him in lieu of Herr Zellenka.[119] Jeffrey Masson suggests that the similarities that Bauer saw between Freud and both her father and Herr Zellenka were not the product of transference but instead real. Freud was as self-interestedly deceitful as Herr Zellenka while also repeating the attitudes of her father in refusing to support her against manipulative men.[120] To call this transference was to distract from the situation in the consulting room itself.

The problem with Freud's approach was that his alternative explanations of Dora's situation were determined to such a degree by his prejudices. As well as substituting his dubious assumptions about masturbation for an exploration of Bauer's own reactions to her experiences, he harbored prejudices about masculine and feminine behavior patterns that made it impossible for him to grasp that Ida Bauer could be active and in control in her own dream. Her dream of a relative freedom (she is somewhere new, her father is dead) is transformed into a fantasy of identifying with her own disempowerment or deflowering. (In a similar interpretative strategy, Freud inverted questions of agency when analyzing the "Wolf Man's" dream. The patient dreamt of six or seven wolves sitting motionless in a tree in front of his window, their ears "pricked like dogs when they pay attention to something."[121] However, just as the woman Bauer could not be interpreted as actively doing something in a dream, so the male patient could not be passive. Freud read the image of the boy being looked at by motionless animals as a distorted record of its opposite—the boy watching "a scene of violent movement at which he looked with strained attention.")[122]

From the evidence of Bauer's case history it is possible to reconstruct something of the development that Freud himself was unwilling or unable to engage with—even Freud's critics acknowledge the descriptive honesty of the case history, despite its interpretative willfulness.[123] To do so reveals parallels between the situations of Ida Bauer and Bertha Pappenheim and so restores something of the behavioral context of which Freud failed to take cognizance. One of Bauer's associations with the dream image of her exploring a new town was a visit to the Gemäldegalerie in Dresden, where she rejected the offer of a male cousin to guide her around and looked at paintings on her own at her own pace. In this visit, she spent two hours in front of Raphael's Sistine Madonna, saying to Freud that it was the figure of the Madonna herself that so fascinated her.[124] Bauer has a number of literary precursors in being struck by the painting, particularly in the Romantic period. These forebears in aesthetic appreciation clarify the fascination that the painting held for Bauer.

The painting was acquired for the gallery in Dresden in 1754 and in Winckelmann's *Reflexions on the Painting and Sculpture of the Greeks* (1755/56) was featured as a painting that inspired the pilgrimages of art lovers in a way comparable only to Praxiteles' Cupid at Thespiae.[125] The painting started to be reproduced in engravings and later as a postcard from 1780 onward and to become an image that embodied the very idea of painting for educated Germans, making it ripe for a parodic restaging by Kurt Schwitters in his 1921 montage picture *Knave Child Madonna with Horse*.[126] When Kleist passed through Dresden on his way to Paris after his nervous collapse early in 1801, it was this painting in particular that caught his imagination. "I have visited the Greek ideals and Italian masterpieces everyday, and each time I've gone into the gallery, I have stood for hours before the one Raphael in the collection, before that mother of God, with her high seriousness and quiet grandeur, oh Wilhelmine, and with features that reminded me simultaneously of two dear people."[127] Novalis was equally struck by the painting when he visited the Gemäldegalerie with Schelling and the Schlegel brothers in August 1798.[128] The conversation about paintings that August Wilhelm Schlegel published in *Athenaeum* in 1799 records something of this impression. The woman character, Louise, barely wants to talk about the image because it has made so deep an impression on her. Indeed, her companion Waller has observed her standing before it for two hours.[129] Later in the century, in a brief discussion in *Human, All Too Human*, Nietzsche returns to the painting as an example of Raphael's honesty. He praises Raphael for painting an image that lent itself to ecclesiastical and sensuous readings simultaneously.[130] Nietzsche is challenging the piety associated with the image, but the very fact that he chooses the painting for his cultural skirmishes betrays something of its place in the minds of educated German-speakers.

The early-nineteenth-century examples prefigure Bauer's extended solitary contemplation of the figure of the Madonna. "For tell me, who would not willingly throw themselves down beside these figures kneeling before the Virgin herself?"[131] The contemplation is not taken to be only religious. Kleist is reminded of people he loves. The Louise character in Schlegel's conversation specifically emphasizes the humanity of the figure.[132] Nietzsche similarly writes of the humanity and challenging immediacy of the image. The Madonna was the focus of a form of cultural pilgrimage as well as being a recurring point of reference for educated young people, and particularly young men. When Bauer went round the Gemäldegalerie alone and stood before the Raphael canvas, she joined this group of cultural aspirants.[133] That this group was predominantly masculine is registered in Freud's assumption that Bauer had adopted a male perspective in the dream. Just as writing entailed for Bertha Pappenheim the persona of the man Paul Berthold, so access to culture had similarly masculine connotations. Although the case history suggests that Bauer found it easier to transform her family position than Pappenheim had done, their cases are similar insofar as the difficulties they experienced were to a large degree the product of assumptions about acceptable behavior, and about femininity.[134]

The responses of their physicians were very different. There is no evidence of a close, cooperative rapport between Freud and Bauer. On the positive side, Freud gave Bauer time (analyzing her for six hours a week over the eleven weeks of the therapy), and he did not share the hypocrisy of her family. However, although the teenage Bauer was as independent of spirit as Pappenheim was, if not more so, this characteristic was not appreciated or fostered by Freud. He preferred to elaborate his theories about infantile masturbation and wish fulfilment rather than to engage with the situation Bauer experienced as a young woman, abused by family and friends but who, as well as wanting love and respect, aspired to having access to culture and to the freedom of development that that entailed. His grasp of the social interaction in which he was participating was so distorted by his theoretical presuppositions that he could grasp the change that Bauer underwent during the encounter only as her recognizing her desire for Herr Zellenka.[135] He could not get a clearer sense of the constraints on the young woman's life or of the mistreatment she had suffered or the aspirations she might have. He described the situation but he did not understand it.

The wider consequence of this attitude was that neither the practice nor the theory of psychoanalysis, as Freud developed it, helped consciously to ameliorate the position of his patients. Psychoanalytic practice retained little of the intense rapport that had characterized the relationship between Breuer and Pappenheim. Indeed, as Abram de Swaan suggests in his reconstruction of the sociogenesis of the psychoanalytic setting, the therapy was designed precisely to control this intensity.[136] In his account, psychoanalysis offered a neutral space in which the individual could acknowledge and reflect on feelings and impulses that his or her social identity otherwise proscribed. During the 1880s and 1890s, Freud still visited his patients in their houses, but he increasingly stayed at home. This reflected the contemporary trend of doctors staying at their practices as their equipment became more bulky. But in the case of psychoanalysis, the doctor's practice offered seclusion as much as it reduced the inconvenience of journeys across town. Freud also made the encounter, as de Swaan sees it, progressively more neutral. He leased time by the hour, eliminated manipulations by the therapist, such as hypnosis or temple massage, sat behind the patient, and turned the emotions that arose between patient and doctor into an analytic tool by treating them as a transference of emotions from earlier relationships. The technique of free association encouraged the patient to let his or her mind wander and explore without reproof. The result was what de Swaan calls a "social null-situation."[137] However, the case of Ida Bauer shows how little the practice could actually be described as neutral. It was marked by Freud's presuppositions. It was also emotionally charged. If one of the key elements of the healing process is the generosity of spirit that one finds in Breuer and Blumhardt or in some of the more open-minded confessors of the fourteenth century, then the absence of such warmth will be as palpable to the patient as will its presence. Rather than being encouraged to grow emotionally, patients who followed Freud's example would learn to distance themselves from their inner life. It is perhaps unfair to brand either Freud or the practice he helped to create as emotionally cold. Bruno Bettelheim has written in spirited defense of the humanity and direct emotional appeal of Freud's texts, and from the reading of a case history such as Winnicott's *The Piggle* it is clear that a commitment to a psychoanalytic vocabulary does not necessarily preclude openness and warmth.[138] Nevertheless there are aspects of both the theory and the practice of psychoanalysis as elaborated by Freud that obstruct rather than facilitate the human encounter, fostering distance rather than nurturing development. Indeed, the next section will show how the problematic aspects of Freud's approach distort the very concepts that he developed to understand the experiences with which he was daily confronted, particularly in his conceptualization of the unconscious.

Unwitting or Inattentive but Not Unconscious

Freud in the essay "The Unconscious" (1915) explicitly described his model of the mind as Kantian.[139] For both Freud and Kant, the individual can know external reality and inner life only through the filter of conscious categories. Like the Kantian "thing in itself," reality, for Freud, including the reality of the unconscious, remains ineffable. "The real will always remain 'unknowable.'"[140] In his view, this is the position of any science, which will always be limited to cataloguing and understanding effects rather than knowing their ultimate causes. To understand the effects of the unconscious, Freud developed a number of metaphorical models for systematizing his observations. He created an imaginary topography to explain how conscious, preconscious, and unconscious relate to each other, as well as developing a model of mental actions along the lines of an economy of fluids (pressure building up, drives being diverted, etc.). He frequently also used, in addition to the spatial and dynamic metaphors, political metaphors to explain how the mind works, such as his image of the (political) censor in *The Interpretation of Dreams*.[141] After 1895, he did not attempt to correlate his models of the mind with biological insights into the functioning of the brain but rather limited himself to refining the description of mental activity. His first major metapsychological statement was the final section of *The Interpretation of Dreams*. The statement is particularly interesting because it suggests how aware he was from the outset of the difficulties presented by his spatial metaphors, especially if they are thought to refer to a particular area of the brain, which they do not.[142] However, the confusion between mind and brain is less important for understanding the limits of Freud's theory than is the association that the spatial metaphors create of the unconscious as a separate alien realm. Strictly speaking, if Freud is seeing the unconscious through the filter of conscious categories, he cannot know that the unconscious is alien. He can only know that to consciousness the unconscious appears, or is made to appear, alien, just as an enemy will be made to appear alien by the propaganda of a government that believes the person or group so vilified to be a threat. However, rather than leave open the question of what the unconscious is, Freud, as his theory develops, progressively distills a set of attributes that radically differentiate it from consciousness. He calls these attributes primary processes and distinguishes them from the secondary processes by which we learn logically to order our thoughts as we grow up. As he sets them out in 1915, the attributes are that the unconscious knows no negation and can entertain contradictory desires without relating them to each other. It knows no degrees of certainty, only weaker or stronger pulses. In order to find a release for impulses, it will displace or condense them beyond recognition. Finally, it has no sense of time, and it is not interested in the practical feasibility of its desires, replacing external reality with the demands of inner life.[143]

The questionable aspects of this model of mental processes become apparent when it is compared with more-recent findings. During the last two decades, research in a number of areas of psychology and cognitive science has drawn attention to so-called subpersonal processes—that is, neurochemical or neurological processes that will necessarily stay below the threshold of our perceptual awareness because they contribute to the construction of our very sense of awareness or because they occur independently of our sense of awareness. The research draws attention, on the one hand, to a level of behavior on which our normal habits of acknowledging or denying responsibility don't function, and, on the other hand, to areas for which there are everyday habits of negotiation and acknowledgment that are comparable to, and indeed useful substitutes for, the psychoanalytic tools of free association and the talking cure. A brief and necessarily selective consideration of recent findings can clarify the limits of the Freudian model of the unconscious and so prepare the way for an exploration, in the concluding chapter, of ways in which, disburdened of Freud's model of the unconscious mind, we can return to the work of Freud and his contemporaries around 1900 to develop an everyday language for acknowledging what we unwittingly or inattentively do to and with other people.

The three areas of investigation I want to look at to contrast with the Freudian model are the research into automatic reactions, by, among other groups, John A. Bargh's lab in Yale; possible connections between automaticity research and the research of cognitive scientists into mirror neurons; and, finally, J. Allan Hobson's findings about dreaming and the neurochemistry of sleep. Bargh and his colleagues have devised experiments to discover habits and expectations that shape our action without our being aware of it. For instance, priming people with the words *rude* or *patient* will make people behave rudely or patiently without their being aware of it or intentionally altering their behavior. Similarly, a subject who has been primed by words associated in their culture with old age (in the American example: *Florida*, *bingo*, *forgetful*) will walk significantly more slowly down a corridor than someone who hasn't, even though the question of speed has not been mentioned nor aging been made an explicit part of the experiment.[144] In such cases, we take on characteristics and behavior patterns associated with the stereotype with which we have been primed. Indeed, it's enough just to see someone to be primed to behave like them: "The very act of perceiving another person's behavior creates the tendency to behave that way oneself."[145] As well as imitating involuntarily, we automatically give, in ways we are not aware of but that then shape our response to a situation, an emotional tone to stimuli, and in particular to faces, that we encounter. Bargh explains this by drawing on experiments that have shown direct neuronal connections in animals between acoustic areas of the brain and the emotion-processing amygdala. He hypothesizes that "affective information is processed immediately and non-consciously by a separate mental system."[146] Finally, Bargh and colleagues also suggest that, in addition to involuntary emotional responses and the acting out of other people's behavior, our more abstract thought patterns, such as moral deliberations, are shaped by more-basic habits—in other words, that the pursuit of goals fundamental to our survival, such as warmth, safety, and cleanliness, establishes a structure that shapes our more-sophisticated actions. Thus, physical feedback on cleanliness affects our moral judgements, so that, even without our being Pontius Pilate, washing our hands can make us feel that a moral goal has been achieved regardless of whether the problem we're faced with has actually been resolved.[147] They conclude: "The subtlety of these effects of the physical environment and hardwired goals on higher-order cognition calls into question how much control human beings actually have over their mental lives."[148]

The research on automatic behavior patterns suggests a model of mental activity in which a number of systems responding independently of each other and also of our conscious deliberations influence our actions. Some of Bargh's formulations suggest an underlying assumption of a brain separated from the world and responding to it by screening and classifying; that is to say, they seem to start from the position of an isolated subject in a way that was criticized in the first part of this book.[149] However, there are other formulations in which our involvement with our environment and with others is clearer. The environment to a certain extent acts through us, prompting automated processes in the same way that, for Dewey, "natural operations like breathing and digesting, acquired ones like speech and honesty, are functions of the surroundings as truly as of a person. They are things done *by* the environment by means of organic structures or acquired dispositions."[150] Similarly, the responses that Bargh and his colleagues document to the appearance and behavior of others suggest that it does not make sense to conceive of people as separate or separable agents of action but rather as participants in an ongoing situation.

Paula Niedenthal and Martha Alibali, who point out the possible connections between the work of Bargh's group and research on mirror neurons, have emphasized this element of participation.[151] Work on automated responses has shown how we are influenced by the behavior of others and by our own sense of typical traits; it has also suggested that our more complex thought patterns depend on the framework established by our pursuit of basic physical goals such as warmth, safety, and cleanliness. Research on mirror neurons brings these two elements together. As we saw in chapter 3, the phenomenon was first noticed at the University of Parma, in monkeys responding to the purposive actions of their human captors with the same neurons that would fire if the monkeys themselves were to perform the actions.[152] Subsequent work has established similar groups of neurons in human brains and also noted that they fire in response not just to motor actions but also to facial expressions and emotions.[153] What links the different responses is the common element of a goal: Our mirror neurons resonate with the meaningful, goal-oriented actions of others. We live in a world of shared goals and participate in the goals even when we are not directly acting ourselves.

The research on automatic responses and on mirror neurons combine to suggest a model of human behavior much of which occurs below the threshold of conscious awareness as we participate in the common goals and shared dispositions of our culture. If we're not aware of this participation, this is for two different reasons. One is that the participation occurs at a subpersonal level, before or alongside our more conscious analyses of a situation. The second is that the participation is too obvious to be noticed. If we imitate the gestures of our interlocutor, or fall in step with our companion when we walk, we don't notice the communality of action because it is part of the tuning in to each other that establishes the shared backdrop that gives us things to notice and reasons for noticing them in the first place.

In relation to Freud's model, it's important to note that we don't, at this level of behavior, follow goals or adopt a logic that are qualitatively distinct from the goals and logic of our more considered responses. On the contrary, our rational deliberations are themselves copies or redeployments of primitive behavior patterns in pursuit of the easily intelligible goals of survival. Furthermore, we don't need an idea of a censor or of repression to explain the unavailability of some areas of mental activity to conscious deliberation. Instead, behavior can be seen to occur "below the radar" for neurological or phenomenological reasons and in both cases can potentially become the focus of our shared attention. Where the cause is neurological, it needs the complex, collective activity of scientific experiment to disclose what's going on; where it's phenomenological we need a reason for changing our habits, and an interlocutor or two to help us think about and draw attention to things that we otherwise take for granted. But in neither case do we need to posit an area that is constitutively unavailable to us or necessarily alien. Instead, we need to ask what prompts Freud, or successors such as Žižek, to follow the Kantian line that individuals are in some disturbing way always at one remove from their experience: assailed by a traumatic immediacy that they can at the same time never immediately encounter.[154] In other words, we need to see the Freudian model of the unconscious as the expression of an attitude, as part of a project and way of being in, or of avoiding, the world, rather than as a neutral description to be reproduced or imitated.

Before moving on to elaborate in more detail an alternative model for the behavior we participate in but do not notice, we might note a third strand of recent research worth mentioning, since it offers an account of the bizarreness of dream images that Freud believed to be the result of primary processes as they eluded the censorship of our conscious mind. J. Allan Hobson's research on dreams at the Harvard Medical School has helped to establish a picture of the changes in the chemical environment that occur in the brain during sleep. The bizarreness of dream images is not the result of a standoff between forbidden desires and our censorious self-image but rather the product of the chemical changes accompanying the brain's nocturnal self-reconstruction during REM sleep.[155] There is a statistical (as opposed to an absolute) correlation between dreaming and REM sleep—that is, most but not all dreams occur at night when our eyes are moving. Hobson's research has helped to establish that "REM sleep dreaming is mediated by [the neurotransmitter] acetylcholine when noradrenalin and serotonin are at very low levels."[156] What this means in practice is an activation of those areas of the brain linked to hyperassociation, instinct, and emotion (areas of the limbic brain such as the amygdala and white matter of the forebrain), and a deactivation of those associated with self-awareness and orientation—in a word: a chemical recipe for the emotional intensity and illogicality of dream images that Freud associated with the id.[157] Desires, therefore, are not concealed in dreams but rather directly disclosed.[158] Dreams are not censored versions of a disguised and alien unconscious but rather contain images of "direct and undisguised emotional salience."[159] At the same time, dreams, for Hobson, help us to learn and adapt. They are part of the process whereby individual memories are transformed into or allowed to revise existing dispositions and habits for acting. As a result: "No longer a cauldron of dread desire, my unconscious procedural repertoire is both rich in sources and ready to respond. I don't have to think about most of what I do. It just happens: automatically, appropriately, and adaptively."[160] Indeed, Hobson goes so far as to hypothesize that, in REM sleep, we are not only learning the patterns of behavior that constitute our response repertoire in waking life but, over the years of development from the start of REM sleep in the third trimester of pregnancy through to the establishment of a mature adult identity, we are also gradually going through the complex process of establishing a sense of self that can take responsibility for the behavior patterns and dispositions that are in the first place—and in fact—automatic.[161]

So where does that leave the Freudian model of the unconscious? We've seen that recent research in the fields of automatic responses, mirror neurons, and the science of sleep confirms how much of our behavior is not governed by conscious deliberation. We act out shared patterns of behavior, in concert with others if often unwittingly, and reinforce and relearn these patterns in our sleep. The patterns are emotionally powerful and often kick in before, and set the tone for, our intellectual appraisal of a situation. However, if we are not aware of the things we do at this level, it is not so much because we repress responses as because they occur independently of our higher-level cognitive processing. Moreover, the distinction between primary and secondary processes does not seem helpful. Not only are patterns of abstract thought redeploying and entangled with habits formed in the pursuit of fundamental bodily needs, but the associative patterns characteristic of dreams and hysterical symptoms are also a normal feature of our waking life. The characteristics that Freud associates with the unconscious or with primary processes are the by-product of the way our brain processes stimuli in different areas simultaneously. Following Daniel Dennett's empirically based model, we might say that consciousness can be understood as "some sort of serial virtual machine implemented on the parallel hardware of the brain."[162] The fragmentary, overdetermined, and associative patterns of our dreams are therefore not the product of a mysterious other logic but are rather a cholinergically heightened version of the usual mental pandemonium of "opportunistic, parallel, evolutionary processes" from which, at any particular moment, a narrative of individual awareness arises.[163]

So why does Freud stress so much the alien nature of the unconscious and put it, metaphorically at least, in a different space from consciousness? So far my argument has not discussed the degree to which behavior is socially policed. There is plenty of behavior that is available to us neurologically and phenomenology but that, because it is socially disapproved of, we relate to in the indirect way of pretending it's not happening or pretending it's got nothing to do with us, just as Freud's patient the governess Miss Lucy R., who was haunted by the smell of burnt pudding, could not admit to herself that she was in love with her employer: "I didn't know—or rather I didn't want to know. I wanted to drive it out of my head and not think of it again; and I believe latterly I have succeeded."[164] Miss Lucy R.'s case is particularly pertinent because her unwillingness to admit being in love is not because she disapproves of sexual desire ("one can't be held to account for one's feelings"), or indeed because her desire is in some sense unknowable, but because of the social consequences of loving above her station: She didn't want to be laughed at by her fellow servants.[165] So in addition to the neurological and phenomenological limits to what we observe, there will also be the area of things we know but don't want to know—that we relate to, as Heidegger might have put it, in the deficient mode of keeping them at a distance.

This is the very tactic Freud deploys in his construction of the unconscious as a separate, alien space, keeping embarrassing impulses at a distance. Freud confuses the sense of alienation that accompanies an unwanted or forbidden thought with the associative process by which the mind works and uses the latter as an erroneous explanation of the former. His theory of the unconscious could be said to be based on a rhetorical figure—hypallage, or the transference of an epithet—that is effective precisely because an individual would prefer to be able to dismiss as alien a thought that contradicts his or her own self-image.

Sartre argued something similar in his brief critique of the idea of the unconscious in *Being and Nothingness* where he suggested that the unconscious was not the product of a radically different mode of functioning of the brain but rather of bad faith—of a subject not wanting to admit something that he or she in fact well knows.[166] But Sartre's self-deceiving individual is fundamentally alone, kidding himself as he struggles to be recognized by other isolated and self-deceiving individuals.[167] The idea of bad faith does not have to remain individualized, as Heidegger's discussion of collective evasiveness under the heading of *das Man* [the They] in *Being and Time* makes clear.[168] A group can, through its shared habits, collude in keeping at bay the things it knows but prefers not to acknowledge, using the shared sense of appropriate behavior to affect this policing. One possible reason for the success of psychoanalysis, therefore, as Wittgenstein saw early on, is that it tells us something we want to hear even if we protest that we don't.[169] It tells us a comfortable uncomfortable truth about ourselves—a scandal we can learn to live with. Karl Kraus's critical quip that psychoanalysis is the malady for which it believes itself to be the cure in this respect seems astute.[170] By conceptualizing the unconscious as a spatially distinct, alien realm, Freud is modifying rather than overturning the habits by which difficult impulses were managed by displacement and denial in the Vienna of 1900. His model of the unconscious distances the patient from impulses and emotions in the same way that the neutrality of the consulting room distances him or her from a lived rapport. Psychoanalysis, as Freud developed it, extended the very social control that his hysterical patients were attempting to escape.

The case histories of Bertha Pappenheim and Ida Bauer give us a sense of what this social policing particularly focused on, or what, in other words, felt most uncomfortable to Freud and his contemporaries. Pappenheim's treatment was given up at the point where it would have been necessary for doctor and patient to transform their roles beyond those of the family doctor helping a young girl maintain her self-understanding as obedient daughter. Freud's reading of the Breuer/Pappenheim case was that the two inadvertently stumbled on the problem of transference—that is, on the patient's living out of unacknowledged sexual desires in the relationship with the therapist—but did not have the courage to confront it.[171] Yet Freud's treatment of Ida Bauer suggests that a sexualized understanding of the etiology of hysteria was not in itself the solution. Talking about sex was not a challenge for Freud; rather, he seems to have relished the provocation. In contrast, it was hard for him to imagine that Ida Bauer could grow beyond the role allotted to her by her father or by her therapist and to acknowledge his own part in the cycles of maltreatment. Both case histories suggest that the two aspects of behavior that needed to be most keenly policed were growth, be it psychological or spiritual, and personal involvement.[172]

In the final chapter, I want to return to texts by Freud and his contemporaries to see what can be learned about the policing of spiritual growth and personal involvement in our everyday interactions if we no longer look at the material through the lens of the Freudian theory of the unconscious. The hope is that by returning to the work of Freud in particular but also to that of other contemporaries such as William James, Arthur Schnitzler, or Jung in the creative period of the 1890s and early 1900s, before the concepts that became psychoanalysis had been firmly established, we can find ideas and resources for revisiting and renewing our own psychological habits. This defamiliarizing view can be achieved if we step back from Freud to reconstruct what he is doing as opposed to what he says he's doing, and to ascertain what role his texts play in the wider attempts of his culture to come to terms with human togetherness. The lead for such a return to context has been set by Frank Sulloway in his article "Reassessing Freud's Case Histories," in which he reconstructs the change observable in Freud's approach after the publication of the *Studies on Hysteria*. Sulloway shows how the authors of the *Studies* still understood themselves to be part of a scientific community, sharing methods and ideas and presenting them for scrutiny and comment. This progressively changed. "Instead of trusting that his methods would withstand critical scrutiny and flourish independent of opposition, Freud privatized the mechanism of their dissemination and trained a movement of loyal adherents."[173]

Sulloway's article opens up the possibility of returning to the beginnings of psychoanalysis and assessing Freud's practice in a language that is not defined by the polemic for and against psychoanalytic theory. Sulloway himself is not very interested in the emotional aspects of this archeological reconstruction. But his study indicates the undogmatic, practical level on which the debate about the historical forms of our relations to others and ourselves could continue. The aim of the debate should be to describe, in an open-minded and sensitive way, the habits and assumptions by which people manage their emotional life, and the sorts of actions and relationships that are helpful for improving their situation. The most significant casualty of this approach is psychoanalytic theory. The concepts people find for their activities are of less importance than what they are actually doing. Methodologically speaking, this returns us to Foucault and his insistence that one study how discourses and institutions function in practice rather than limiting oneself to what a culture says about itself.[174] However, the focus has moved to psychological and emotional practices in a way that was never the case in Foucault's work.

Before embarking on this return to fin-de-siècle Vienna, however, I need to make explicit an assumption about how people work that has informed and been strengthened by the critique of Freud; that will be central to the defamiliarizing reassessment of Freud in the next chapter; and that can be further clarified by a brief consideration of Jung's version of the unconscious: That is the assumption of a certain dynamism in our psychological and spiritual lives. The encounters between Breuer and Pappenheim and between Freud and Bauer appear, in retrospect, to betray the expectations they arouse, because the physician in both cases does not finally support the development of his patient. Where the confessor in the *Sister Catherine* treatise lets the beguine go against expectations and himself is willing to transform his role, or where Eckhart insists that there is no single model for spiritual development but rather enjoins his listeners to attend to and abandon what specifically limits them, Breuer does not pursue the therapy with Pappenheim beyond the point where it demands more change than he believes to be socially responsible, and Freud develops a theory of what's going on in place of attending to the specifics of the case before him.

My critique of Breuer and Freud is thus premised on the idea that Breuer and Pappenheim and Freud and Bauer were engaged in a ongoing process that they interrupted—in other words, that their encounters were dynamic and that human interaction can be evaluated according to how it relates to this dynamism. Is it fostered, displaced, or constrained? Does everyone involved change equally, or is change delegated to one more than others? How is the change understood? Is it a spiritual growth (God moving through an individual; an individual moving closer to God)? Is it psychological (the flourishing a specific life; the overcoming of personal obstacles)? Is it feared? Celebrated? Or mistrusted? Such questions and the concomitant commitment to an idea of psychological or spiritual momentum are not something I can delay until I have enough evidence to know whether growth actually occurs, since I will never stand outside my life to see if it is finally going anywhere. At the same time, it's not just an article of faith. Rather, it's something I cannot avoid, since in the process of socialization I become aware that I'm joining a group activity that is already in full swing. Moreover, my own body and the bodies of those around me are also in a state of change. Change is what happens to me and what I must take a stance on, even though it will continue regardless of my attitude to it.

Jung's model of the unconscious includes something like this emphatic sense of change, where Freud, whatever his practice, in his theory hopes at best for a cure and an element of self-understanding, and, in the later writings such as *Civilization and Its Discontents*, adopts the bleaker picture of a humanity turned constitutively against itself, with individuals venting on themselves the aggressive drives that their dependence on others prevents them from taking out on their companions.[175] For Jung, the unconscious follows a dynamic of its own, or is, as he calls it, purposive.[176] Something is moving through us that Jung encourages us to treat with respect and curiosity rather than attempting to control it. Whatever unfolds through us will follow a purpose, even if it is not one that we would have initially recognized as our own. The individual's task is to be open-minded enough to hear what it is saying without being overwhelmed by it or trying to translate it into images or a vocabulary other than the ones it chooses to use.[177] As Jung says of the therapist's response to dreams: "The doctor should regard every dream as something new, as a source of information about conditions whose nature is unknown to him, concerning which he has as much to learn as the patient. It goes without saying that he should give up all his theoretical assumptions and should in every case be ready to construct a totally new theory of dreams."[178] As individuals learn to understand what is moving through them, they will also let their conscious control be displaced. Like mystical texts of the fourteenth century, Jung uses a phrase from St. Paul's letter to the Galatians to describe this attitude: "And I no longer live but Christ lives in me" (Galatians 2:20).[179] The Christian vocabulary is no accident. Jung's view of the unconscious is, in the broadest sense, religious. In his view, every society is cultivating a relationship with what he calls the "numinous," be it in the form of spirits, gods, a God, or ideals. Such behavior is an anthropological given.[180] Psychotherapy, and the process of individuation it supports, means learning to allow the numinous to move through us unhindered.

The purposive unfolding that Jung presupposes in his account of the unconscious seems quaintly old-fashioned in a world in which teleology has been abandoned in favor of open-ended Darwinian evolution. However, the idea lends itself to being formulated in other terms, such as those of Hobson's hypothesis about the function of REM sleep and dreaming in the development of habitual dispositions and of a sense of self to take responsibility for them. Hobson's account allows for a growth that is adaptive, and it has an end point—an accountable self—without being as explicitly teleological as Jung's: Our dispositions and sense of self will be revised and altered as circumstances demand. Of course, if we take seriously Jung's comments about not having a theory in advance, the teleological aspect of his approach is not a problem anyway. Growth and a sense of purposive unfolding can be acknowledged without the claim being made that the end point is known. Indeed, one aspect of real growth is that we don't know where it's going; it's an expansion that takes us beyond what we're used to and forces us to improvise new habits and ways of acting.

If there is a limit to Jung's approach, it is the focus on inner impulses as opposed to things that we do with other people. Jung no less than Freud separates what he calls the unconscious from the historical encounters through which it will be experienced. On the one hand, there are many ways his approach, with its refreshing insistence on literal readings, seems to promise more specificity. Jung criticizes the process of free association because it leads away from the material explicitly presented in a dream.[181] He also insists that the issues that cause an individual to be sick arise from his or her situation in the present rather than from an unacknowledged past.[182] Both of these ideas fit with his general desire to engage undogmatically with what is before him rather than jump to a meaning hidden behind it. On the other hand, these theoretical insights are in themselves no sure indicator that Jung could be that receptive in practice. His texts tend to overlook the element of human interaction, amplifying a dream image with its mythical resonances but not being especially interested in the social structures that shape an individual's relationship to their inner life. The archetypal images of the collective unconscious are for Jung hereditary.[183]

This suggests a blindness to the day-to-day habits through which the management of emotions occurs. Indeed one could speculate that it was in particular a blindness to gender patterns that turned Jung's attention away from the day-to-day habits through which the relationship to our dynamic involvements is managed to the more grandiose territory of its mythological genealogy. His comments on the "animus," the masculine part of woman's psyche and the equivalent to the "anima" in a man, are tritely misogynist. When controlled by his anima, a man is the victim of mood swings and irrational outbursts for which his conscious self can give no rational account. In the case of women it is the very ability to think that is banished to the unconscious to be taken over by collective forces. A man surrenders to uncontrollable emotions, a woman is the helpless victim of received opinions and beliefs that she cannot rationally defend but that possess her with the same violence as an uncontrolled passion.[184] Even if we agree that Jung is accurately observing the behavior of his contemporaries, other explanations are imaginable than the one he gives; ones that look at the shared habits through which different psychological duties are delegated to the different sexes or at the symbiotic division of labor that often establishes itself in couples or between siblings. Jung's approach is useful where it offers tools for coming to terms with the dynamism of our spiritual and psychological lives, but to develop a more specific sense of the relationships, routines and rituals through which the dynamic is managed, we need to look elsewhere.

The elsewhere that we need to look is not another text or a better theory. Rather than looking elsewhere, it is more accurate to say we need to look differently and focus our attention on habits and relationships and on what people do with their words as much as what they say. Guided by the assumption of something unfolding through people's shared activities, we need to pay attention to how we relate to this unfolding. In principle this change of view could start anywhere. The next chapter will turn to psychological vocabulary around 1900 and in particular to Freud's *The Psychopathology of Everyday Life*, for two reasons. First, it is a text in which the way of life from which the deliberations emerge is particularly visible, as Freud collects encounters from his everyday life and adds those of other people sent to him for later editions of the book. It is a book that makes the step from the words to what people were doing with them relatively easy. Second, the context it was written in is particularly illuminating, since it's one in which there was the desire to establish a psychological vocabulary—even the hope of a common vocabulary in Esperanto with which psychologists all over the world could share their ideas—but the vocabulary had not yet been fixed, nor had the institutions, practical methods, and rituals that were to become the basic forms of the discipline finally established themselves.[185] It's a moment of exploration, discovering what psychology might yet be, and to that extent it is a fruitful place to explore if we want to revise and revitalise our psychological assumptions.

However, if returning to this context we are blinded by what subsequently happened, it won't be possible to surprise ourselves out of our preconceptions. So the chapter approaches Freud's text by the historical detour of the first recorded analysis of a slip of the tongue, that of the satirist Lucian of Samosata, of the Second Sophistic, some time toward the end of the second century of the Common Era.

9

Everyday Acknowledgments

A Classical Slip of the Tongue

With *The Psychopathology of Everyday Life*, Freud hoped to transform everyday interactions, as he drew attention to the unacknowledged impulses that accompany and interrupt our day-to-day exchanges and challenged us to face up to them. To put Freud's approach in context and so come to a revised sense of how we might transform our relationship with our everyday life, I want to start with a slip of a literal kind and then move on to a text that could literally be called the locus classicus for analyses of slips of the tongue, Lucian's second-century dissection of his own "Slip of the Tongue in Greeting." The discussion of the literal and the classical slips will allow me to elaborate a phenomenological account of what makes slips possible, setting out the context that we have to presuppose in order for a slip even to be noticeable as a slip. When we have established this background, it will be easier to avoid the false choice of supporting or opposing Freud's account of everyday life and so to see more clearly the wider project of which his approach was one influential variant: negotiating the shared space of our physical and emotional life.

To start with the literal slip: In the senior common room of my college in Oxford, the floor of the loo very often has on it drops of urine left behind by the inattention of whichever of my male colleagues still stand when they pee. This urinary incompetence occurs often enough to be more than a random event, there is a certain logic or intentionality behind the phenomenon—but of what sort? It's an action that could lend itself to a psychological reading, as a marking of territory, or a reestablishing of power in a secure place where there are no social witnesses to contradict or intervene.[1] But rather than presupposing a psychological framework into which we can slot the habit, the habit itself can be used to help us get a clearer view of how our psychological frameworks themselves function.

To get the issue in focus, it helps to quickly rule a few options out, using as a guide J. L. Austin's reflections on the language of individual agency as they are recorded in the notes for his lecture "Three Ways of Spilling Ink." Austin considers three everyday adverbs used to qualify accounts of people's actions—the terms *intentionally*, *deliberately*, and *on purpose*—hoping in the process to make explicit some of the shades of variation in the way we act that are acknowledged in everyday language. He starts from the assumption that "questions of whether a person was responsible for this or that are prior to questions of freedom"; in other words, that we look at the circumstances of an action before proceeding to an analysis of free agency.[2] The three adverbs he focuses on are the tools developed by ordinary language for mulling such issues over: Was the person who peed on the floor responsible for his action? Did he do it intentionally, deliberately, or on purpose? The comparison with Austin's reflections is illuminating because it highlights the degree to which the terms he is investigating for everyday reflections on responsibility don't apply in this case. In most circumstances we wouldn't say that my colleagues peed on the floor intentionally, deliberately or on purpose, since peeing on the floor was not one of the intended effects of their actions, it was not something they particularly thought about, and it was not something they did to achieve a particular effect. Rather, they didn't need to think about it at all. It was an action that wasn't managed or controlled in that much detail. Since no one was observing them and they are not responsible for cleaning the toilet themselves, it's likely that they did not even notice it had happened, indeed that they didn't even notice that there was anything they should be noticing. In order for peeing on the ground to be an embarrassing mistake and so to qualify as a slip, there would need to be others around to call us to account for it. Slips thus need not only a shared space and a sense of what is appropriate but also a witness. They are a form of bungled togetherness.

The toilet example also suggests that there is a way of routinely inhabiting and using a space for which the idea of a slip is meaningless. Where our right or power to use a space is unchallengeable and the issue of taking responsibility for what we do doesn't arise, we can't meaningfully be said to make a slip. Or rather, to call something a slip in these circumstances means trying to initiate a conversation about a new area of behavior for which we should allow ourselves to be called to account. Slips are thus a form of bungled togetherness which, at the same time, draw attention to the way our behavior falls, to speak loosely, into two categories: things we do for which we can be called to account, and things that slip under the radar of accountability. Slips can occur only in those areas for which we generally take responsibility.

Having discussed these basic phenomenological markers for the situation of making a mistake, we can turn to Lucian, whose exploration of why he used the wrong greeting when he paid a morning visit to his patron is the first written examination of such a slip.[3] Lucian of Samosata (ca. 120–190) was a Syrian writing in a cultured, Attic Greek whose satirical and ethnological observations of his contemporaries return again and again to the question of what counts as appropriate, cultured, Greek behavior in the context of the Roman Empire.[4] In their sensitivity to what Tim Whitmarsh has called the "performance" of Greek identity—that is to say, in their awareness of the changing and learnable framework that constitutes social interaction—Lucian's texts add a further element to the phenomenology of slips.[5] In addition to the bungling of togetherness in the arena of shared action, they suggest, as we shall see, that the question of what counts as bungled and which behavior belongs in the arena of shared acknowledgment is being constantly negotiated. Before we look at Lucian's text, it should be added that if Lucian explicitly reflects on the construction of appropriate behavior, thus preparing the way for a discussion of slips in turn-of-the-century Vienna, his texts were also a feature in the cultural landscape in which Freud was writing. Paul Lindau published three stage adaptations of a Lucian's satires in 1902.[6] A version of Lucian's dialogue *Die Fahrt über den Styx* (*The Downward Journey, or the Tyrant*) was subsequently performed at Vienna's *Lustspieltheater* and discussed in 1906 in Karl Kraus's journal *Die Fackel* (The torch) in the same short entry in which Kraus clarifies that the pseudonym Lucianus being used by one of his collaborators since 1905 is not actually Lucian.[7] While Lucian was available as a cultural reference to Freud's contemporaries, Freud himself did not cite him, despite the classical writer's treatment of the very subject matter of *The Psychopathology of Everyday Life*, but drew instead on Ovid, Plato, and Sophocles, perhaps because Lucian had been dismissed as a figure of intellectual merit in an influential book published by Jacob Bernays, the uncle of Freud's future bride, in 1879.[8] Where the *Interpretation of Dreams* discussed historical precursors in dream interpretation and offered a first version of Freud's reading of the Oedipus myth, *The Psychopathology of Everyday Life* makes reference only to some contemporary psychologists and a few literary precursors, such as Shakespeare and Schiller, but makes no mention of Freud's classical forebear.[9] What we learn about slips from looking in more detail at Lucian's text was thus something potentially available to Freud's contemporaries but not explicitly thought: a significant absence not filled until Halpern's Freudian reading of Lucian's text in 1962.[10]

Lucian discusses the slip (*to ptaisma*) he made when greeting his patron, wishing him health (*hugiainein*) (the greeting appropriate in the evening or when taking leave) when the situation called for him to wish him joy (*chairein*); so he made a slip a little like walking into the boss's office at the start of the day and saying goodbye or cheers rather than wishing him or her good morning.[11] The mistake is one for which Lucian feels he does not need to apologize, since what he said by accident was not bad. Nevertheless, he wishes to comfort himself for the error by writing.[12] The result of the process is Lucian taking responsibility for what he said: He may not have said it deliberately, but something made him say it on purpose, and he can stand by what it was he said ("A Slip of the Tongue," 185).

The bulk of the text is given over to exploring what it is he has accidentally said when he wished his patron health. A psychological explanation of the blunder is briefly considered toward the end of the argument when Lucian declares that "there is nothing strange if a fervent desire for your good opinion in all that is best was too strong and in my utter confusion I stumbled into the opposite effect" ("A Slip of the Tongue," 187). He suggests that an individual can be tripped up by the very desire to please, and illustrates this confusion by drawing an analogy with someone who is distracted from his or her thought processes by people pushing to the front of a crowd ("A Slip of the Tongue," 187). However, this psychological explanation is not what dominates the essay. The explanation in terms of human psychology is framed and displaced by a consideration of what a higher power (*daimōn*) or even a god may have led him to say.

To prepare this line of thought, Lucian first gives examples from Homer and elsewhere that show that, in the past at least, the greeting he failed to give was not as rigidly associated with a particular occasion or time of day as it is now ("A Slip of the Tongue," 175–77). He shows that alternatives have been possible, even if the mistake he made can later be likened to the obviously nonsensical action of putting a helmet on one's shin ("A Slip of the Tongue," 185). Having established that alternatives to the norm are conceivable, he goes on to cite authorities who preferred not to wish people joy at all: Plato opted for wishing that people do well ("A Slip of the Tongue," 177), while Pythagoras in the distant past and Epicurus more recently wished people health ("A Slip of the Tongue," 177–79). This leads to the main point of Lucian's reflections—namely, that there is no point having other goods if you don't have health.

As well as establishing this point, Lucian also wants to establish a connection between his own error and the different behaviors he records from the past. He achieves this in part by occasionally slipping first-person comments into his presentation of unchallengeable authorities, such as when he personally approves the approach of the general Pyrrhus of Epirus, who prayed only for health rather than for other goods ("A Slip of the Tongue," 183). He affirms Pyrrhus's actions only in fact to bolster his own. In a similar vein, his reflections include the report of an error that becomes the model for understanding his slip. Hephaestion, by wishing Alexander health on the morning of the Battle of Issus, erroneously greeted him with the evening salutation, upsetting everyone except Alexander, who saw the slip as a good omen—a sign that they would return safely from battle ("A Slip of the Tongue," 183). Hephaestion is said specifically to have been confused, as Lucian was, and to have given Lucian's evening greeting, suggesting that the positive response he prompted should also be the one prompted by Lucian's perplexity. If Lucian said the wrong thing, it was because the goddess Health or perhaps even her father Asclepius himself inspired him on purpose ("A Slip of the Tongue," 185).

Lucian's discussion of his slip thus acknowledges that he has perpetrated a social blunder (putting a helmet on a leg), but at the same time it makes sense of the senseless action. While he is not responsible for what happened, he can nevertheless take responsibility for his words without wanting at the same time to take the credit. Lucian realizes that his explanation lays him open to the charge that he made the blunder on purpose in order to prepare the way for his grandiloquent defense, but he maintains that this was not the point ("A Slip of the Tongue," 189). Instead he asks the god Asclepius that his text might be taken "as a starting point of display, not as a defense" ("A Slip of the Tongue," 189). Lucian thus concludes by praying that he might so successfully have shifted the terms being used to evaluate his behavior that the bungled greeting becomes instead a moment of inspiration to be proudly shown to his peers; the birth of a new social meaning.

One tactic Lucian has deployed to change the terms of the debate is to present the cultural credentials of his blunder. If the witnesses of the error thought him to be senile or hung over ("A Slip of the Tongue," 173), or to lack education ("A Slip of the Tongue," 187), he has demonstrated the cultural pedigree of the phrase he mistakenly used. The second tactic is to invoke the idea of something speaking through him. There are thus two ways in which Lucian can understand how he is part of something he previously wasn't aware of. Before he sat down to write, he didn't know what he was going to say ("Slip of the Tongue," 173). But on sitting down, he uncovers the history he was unwittingly part of. He then doesn't take credit for what he's done, but allows something to have moved through him to this beneficial effect.

So what does Lucian's essay add to our phenomenology of making a slip? His slip fits the model so far established, since it is in front of witnesses, and doing something for which he can be called to account.[13] The first thing Lucian adds to the model is the sense that the slip can be a discovery: You can find out that you belong to something you were not previously aware of. Through his cultural history of salutations in the ancient world, Lucian constructs the context that makes his nonsensical act make sense. The second thing he adds to the model so far established is the qualification of the question of responsibility: Lucian can become responsible for something he didn't do. In this sense, taking responsibility means coming to understand how your act is meaningful. It has nothing to do with agency but is more a question of understanding: Lucian sees the wider picture of which the act could be a part. Of course, the Lucian who writes the essay is not out of control. His prose is carefully molded, the shape of his argument poised and elegant, even to the point that at the end he must add the disclaimer that he hasn't made the slip as an excuse to stage his rhetorical skill. But his facility with language is control only insofar as it allows him to place and understand what happened to him. The essay ends with a short prayer to Asclepius ("Slip of the Tongue," 189), and it is the god who in the end will be responsible for how the event, of which Lucian now knows himself to be a part, continues to unfold. Lucian's text thus enriches the model of what makes a slip, by qualifying the question of accountability. A slip can occur only for those actions for which we can be held responsible. But the idea of being responsible doesn't require an elaborate theory of volition or assumptions about what it means to be an agent. Being held responsible simply means being called to answer the schoolmasterly question: "What is the meaning of this?" Does Lucian's slip mean that he is hung over, senile, or ill educated? No, it means that he can recognize that health is the most important of all goods.

Lucian can use his rhetorical skills to become part of what he is already involved in. This is only one possible reaction to a social blunder. Another text, the "Apology for the 'Salaried Posts in Great Houses' "—written at a similar time in Lucian's life, if the reference to his being old in both texts is to be trusted—shows that other reactions were conceivable in response to a course of action likely to provoke the disapproval of one's peers.[14] The text was written because Lucian, having previously composed a biting satire of people who take up salaried posts and thus give up their independence, has now taken a post in the Egyptian administration. He imagines how the addressee of his text, Sabinus, might mock his inconsistency—for instance, by pointing out how Lucian could be likened to Cleopatra's trained monkey that can dance elegantly until it is distracted by a fig or an almond, at which point it tears off or even tears up its mask, grabs the food, and lapses back into animality ("Apology," 199–201). Lucian's behavior is potentially legible as a moment when culture is stripped away to show a merely instinctual reaction. Lucian considers how he might, in his defense, use an excuse comparable to his response, in the essay, on the slip of the tongue—namely, that no man is in control of his life ("Apology," p. 203). But this is not the line he takes. His alternative strategy is to give a redescription of the everyday life he shares with his interlocutor and to say: What you're doing is no different from what I'm doing, even the emperor works for a reward ("Apology," 209). Activity is a good thing, being rewarded is normal, and Lucian makes no claim to being wise, and indeed himself has never come across someone who "fulfilled the promise of wisdom" ("Apology," 211), so maybe wisdom isn't an alternative to working for money but a false standard.

If in the slip-of-the-tongue essay Lucian could understand what he was part of, here his response is to stand up for what he knows he's already involved in. The "Apology" thus shows that there are two sides to a blunder. A slip can surprise you beyond what you know; or it can confront you with a view of the world that, by being too narrow, tries to overlook what you're all involved in anyway. A view of life will be too narrow where it takes refuge in a false abstraction (for instance, that it is possible to avoid acting for a reward). Lucian's preference is to encourage people to acknowledge their involvements and give up the pursuit of philosophical abstractions. As his dialogue with Hermotimus, that aspiring Stoic, makes clear, we can discover whether a philosophy is true only by living it, but there isn't time to live all the different philosophies, and it's also not clear how we would know which version of a particular philosophy was the real thing. So rather than latching on to the first sect that seems to have a good reputation, as Hermotimus has done, Lycinus, Lucian's mouthpiece in the dialogue, suggests joining in the shared everyday life of the city ("Hermotimus," 413) and focusing on the question of how to act justly, wisely, and bravely ("Hermotimus," 405), giving up the illusory quest for a certainty beyond or outside everyday life.[15] The essay on the slip of the tongue and the "Apology" give us examples of how, if we can't appeal to an outside position, we might negotiate over which of our actions are just, wise, and brave. They show Lucian using his rhetorical accomplishments to investigate and acknowledge the meaning of his actions, and trying to get his interlocutors to acknowledge the meaning of theirs. To understand and evaluate our actions, we don't have to position ourselves somewhere different from where we are (we're already living the shared life of the city), nor indeed do we have to do anything other than what we're already doing or what the gods are doing through us. Instead, we need to stop taking refuge in false abstractions. Slips and social faux pas are an opportunity to notice our unhelpful attachments, to let go of them and participate more fully in what we're actually involved in anyway.

So how does this change the phenomenology of the slip? In addition to the aspect of bungled togetherness, and the division of our activity loosely into those things we might be called to account for and those for which we generally will not, Lucian's analysis of his own mistake adds the element of acknowledging what we're doing and making sense of it. A slip is not so much an opportunity to ask who or what did something but rather to investigate "what did it mean?"; to explore what is available to me in terms of a shared culture—be it literary or practical—that could help me own up to and understand what has occurred. There are ways in which this model that is derived from a second-century analysis is illuminating when contrasted with Freud's in *The Psychopathology of Everyday Life.* Where we find in Lucian's text the affirmation of a shared way of life, we find in Freud's a contrasting tendency to privatize the slip and so to draw our attention away from the common project to which an analysis of the slip could contribute as it did for Lucian.

Some Different Ways of Having a Cultured Conversation

The Psychopathology of Everyday Life was first published in 1901 in the *Monatsschrift für Psychiatrie und Neurologie.* The text was reissued as a book in 1904 and went through eleven editions in Freud's lifetime, many of which included new material that comprised either observations of Freud's or further examples and anecdotes that had been sent him by colleagues and correspondents.[16] The book is thus something like the family photo album of the early psychoanalytic movement in which Freud and others recorded everyday events that seemed to them to demonstrate the legitimacy of psychoanalysis as a tool for understanding the dynamics of our day-to-day encounters. Like Lucian, Freud and his coauthors assume that the mistakes can be made sense of. His tools for making sense are, first, the guiding assumption that the blunders are not arbitrary but follow predictable paths, the logic of which can be uncovered, and, second, free association is a means of uncovering this logic (*Psychopathology*, 38/13). That there was a certain uncomfortable insistence in this approach as it was cultivated by Freud and his colleagues is recorded in Kraus's 1908 satire of the stock phrase of the psychoanalyst: "Does anything occur to you in relation to the matter [Was fällt Ihnen dazu ein]?" with Kraus objecting to the fact that the psychoanalyst knows the answer in advance—namely, sex—and won't listen to an answer that isn't the one expected.[17] However, the parallel with Lucian suggests a different limitation to Freud's method, the exploration of which will help us reconstruct how Freud's reflections on everyday slips fitted into the wider culture.

At the start of the *Psychopathology*, Freud famously analyzes the forgetting of a name, an event that occurred when he was staying in Ragusa (modern day Dubrovnik) with his wife on the Adriatic coast in September 1898. He made an excursion into Herzegovina with a civil servant from Berlin.[18] During the trip, the conversation turned to art and traveling in Italy. Freud wished to ask his companion if he had seen Signorelli's frescoes in Orvieto, but he could not remember the artist's name (*Psychopathology*, 38–39 / 14). When Lucian made a mistake in greeting, he turned his thoughts to what people do when they greet and investigated the different forms and functions of greeting in the culture of which he was a part. When Freud makes a mistake in talking about art, he does not ask himself what people are doing when they talk about art with their traveling companions, or the different functions that this aesthetic conversation can serve, but instead he thinks about his own thoughts and associations in relation to the word he has forgotten and about the circumstances of a trip through Muslim Bosnia that's playing on his mind as he talks. Compared to Lucian's approach, Freud's thus involves a narrowing of focus, away from the encounter in which the mistake occurred and toward the private concerns of the blunderer himself.

For all Freud's apparent indifference to the circumstances in which the blunder arose, a similar context crops up frequently in the *Psychopathology* as Freud and his peers make mistakes when talking about culture. The second slip Freud analyzes is also a cultural slip that occurs in a conversation that develops on a journey. A younger colleague who eventually admits that he is worried about a woman, whom he is having an affair with, missing her period forgets the word *aliquis* in a line of Virgil that he quoted as the peroration to an impassioned speech about the overcoming of professional obstacles put in the way of Jews (*Psychopathology*, 46–47 / 18–19). In a similar vein, Freud and another colleague investigate failings of memory by reciting a famous Goethe poem, "The Bride of

Corinth" (*Psychopathology*, 53–57 / 23–25). Schiller's *The Robbers* provides the link for another misremembering of names (*Psychopathology*, 62–63 / 29), while misremembering the poet's birthplace is also the occasion for Freud being confused (*Psychopathology*, 276–78 / 173–74). A patient's dream is unpacked with reminiscences about Cleopatra and Antony, and about Gretchen from Goethe's *Faust* (*Psychopathology*, 108–9 / 59). And so the list continues. Freud lived in a world where people negotiated their encounters with each other by talking about the culture that they had in common. It didn't always have to be high culture. Lewis Wallace's *Ben Hur* features as a shared text (*Psychopathology*, 81–82 / 42–43), as do the journalistic portraits of Vienna collected in Daniel Spitzer's *Wiener Spaziergänge* (Viennese strolls) (*Psychopathology*, 63/29). The common denominator in these encounters is social interaction mediated by the discussion of art.

Freud's own analyses suggest that a slip occurs because we're trying not to think about, or not to do, something other than what we're saying or doing. The stifled impulse finds indirect expression in our mistake, be it that we forget something, say or do something other than we intended, or bungle our actions by stumbling or breaking something. The model of the mind that we saw in the work of John Bargh and colleagues confirms that we could be involved in conflicting tasks simultaneously, or that things that we understood in one way (such as moral deliberations) might turn out to be redescribable in another (attempts to manage our physical cleanliness, for instance). The problem with Freud's account of everyday mistakes is not that it is implausible but rather that it is only part of a wider picture. The slips that Freud analyzes occur in the context of people managing their social encounters by talking about culture. Such conversations are a delicate negotiation of the gradations of intimacy, an instrument by which middle-class Europeans at the turn of the twentieth century could vary how much of what they care about they allowed to be visible and how much of the life they were in the processes of sharing with other people they were willing to acknowledge. When Freud describes the Signorelli slip in the letter to Fließ, he calls the frescoes in Orvieto "the greatest work he has seen" in his life thus far.[19] So the conversation has approached a point at which he is talking about experiences in which he has a strong emotional investment. When he makes a slip and subsequently analyzes it, he is offering a way of carrying on the process of cultural negotiation in a new form, a different way of doing aesthetic conversation. His analyses don't radically change the framework, since the conversation was already a way of dealing with intimacy. They are not even necessarily a way of being more frank about this process, since the people involved in the conversation will already have a tacit sense of what makes for a good conversation in different circumstances; of the contextually appropriate combination of solicitude, personal engagement, and distance. Freud's analyses are a way of continuing and taking responsibility for a cultured conversation just as Lucian's essay was a way of continuing and taking responsibility for his salutation.

The change of perspective from concentrating on the forbidden impulse to considering the shared conversation shifts the emphasis of Freud's analysis in two ways. The first is that it explicitly brings other people into the discussion. The focus is no longer my impulses and my failing strategies for control but rather the shared process being negotiated as we talk about culture. Freud observed in *The Psychopathology of Everyday Life* that slips of the tongue are contagious: His daughter mispronounced something a few minutes after Freud himself had made a slip as he tried to scold her for pulling a face while eating her apple (*Psychopathology*, 103–04 / 55–56). Freud can't explain the mechanism for this process, but if our conversations are negotiating our togetherness, then it does not seem so odd that my mistake should produce mistakes in others. Speaking in unison with others has been found to ameliorate stuttering, suggesting that, prior to our own habits of speaking, our mirror neurons are tuning in to the way those around us are talking.[20] If the tuning in to others has priority over execution of our own actions, then it makes sense that other people's stumbling over their words might be as infectious as their yawning, as we mirror the responses of our interlocutor. The cultural conversation is the means of our being attuned to others and of engaging with or keeping at a distance from our being together, so mistakes and bungles will tell me about this shared life as much as they tell me about my own private management of impulses.

The second change of emphasis entails recognizing that the acknowledgment of an interlocutor's hidden motives is not something that Freud alone has added to the conversation. While a portion of *The Psychopathology of Everyday Life* is given over to presenting and vindicating Freud's specific approach, including a number of episodes reported to Freud and included in later editions of the book in which the significance of a blunder becomes clear only after reading *The Psychopathology of Everyday Life* (*Psychopathology*, 207–08 / 125–26), other parts of the book stress the degree to which Freud is only saying what poets have said before him. The culture about which Freud is having his conversations already contains the idea of a meaningful mistake. For the 1907 and 1910 editions of the work, Freud quotes examples from *Wallenstein* and *The Merchant of Venice* in which Schiller and Shakespeare communicate something to the audience by having a character make a slip of the tongue (*Psychopathology*,

142–44 / 81–83). The Shakespeare example is borrowed from Otto Rank, who points out that the playwright could presume that his audience knew how to interpret the character's mistake (*Psychopathology*, 143/82). Not only the poets but audiences themselves had as part of their everyday repertoire for dealing with other people the option of putting a mistake in the context of a person's wider motivations.

These references to Schiller and Shakespeare fit the account of Freud's literary culture offered by Graham Frankland, but they also draw attention to the wider context of Freud's undertaking. Frankland documents the degree to which Freud's texts are in dialogue with the literary tradition and suggests that the frequent allusions partly have the function of legitimating Freud's claims by showing that his ideas stand in the tradition of such august figures as Sophocles or Goethe. The engagement with literary culture also helps Freud to formulate his concepts: Freud's "literary culture is *prior* to his analytic insights."[21] Each time he meets a problem in his metapsychological theorizations, it is to literary sources that he turns to think the problems through. Frankland thus suggests that there is a literary framework that establishes the territory for Freud's psychology theory. However, the references to Shakespeare, Schiller, and their audiences in *The Psychopathology of Everyday Life* invite us to go a step further, suggesting that not only Freud but his contemporaries, and indeed the contemporaries of Shakespeare and Schiller, were already involved in the process, using culture to reflect on people's motivations and expand the realm of what we can take responsibility for or make meaningful. We're already involved in the shared cultural conversation that negotiates our togetherness. Indeed, Freud bemoans the impression he has that "everything that can be said about forgetting and about parapraxes is already familiar and self-evident to everyone" (*Psychopathology*, 213/129).

This raises the question of what Freud's analyses add. From reading the *Psychopathology*, it seems that his interventions in the cultural conversation contribute a combination of heightened intimacy, bullying, and self-vindication. On the one hand, his interrogations allow his (generally male) interlocutors to broaden the range of what can meaningfully be included in the conversation, talking about their worries in particular in relation to a woman they might have made pregnant (the *aliquis* / Virgil example) or a woman they had a relationship with who was older than them (the "Bride of Corinth" example). The book is an anthology of social worries, embarrassments, and mishaps, documenting the sensitive points of private encounters in Vienna of the first decade of the twentieth century. On the other hand, the conversation does not make explicit what both parties are contributing to the emotional exchange but remains one-sided.

For while Freud's analyses promote a certain acknowledgment of the undercurrents negotiated by the conversations, it's not clear how much they are acknowledging his involvement with the situations he analyzes. It is perhaps unfair to say that Freud is requiring his interlocutors to speak the language of the inquisitor in the way that Bernard Gui did suspected heretics (although that seems to have been Kraus's objection to the analysts' leading question, "Does anything occur to you?" (Was fällt Ihnen dazu ein?).[22] The book is in fact more pluralistic than Freud himself would have liked, because the autobiographical nature of much of the material that he relied on in its composition made him focus less on sexual motivation than his theoretical model demanded (*Psychopathology*, 340–41 / 216). Instead it includes impatience, anger, professional worries and rivalries, concerns about being too fat or getting old, and the changes in thought patterns occasioned by being at war, to name but a few of the motivations Freud and his colleagues draw attention to.

However, even more important than the range of motives admitted to the conversation is the question of what happens to them when they are acknowledged. The therapies of Bertha Pappenheim and Ida Bauer were, on the one hand, successful to the degree they allowed the women to develop, and, on the other, constrained by the difficulties experienced by patient and physician alike in reconfiguring the terms of their interaction. Similarly, we have seen how the fourteenth-century relations between confessor and visionary were productive or constraining, depending on the degree to which the participants remained attached to received forms of interaction as opposed to allowing the situation to unfold as necessary. Freud in *The Psychopathology of Everyday Life* is no more interested in the spiritual or psychological growth of his interlocutors than he was in fostering the cultural conversation he might have had with Ida Bauer about Raphael's Sistine Madonna. Instead, the conclusion of the conversation seems often to be simply that Freud's theory is right. For example, the Virgil analysis starts off as a challenge from his interlocutor that Freud demonstrate his theory that nothing is forgotten without a reason: "I took up the challenge most readily, for I was hoping for a contribution to my collection" (*Psychopathology*, 46/19). As Heidegger might have said, Freud relates to the experiences he draws out of his partner in the deficient mode of using them to vindicate himself.

The desire to be vindicated is perhaps not surprising, given the situation in which his approach to slips and blunders was first elaborated in the summer of 1898. Freud was on holiday with his family at Bad Aussee, slightly bored because he knew the small resort well, reading Theodor

Lipps's book *Grundtatsachen des Seelenlebens* ("Fundamental Facts of Psychology") as he continued thinking about the metapsychological chapter of *The Interpretation of Dreams*, a draft of which he had just sent to Fließ, in the hope that this would prove more fruitful territory to establish a name for himself than were his attempts to understand hysteria—attempts with which, three years after the publication of the *Studies* with Breuer, he was no longer happy. Reading Lipps's account of unconscious processes in the mind, he was aware of possible parallels to his own position and looking for ways of making his theory more distinctive.[23] Freud's interest in forgetting bears the mark of this context. He is trying to establish himself in the shared conversation of his era and uses the analysis of slips and blunders to further this aim.

We don't have to be constrained by Freud's narrow agenda, nor would it be accurate to say that Freud himself was. One of his observations is a recognition of the inevitable and often unwanted degree of honesty in our everyday interactions: "It may, in general, seem astonishing that the urge to truth [*Wahrheitsdrang*] is so much stronger than is usually supposed" (*Psychopathology*, 280/176, translation modified). In Freud's account, people are driven by a will to consistency of purpose that can surprise them into doing things they do not expect or even into performing physical actions more skilful than they are aware they can accomplish (*Psychopathology*, 223/134). This will to truthful consistency is as close as Freud comes to a model of the unconscious, which, rather than following an alien logic with no notion of time, is smart, purposive, and adaptive in the way many subpersonal processes now appear from experimental investigation.[24] It's also the closest he comes to articulating a sense of purposive unfolding. What's particularly striking about Freud's formulations is that, although they might initially seem to suggest a model of identity as unified, controlled, and autonomous, they in fact displace individual control with a relational view of human action, in which individuals key into a situation and rise to the occasion: "I do not really think that anyone would make a slip of the tongue in an audience with his Sovereign, in a serious declaration of love or in defending his honour and name before a jury—in short, on all those occasions in which a person is heart and soul engaged [*ganz dabei ist*]" (*Psychopathology*, 147/85). Just as in Austin's theory of speech acts it takes the right context for utterances like "I promise" or "I now declare you man and wife" to have their effect—the situation speaks through us—so, too, for Freud, we can let things be done through us, as the vehicle for the occasion.[25] In fact, we have no choice. We can deceive ourselves and try to do otherwise, but the situation will show us up, and others will be aware of our "internal dishonesty [*innere Unaufrichtigkeit*]" (*Psychopathology*, 269/169).

Freud's account of slips thus pulls in two directions. On the one hand, Freud is concerned to collect examples that fit his theoretical construction and is not interested in participating in the shared event of which the slip is a part. On the other hand, he acknowledges a certain dynamism—a will to truthfulness, or *Wahrheitsdrang*—moving through encounters regardless of the self-image or conscious intentions of the speakers. As we encounter each other, we're part of an event that will unfold regardless, and we can align ourselves with this unfolding, or can find ways to keep it at a distance, developing the habits and ways of relating to the situation that Freud calls "inner dishonesty."

The German word Freud uses for *dishonesty*—*Unaufrichtigkeit*—is also part of the moral vocabulary employed by Arthur Schnitzler as he records the self-deception and callousness but also contrasting moments of honesty, or *Aufrichtigkeit*, in the Viennese milieu he shared with Freud. It's a term Schnitzler's narrator can use to gloss the unease of his characters.[26] But it's also a word the characters themselves use as they understand and evaluate their own behavior and the actions of friends and lovers.[27] Thus Freud's analyses draw on the sorts of vocabulary available to educated people for thinking about their social behavior. The shared vocabulary brings us back to the question of what Freud's approach to the slips and blunders of human togetherness adds to the stock of tacit knowledge that he is aware already informs people's day-to-day interactions.

A number of scholars have noted a tension in Freud's analyses between the development of a specialist discourse and the empowering of the vocabulary that his patients used to come to terms with their predicament. For instance, Rachel Bowlby has noted the contrast from the very earliest days of psychoanalysis between the terms that Bertha Pappenheim chose for her therapeutic encounters with Breuer (the English words the "talking cure" and "chimney sweeping") and the more specialist vocabulary of the "cathartic method" and "abreacting" [*abreagieren*] that Breuer and Freud employed in their theoretical deliberations. For Bowlby, the advantage of the term "chimney sweeping" is that it uses the patient's own words to describe a necessary, regular activity, rather than deploying the therapist's vocabulary to depict a dramatic, final expulsion of a foreign body.[28] Bowlby's reading is partly shaped by the assumption, questioned by Richard Skues, that Breuer and Freud overplayed the efficacy of their cathartic method in *Studies on Hysteria*, so she is keen to emphasize, not the dramatic finale suggested by a cathartic purging, but the ongoing, unfinished nature of the encounter with unacknowledged desires.[29] Nevertheless, even if one takes into account Skues's reminder that the claims made for the talking cure were not as overstated as has been maintained, the tension Bowlby notes is important insofar as it bespeaks an unwillingness on the part of Breuer and Freud to allow the patient's words and the patient's perspective to set the agenda. This unwillingness, among other things, was remarked on by one of the very first reviewers of the *Studies*, Adolf Strümpell. Strümpell was sympathetic to the attempt to give a psychogenic rather than physiological account of hysteria and thought the method described by Freud and Breuer could be clinically effective. However, he wondered whether it was necessary for Freud and Breuer to use so many terms of foreign origin (*Fremdwörter*) and also whether it was necessary to abstract and generalize about affects being stored up in the mind as opposed to developing a theory that was practically effective. He also asked whether it is necessary for the physician to pry into the private lives of his patients, especially their sex lives, whether the use of hypnosis was necessary, and what the status was of the events acted out or remembered under hypnosis.[30]

Strümpell's review is interesting because it confirms that the tendency to abstraction in Freud's language is not, as Bettelheim suggested, just a function of the Latinate translation of Strachey's Standard Edition but was also noticed by German-speaking contemporaries of Freud and Breuer.[31] More important is that it shows someone deliberating about the most productive ways to manage the encounter between patient and physician. Clinical effectiveness is more important than theorizing, and questions are raised about how to structure the encounter, what language to use, what techniques, and about how to deal with social taboos. We don't need to agree with Strümpell about where to draw the boundaries of appropriate behavior. Nevertheless, the review takes us back to the process of negotiation, and reminds us how Freud and Breuer were part of this process, and gives us the freedom to renegotiate ourselves. Sulloway, as we have seen, values the *Studies* as a record of Freud's thinking before the boundaries had been fixed and while he was still a willing participant in a shared debate.[32]

The framework is no more fixed in *The Psychopathology of Everyday Life* than it is in the *Studies*. Indeed, precisely because it engages with quotidian encounters and the continuing management of our emotional involvements, it is easier to connect the text with the program of finding ways of being honest and of aligning ourselves with the situation moving through us in ways that draw on the riches of ordinary language, or, as Austin phrased it, "the distinctions men have found worth drawing, and the connexions they have found worth marking."[33] We draw on these distinctions because, as Michel de Certeau insists, there is no alternative to them. The dream of a theory that stands back to document an involvement in which it does not itself participate is as illusory as the progress of a cartoon character after it's run off a cliff but before it realizes the situation it's in.[34] In some of the examples in *The Psychopathology of Everyday Life*, Freud acknowledges that the undercurrents of our interactions don't disappear when we adopt a specialist language or take on a public role. Instead they continue to disrupt the efforts of a printer typesetting a text, a doctor writing a prescription, or witnesses in a court of law (*Psychopathology*, 178/106, 170–71 / 100, 199/120). At one point, Freud suggests that making things conscious is the key to establishing or reestablishing control (*Psychopathology*, 299/189). But, as we have seen, when we are before our Sovereign or making a declaration of love, we speak well not because we make our impulses conscious but because we are aligned with the situation and allow it to speak through us.

This alignment is an aspect of *The Psychopathology of Everyday Life* that does not get developed much further by Freud in his later work. It's taken up more explicitly by Jung, who, as we have seen, sums up the sense of alignment by borrowing a formulation from Paul's Epistle to the Galatians: "And I no longer live, but Christ lives in me" (Galatians 2:20).[35] Acknowledging our situation and resolutely allowing it to unfold is also an idea that features in *Being and Time*.[36] But returning to the Freud text keeps the connection between the pursuit of alignment and the involvements of everyday life more clearly than either in Jung's account of the collective archetype or in Heidegger's adopting of the archetype of the lone male hero. It allows the project of spiritual and psychological growth to remain rooted in our normal lives, as Meister Eckhart suggested it should be when he preferred Martha's activity to Mary's contemplation.[37] We do not need a specialist vocabulary or a special heroism to unpack our involvements or to articulate what the situation already contains anymore than Lucian did as he came to understand and take responsibility for the greeting that had been spoken through him when he went to visit his patron. Rather, as the Lucian example suggests, we need tact, historical knowledge, a form of honesty, and a capacity for bearing social embarrassment.

A reading of *The Psychopathology of Everyday Life* thus uncovers a radical project to which we can return: that of acknowledging what we already know but don't want to know, to borrow the phrase of Freud's patient Miss Lucy R.[38] Of course, this project is radical only in the sense of taking us back to the root of our interaction and reflects a radicality that we are in fact daily involved in as we reaffirm or alter the terms of our engagement with others and with ourselves. Nevertheless, the Freud text can assist us by drawing our attention to the aspects of our life we engage in without necessarily taking note of them, like the pee on the floor that is left for someone else to clean up. It can help us be honest about things we all already agree we can be called to account for but are hoping to keep at a distance. But it can also help to start conversations about aspects of our shared life that we are involved in together but that previously took place below the radar of accountability. For these new conversations we will need to leave Freud behind and to draw on other writers, be they feminist theorists like Beauvoir and Butler, experimentalists working in the fields of cognitive science and social psychology, or from the phenomenological or mystical traditions. But if we leave Freud's text behind, we shouldn't leave the places where it so firmly located its analyses: in train compartments, on the street, at the family dinner table, or at our desk.

"Neither a Be-All nor an End-All Be": Conclusions

The motto for my conclusion is taken from Austin's essay "Pretending" (1957–58) and is appropriately enough a phrase that occurred to him in a dream and that he records as "a motto for a sober philosophy."[39] For Austin, the phrase is a reminder that making grand claims for the importance of one's arguments is not so important and certainly shouldn't be preferred to the careful analysis of the multiple forms of human interaction. The book has not offered a new theory of the modern subject. But I hope that it's shown the plausibility and productivity of some changes of perspective—most important, that of taking being-together-in-the-world-with-others as our theoretical starting point, despite the constant temptation to take the "mineness" of our own conscious cogitations to be the irrefragable foundation of our thoughts and actions. If we step aside from our own conscious perspective, then there's plenty that we can take note of about our interaction with each other and our way of being in the world—especially if we stay in dialogue with other people. Finding ways to surprise ourselves into new and fuller descriptions of these shared patterns of behavior could then be our goal. The descriptions won't necessarily make the interactions we document any the nicer or more humane, but they might help the situation continue to unfold, and I share Dewey's optimism that we don't need to import moral standards from the outside to make the world better but can draw on the resources a situation—whatever situation we find ourselves in—already contains.[40] And if it doesn't contain them, then importing them won't help anyway.

My argument started out from the desire to understand what a late medieval mystic might mean when he or she claims to have "become God," assuming that we approach the phrase charitably, as the best way of talking about the experiences and aspirations of the people who used it.

Recent engagements with the texts of late medieval mystics by, for example, Lacan, Irigaray, and Amy Hollywood were shown to be hampered by their commitment to a model of human identity and of human freedom not shared by the mystical writers. This problem was not a local problem of "mysticism studies" but could seen, in various guises, in the attempts by theorists in the postwar period to imagine an alternative to the forms of behavior they criticized: Lyotard, Žižek, Derrida, and Adorno could appear to be prevented by their own assumptions from formulating their alternative as something other than an empty epiphany. To overcome these conceptual obstacles to engaging with the texts of the mystical tradition, it was necessary to change the assumptions with which the notion of identity was approached; and, as a consequence of these changed assumptions, to rethink what we are studying when we study the history of modern forms of identity. The change of orientation built on Heidegger's analyses of our being-with-others to insist that our individual identity must be approached as a way of coping with being delivered up to a shared world rather than as something that magically preexists our involvement in the stream of human behavior.

Heidegger was seen not to follow through the idea of a fundamental layer of shared experience as far as he might, since he harbored a residual commitment to the archetype of the lone male hero. Beauvoir's arguments added to Heidegger's the insistence that the experience of connection will be shaped by the data of biology and by the reminder that social forms of connection will be colored by the way a society interprets sexual difference. Butler's arguments in *Gender Trouble* put the case for the contingency and malleability of the social habits by which our shared experience of embodiment is regulated. At the same time, we saw how her concept of "primary impressionability" betrayed the degree to which, even in a theoretical position as self-questioning as hers, there was a commitment to a preexisting self that could be damaged by contact with other human beings. Finally, we saw how the position developed by Heidegger, and differentiated with the help of Beauvoir and Butler, finds empirical confirmation in recent work in neuroscience, giving us a clearer sense of the sorts of interactions in day-to-day life that it is helpful to study if we want to understand our involvement in shared patterns of behavior that are the background and precondition of our sense of individual identity.

To avoid the recurring problem of assuming a subject even as we attempt to go beyond isolated subjectivity, therefore, we need to develop a model of human connectedness that does not presuppose a prior separation of the human beings. Rather, the connection needs to be seen as something that is always already there and that doesn't require a single label to name it but is the constant accompaniment of our social behavior and, indeed, the thing that many habits—from talking about the weather to, as we've just seen in the analysis of Freud's *Psychopathology of Everyday Life*, talking about art—have grown up to negotiate. This stream of shared human activity is dynamic: It is a form of shared growth. Many forms of behavior can be seen as more or less creative ways of engaging with this unfolding predicament. Some habits stifle the development of the shared, ongoing situation, others nurture it; some situations we will want to foster, others we will decide are better contained or redirected. We will decide this by using the tools we have inherited for thinking about how the activity we're engaged with could be better or worse, and by trying to be as honest as possible about our motives for preferring one course of action over another, or, as Dewey puts it: "Every situation has its own measure and quality of progress, and the need for progress is recurrent, constant."[41]

Once we've adopted this perspective, then we will no longer want to write the history of this special thing called modern identity but will rather see a greater continuity in the different sorts of habits human societies have developed, and continue to develop, for the regulation and control, or the fostering and nurturing, of human togetherness. We will write the history not so much of techniques of the self as of techniques of coexistence. A history of identity will take the form of an account of the varied ways in which people, in their everyday life, have lived with and alongside each other, participating in the shared habits that allow others to become closer or less close in different situations and that permit more or less growth.

The texts of Eckhart and his contemporaries were turned to because they offered an example of a culture in which the maximum of growth was aspired to and given the name "being in" or "becoming" God. Eckhart's spiritual project was one that it was hard to classify historically, because it combines two forces—first, an apparently modern interest in an individualized spiritual program that questions received structures, and then a relationship with God that displaces or disregards ideas of individual agency and individual consciousness to replace them with a form of surrender: with freedom before God. At the same time, it is very much the product of the milieu in which he was preaching, as a radical form of the *vita apostolica* adopted by friars, nuns, beguines, and other laypeople from the twelfth century onward. Turning to study examples of this social movement in more detail, we saw that gender roles were one of the social structures through which the experience of connection was negotiated. Gendered habits of behavior could be questioned and redeployed as a confessor and beguine allowed their shared longing for God to develop, as we saw in the *Sister Catherine* treatise. But the habits could also be used as a way of limiting spiritual development, as we saw with Margaretha Ebner and Heinrich von Nördlingen. In the case of Heinrich Seuse and Elsbeth Stagel, the woman's longing was encouraged to submit to the form her male confessor had already imposed on his own desire for God. In this partnership, we saw habits and ways of talking that prefigured those that come to dominate, without being the only possible options, in the modern period. Faced with the condemnation of Eckhart's teachings as heretical, but unwilling to give up his desire for God, Seuse seems to have opted to police his longing himself and to have come, in the process, to identify strongly enough with the habits of self-policing for these habits to crystallize into something comparable to modern self.

In Seuse's case, self-policing replaced self-abandonment as the individual's ultimate aim. This shifts the orientation of day-to-day life away from God, away from external embodiments of authority, and toward the individual's own strategies for regulating his or her longing. If Seuse's texts suggest the circumstances in which something like the habits of modern identity come to be fostered, the case of Seuse and Stagel also gave a historical inflection to the bleak model of gender proposed by Irigaray in her *Speculum*. Stagel is exhorted to speak the language of her confessor and to give up the specificity of her experience to participate instead in his more self-controlling practices. This renders femininity either identical to male habits of self-regulation or casts it as a terrifying menace beyond the pale of civilized identity. By contrast, in the texts of Eckhart and Margaretha Ebner, as in the *Sister Catherine* treatise, the women are not reduced to this stark choice. In these other texts, the male cleric and the woman visionary share an experience for which they are both trying to find an appropriate vocabulary. Neither the women's voice nor the experience of "being in" or "becoming" God have yet been relegated to the status of an incomprehensible alterity. By the same token, Seuse's habits themselves can be seen as an alternative, and more controlling, way of managing communion, with others and with God, by keeping it at a permanent distance.

This account of habits of identity enables us to return to and reconsider the psychoanalytic vocabulary that in the works of Lacan, Irigaray, and Hollywood had trouble engaging with the mystical tradition and with the fostering of freedom and surrender that it represents. Psychoanalysis can be seen against the larger background of habits, developed in different cultures, for coming to terms with and acknowledging the commitments of our shared predicament. The practices developed by Breuer and Freud were radical where they respected the vocabulary and creativity of the patient and established a collaborative relationship for coming to terms with the legacy of inherited patterns of behavior and inhibiting models of how it was appropriate for men and women, as men and women, to behave. At the same time, there were limits to how far both men were willing to go in challenging habits. In both we saw an attachment to models of behavior that constrained the patient's and the doctor's capacity for growth. Indeed, the idea of alien unconscious processes can be understood as limiting and putting at a distance the very aspects of experience it purports to name. Despite the limitations of Freud's and Breuer's theorization of their therapeutic practice, we can return to the period around 1900 to see what habits and what vocabulary we might develop if we were to follow through the intuitions of the early psychoanalysts and their contemporaries without reinforcing structures of self-control. In particular, Freud's turn to day-to-day encounters in *The Psychopathology of Everyday Life* and his recognition of a plurality of different impulses and of an urge to truth—that is to say, an urge to acknowledge what our day-to-day behavior is involved in negotiating—are particularly promising for a reengagement with our shared predicament.

What I hope to have drawn attention to with my account is the historical legacy of our current habits, showing how the sense of autonomy that, as Taylor suggests, is a value we will find it hard to simply cast aside arose in part as individuals acquired the habits of policing their own sense of connectedness themselves. It's not clear that we all feel to the same degree the sense of connection to others and to our shared predicament. The religious tradition optimistically supposes that we all stand equal before God, but it's possible that a connection experienced through hormones, smells, mirror neurons, touch, voice, and other bodily systems is as variable as musicality or the sense of vision.[42] If we are all connected, we perhaps do not all have the same facility for acknowledging the fact; or, to put the same thought in another way, when we engage with our shared predicament, it is probably useful to be willing to operate with different assumptions, depending on which seems most profitable in different contexts—on the one hand, the assumptions that we are all equally connected, all participating in God's creation; on the other hand, the possibility that some may have more talent for connecting than do others, just as some are more musical, more visually or numerically adept, or more athletic. As well as drawing attention to the level of our shared participation in human unfolding, my argument has suggested that gender is one of the explanatory frameworks used in everyday life to police and structure forms of togetherness, as we learn to be as connected or as reserved as is proper for a man or a woman. I hope that the perspective opened up by this book allows us to describe the processes in more detail in order to see the ways in which our actual behavior, beneath the radar of the gender police, does not neatly conform to the patterns, just as our bodies don't.

There is no special place for starting or continuing the work of description and collation. Or rather the place for starting will have already been decided for us by life. We'll be somewhere, coping with problems with varying degrees of honesty and courage, and our only task is to continue what we're doing already, being as clear as possible about what that is, and allowing ourselves to be surprised if it turns out that less flattering descriptions of our problems and embroilments are possible than the ones we currently use. The title of the book mentions God because the medieval aspiration to "become God" exemplifies so well the process of allowing the longing of being thrown into the world to take its course. It's possible that in adopting our own honest descriptions of our predicament we won't find the term useful, just as, in carrying on the cultural conversation of which Freud's *The Psychopathology of Everyday Life* is a part, we might not choose to focus on works of literature like those of Virgil or Schiller because they are no longer the way we negotiate the space of our shared emotions. In neither case is it important to be attached to particular words: If God and art are not the way we let life unfold through us, then so be it.[43] More important than the words is the project: of acknowledging what we're involved in and letting it unfold as much as we can bear.

Notes

Introduction

1. Franz-Josef Schweitzer, *Der Freiheitsbegriff der Deutschen Mystik: Seine Beziehung zur Ketzerei der "Brüder und Schwestern vom Freien Geist," mit besonderer Rücksicht auf den pseudoeckartischen Traktat "Schwester Katrei" (Edition), Europäische Hochschulschriften: Reihe I, Deutsche Sprache und Literatur,* Bd. 378 (Frankfurt am Main: Peter Lang, 1981), 334; Bernard McGinn, ed., *Meister Eckhart: Teacher and Preacher* (New York: Paulist Press, 1986), 358.

2. Franz Josef Schweitzer, "Schwester Katrei," in *Die Deutsche Literatur des Mittelalters: Verfasserlexikon*, ed. Wolfgang Stammler, Karl Langosch, and Kurt Ruh, 2nd ed. (Berlin: Walter de Gruyter, 1977–), 8:947.

3. For a reading of mystical writings from this context as pedagogic manuals, see Ursula Peters, *Religiöse Erfahrung als Literarisches Faktum : Zur Vorgeschichte und Genese frauenmystischer Texte des 13. und 14. Jahrhunderts* (Tübingen: Niemeyer, 1988).

4. Alfred Schütz, "The Problem of Transcendental Intersubjectivity in Husserl," in *Phenomenology: Critical Concepts in Philosophy*, ed. Dermot Moran et al. (Abingdon: Routledge, 2004), 2:143–78 (66). For more-recent empirical research on the shared activity out of which children develop a sense of their own and other people's minds, see R. Peter Hobson, *The Cradle of Thought* (London: Macmillan, 2002); Jeremy I. M. Carpendale and Charlie Lewis, *How Children Develop Social Understanding* (Oxford: Blackwell, 2006). Vasudevi Reddy and Paul Morris, "Participants Don't Need Theories: Knowing Minds in Engagement," *Theory and Psychology* 14 (2004): 647–65.

5. Toril Moi suggests that it's not, Toril Moi, *What Is a Woman? And Other Essays* (Oxford; New York: Oxford University Press, 1999), 72–83.

6. Simone de Beauvoir, *The Second Sex*, trans. H. M. Parshley (London: Vintage, 1997), 67 (translation amended); Simone de Beauvoir, *Le deuxième sexe*, 2 vols. (Paris: Gallimard, 2006), 1:77: "Ce n'est pas comme individus que les hommes se définissent d'abord; jamais hommes et femmes ne se sont défiés en combats singuliers; le couple est un *mitsein* original." For discussions of the relationship between Beauvoir and Heidegger and in particular her treatment of the idea of *Mitsein*, see Eva Gothlin, "Reading Simone de Beauvoir with Martin Heidegger," in *The Cambridge Companion to Simone de Beauvoir*, ed. Claudia Card (Cambridge: Cambridge University Press, 2003), 45–65; and Nancy Bauer, "Must We read Simone de Beauvoir?", in *The Legacy of Simone de Beauvoir*, ed. Emily Grosholz (Oxford: Clarendon Press, 2004), 115–35, esp. 32–34.

7. Iris Marion Young, *On Female Body Experience: "Throwing Like a Girl" and Other Essays* (Oxford; New York: Oxford Uuniversity Press, 2005), 145.

8. Elisabeth Bronfen's Cavellian reading of the femme fatale figure similarly suggests that male and female identities are both actively involved in the shared project of not acknowledging each other. Elisabeth Bronfen, "Femme Fatale—Negotiations of Tragic Desire," *New Literary History: A Journal of Theory and Interpretation* 35, no. 1 (2004): 103–16.

9. Prudence Allen, *The Early Humanist Reformation, 1250–1500*, vol. 2 of *The Concept of Woman* (Grand Rapids, Mich.: William B. Eerdmans, 2002), 21. The idea of "doing gender" draws on an article to which I'll return later in the discussion: Candace West and Don H. Zimmerman, "Doing Gender," *Gender and Society* 1, no. 2 (1987): 125–51.

10. See Sigmund Freud, "Die Zukunft einer Illusion," in *Studienausgabe*, ed. Alexander Mitscherlich, Angela Richards, and James Strachey, 11 vols. (Frankfurt am Main: S. Fischer, 1969), 9:135–89; Richard Dawkins, *The God Delusion* (London: Bantam, 2006); Daniel C. Dennett, *Breaking the Spell: Religion as a Natural Phenomenon* (London: Allen Lane, 2006).

11. Dennett, *Breaking the Spell: Religion as a Natural Phenomenon*, 303.

12. Stanley Cavell, *Must We Mean What We Say? A Book of Essays*, updated ed. (Cambridge: Cambridge University Press, 2002), xxxiii.

13. Todd May, "Foucault's Relation to Phenomenology" in *The Cambridge Companion to Foucault*, 2nd ed., Gary Gutting (Cambridge: Cambridge University Press, 2005), 284–311.

14. For a discussion of the way modern preconceptions of agency in particular can inhibit readings of mystical texts, see A. Hollywood, "Gender, Agency, and the Divine in Religious Historiography," *Journal of Religion* 84, no. 4 (2004): 514–28.

1. Some Recent Versions of Mysticism

1. Uwe Spörl, "Mystisches Erleben, Leben Und Schreiben Um 1900: Überlegungen Zu Den Grenzen Der Literaturwissenschaft," *KulturPoetik: Zeitschrift für kulturgeschichtliche Literaturwissenschaft/Journal of Cultural Poetics* 1, no. 2 (2001): 214–30.

2. Jung discusses his experience of having a spirit as a guru in "The Confrontation with the Unconscious," Carl Gustav Jung, *Memories, Dreams, Reflections*, ed. Aniela Jaffé, trans. Richard Winston and Clara Winston (London: Fontana, 1983), 194–225. On the construction of this supposed autobiography by Jung's publisher after his death, see Sonu Shamdasani, "Misunderstanding Jung: The Afterlife of Legends," *Journal of Analytic Psychology* 45 (2000): 459–72. For the reliability of many sections nevertheless, see Alan C. Elms, "Jung's Lives," *Journal of the History of the Behavioral Sciences* 41, no. 4 (2005): 331–46.

3. Jacques Derrida, "How to Avoid Speaking: Denials," in *Derrida and Negative Theology*, ed. Harold G. Coward and Toby Foshay (Albany: State University of New York Press, 1992), 73–142.

4. John D. Caputo, *The Mystical Element in Heidegger's Thought*, rev. ed. (New York: Fordham University Press, 1986), 174–75. Reiner Schürmann, "Heidegger and Meister Eckhart on Releasement," *Research in Phenomenology* 3 (1973): 95–119. Friedrich-Wilhelm von Herrmann, "'Gelassenheit' bei Heidegger und Meister Eckhart," in *From Phenomenology to Thought, Errancy, and Desire: Essays in Honor of William J. Richardson, S.J.*, ed. Babette E. Babich (Dordrecht: Kluwer, 1995), 115–27.

5. For bibliographical information on the reception of German mysticism in particular, see Niklaus Largier, "Meister Eckhart: Perspektiven der Forschung, 1980–1993," *Zeitschrift fur Deutsche Philologie* 114, no. 1 (1995): 29–98. For a recent account of Musil's reading of Eckhart, see Niklaus Largier, "A 'Sense of Possibility': Robert Musil, Meister Eckhart and the 'Culture of Film,'" in *Religion: Beyond a Concept*, ed. Hent de Vries (New York: Fordham University Press, 2008), 739–49.

6. Janet Sayers, *Divine Therapy: Love, Mysticism, and Psychoanalysis* (New York: Oxford University Press, 2003); Morny Joy, Kathleen O'Grady, and Judith L. Poxon, eds., *Religion in French Feminist Thought: Critical Perspectives* (London: Routledge, 2003).

7. Sudhir Kakar, *The Analyst and the Mystic: Psychoanalytic Reflections on Religion and Mysticism* (Chicago: University of Chicago Press, 1990), 28.

8. A. Hollywood, "Gender, Agency, and the Divine in Religious Historiography," *Journal of Religion* 84, no. 4 (2004): 519.

9. For an account of the Freud/Rolland debate, see chapter 2 in Sayers, *Divine Therapy: Love, Mysticism, and Psychoanalysis.*

10. Oskar Pfister, "Hysterie und Mystik bei Margaretha Ebner (1291–1351)," *Zentralblatt für Psychoanalyse* 1, no. 10/11 (1911): 468–85.

11. C. G. Jung, *Psychological Types, or, the Psychology of Individuation*, trans. H. Godwin Baynes (London: Routledge & Kegan Paul, 1923), 299–316.

12. Jacques Lacan, *On Feminine Sexuality: The Limits of Love and Knowledge*, trans. Bruce Fink (New York: Norton, 1998), 76.

13. Ibid., 77.

14. Ibid., 76.

15. Ibid., 72.

16. Malcolm Bowie, *Lacan* (London: Fontana, 1991), 153–54.

17. "There is no such thing as woman because, in her essence—I've already risked using that term, so why should I think twice about using it again?—she is not whole." Lacan, *On Feminine Sexuality: The Limits of Love and Knowledge*, 72–73.

18. Ibid.

19. Ibid., 76.

20. Elisabeth Roudinesco, *Jacques Lacan: Outline of a Life, History of a System of Thought*, trans. Barbara Bray (New York: Columbia University Press, 1997), 369–70.

21. Stanley Cavell, *Contesting Tears: The Hollywood Melodrama of the Unknown Woman* (Chicago: University of Chicago Press, 1996), 99.

22. Toril Moi, "From Femininity to Finitude: Freud, Lacan, and Feminism, Again," *Signs* 29, no. 3 (2004): 841–78.

23. Jacques Lacan, *Écrits: A Selection*, trans. Alan Sheridan (London: Routledge, 1977), 6.

24. Ibid., 4.

25. Elisabeth Roudinesco, "The mirror stage: an obliterated archive," in Jean-Michel Rabaté, ed., *The Cambridge Companion to Lacan* (Cambridge: Cambridge University Press, 2003), 25–34, 33.

26. Martin Jay, *Downcast Eyes: The Denigration of Vision in Twentieth-Century French Thought* (Berkeley: University of California Press, 1993), 343–45.

27. For a sympathetic reading of Lacan which uses a combination of Merleau-Ponty and Winnicott to re-introduce human interaction and plug the theoretical gaps in Lacan's account, see John O'Neill, "The Specular Body: Merleau-Ponty and Lacan on Infant Self and Other," *Synthese* 66, no. 2 (1986): 201–17.

28. D. W. Winnicott, *Playing and Reality* (London: Routledge, 1989), 111–18.

29. Ibid., 112.

30. Colwyn Trevarthen, "Communication and cooperation in early infancy: a description of primary intersubjectivity," in Margaret Bullowa, ed., *Before Speech: The Beginning of Interpersonal Communication* (Cambridge: Cambridge University Press, 1979), 321–47. Colwyn Trevarthen, "The Concept and Foundations of infant intersubjectivity," in Stein Bråten, ed., *Intersubjective Communication and Emotion in Early Ontogeny, Studies in Emotion and Social Interaction. Second Series* (Cambridge: Cambridge University Press, 1998), 15–46. R. Peter Hobson, *The Cradle of Thought* (London: Macmillan, 2002), 59.

31. Amy Hollywood emphasizes the degree to which Lacan's discuss of gender can be separated from biological sex. Amy M. Hollywood, *Sensible Ecstasy: Mysticism, Sexual Difference, and the Demands of History, Religion and Postmodernism* (Chicago: University of Chicago Press, 2002), 155–56. I discuss Hollywood's position in more detail below.

32. Luce Irigaray, *Speculum of the Other Woman*, trans. Gillian C. Gill (Ithaca: Cornell University Press, 1985), 227.

33. Ibid., 143.

34. Ann-Marie Priest, "Woman as God, God as Woman: Mysticism, Negative Theology, and Luce Irigaray," *Journal of Religion* 83, no. 1 (2003): 1–23.

35. Luce Irigaray, *I Love to You: Sketch for a Felicity within History*, trans. Alison Martin (New York; London: Routledge, 1996), 63.

36. Ibid., 64.

37. Luce Irigaray, *Sexes and Genealogies*, trans. Gillian C. Gill (New York: Columbia University Press, 1993), 57–72.

38. Ibid., 67–68.

39. Ibid., 62.

40. Ibid.

41. Ibid., 64.

42. Ibid., 72, 68.

43. Franz-Josef Schweitzer, *Der Freiheitsbegriff der deutschen Mystik: Seine Beziehung zur Ketzerei der "Brüder und Schwestern vom Freien Geist," mit besonderer Rücksicht auf den pseudoeckartischen Traktat "Schwester Katrei" (Edition), Europäische Hochschulschriften. Reihe I, Deutsche Sprache Und Literatur; Bd. 378* (Frankfurt am Main: Peter Lang, 1981), 323.

44. Eckhart, *German Sermons & Treatises*, trans. Maurice O'C Walshe, 3 vols. (Shaftesbury: Element Books, 1979), 1:72–73.

45. Marguerite Porete, *The Mirror of Simple Souls*, trans. Ellen L. Babinsky, *Classics of Western Spirituality* (New York: Paulist Press, 1993), 145.

46. Irigaray, *Sexes and Genealogies*, 63.

47. Mary L. Keller, "Divine Women and the Nehanda Mhondoro: Strengths and Limitations of the Sensible Transcendental in a Post-Colonial World of Religious Women" in *Religion in French Feminist Thought: Critical Perspectives*, ed. Joy, O'Grady, and Poxon, 68–82. Phyllis Mack has similarly commented on the difficulties for feminist approaches committed to the idea of autonomy when trying to understand cultures, especially religious cultures, in which a sense of agency is not necessarily linked to autonomy. Phyllis Mack, "Religion, Feminism, and the Problem of Agency: Reflections on Eighteenth-Century Quakerism," *Signs* 29, no. 1 (2003): 149–77.

48. Irigaray, *Sexes and Genealogies*, 71.

49. Penelope Deutscher, *A Politics of Impossible Difference: The Later Work of Luce Irigaray* (Ithaca, N.Y.: Cornell University Press, 2002), 97.

50. Pamela Sue Anderson, "Life, Death and (Inter)Subjectivity: Realism and Recognition in Continental Feminism," *International Journal for Philosophy of Religion* 60, no. 1–3 (2006): 48.

51. Patrice Haynes, "The Problem of Transcendence in Irigaray's Philosophy of Sexual Difference," in *New Topics in Feminist Philosophy of Religion: Contestations and Transcendence Incarnate*, ed. Pamela Sue Anderson (Dordrecht: Springer Netherlands, 2009), 279–96.

52. Hollywood, *Sensible Ecstasy*, 155–56. Quoting Lacan, *On Feminine Sexuality: The Limits of Love and Knowledge*, 76.

53. Hollywood, *Sensible Ecstasy*, 168.

54. Examples would be the 1983 essay "A critique of the sex/gender distinction," reprinted in Moira Gatens, *Imaginary Bodies: Ethics, Power and Corporeality* (London: Routledge, 1995), 3–20, esp. p. 19. Judith Butler, *Gender Trouble: Feminism and the Subversion of Identity* (New York: Routledge, 1990). The idea of the sliding scale is confirmed by experiments showing that sexual attributes are not binary (more femaleness implies less maleness) but that male and female attributes can be independently triggered. Sexual differentiation of behavior thus occurs in a "multidimensional space," an individual can exhibit both male and female characteristics, and both to varying degrees. Melissa Hines, *Brain Gender* (Oxford: Oxford University Press, 2004), 62–64.

55. Hollywood, *Sensible Ecstasy*, 214.

56. Ibid., 277.

57. Ibid., 234–35.

58. Georges Bataille, *La somme athéologique.*, vols. 5–6 of *Œuvres complètes* (Paris: Gallimard, 1970).

59. "Bataille argues that woundedness and its recognition are necessary for opening one human being to the other. The greater the woundedness and laceration—the more the self is exploded and ripped apart—the fuller the communication that occurs between the nonself and the now ruined other." Hollywood, *Sensible Ecstasy*, 82.

60. Ibid., 58–59.

61. Ibid., 65.

62. Ibid., 118.

63. Ibid., 105.

64. Ibid., 123.

65. Simone de Beauvoir, *The Second Sex*, trans. H. M. Parshley (London: Vintage, 1997), 639.

66. Ibid., 687.

67. Hollywood, *Sensible Ecstasy*, 272.

2. Empty Epiphanies in Modernist and Postmodernist Theory

1. I use Derrida's "Geschlecht" essay to establish a framework for rethinking questions of sexual difference in Ben Morgan, "The Limits of Human Togetherness," *Limbus: Australian Yearbook of German Literary and Cultural Studies* 3 (2010): 159–76. I offer a reading of Adorno's and Horkheimer's concept of mimesis that tries to disentangle it from their Hegelian habits of thought in Ben Morgan, "The Project of the Frankfurt School," *Telos*, no. 119 (2001): 75–98.

2. Andrew E. Benjamin, ed., *The Lyotard Reader* (Oxford: Basil Blackwell, 1989), 196–211.

3. Ibid., 197.

4. Ibid., 198.

5. Ibid.

6. Carroll Jerome, "The Limits of the Sublime, the Sublime of Limits: Hermeneutics as a Critique of the Postmodern Sublime," *Journal of Aesthetics and Art Criticism* 66, no. 2 (2008): 173.

7. Slavoj Žižek, *The Sublime Object of Ideology* (London: Verso, 1989), 2.

8. Ibid., 31.

9. Ibid., 49.

10. Slavoj Žižek, *Liebe deinen Nächsten? Nein, Danke: Die Sackgasse des Sozialen in der Postmoderne* (Berlin: Volk u. Welt, 1999). See also Alenka Zupancic, "The Subject of the Law," in *Cogito and the Unconscious*, ed. Slavoj Žižek (Durham, N.C.: Duke University Press, 1998), 41–73.

11. Judith Butler, *Bodies That Matter: On the Discursive Limits Of "Sex"* (New York: Routledge, 1993) 207.

12. Claudia Breger, "The Leader's Two Bodies—Slavoj Žižek's Postmodern Political Theology," *Diacritics* 31, no. 1 (2001): 88.

13. Hubert L. Dreyfus, *On the Internet* (London: Routledge, 2001), 6.

14. Slavoj Žižek, "The Rhetorics of Power," *Diacritics* 31, no. 1 (2001): 99.

15. Ibid., 99–100.

16. Ibid., 100.

17. "Alsô sprechen wir, daz der mensche alsô arm sül stân, daz er niht ensî noch enhabe deheine stat, dar got inne müge würken. Dâ der mensche stat beheltet, dâ beheltet er underscheit. Her umbe sô bite ich got, daz er mich quît mache gotes. . . ." Georg Steer and Loris Sturlese, eds., *Lectura Eckhardi: Predigten Meister Eckharts von Fachgelehrten gelesen und gedeutet* (Stuttgart: Kohlhammer, 1998), 179; Niklaus Largier and Josef Quint, eds., *Meister Eckhart Werke*, 2 vols., vol. 20–21, *Bibliothek des Mittelalters* (Frankfurt am Main: Deutscher Klassiker Verlag, 1993), 1:560. Steer and Sturlese give the revised reading of the manuscripts, which I'm following.

18. Žižek, "The Rhetorics of Power," 100.

19. For example: "We all know very well that bureaucracy is not all-powerful." Žižek, *The Sublime Object of Ideology*, 36.

20. Theodor W. Adorno and Max Horkheimer, *Dialectic of Enlightenment*, trans. John Cumming (London: Verson, 1979), 118.

21. Jacques Derrida, *Margins of Philosophy*, trans. Alan Bass (Brighton: Harvester, 1982), 26–27.

22. Eduardo Cadava, Peter Connor, and Jean-Luc Nancy, *Who Comes after the Subject?* (London: Routledge, 1991), 100.

23. Jacques Derrida and John D. Caputo, *Deconstruction in a Nutshell: A Conversation with Jacques Derrida* (New York: Fordham University Press, 1997), 24–25. The story is dealt with at greater length in Jacques Derrida, *The Politics of Friendship*, trans. George Collins (London: Verso, 1997), 37, 46, 173.

24. Derrida and Caputo, *Deconstruction in a Nutshell: A Conversation with Jacques Derrida*, 22.

25. Ibid., 27–28.

26. Samuel Beckett, *Worstward Ho* (London: John Calder, 1983), 7.

27. John D. Caputo, *The Prayers and Tears of Jacques Derrida: Religion without Religion* (Bloomington: Indiana University Press, 1997), xix.

28. Dan Zahavi, *Subjectivity and Selfhood: Investigating the First-Person Perspective* (Cambridge, Mass.: MIT Press, 2005), 69–72.

29. Michael Stone, "Wittgenstein on Deconstruction," in Alice Crary and Rupert Read, *The New Wittgenstein* (London: Routledge, 2000), 83–117.

30. "Narretei ist Wahrheit in der Gestalt, mit der die Menschen geschlagen werden, sobald sie inmitten des Unwahren nicht von ihr ablassen." Theodor W. Adorno, *Gesammelte Schriften*, ed. Rolf Tiedemann, 20 vols. (Frankfurt am Main: Suhrkamp, 1970–), 6:396.

31. "Reflektierte Menschen, und Künstler, haben nicht selten ein Gefühl des nicht ganz Dabeiseins, nicht Mitspielens aufgezeichnet; als ob sie gar nicht sie selber wären, sondern eine Art Zuschauer." Adorno, *Gesammelte Schriften*, 6:356.

32. John Dewey, *Human Nature and Conduct* (Amherst, N.Y.: Prometheus, 2002), 167.

33. Amy M. Hollywood, *Sensible Ecstasy: Mysticism, Sexual Difference, and the Demands of History, Religion and Postmodernism* (Chicago: University of Chicago Press, 2002), 265.

34. Ibid.

35. Charles Taylor, *Sources of the Self: The Making of the Modern Identity* (Cambridge: Cambridge University Press, 1989); Jerrold E. Seigel, *The Idea of the Self: Thought and Experience in Western Europe since the Seventeenth Century* (Cambridge: Cambridge University Press, 2005). Taylor's failure systematically to address the question of gender has been pointed out by Elizabeth Frazer and Nicola Lacey, *The Politics of Community: A Feminist Critique of the Liberal–Communitarian Debate* (London: Harvester Wheatsheaf, 1993), 159. Seigel's omission of gender is commented on by a number of reviewers: William Breckman, "The Idea of the Self Thought and Experience in Western Europe since the Seventeenth Century," *Journal of British Studies* 46, no. 1 (2007): 158–61; Peter Mandler, "The Idea of the Self Thought and Experience in Western Europe since the Seventeenth Century," *American Historical Review* 112, no. 2 (2007): 575–76.

36. Colin Morris, *The Discovery of the Individual, 1050–1200*, Medieval Academy Reprints for Teaching 19 (Toronto: University of Toronto Press with the Medieval Academy of America, 1987), 96.

37. Michel Foucault, *The Use of Pleasure*, vol. 2 of *The History of Sexuality*, trans. Robert Hurley (Harmondsworth: Viking, 1986), 58.

38. Hollywood, *Sensible Ecstasy: Mysticism, Sexual Difference, and the Demands of History*, 259–60.

39. Sudhir Kakar, *The Analyst and the Mystic: Psychoanalytic Reflections on Religion and Mysticism* (Chicago: University of Chicago Press, 1990), 28.

40. For an overview of the treatment of intersubjectivity in the phenomenological tradition, see Dan Zahavi, *Husserl and Transcendental Intersubjectivity: A Response to the Linguistic-Pragmatic Critique*, trans. Elizabeth A. Behnke (Athens: Ohio University Press, 2001). As the title suggests, Zahavi's main point of orientation is Husserl, so he is less interested than I in the changing historical forms of human togetherness.

41. Rorty uses the tool metaphor even for scientific discoveries: "Whereas the positivist sees Galileo as making a discovery—finally coming up with words which were needed to fit the world properly, words Aristotle missed—the Davidsonian sees him as having hit upon a tool which happened to work better for certain purposes than any previous tool." Richard Rorty, *Contingency, Irony, and Solidarity* (Cambridge: Cambridge University Press, 1989), 19.

42. "Was für eine Philosophie man wähle, hängt sonach davon ab, was man für ein Mensch ist." Johann Gottlieb Fichte, "Erste Einleitung in die Wissenschaftslehre" (1797), in *Deutscher Idealismus*, ed. Rüdiger Bubner, vol. 6 of *Geschichte der Philosophie in Text und Darstellung* (Stuttgart: Reclam, 1978), 138.

3. The Gender of Human Togetherness

1. Hubert L. Dreyfus, *Being-in-the-World: A Commentary on Heidegger's Being and Time, Division I* (Cambridge, Mass.: MIT Press, 1991), 143–44. Three recent studies that use Heidegger's approach to togetherness, or *Mitsein*, to, as it were, take Heidegger beyond Heidegger are Frederick A. Olafson, *Heidegger and the Ground of Ethics: A Study of Mitsein* (Cambridge: Cambridge University Press, 1998); Jean-Luc Nancy, *Being Singular Plural*, trans. Robert D. Richardson and Anne E. O'Byrne (Stanford, Calif.: Stanford University Press, 2000); and Michael Lewis, *Heidegger and the Place of Ethics: Being-with in the Crossing of Heidegger's Thought* (London: Continuum, 2005).

2. Martin Heidegger, *Being and Time*, trans. John Macquarrie and Edward Robinson (Oxford: Basil Blackwell, 1962), 156 (§26).

3. Ibid., 156–57 (§26).

4. Jean-Paul Sartre, *Being and Nothingess: An Essay on Phenomenological Ontology*, trans. Hazel E. Barnes (London: Routledge, 1969), 334. Nancy Bauer discusses Sartre's reading of *Mitsein* and quotes this passage in her essay "Must We Read Simone de Beauvoir?" in *The Legacy of Simone de Beauvoir*, ed. Emily Grosholz (Oxford: Clarendon Press, 2004), 132.

5. "Partir du *Dasein* ou partier du J. . . . J. comme catégorie." Emmanuel Levinas, *Carnets de captivité et autres inédits*, ed. Rodolphe Calin and Catherine Chalier (Paris: Bernard Grasset / IMEC, 2009), 75 (C2, 35). The editors gloss the "J" unambiguously as Judaism. An identity simultaneously produced and disrupted by an accusatory address returns in Levinas's later work. "La persecution ne vient pas s'ajouter à la subjectivité du sujet et à sa vulnérabilité; elle est le mouvement même de la recurrence." Emmanuel Levinas, *Autrement qu'être ou au-delà de l'essence* (The Hague: Nijhoff, 1978), 176.

6. "Participation véritable forme de relation avec autrui . . ." Levinas, *Carnets de captivité et autres inédits*, 55 (C1, 12).

7. Ibid., 52 (C1, 4–5). "En transformant la solitude en une forme de l'*In-der-Welt-Sein* Heidegger s'interdit de voir dans la solitude une insuffisance le néant du fait meme de l'être at la voie du salut."

8. Emmanuel Levinas, *Time and the Other*, trans. Richard A. Cohen (Pittsburgh: Duquesne University Press, 1987), 42. Emmanuel Levinas, *Le temps et l'autre* (Paris: Quadrige/PUF, 1983), 21. Levinas's critique of Heidegger is discussed in: Tina Chanter, *Time, Death, and the Feminine: Levinas with Heidegger* (Stanford: Stanford University Press, 2001), 105–8.

9. Levinas, *Time and the Other*, 55. "L'identité n'est pas une inoffensive relation avec soi, mais un enchaînement à soi." Levinas, *Le temps et l'autre*, 36.

10. Heidegger, *Being and Time*, 176 (§29).

11. Martin Heidegger, *Die Grundbegriffe der Metaphysik: Welt—Endlichkeit—Einsamkeit*, ed. Friedrich-Wilhelm von Hermann (Frankfurt am Main: Klostermann, 1983), 100.

12. Heidegger, *Being and Time*, 175 (§29).

13. Ibid., 178 (§29).

14. "Mitdasein ist wesenhaft schon offenbar in der Mitbefindlichkeit und im Mitverstehen." Ibid., 205 (§34).

15. Dan Zahavi, *Husserl and Transcendental Intersubjectivity: A Response to the Linguistic-Pragmatic Critique*, trans. Elizabeth A. Behnke (Athens: Ohio University Press, 2001), 136, 63–64.

16. "Weil die Stimmung das ursprüngliche Wie ist, in dem jedes Dasein ist, wie es ist, ist sie nicht das Unbeständigste, sondern das, was dem Dasein von Grund auf *Bestand und Möglichkeit* gibt." Heidegger, *Die Grundbegriffe der Metaphysik: Welt—Endlichtkeit—Einsamkeit*, 101.

17. For an accessible introduction to the research group in Parma and their discoveries, see Marco Iacoboni, *Mirroring People: The New Science of How We Connect with Others* (New York: Farrar, Straus and Giroux, 2008), 3–46.

18. G. Pellegrino et al., "Understanding Motor Events: A Neurophysiological Study," *Experimental Brain Research* 91, no. 1 (1992): 176–80.

19. The best account for the general reader is Iacoboni, *Mirroring People: The New Science of How We Connect with Others*. For a more specialist review of literature on mirror neurons and their relation to research on empathy and mind-reading, see Tania Singer, "The Neuronal Basis and Ontogeny of Empathy and Mind Reading: Review of Literature and Implications for Future Research," *Neuroscience and Biobehavioral Reviews* 30, no. 6 (2006): 855–63. For a discussion of research on mirror neurons and language, see Giacomo Rizzolatti and Laila Craighero, "The Mirror-Neuron System," *Annual Review of Neuroscience* 27, no. 1 (2004): 169–92. For hand gestures, see Kimberly J. Montgomery, Nancy Isenberg, and James V. Haxby, "Communicative Hand Gestures and Object-Directed Hand Movements Activated the Mirror Neuron System," *Social Cognitive and Affective Neuroscience* 2, no. 2 (2007): 114–22.

20. For an intervention that gives bibliographical information for the early stages of the debate in the 1990s see Rebecca Saxe, "Against Simulation: The Argument from Error," *Trends in Cognitive Sciences* 9, no. 4 (2005): 174–79.

21. Vittorio Gallese, "Intentional Attunement: A Neurophysiological Perspective on Social Cognition and Its Disruption in Autism," *Brain Research* 1079 (2006): 15.

22. Peter Carruthers, "Simulation and Self-Knowledge: A Defence of Theory-Theory," in *Theories of Theories of Mind*, ed. Peter Carruthers and Peter K. Smith (Cambridge: Cambridge University Press, 1996), 22–38, 22.

23. Pierre Jacob and Marc Jeannerod, "The Motor Theory of Social Cognition: A Critique," *Trends in Cognitive Sciences* 9, no. 1 (2005): 21–25.

24. V. Gazzola et al., "The Anthropomorphic Brain: The Mirror Neuron System Responds to Human and Robotic Actions," *NeuroImage* 35, no. 4 (2007): 1674–84.

25. Shaun Gallagher, "Direct Perception in the Intersubjective Context," *Consciousness and Cognition* 17 (2008): 540.

26. To give an example from recent literature, James Kilner, discussing the ability of the mirror neuron system to predict people's behavior, writes: "Social interaction depends upon our ability to infer beliefs and intentions in others." James M. Kilner, Karl J. Friston, and Chris D. Frith, "The Mirror-Neuron-System: A Bayesian Perspetctive," *NeuroReport* 18, no. 6 (2007): 622. The model of separated subjects making inferences and having theories, simulations, or direct perceptions of the actions of other, separated subjects returns again and again. Shaun Gallagher's examples are similarly those of a disengaged observer: Looking at his car, watching someone get a drink, or watching someone walk away angrily. Gallagher, "Direct Perception in the Intersubjective Context," 536.

27. For an explicit appeal that theorizations of mirror neurons move beyond the image of an isolated subject inherited from the Cartesian tradition, see Marco Iacoboni, "The Quiet Revolution of Existential Neuroscience," in *Social Neuroscience: Integrating Biological and Psychological Explanations of Social Behavior*, ed. Eddie Harmon-Jones and Piotr Winkielman (New York: Guilford Press, 2007), 439–53.

28. Pellegrino et al., "Understanding Motor Events: A Neurophysiological Study," 176.

29. See the discussion of macaque monkeys expanding their repertoire to include tool use when they come into contact with human experimenters. Iacoboni, *Mirroring People: The New Science of How We Connect with Others*, 38–42.

30. V. Gallese, "The Roots of Empathy: The Shared Manifold Hypothesis and the Neural Basis of Intersubjectivity," *Psychopathology* 36, no. 4 (2003): 172.

31. Peter Carruthers, "Simulation and Self-Knowledge: A Defence of Theory-Theory," *Theories of Theories of Mind*, ed. Carruthers and Smith, 22–38.

32. Gazzola et al., "The Anthropomorphic Brain: The Mirror Neuron System Responds to Human and Robotic Actions," 1674.

33. Valeria Gazzola et al., "Aplasics Born without Hands Mirror the Goal of Hand Actions with Their Feet," *Current Biology* 17, no. 14 (2007): 1235–40.

34. Yawei Cheng, Andrew N. Meltzoff, and Jean Decety, "Motivation Modulates the Activity of the Human Mirror-Neuron System," *Cerebral Cortex* 17, no. 8 (2007): 1979–86.

35. Frederique de Vignemont and Tania Singer, "The Empathic Brian: How, When, Why?" *Trends in Cognitive Sciences* 10, no. 10 (2006): 435–41.

36. For instance, Tania Singer insists that "affect sharing" does not suggest one feeling felt by two people but two people separately feeling the same thing: "At this point it is important to stress that although empathizing is defined as 'affect sharing' the affective state in self and others is not simply shared but has to be induced in the self by the perception or imagination of an emotional state in another person and, even if it feels similar, is nevertheless distinguishable from the same feeling originated in ourselves." Singer, "The Neuronal Basis and Ontogeny of Empathy and Mind Reading: Review of Literature and Implications for Future Research," 858.

37. John Dewey's pragmatist position is similarly helpful, if a little less explicit about the fundamental nature of our interconnectedness. "Conduct is always shared," Dewey insists. "Even letting a man alone is a definite response. Envy, admiration and imitation are complicities." John Dewey, *Human Nature and Conduct* (Amherst, N.Y.: Prometheus, 2002), 17.

38. Theodore R. Schatzki, "Early Heidegger on Sociality," in *A Companion to Heidegger*, ed. Mark A. Wrathall and Hubert L. Dreyfus (Oxford, UK; Malden, Mass.: Blackwell, 2005), 245.

39. Jürgen Habermas, *The Philosophical Discourse of Modernity: Twelve Lectures*, trans. Frederick Lawrence (Cambridge, Mass: MIT Press, 1987), 148–50; Patricia J. Huntington, *Ecstatic Subjects, Utopia, and Recognition: Kristeva, Heidegger, Irigaray* (Albany, N.Y.: State University of New York Press, 1998), 22.

40. Dreyfus, *Being-in-the-World: A Commentary on Heidegger's Being and Time, Division I*, 154.

41. "We enjoy ourselves and take pleasure as *one* is meant to enjoy oneself; we read, look at and have an opinion about literature and art as *one* looks at things and forms an opinion. But we also withdraw from the 'madding crowd' in the way *one* withdraws. We are 'outraged' at the things that *one* finds outrageous." Heidegger, *Being and Time*, 164, (§27) (translation amended.)

42. Chanter, *Time, Death, and the Feminine.*

43. "Le sujet reposant sur soi est désarçonné par une accusation sans paroles." "Subjectivité comme otage." Levinas, *Autrement qu'être ou au-delà de l'essence*, 202.

44. Eva Gothlin, "Reading Simone de Beauvoir with Martin Heidegger," in *The Cambridge Companion to Simone De Beauvoir*, ed. Claudia Card (Cambridge: Cambridge University Press, 2003), 58.

45. Simone de Beauvoir, *The Second Sex*, trans. H. M. Parshley (London: Vintage, 1997), I, 17, 29.

46. Herman Philipse has pointed out that a range of issues such as gender, ageing, love, and procreation, which are vital to an understanding of what fundamentally structures a human life, are not adequately addressed by Heidegger. Herman Philipse, "Heidegger and Ethics," *Inquiry* 42 (1999): 444. He doesn't mention Beauvoir's adoption of the term *Mitsein*.

47. Beauvoir, *The Second Sex*, 67 (translation amended); Simone de Beauvoir, *Le deuxième sexe*, 2 vols. (Paris: Gallimard, 2006), 1:77: "le couple est un *mitsein* original."

48. Beauvoir, *The Second Sex*, 19–20 (translation amended); Beauvoir, *Le deuxième sexe*, 1:21–22.

49. Toril Moi, *What Is a Woman? And Other Essays* (Oxford; New York: Oxford University Press, 1999), 65.

50. Beauvoir, *The Second Sex*, 78–79. Beauvoir, *Le deuxième sexe*, 1:91.

51. Heidegger, *Being and Time*, 269 (§44c).

52. D. W. Winnicott, *Playing and Reality* (London; New York: Routledge, 1989), 79.

53. Ibid., 80.

54. Ibid., 137.

55. Ibid., 130.

56. Ibid., 80.

57. Timothy P. Racine and Jeremy I. M. Carpendale, "The Role of Shared Practice in Joint Attention," *British Journal of Developmental Psychology* 25 (2007): 3–25.

58. Judith Butler, *Gender Trouble: Feminism and the Subversion of Identity* (New York: Routledge, 1990), 25.

59. Judith Butler, *Bodies That Matter: On the Discursive Limits of "Sex"* (New York: Routledge, 1993), 222.

60. Ibid., 8.

61. For a summary of his position, see Habermas, *The Philosophical Discourse of Modernity: Twelve Lectures*, 294–367.

62. "What is Critique? An Essay on Foucault's Virtue," in *The Judith Butler Reader*, ed. Sara Salih and Judith Butler (Oxford: Blackwell, 2004), 306.

63. The self, for Butler, "is compelled to form itself within practices that are more or less in place. But if that self-forming is done in disobedience to the principles by which one is formed, then virtue becomes the practice by which the self forms itself in desubjugation, which is to say that it risks its deformation as a subject, occupying that ontologically insecure position which poses the question anew: who will be a subject here, what will count as a life, a moment of ethical questioning which requires that we break the habits of judgment in favor of a riskier practice that seeks to yield artistry from constraint." Ibid., 321.

64. Moi, *What Is a Woman? And Other Essays*, 56.

65. Judith Butler, *The Psychic Life of Power: Theories in Subjection* (Stanford, Calif.: Stanford University Press, 1997), 30.

66. Frances L. Restuccia similarly argues that "Butler takes up melancholia, a painful pathology, as if it were the condition of all subjects—the constitutive condition, no less." "The Subject of Homosexuality: Butler's Elision," in *Lacan in America*, ed. Jean-Michel Rabaté (New York: Other Press, 2000), 351.

67. Butler, *The Psychic Life of Power: Theories in Subjection*, 66–67.

68. Judith Butler, "Giving an Account of Oneself," *Diacritics* 31, no. 4 (2001): 36.

69. Ibid., 38.

70. D. W. Winnicott, *The Maturational Processes and the Facilitating Environment: Studies in the Theory of Emotional Development* (London: Karnac and the Institute of Psycho-Analysis, 1990), 43.

71. Butler, "Giving an Account of Oneself," 34.

72. Judith Butler in *Undoing Gender* (2004) uses grief as a very vivid way of showing how we're constituted, in ways we don't fully control, by our relations with others. But because Butler retains her commitment to autonomy and agency, our being undone can only be thought of as a paradox rather than as a way of rethinking identity and moving beyond terms like *agency* and *autonomy.* "Beside Oneself: On the Limits of Sexual Autonomy," Judith Butler, *Undoing Gender* (New York; London: Routledge, 2004), 17–39.

73. D. W. Winnicott, *The Child, the Family, and the Outside World* (Harmondsworth: Penguin Books, 1964), 75–79.

74. Ibid., 79.

75. Butler explicitly engages with Hegel in Judith Butler, *Antigone's Claim: Kinship between Life and Death* (New York: Columbia University Press, 2000), 12–14, 28–40. In this text, she presents the trope of catachresis (Antigone's misapplication of the idea of the human) as a way of moving beyond oppositions (the human versus the nonhuman) (82).

76. Heidegger, *Being and Time*, 156–57 (§26).

77. Simone de Beauvoir, *Journal De Guerre: Septembre 1939–Janvier 1941*, ed. Sylvie Le Bon de Beauvoir (Paris: Gallimard, 1990), 362.

78. Beauvoir, *The Second Sex*, 17; Beauvoir, *Le deuxième sexe*, 1:19.

79. Beauvoir, *The Second Sex*, 19; Beauvoir, *Le deuxième sexe*, 1:22.

80. "L'amour authentique devrait être fondé sur la reconnaissance réciproque de deux libertés; chacun des amants s'éprouverait alors comme soi-même et comme l'autre." Beauvoir, *Le deuxième sexe*, 2:571.

81. Beauvoir, *The Second Sex*, 655; Beauvoir, *Le deuxième sexe*, 2:543.

82. Beauvoir, *The Second Sex*, 79: Beauvoir, *Le deuxième sexe*, 1:92.

83. Melissa Hines, *Brain Gender* (Oxford: Oxford University Press, 2004), 19.

84. Habermas, *The Philosophical Discourse of Modernity: Twelve Lectures*, 284–86; Charles Taylor, "Foucault on Freedom and Truth," in *Philosophy and the Human Sciences* (Cambridge: Cambridge University Press, 1985), 174–77; Peter Dews, "The Return of the Subject in Late Foucault," in *Michel Foucault: Critical Assessments*, 7 vols., ed. Barry Smart (London: Routledge, 1994), 6:150–

52; Judith Butler, "What Is Critique? An Essay on Foucault's Virtue," in *The Judith Butler Reader*, ed. Salih and Butler, 302–22.

85. Heidegger, *Being and Time*, 167 (§27).

86. Ibid., 213 (§35).

87. Ibid., 167 (§27).

88. Ibid., 234 (§40).

89. Franz Kafka, "Eine kleine Frau," in *Drucke zu Lebzeiten*, ed. Wolf Kittler, Hans-Gerd Koch, and Gerhard Neumann (Frankfurt am Main: S. Fischer, 1994), 321–33. Further references will be given parenthetically in the text. For information about the text's composition, see Franz Kafka, *Drucke zu Lebzeiten: Apparatband*, ed. Wolf Kittler, Hans-Gerd Koch and Gerhard Neumann (Frankfurt am Main: S. Fischer, 1996), 418–20. The translations are my own.

90. Dora Diamant, "Mein Leben mit Franz Kafka," in *"Als Kafka mir entgegenkam . . .": Erinnerungen an Franz Kafka*, ed. Hans-Gerd Koch (Berlin: Wagenbach, 1995), 174–85; Stanley Corngold, "Kafka's Later Stories and Aphorisms," in *The Cambridge Companion to Kafka*, ed. Julian Preece (Cambridge: Cambridge University Press, 2002), 95–110; Sander L. Gilman, *Franz Kafka, the Jewish Patient* (New York: Routledge, 1995), 167–78.

91. Elisabeth Bronfen, "Femme Fatale—Negotiations of Tragic Desire," *New Literary History: A Journal of Theory and Interpretation* 35, no. 1 (2004): 114.

92. Roy Pascal, *Kafka's Narrators: A Study of His Stories and Sketches*, (Cambridge: Cambridge University Press, 1982), 186.

93. Stanley Cavell, *Must We Mean What We Say? A Book of Essays*, updated ed. (Cambridge: Cambridge University Press, 2002), 265–66.

94. For a very productive, comparative approach to the history of selfhood, see Thomas P. Kasulis with Roger T. Ames and Wimal Dissanayake, eds., *Self as Body in Asian Theory and Practice* (Albany: State University of New York Press, 1993); Roger T. Ames, with Wimal Dissanayake and Thomas P. Kasulis, eds. *Self as Person in Asian Theory and Practice* (Albany: State University of New York Press, 1994); and Roger T. Ames with Thomas P. Kasulis and Wimal Dissanayake, eds., *Self as Image in Asian Theory and Practice*, (Albany, N.Y.: State University of New York Press, 1998).

95. Terence Cave's defamiliarizing investigation of what he calls the prehistory of modern identity hopes to avoid imposing our current agenda on the fragments from the past, forgoing the temptations of analepsis, or looking back to see ourselves prefigured. Terence Cave, *Pré-Histoires: Textes troublés au seuil de la modernité* (Geneva: Droz, 1999), 17. I question whether it is desirable to detach our current involvements from the investigation of the past, in Ben Morgan, "Abandoning Selfhood with Medieval Mystics," in *Pre-Histories and Afterlives: Studies in Critical Method*, ed. Anna Holland and Richard Scholar (London: Legenda, 2009), 29–43.

4. Histories of Modern Selfhood

1. Michel Foucault, *The Use of Pleasure*, vol. 2 of *The History of Sexuality* trans. Robert Hurley (Harmondsworth: Viking, 1986), 9.

2. Ibid., 8.

3. Michel Foucault, *Ethics: Subjectivity and Truth*, ed. Paul Rabinow (London: Penguin, 2000), 12.

4. Ibid., 34.

5. Sonia Kruks, "Reading Beauvoir with and against Foucault," in *Simone de Beauvoir's Political Thinking*, ed. in Lori Jo Marso and Patricia Moynagh (Urbana, Ill.: University of Illinois Press, 2006), 62.

6. Michel Foucault, *Discipline and Punish: The Birth of the Prison*, trans. Alan Sheridan (Harmondsworth: Penguin, 1977), 30.

7. Foucault, *Ethics: Subjectivity and Truth*, 34–35.

8. Kruks comments on Foucault's tendency to personify or anthropomorphize abstract social forces and thereby mask human activity, in "Reading Beauvoir with and against Foucault," ed. Marso and Moynagh, 56–58.

9. Michel Foucault, *The History of Sexuality: An Introduction*, trans. Robert Hurley (Harmondsworth: Penguin, 1979), 92–96.

10. Michel de Certeau, *The Practice of Everyday Life*, trans. Steven Rendall (Berkeley: University of California Press, 1984), xix.

11. Foucault, *Ethics: Subjectivity and Truth*, 77.

12. Ibid., 81.

13. Foucault, *The Use of Pleasure*, 27.

14. Michel Foucault, *The Care of the Self*, vol. 3 of *The History of Sexuality*, trans. Robert Hurley (Harmondsworth: Penguin, 1988), 58–64.

15. Foucault, *Ethics: Subjectivity and Truth*, 87.

16. Foucault, *The Use of Pleasure*, 23.

17. Ibid., 83.

18. Ibid., 9.

19. "If we are asked to relate to the question of identity, it must be an identity to our unique selves. But the relationships we have to have with ourselves are not ones of identity, rather, they must be relationships of differentiation, of creation, of innovation." Foucault, *Ethics: Subjectivity and Truth*, 166.

20. Ibid., 97.

21. Ibid., 301.

22. "Inescapable Frameworks," Charles Taylor, *Sources of the Self: The Making of the Modern Identity* (Cambridge: Cambridge University Press, 1989), 3–24.

23. Ibid., 32.

24. Ibid., 34–35.

25. Ibid., 502.

26. Ibid., 488–90.

27. Ibid., 504.

28. Ibid., 503.

29. Ibid., 28, 29, 112. Taylor is aware that he is using a spatial metaphor. Taylor, 44.

30. Taylor, 199. A history of personal identity that similarly focuses on distilling arguments from texts ("the most consequential core of each theorist's views"), as opposed to looking at the wider activities of which philosophical arguments are a part, can be found in Raymond Martin and John Barresi, *The Rise and Fall of Soul and Self: An Intellectual History of Personal Identity* (New York: Columbia University Press, 2006), 5.

31. Taylor, chap. 13, " 'God Loveth Adverbs' "; Taylor, chap. 17, "The Culture of Modernity"; Taylor, 211–33, 285–302.

32. Ibid., 58.

33. "A self exists only within what I call 'webs of interlocution.' " Ibid., 36. I would prefer a formulation such as "webs of interaction, of which interlocution is a part." The activity is more than the language. For a discussion of shared meaningful action as the basis for language rather than vice versa, see Martin Heidegger, *Being and Time*, trans. John Macquarrie and Edward Robinson (Oxford: Basil Blackwell, 1962), §34.

34. Taylor, 35.

35. Jerome S. Bruner, *Child's Talk: Learning to Use Language* (Oxford: Oxford University Press, 1983), 24. More recent research into language acquisition has similarly focused on the activity that precedes language. John V. Canfield, "The Living Language: Wittgenstein and the Empirical Study of Communication," *Language Sciences* 15, no. 3 (1993): 165–93; Jeremy I. M. Carpendale and Charlie Lewis, "Constructing an Understanding of Mind: The Development of Children's Social Understanding within Social Interaction," *Behavioral and Brain Sciences* 27 (2004): 79–151.

36. Taylor, 514–15.

37. Ibid., 44.

38. Ibid., 481–82.

39. Ibid., 512.

40. Ibid., 39.

41. Ibid., 511.

42. Pierre Bourdieu, *The Logic of Practice*, trans. Richard Nice (Cambridge: Polity, 1990), 68.

43. Ibid.

44. Ibid., 69.

45. Ibid., 68.

46. Taylor, 389–90.

47. On the reification of these metaphors, see J. I. M. Carpendale et al., "Talking and Thinking: The Role of Speech in Social Understanding," in *Private Speech, Executive Functioning, and the Development of Verbal Self-Regulation*, ed. A. Winsler, C. Fernyhough, and N. Montero (Cambridge: Cambridge University Press, 2008), 6.

48. Ibid., 8.

49. "Foucault on Freedom and Truth," Charles Taylor, *Philosophy and the Human Sciences* (Cambridge: Cambridge University Press, 1985), 83.

50. Niklaus Largier and Josef Quint, eds., *Meister Eckhart Werke*, 2 vols., vol. 20–21 of *Bibliothek des Mittelalters* (Frankfurt am Main: Deutscher Klassiker Verlag, 1993), 2:340 (Die rede der underscheidunge, §1).

51. Taylor revisits the territory he covered in *Sources of the Self*, in Charles Taylor, *A Secular Age* (Cambridge, Mass.: Harvard University Press, 2007), 25–145. The more recent book investigates more explicitly the self-controlling habits that developed during the late medieval and early modern periods as part of an attempt to step back from the secularizing legacy of modernity. However, Taylor still tends to focus on ideas and what we say rather than on what we do together (e.g., 544).

52. For Taylor's treatment of woman's identity, see Elizabeth Frazer and Nicola Lacey, *The Politics of Community: A Feminist Critique of the Liberal–Communitarian Debate* (London: Harvester Wheatsheaf, 1993), 159. See also Melissa Orlie, "Taylor and Feminism: From Recognition of Identity to a Politics of the Good," in *Charles Taylor*, ed. Ruth Abbey (Cambridge: Cambridge University Press, 2004), 140–65. For Foucault and feminism, see Lois McNay, *Foucault and Feminism: Power, Gender, and the Self* (Cambridge: Polity Press, 1992); Dianna Taylor and Karen Vintges, *Feminism and the Final Foucault* (Urbana: University of Illinois Press, 2004).

53. Toril Moi, *What Is a Woman? And Other Essays* (Oxford; New York: Oxford University Press, 1999), 11–30.

54. Quentin Skinner, "Modernity and Disenchantment: Some Historical Reflections," in *Philosophy in an Age of Pluralism: The Philosophy of Charles Taylor in Question*, ed. James Tully and Daniel M. Weinstock (Cambridge: Cambridge University Press, 1994), 42–45.

55. Alasdair MacIntyre, "Critical Remarks on *Sources of the Self* by Charles Taylor," *Philosophy and Phenomenological Research* 54, no. 1 (1994): 189.

56. Taylor, *Sources of the Self*, 61, 67–68.

57. Ibid., 526–27.

58. Ibid.

59. I discuss possible constraints on this project of acknowledgment in Ben Morgan, "The Limits of Human Togetherness," *Limbus: Australian Yearbook of German Literary and Cultural Studies* 3 (2010): 159–76.

60. Peter Bürger, *Das Verschwinden des Subjekts: Eine Geschichte der Subjektivität von Montaigne bis Barthes* (Frankfurt am Main: Suhrkamp, 1998). Christa Bürger, *"Diese Hoffnung, eines Tages nicht mehr allein zu denken": Lebensentwürfe von Frauen aus vier Jahrhunderten* (Stuttgart: J. B. Metzler, 1996).

61. Bürger, *Das Verschwinden des Subjekts*, 44.

62. Ibid., 70–71, 157.

63. Ibid., 52–63.

64. "En verité il faut sortir un peu de soi pour n'être pas trop malheureux." Ibid., 93–94.

65. "Der Ort der Frau." Ibid., 238–48.

66. Ibid., 244–45.

67. Ibid., 248.

68. Georges Bataille, *L'expérience intérieure* (Paris: Gallimard, 1954), 176.

69. "Our Lord says truthfully that eternal life consists in this, in knowing God as the one true God (John 17:3) and not in knowing that we know God. For how should we know ourselves to know God when we do not even know ourselves." Eckhart, *Selected Writings*, trans. Oliver Davies (Harmondsworth: Penguin, 1994), 106–7; Largier and Quint, eds., 2:330 ("Von dem edeln menschen").

70. Ruth Anthony El Saffar, *Rapture Encaged: The Suppression of the Feminine in Western Culture* (London: Routledge, 1994), 97–99.

71. "Ein anderes Denken, das es geben muß, weil wir es brauchen, und für das ich [Christa Bürger] . . . vorläufig nur den Begriff der Immanenz vorschlagen kann." Bürger, *Diese Hoffnung*, 29.

72. Ibid., 67.

73. Taylor, *Sources of the Self*, 460, 343–47.

74. Jerrold E. Seigel, *The Idea of the Self: Thought and Experience in Western Europe since the Seventeenth Century* (Cambridge: Cambridge University Press, 2005), 631.

75. Ibid., 31.

76. Ibid., 166.

77. Ibid., 599.

78. Ibid., 60–62.

79. Ibid., 208–9.

80. Ibid., 43.

81. Ibid., 26–28.

82. Dan Zahavi, *Subjectivity and Selfhood: Investigating the First-Person Perspective* (Cambridge, Mass.: MIT Press, 2005), 11–12.

83. Martin Heidegger, *Phänomenologische Interpretationen zu Aristoteles* (Stuttgart: Reclam, 2002).

84. Seigel, 29.

85. Ibid., 28.

86. Ibid., 31.

87. The idea that only reflective consciousness is smart enough to hold the different parts of our life meaningfully together has been challenged by recent empirical work on the intelligent, adaptive subpersonal processes by which we manage our day-to-day life. John A. Bargh and Ezequiel Morsella, "The Unconscious Mind," *Perspectives on Psychological Science* 3, no. 1 (2008): 73–79. This new model of the unconscious will be discussed in more detail below, in chapter 8.

88. Seigel, 108.

89. Ibid., 595.

90. Ibid., 44, 31.

91. Ibid., 29, 129.

92. Martin Heidegger, *Die Grundprobleme der Phänomenologie*, vol. 24 of *Gesamtausgabe* (Frankfurt am Main: Klostermann, 1975), 224, 225.

93. Ibid., 226.

94. "[In] unmittelbarem leidenschaftlichen Ausgegebensein an die Welt scheint das eigene Selbst des Daseins aus den Dingen wider." Ibid., 227.

95. Shaun Gallagher, *How the Body Shapes the Mind* (Oxford: Clarendon Press, 2005), 81.

96. Manfred Frank, "Selbstbewußtsein und Selbsterkenntnis oder über einige Schwierigkeiten bei der Reduktion von Subjektivität," in *Die Öffentlichkeit der Vernunft und die Vernunft der Öffentlichkeit: Festschrift für Jürgen Habermas*, ed. Lutz Wingert and Klaus Günther (Frankfurt am Main: Suhrkamp, 2001), 223.

97. "[A]nonyme Vertrautheit." Ibid.

98. Gerhard Wahrig, *Deutsches Wörterbuch*, ed. Ursula Hermann et al., 3rd ed. (Munich: Mosaik Verlag, 1986), 1378.

99. Manfred Frank, ed., *Selbstbewußtseinstheorien von Fichte bis Sartre* (Frankfurt am Main: Suhrkamp, 1991), 516–18.

100. Charles Taylor, "Engaged Agency and Background in Heidegger," in *The Cambridge Companion to Heidegger*, 2nd ed., ed. Charles B. Guignon (Cambridge: Cambridge University Press, 2006), 202–21.

101. Seigel, 40.

5. Meister Eckhart's Anthropology

1. For historical background, see Yoshiki Yoda, "Mystische Lebenslehre zwischen Kloster und Stadt: Meister Eckharts 'Reden der Unterweisung' und die spätmittelalterliche Lebenswirklichkeit," in *Mittelalterliche Literatur im Lebenszusammenhang*, ed. Eckart Conrad Lutz, Scrinium Friburgense 8 (Freiburg, CH: Universitätsverlag, 1997), 225–64.

2. Niklaus Largier and Josef Quint, eds., *Meister Eckhart Werke*, 2 vols., vol. 20–21, *Bibliothek des Mittelalters* (Frankfurt am Main: Deutscher Klassiker Verlag, 1993), 2:793 (editorial commentary).

3. For a summary of Eckhart's pastoral functions, see Winfried Trusen, *Der Prozeß gegen Meister Eckhart: Vorgeschichte, Verlauf und Folgen* (Paderborn: Ferdinand Schöningh, 1988), 14–19. I follow critics such as Koch, Ruh, or Langer, who make Eckhart's pastoral concerns, or what Langer calls the "praktische Zwecksetzung," the central focus of his thought. Scholastic concepts, be they in the commentaries or the sermons, are in Eckhart's texts ultimately a tool to help Eckhart and his charges in their spiritual endeavors. Joseph Koch, "Sinn und Struktur der Schriftauslegung Meister Eckharts," in *Kleine Schriften*, 2 vols. (Rome: Edizioni di Storia e Letteratura, 1973), 1:399–428. Kurt Ruh, *Meister Eckhart: Theologe, Prediger, Mystiker* (Munich: Beck, 1985). Otto Langer, *Mystische Erfahrung und spirituelle Theologie: Zu Meister Eckharts Auseinandersetzung mit der Frauenfrömmigkeit seiner Zeit* (Munich: Artemis Verlag, 1987).

4. "Nim dîn selbes war, und swâ dû dich vindest, dâ lâz dich; daz ist daz aller beste." Eckhart, *Selected Writings*, trans. Oliver Davies (Harmondsworth: Penguin, 1994), 7; Largier and Quint, eds., *Eckhart Werke*, 2:340 (Die rede der underscheidunge, §1).

5. Immanuel Kant, *Critique of Pure Reason*, ed. Vasilis Politis, trans. J. M. D. Meiklejohn and Vasilis Politis (London: Dent, 1993), 99 (B 131–32).

6. Friedrich Nietzsche, *Zur Genealogie der Moral*, ed. Giorgio Colli and Mazzino Montinari, in *Kritische Gesamtausgabe* (Berlin: de Gruyter, 1968–), 6.2:285 ("Erste Abhandlung," § 13); Michel Foucault, *The Order of Things: An Archaeology of the Human Sciences*, trans. Alan Sheridan (London: Tavistock, 1971), 342–43.

7. Manfred Frank, *Selbstbewußtsein und Selbsterkenntnis: Essays zur Analytischen Philosophie der Subjektivität* (Stuttgart: Reclam, 1991), 7, 161.

8. Anthony Cohen, *Self Consciousness: An Alternative Anthropology of Identity* (London: Routledge, 1994), 23.

9. "Enmeine nihtes dan in, und bis unbeworren, ob got dîniu werk würke oder ob dû sie würkest." Eckhart, *Selected Writings* 51; Largier and Quint, eds., *Eckhart Werke*, 2:430 (Die rede der underscheidunge, §23).

10. The following analysis was inspired by Terence Cave's study of the emergence of the French term *le moi*. Terence Cave, "Fragments d'un moi future: de Pascal à Montaigne," in *Pré-Histoires: Textes troublés au seuil de la modernité* (Geneva: Droz, 1999), 111–27.

11. Jacob Grimm and Wilhelm Grimm, *Deutsches Wörterbuch*, ed. M. Heyne, et al. (Leipzig: S. Hirzel, 1905), vol 10.1, col. 451.

12. Karl Bihlmeyer, ed., *Heinrich Seuse: Deutsche Schriften im Auftrag der württembergischen Kommission für Landesgeschichte* (Frankfurt am Main: Minerva, 1961), 180, ll. 1–2.

13. Bihlmeyer, ed., *Heinrich Seuse: Deutsche Schriften im Auftrag der württembergischen Kommission für Landesgeschichte*, 187, l. 22. For the details of Seuse's acquaintance with Eckhart, see Alois M. Haas and K. Ruh, "Seuse, Heinrich, OP," in *Die Deutsche Literatur des Mittelalters: Verfasserlexikon*, 2 ed., ed. Wolfgang Stammler, Karl Langosch, and Kurt Ruh (Berlin: Walter de Gruyter, 1977–), vol. 8, cols. 1109–10.

14. "Er sol aller vrîest sîn, alsô daz er vergezze sîn selbesheit unde vlieze mit alle dem, daz er ist, in daz gruntlôse abgründe sînes urspringes." Franz Pfeiffer, *Meister Eckhart*, vol. 2 of *Deutsche Mystiker des Vierzehnten Jahrhunderts* (Leipzig: G. J. Göschen'sche Verlagsbuchhandlung, 1857), 393.

15. Largier and Quint, eds., *Eckhart Werke*, 2:336, 2:340 (Die rede der underscheidunge, §1, §3).

16. Ibid., 2:564 (Q53).

17. Georg Steer, "*würken vernünfticlîchen*. Das 'christliche' Leben nach den 'Reden der Unterweisung' Meister Eckharts," in *Heinrich Seuses Philosophia Spiritualis: Quellen, Konzept, Formen und Rezeption. Tagung Eichstätt 2.–4: Oktober*

1991, ed. Rüdiger Blumrich and Philipp Kaiser (Wiesbaden: Dr. Ludwig Reichert, 1994), 101–02. For details of Humbert's biography, see Fritz Heinkle, *Humbert Von Romans, der fünfte Ordensmeister der Dominikaner, Historische Studien* (Berlin: Dr. Emil Ebering, 1933).

18. "Epistola," in *B. Humberti de Romanis Quinti Praedicatorum Magistri Generalis Opera de Vita Regulari*, ed. Joseph Joachim Berthier, 2 vols. (Rome: A. Befani, 1888/89), 1:6. Quoted by Steer, Blumrich, and Kaiser, eds., *Heinrich Seuses Philosophia Spiritualis: Quellen, Konzept, Formen und Rezeption. Tagung Eichstätt 2.–4. Oktober 1991*, 102.

19. "Swâ der mensche in gehôrsame des sînen ûzgât und sich des sînen erwiget, dâ an dem selben muoz got von nôt wider îngân." Largier and Quint, eds., *Eckhart Werke* 2:334 (Die rede der underscheidunge, §1). Quoted by Steer, Blumrich, and Kaiser, eds., *Heinrich Seuses Philosophia Spiritualis: Quellen, Konzept, Formen und Rezeption. Tagung Eichstätt 2.–4. Oktober 1991*, 102.

20. Bihlmeyer, ed., *Heinrich Seuse: Deutsche Schriften im Auftrag der württembergischen Kommission für Landesgeschichte*, 39–53 (chapters 15–18).

21. Georg Wolfgang Karl Lochner, ed., *Leben und Gesichte der Christina Ebnerin, Klosterfrau zu Engelthal* (Nuremberg: Aug. Recknagel's Buchandlung, 1872), 11.

22. Caroline Walker Bynum, *Holy Feast and Holy Fast: The Religious Significance of Food to Medieval Women* (Berkeley: University of California Press, 1987), 193.

23. Winfried Trusen writes of "der von Eckhart eingeschlagene Weg einer rationalen Erfassung der Mystik." Trusen, *Der Prozeß gegen Meister Eckhart*, 52.

24. "Und hindert dich des dehein ûzerlich werk, ez sî vasten, wachen, lesen oder swaz ez sî, daz lâz vrîlîche âne alle sorge, daz dû hie mite iht versûmest deheine pênitencie; wan got ensihet niht ane, waz diu werk sîn, dan aleine, waz diu minne und diu andâht und daz gemüete in den werken sî." Eckhart, *Selected Writings*, 27; Largier and Quint, eds., *Eckhart Werke*, 2:382 (Die rede der underscheidunge, §16) (translation amended).

25. "Kristus hât gevastet vierzic tage. Dar ane volge im, daz dû war nemest, war zuo dû allermeist sîst geneiget oder bereit: dâ verlâz dich ane und nim wol dîn selbes war. Daz gebürt dir dicke mêr und unbekümbert ze lâzenne, dan ob dû zemâle vastet aller spîse. Und alsô ist dir etwenne swærer ein wort ze verswîgenne, dan ob man zemâle swîge von aller rede." Eckhart, *Selected Writings*, 30; Largier and Quint, eds., *Eckhart Werke*, 2:388 (Die rede der underscheidunge, §17) (translation amended).

26. Bihlmeyer, ed., *Heinrich Seuse: Deutsche Schriften im Auftrag der württembergischen Kommission für Landesgeschichte*, 10; Philipp Strauch, ed., *Margaretha Ebner und Heinrich von Nördlingen: Ein Beitrag zur Geschichte der Deutschen Mystik* (Freiburg i.B. / Tübingen: J.C.B. Mohr, 1882), 41.

27. Sigmund Freud, *Massenpsychologie und Ich-Analyse* (1921), in *Studienausgabe*, ed. Alexander Mitscherlich, Angela Richards, and James Strachey, 11 vols., (Frankfurt am Main: S. Fischer, 1969), 9:67–76.

28. "[Der mensche] muoz ein innerlich einœde lernen." Eckhart, *Selected Writings*, 11; Largier and Quint, eds., *Eckhart Werke*, 2:350 (Die rede der underscheidunge, §6).

29. "Diz wærlîche haben gotes liget an dem gemüete und an einem inniclîchen vernünftigen zuokêrenne und meinenne gotes, niht an einem stæten anegedenkenne in einer glîchen wîse, wan daz wære unmügelich der natûre in der meinunge ze habenne und sêre swære und ouch daz aller beste niht. Der mensche ensol niht haben noch im lâzen genüegen mit einem gedâhten gote, wan, swenne der gedank vergât, sô vergât ouch der got. Mêr: man sol haben einen gewesenden got, der verre ist obe den gedenken des menschen und aller crêatûre." Eckhart, *Selected Writings*, 10 (translation amended); Largier and Quint, eds., *Eckhart Werke*, 2:348 (Die rede der underscheidunge, §6).

30. Otto Langer "*Sich lâzen, sîn selbes vernihten*: Negation und 'Ich-Theorie' bei Meister Eckhart," in Walter Haug and Wolfram Schneider-Lastin, *Deutsche Mystik im abendländischen Zusammenhang: Neu erschlossene Texte, neue methodische Ansätze, neue theoretische Konzepte. Kolloquium Kloster Fischingen 1998* (Tübingen: Niemeyer, 2000), 328.

31. Largier and Quint, eds., *Eckhart Werke*, 2:350–52.

32. Haug and Schneider-Lastin, *Deutsche Mystik im abendlandischen Zusammenhang*, 174–75.

33. Largier and Quint, eds., *Eckhart Werke*, 2:348–50 (Die rede der underscheidunge, §6).

34. Critics who read Eckhart as a proto-deconstructionist overlook the theoretical point that Eckhart does not separate the individual from God (God is not permanently deferred) and the practical point that his preaching works to break the attachments that prevent his listeners from acquiring the habit of openness. They do not put Eckhart's work in the context of the habits of identity that prevailed in the milieu in which he wrote, but read it retrospectively as a confirmation of deferral and distance as positive terms. John D. Caputo, *Radical Hermeneutics: Repetition, Deconstruction, and the Hermeneutic Project* (Bloomington: Indiana University Press, 1987); Niklaus Largier, "Repräsentation und Negativität: Meister Eckharts Kritik als Dekonstruktion," in *Contemplata Aliis Tradere: Studien zum Verhältnis von Literatur und Spiritualität*, ed. Claudia Brinker et al. (Bern: Peter Lang, 1995), 371–90; Amy Hollywood, "Preaching as Social Practice in Meister Eckhart," in *Mysticism and Social Transformation*, ed. Janet K. Ruffing (Syracuse, N.Y.: Syracuse University Press, 2001), 76–90.

35. "Wan als vil bist dû in gote, als vil dû bist in vride, und als vil ûz gote, als vil dû bist ûz vride." Largier and Quint, eds., *Eckhart Werke*, 2:432.

36. I. M. Lewis, *Ecstatic Religion: A Study of Shamanism and Spirit Possession*, 2nd ed. (London: Routledge, 1989).

37. For a discussion of Horkheimer and Adorno, see Ben Morgan, "The Project of the Frankfurt School," *Telos*, no. 119 (2001): 75–98.

38. For an argument in favor of retaining experience as a concept of analysis, see Peter Dinzelbacher, "Zur Interpretation erlebnismysticher Texte Des

Mittelalters," *Zeitschrift für deutsches Altertum und deutsche Literatur* 117 (1988): 1–12. Frank Tobin summarizes the debate in "Henry Suso and Elsbeth Stagel: Was the Vita a Cooperative Effort?" in *Gendered Voices: Medieval Saints and Their Interpreters*, ed. Catherine M. Mooney (Philadelphia: University of Pennsylvania Press, 1999), 126–28.

39. Largier and Quint, eds., *Eckhart Werke*, 1:759 (editorial comments).

40. Corp. altdt. Originalurk. 4, 146 (1297): "zv vrkrnde dirre vorbenanten eigenschefte, vnde zv vestenvnge disses kőfes . . . habe wir der vrowen samenunge disen brief gegeben." Corp. altdt. Originalurk., 2, 358 (1288): "diser prief vnde disev eigenschaft ist geben ze Mçrekge, an sant Augustines tage." Jacob Grimm and Wilhelm Grimm, *Deutsches Wörterbuch*, ed. Berlin-Brandenburgische Akademie der Wissenschaften and Akademie der Wissenschaften zu Göttingen (Stuttgart: S. Hirzel, 1993), vol. 7, col. 407.

41. Ibid., vol. 7, col. 406.

42. "Êlîche liute die bringent des jâres lützel mê dan éine vruht. Aber ander êlîche liute die meine ich nû ze disem mâle: alle die mit eigenschaft gebunden sint an gebete, an vastenne, an wachenne und aller hande ûzerlîcher üebunge und kestigunge. Ein ieglîchiu eigenschaft eines ieglîchen werkes, daz die vrîheit benimet, in disem gegenwertigen nû gote ze wartenne und dem aleine ze volgenne in dem liehte, mit dem er dich anwîsende wære ze tuonne und ze lâzenne in einem ieglîchen nû vrî und niuwe, als ob dû anders niht enhabest noch enwellest noch enkünnest: ein ieglîchiu eigenschaft oder vürgesetzet werk, daz dir dise vrîheit benimet alle zît niuwe, daz heize ich nû ein jâr; wan dîn sêle bringet dekeine vruht, si enhabe daz werk getân, daz dû mit eigenschaft besezzen hâst, noch dû engetriuwest gote noch dir selber, dû enhabest dîn werk volbrâht, daz dû mit eigenschaft begriffen hâst; anders sô enhâst dû dekeinen vride." Eckhart, *German Sermons and Treatises*, trans. Maurice O'C Walshe, 3 vols. (Shaftesbury: Element Books, 1979), 1:72–73; Largier and Quint, eds., *Eckhart Werke*, 1:26–28 (sermon 2).

43. Georg Misch, *Geschichte der Autobiographie* (Frankfurt am Main: Schulte-Bulmke, 1967), 4.1:91–93; Siegfried Ringler, *Viten-und Offenbarungsliteratur in Frauenklöstern des Mittelalters: Quellen und Studien*, vol. 72 of *Münchener Texte und Untersuchungen zur Deutschen Literatur des Mittelalters* (Munich: Artemis Verlag, 1980), 380.

44. Kurt Flasch, *Das philosophische Denken im Mittelalter* (Stuttgart: Reclam, 1986), 408; Burkhard Mojsisch, "Die Theorie des Ich in seiner Selbst- und Weltbegründung bei Meister Eckhart," in *L'homme et son univers au moyen âge. Actes du septième congrès international de philosophie médiévale*, ed. Christian Wenin, 2 vols. (Louvain-la-Neuve: Éditions de l'institut supérieur de philosophie, 1986), 1:267–72; Burkhard Mojsisch, " 'Dieses Ich': Meister Eckharts Ich-Konzeption: Ein Beitrag zur 'Aufklärung' im Mittelalter," in *Sein—Reflexion—Freiheit. Aspekte der Philosophie Johann Gottlieb Fichtes*, ed. Christian Wenin, *Bochumer Studien zur Philosophie* (Amsterdam: Grüner, 1997), 25:239–52.

45. Otto Langer gives a detailed critique of Mojsisch's position in "*Sich lâzen, sîn selbes vernihten*: Negation und 'Ich-Theorie' bei Meister Eckhart," in Haug and Schneider-Lastin, *Deutsche Mystik im Abendländischen Zusammenhang*, 332–40.

46. "Nû suln wir glîch sîn den engeln, und alsô suln wir ein bilde gotes sîn, wan got hât uns genachet ein bilde sîn selbes. Der meister, der ein bilde machen wil nâch einem menschen, der enmachet ez niht nâch Kuonrâte oder nâch Heinrîche. Aber, machete er ein bilde nâch Kuonrâte oder nâch Heinrîche, sô enmeinete er niht dén menschen, er meinete Kuonrât oder Heinrich. Aber machete er ein bilde nâch Kuonrâte, so enmeinete er niht Heinrich; wan, möhte und künde er, er machete alzemâle Kuonrât und den selben und alzemâle im glîch. Nû mac got alzemâle und kan, und dar umbe sô hât got dich im alzemâle glîch gemachet und ein bilde sîn selbes." Eckhart, *German Sermons & Treatises*, 2:40; Largier and Quint, eds., *Eckhart Werke*, 2:144 (Q77).

47. In the analysis that follows I am drawing on Georgia Sommers Wright, "The Reinvention of the Portrait Likeness in the Fourteenth Century," *Gesta: International Center of Medieval Art* 39, no. 2 (2000): 117–34.

48. "[W]er daz wolde schouwen, / der muoste im des jehen, / daz er nie bild hiet gesehen / einem manne sô gelîch." Joseph Seemüller, ed., *Ottokars Österreichische Reimchronik, nach den Abschriften Franz Liechtensteins*, 2 vols. (Hanover: Hahnsche Buchhandlung, 1890/93), 1:509, ll. 39129–32.

49. Ibid., 509, ll. 39150–171. This passage is discussed by Wright, "The Reinvention of the Portrait Likeness in the Fourteenth Century," 118–19.

50. Joan A. Holladay, "Portrait Elements in Tomb Sculpture: Identification and Iconography," in *Europäische Kunst um 1300 (Akten der XXV. Internationalen Kongress für Kunstgeschichte, Wien 4–10.9.1983)*, ed. Elisabeth Liskar (Vienna: Hermann Böhlhaus, 1986), 220.

51. Wright, "The Reinvention of the Portrait Likeness in the Fourteenth Century," 118.

52. "Ich enweiz noch enkan niht mê; dâ mite sî dirre rede ein ende. Aber ich gedâhte eines ûf dem wege. . . ." Eckhart, *German Sermons & Treatises*, 2:40; Largier and Quint, eds., *Eckhart Werke*, 2:144 (sermon 77).

53. Giles Constable, *Three Studies in Medieval Religious and Social Thought* (Cambridge: Cambridge University Press, 1995), 181.

54. Wright, "The Reinvention of the Portrait Likeness in the Fourteenth Century," 125.

55. "Wir hân sie arcwænic, die lieben Marîen, si sæze etwenne mê durch lust dan durch redelîchen nutz." Eckhart, *German Sermons & Treatises*, 1:81; Largier and Quint, eds., *Eckhart Werke*, 2:212 (sermon 86).

56. "Unser herre Jêsus Kristus wart dicke beweget und andere sîne heiligen; sie enwurden aber niht entworfen an untugenden." Eckhart, *German Sermons & Treatises*, 2:124; Largier and Quint, eds., *Eckhart Werke*, 2:168 (sermon 81).

57. The phrase appears in a text called "Von der anmynnent gnad" ["Of loving grace"] in a fifteenth-century manuscript that contains, among other things, Eckhart sermons and a Seuse excerpt. Georg Steer, *Scholastische Gnadenlehre in*

Mittelhochdeutscher Sprache, vol. 14 of *Münchener Texte und Untersuchungen zur Deutschen Literatur des Mittelalters* (Munich: Beck, 1966), 78.

58. Wayne A. Meeks and John T. Fitzgerald, eds., *The Writings of St Paul: Annotated Texts, Reception, and Criticism*, 2nd ed. (New York: Norton, 2007), 15.

59. Robert E. Lerner, *The Heresy of the Free Spirit in the Later Middle Ages* (Berkeley: University of California Press, 1972), 58.

60. M. Michèle Mulchahey, *"First the Bow Is Bent in Study . . .": Dominican Education before 1350* (Toronto: Pontifical Institute of Medieval Studies, 1998), 11, 18, 38.

61. Ruh, *Meister Eckhart: Theologe, Prediger, Mystiker*, 165.

62. Joel Kaye, *Economy and Nature in the Fourteenth Century: Money, Market Exchange, and the Emergence of Scientific Thought* (Cambridge: Cambridge University Press, 1998), 17.

63. "Ez ist rehte ein glîch widergelt und glîcher kouf: als vil dû ûzgâst aller dinge, als vil, noch minner noch mêr, gât got în mit allem dem sînen, als dû zemâle ûzgâst in allen dingen des dînen." Eckhart, *Selected Writings*, 7; Largier and Quint, eds., *Eckhart Werke*, 2:342 (Die rede der underscheidunge §4) (translation amended).

64. "Sehet, diz sint allez koufliute, die sich hüetent vor groben sünden und wæren gerne guote liute und tuont ir guoten werk gote ze êren, als vasten, wachen, beten und swaz des ist, aller hande guotiu werk, und tuont sie doch dar umbe, daz in unser herre etwaz dar umbe gebe, oder daz in got iht dar umbe tuo, daz in liep sî: diz sint allez koufliute. Daz ist grop ze verstânne, wan sie wellent daz eine umbe daz ander geben und wellent alsô koufen mit unserm herren." Eckhart, *German Sermons & Treatises*, 1:56; Largier and Quint, eds., *Eckhart Werke*, 1:12 (sermon 1).

65. Largier and Quint, eds., *Eckhart Werke*, 2:392 (Die rede der underscheidunge, §18).

66. Jung's summary of analytical psychology in *The Relations between the Ego and the Unconscious* explicitly quotes the statement from Galatians 2:20—"I do not live, but Christ lives in me"—to explain the self-relationship that Jungian therapy aims at. Carl Gustav Jung, *Die Beziehungen zwischen dem Ich und dem Unbewußten* (Munich: dtv, 1990), 106. Fromm draws on Eckhart in *To Have or to Be?* (London: Abacus, 1979), 65–71.

67. "Wer dise rede niht enversât, der enbekümber sîn herze niht dâ mite. Wan als lange der mensche niht glîch enist dirre wârheit, als lange ensol er dise rede niht verstân; wan diz ist ein unbedahtiu wârheit, diu dâ komen ist ûz dem herzen gotes âne mittel." Eckhart, *German Sermons & Treatises*, 2:276; Largier and Quint, eds., *Eckhart Werke*, 1:562 (sermon 52).

68. For the classic account of this history, see Herbert Grundmann, *Religious Movements in the Middle Ages: The Historical Links between Heresy, the Mendicant Orders, and the Women's Religious Movement in the Twelfth and Thirteenth Century, with the Historical Foundations of German Mysticism*, trans. Steven Rowan (Notre Dame, Ind.: University of Notre Dame Press, 1995).

69. "Fröwent uch mitt mir, ich bin gott geworden!" "The 'Sister Catherine' Treatise," trans. by Elvira Borgstädt, in *Meister Eckhart: Teacher and Preacher*, ed. Bernard McGinn (New York: Paulist Press, 1986), 358; Franz–Josef Schweitzer, *Der Freiheitsbegriff der deutschen Mystik: Seine Beziehung zur Ketzerei der "Brüder und Schwestern vom Freien Geist," mit besonderer Rücksicht auf den pseudoeckartischen Traktat "Schwester Katrei" (Edition)*, vol. 378 of *Europäische Hochschulschriften: Reihe I, Deutsche Sprache und Literatur* (Frankfurt am Main: Peter Lang, 1981), 334.

70. Bernard McGinn, *The Harvest of Mysticism in Medieval Germany (1300–1500)*, vol. 4 of *The Presence of God: A History of Western Christian Mysticism* (New York: Herder and Herder, 2005), 87.

71. For a detailed study of the life and ideas of al-Hallaj in their medieval context, see Louis Massignon, *The Passion of Al-Hallaj: Mystic and Martyr of Islam*, 4 vols., Bollingen Series 98 (Princeton, N.J: Princeton University Press, 1982). It has recently been disputed whether the phrase was uttered by al-Hallaj rather than attributed to him by later sources. Ahmet T. Karamustafa, *Sufism: The Formative Period*, ed. Carole Hillenbrand, *The New Edinbugh Islamic Surveys* (Edinburgh: Edinburgh University Press, 2007), 25–26. Massignon notes parallels between al-Hallaj and Eckhart; see his "Muslim and Christian Mysticism in the Middle Ages," in *Testimonies and Reflections: Essays of Louis Massignon*, ed. Herbert Mason (Notre Dame, Ind.: University of Notre Dame Press, 1989), 128.

72. Lewis, *Ecstatic Religion*; Shizuteru Ueda, *Die Gottesgeburt in der Seele und der Durchbruch zur Gottheit: Die mystische Anthropologie Meister Eckharts und ihre Konfrontation mit der Mystik des Zen-Buddhismus* (Gütersloh: Mohn, 1965).

6. Becoming God in Fourteenth-Century Europe

1. "Diz bîspil ist meister Eckehartes tohter genant." Josef Quint, ed., *Meister Eckehart: Deutsche Predigten und Traktate* (Munich: Carl Hanser, 1963), 528.

2. Completed by Quint from the manuscripts. Quint, *Meister Eckehart: Deutsche Predigten und Traktate*. 443, 528.

3. Ibid., 528.

4. "Ein tohter kom ze einem predierklôster und vordert meister Eckeharten. Der portenêre sprach 'von weme sol ich im sagen?' Si sprach 'ich enweiz.' Er sprach 'wâ von wizzent ir sîn niht?' Si sprach 'dâ enbin ich niht ein maget noch ein wîp noch ein man noch ein frowe noch ein witwe noch ein juncfrowe noch ein herre noch ein dierne noch ein kneht.' Der portenêre gienc zuo meister Eckehart. 'Kument her ûz zuo der wunderlîchesten crêatûre, die ich nie gehôrte, und lânt mich mit iu gân unde bietent iuwer houbet hin unde sprechent "wer vordert mich?" Er tet alsô. Sie sprach zuo im, als si zuo dem portenêre gesprochen hete. Er sprach 'liebez kint, dîn rede ist wârhaftig unde behende: berihte mich baz, wie dû ez meinest.' Sie sprach 'wêr ich ein maget, sô stüende ich in mîner êrsten unschulde; wêr ich denne ein wîp, sô gebêre ich daz êwige wort âne underlâz in mîner sêle; wêr ich denne ein man, sô hête ich ein kreftigez widerstân wider alle gebresten; wêr ich danne ein frowe, sô hielte ich mînen lieben einigen gemahel

triuwe; wêr ich danne ein witwe, sô hête ich ein stêtez senen nâch mînem einigen liebe; wêr ich danne ein juncfrowe, sô stüende ich in einem vorhtlîchen dienste; wêr ich danne ein dierne, sô hêt ich einen diemüetigen underwurf under got und alle crêature, unde wêr ich ein kneht, sô stüende ich in starken werken unde diente mînem herren nâch allem mînen willen âne widerrede. Der allersament bin ich einez niht unde bin ein dinc als ein ander dinc und loufe dâ hin.' Der meister gienc hin und sprach zuo sînen jungern 'ich hân den aller lûtersten menschen gehôrt, den ich nie funden hân nâch mînem dunken.'—Diz bîspil ist meister Eckehartes tohter genant." Franz Pfeiffer, ed., *Meister Eckhart (Deutsche Mystiker des 14. Jahrhunderts Bd. II)* (Leipzig: Göschen, 1857), 625 (§69).

5. For the pedagogical argument, see Ursula Peters, *Religiöse Erfahrung als Literarisches Faktum : Zur Vorgeschichte und Genese Frauenmystischer Texte des 13. und 14. Jahrhunderts* (Tübingen: Niemeyer, 1988). For a clear critique of this approach, see Peter Dinzelbacher, "Zur Interpretation erlebnismysticher Texte des Mittelalters," *Zeitschrift für deutsches Altertum und deutsche Literatur* 117 (1988): 1–23. For a countercritique of Dinzelbacher, pointing out his tendency to overemphasize the opposition between experience and literary form, see Susanne Köbele, *Bilder der unbegriffenen Wahrheit: Zur Struktur Mystischer Rede im Spannungsfeld von Latein und Volkssprache* (Tübingen: Francke, 1993), 21–24.

6. Herbert Grundmann, *Religious Movements in the Middle Ages: The Historical Links between Heresy, the Mendicant Orders, and the Women's Religious Movement in the Twelfth and Thirteenth Century, with the Historical Foundations of German Mysticism*, trans. Steven Rowan (Notre Dame: University of Notre Dame Press, 1995), 7–8.

7. Ibid., 13.

8. John B. Freed, "Urban Development and the 'Cura Monialium' in Thirteenth-Century Germany," *Viator* 3 (1972): 317. The dates of the reforms are set out in Giles Constable, *The Reformation of the Twelfth Century* (Cambridge: Cambridge University Press, 1996), 4–7.

9. Grundmann, 87.

10. Lester K. Little, *Religious Poverty and the Profit Economy in Medieval Europe* (London: Paul Elek, 1978).

11. Marie-Dominique Chenu, *Nature, Man, and Society in the Twelfth Century: Essays on New Theological Perspectives in the Latin West*, trans. Jerome Taylor and Lester K. Little (Chicago: University of Chicago Press, 1986), 265.

12. Erich Auerbach, *Mimesis: The Representation of Reality in Western Literature*, trans. Willard R. Trask (Princeton, N.J.: Princeton University Press, 1968), 168.

13. "Fratres mei, fratres mei, Deus vocavit me per viam simplicitatis et humilitatis, et hanc viam ostendit mihi in veritate pro me et pro illis qui volunt mihi credere et me imitari. Et ideo nolo quod nominetis mihi aliquam regulam, neque sancti Benedicti, neque sancti Augustini, neque sancti Bernardi, nec aliquam viam et forman vivendi, praeter illam quae mihi a Domino est ostensa misericorditer et donata." Quoted in Chenu, 257–58. There is a shorter version in Rosalind B. Brooke, ed., *Scripta Leonis, Rufini et Angeli, Sociorum S. Francisci*

(Oxford: Clarendon Press, 1970), 288: "Fratres mei! fratres mei! Deus uocauit me per uiam simplicitatis et ostendit michi uiam simplicitatis. Nolo quod nominetis michi regulam aliquam neque sancti Augustini, nec sancti Bernardi, nec sancti Benedicti. Et dixit Dominus michi quod uolebat quod ego essem unus nouellus pazzus in mundo; et noluit nos ducere Deus per aliam uiam quam per istam scientiam; sed per uestram scientiam et sapientiam Deus uos confundet."

14. Auerbach, 169, Rosalind B. Brooke, ed., 144–47.

15. Grundmann, 89.

16. Theodor W. Adorno and Max Horkheimer, *Dialectic of Enlightenment*, trans. John Cumming (London: Verso, 1979). Horkheimer's and Adorno's position is assessed in more detail in Ben Morgan, "The Project of the Frankfurt School," *Telos*, no. 119 (2001): 75–98.

17. "Wan min snődeste notdurft wil ich vor gotte also hohe reiten als ob ich were in der hohesten contemplacie, da ein mensche in komen mag. Warumbe? Tůn ich es in einer liebiu gotte ze eren, so ist es alles ein. Swenne ich aber súnde, so bin ich nit an disem wege." Mechthild von Magdeburg, *The Flowing Light of the Godhead*, trans. Frank Tobin (New York: Paulist Press, 1998), 53; Hans Neumann, ed., *Das fließende Licht der Gottheit*, vol. 100 of *Münchener Texte und Untersuchungen zur deutschen Literatur des Mittelalters* (Munich: Artemis, 1990), 21 (book 1, §27).

18. "Ihre Lebensweise bedeutete einen Affront gegen mittelalterliche Ordnungsvorstellungen." Uta C. Schmidt: ", . . . que begine appellantur', oder: Die Beginen als Frauenfrage in der Geschichtsschreibung," in *Lustgarten und Dämonenpein: Konzepte von Weiblichkeit in Mittelalter und Früher Neuzeit*, ed. Annette Kuhn and Bea Lundt, eds. (Dortmund: Edition Ebersbach, 1997), 62.

19. Walter Simons, *Cities of Ladies: Beguine Communities in the Medieval Low Countries, 1200–1565* (Philadelphia: University of Pennsylvania Press, 2002), 122.

20. Dayton Phillips, "Beguines in Medieval Strasbourg: A Study of the Social Aspect of Beguine Life" (PhD, Stanford University, 1941), 20–21. Some beguine houses also had enough wealth in common to support their members without work.

21. *Nikolai de Bibera Carmen Satiricum*, ed. Theobald Fischer, in *Erfurter Denkmäler* (*Geschichtsquellen der Provinzsachsen und angrezender Gebiete* 1.2) (Halle, 1870), pp. 1–176, book 5, ll. 1600–27; quoted in Yoshiki Yoda, "Mystische Lebenslehre zwischen Kloster und Stadt: Meister Eckharts 'Reden der Unterweisung' und die spätmittelalterliche Lebenswirklichkeit," in *Mittelalterliche Literatur im Lebenszusammenhang*, ed. Eckart Conrad Lutz, vol. 8 of *Scrinium Friburgense* (Freiburg, CH: Universitätsverlag, 1997), 252.

22. "Die wile dat si sijn over mi / wie sal hare lief dan minnen." Marieke J. E. H. T. van Baest, ed., *Poetry of Hadewijch, Studies in Spirituality Supplement 3* (Leuven: Peters, 1998), 44, ll. 61–62.

23. "[N]ulli promittant obedientiam, . . . neque profiteantur aliquam regulam approbatam." H. J. Schroeder, ed., *Disciplinary Decrees of the General Councils*

(London: Herder, 1937), 388. The book contains translations of all the decrees issued by the Council of Vienne (1311–12). The Latin texts can be found in Charles-Joseph Hefele, *Histoires des conciles d'après les documents originaux*, trans. H. Leclercq, vol. 6, pt. 2 (Paris: Librairie Letouzey et Ané, 1915), 672–715, here 681.

24. Simons, 125–28.

25. "[E]arum aliquæ, quasi perductæ in mentis insaniam, de summa Trinitate ac divina essentia disputent et prædicent." Hefele, 681; Schroeder, ed., 388.

26. I. M. Lewis, *Ecstatic Religion: A Study of Shamanism and Spirit Possession*, 2nd ed. (London: Routledge, 1989), 169.

27. Ibid., 71–77.

28. Ibid., 79.

29. Joan Cadden, *Meanings of Sex Difference in the Middle Ages: Medicine, Science, and Culture* (Cambridge: Cambridge University Press, 1993), 163.

30. Grundmann, 85.

31. Uta C. Schmidt, ", . . . que begine appellantur', oder: Die Beginen als Frauenfrage in der Geschichtsschreibung," in Kuhn and Lundt, eds., 54–77.

32. Martha C. Howell, *Women, Production, and Patriarchy in Late Medieval Cities* (Chicago: University of Chicago Press, 1986), 155–56.

33. Ibid., 172.

34. Edith Ennen, *Frauen Im Mittelalter*, 5th ed. (Munich: Beck, 1994), 139–40.

35. Lewis, 156.

36. C. H. Lohr, "The Medieval Interpretation of Aristotle," in *The Cambridge History of Later Medieval Philosophyi*, ed. Norman Kretzmann, Anthony Kenny, and Jan Pinborg (Cambridge: Cambridge University Press, 1982), 82–84.

37. Loris Sturlese, *Die Deutsche Philosophie im Mittelalter: Von Bonifacius bis zu Albert dem Großen*, trans. Johanna Baumann (Munich: Beck, 1993), 284–87.

38. "Nec nos in naturalibus habemus inquirere, qualiter deus opifex secundum suam liberrimam voluntatem creatis ab ipso utatur ad miraculum, quo declaret potentiam suam, sed potius quid in rebus naturalibus secundum causas naturae insitas naturaliter fieri possit." Albertus Magnus, De *caelo et mundo*, ed. Paul Hossfeld, vol. 5.1 of *Opera omnia*, ed. Albertus Magnus Institute, Cologne (Aschendorf: Monasterii Westfalorum, 1971), lib. 1, tract. 4, cap. 10, p. 103, ll. 7–12; quoted in *Albertus Magnus Ausgewählte Texte*, ed. Albert Fries (Darmstadt: Wissenschaftliche Buchgesellschaft, 1981), 6.

39. Sturlese, 341–42.

40. "Unde sciendum, quod Augustino in his quæ sunt de fide et moribus plusquam Philosophis credendum est, si dissentiunt. Sed si de medicina loqueretur, puls ego crederem Galeno, vel Hipocrati: et si de naturis rerum loquatur, credo Aristoteli plus vel alii experto in rerum naturis." *B. Alberti Magni Ratisbonensis Episcopi Ordinis Praedicatorum Opera Omnia*, ed. Augustus Borgnet, 38

vols. (Paris: Ludovicus Vivès, 1890–99), vol. 27, p. 247 (2 sentent. dist. 13, C, art. 2), cited in Fries, ed., 8.

41. *Alberti Magni ex ordine praedicatorum De vegetabilibus libri vii*, ed. Ernest Meyer and Carl Jessen (Berlin: Georg Reimer, 1867), 563 (lib. 6, tract. 2, cap.17, §434), cited in Fries, ed., 56.

42. Claude Thomasset, "The Nature of Woman," in *Silences of the Middle Ages*, ed. Christiane Klapisch-Zuber, vol. 2 of *A History of Women in the West* (Cambridge, Mass.: Harvard University Press, 1992), 53.

43. Cadden, passim.

44. Walter Simons, "The Beguine Movement in the Southern Low Countries: A Reassessment," *Bulletin de l'institut historique belge de Rom* 59 (1989): 72–77.

45. Kari Elisabeth Børresen, *Subordination and Equivalence: The Nature and Role of Woman in Augustine and Thomas Aquinas*, trans. Charles H. Talbot (Washington, D.C.: University Press of America, 1981), 174.

46. "Feminam enim indiget mare non solum propter generationem, sicut in aliis animalibus, sed etiam propter gubernationem: quia mas est et ratione perfectior, et virtute fortior . . . . [M]ulier naturaliter viro subiecta sit tanquam gubernatori." *Summa contra Gentiles*, ed. Robertus Busa, in *Thomas Aquinas Opera Omnia*, 7 vols. (Stuttgart-Bad Cannstatt: Frommann-Holzboog, 1980), vol. 2, p. 101 (lib. 3, cap. 23, n. 3 / n. 4).

47. *Summa theologiæ*, in *Thomas Aquinas Opera Omnia*, vol. 2, p. 320 (1 qu. 92, art. 1).

48. Børresen, 177; Thomas Aquinas, *Supplementum Tertiæ Partis Summæ Theologiæ*, *Opera Omnia* (Rome: Typographia Polyglotta, 1888–), 73 (qu. 39, art. 1, ad 1).

49. "Ich han die wisheit bî mir hie, da mitte wil ich ie zem besten kiesen." Neumann, ed., 30 (book 1, §44; English trans. 60).

50. See the discussion in chapter 3.

51. For a differentiated account of the hormonal mechanisms by which the complex mosaic of gendered behavioral traits is reproduced, see Melissa Hines, *Brain Gender* (Oxford: Oxford University Press, 2004).

52. For the metaphor of the mosaic, see Hines, 19.

53. John Coakley, "Friars as Confidants of Holy Women in Medieval Dominican Hagiography," in *Images of Sainthood in Medieval Europe*, ed. Renate Blumenfeld-Kosinski and Timea Szell (Ithaca, N.Y.: Cornell University Press, 1991), 225. See also John Wayland Coakley, *Women, Men, and Spiritual Power: Female Saints and Their Male Collaborators* (New York: Columbia University Press, 2006).

54. Uta C. Schmidt, ",. . . que begine appellantur', oder: Die Beginen als Frauenfrage in der Geschichtsschreibung," in Kuhn and Lundt, eds., 54–77.

55. Caroline Walker Bynum, *Jesus as Mother: Studies in the Spirituality of the High Middle Ages* (Berkeley: University of California Press, 1982), 250. Coakley, like Bynum, sees a "permanent dialectical tension" between women's charisma

and the clerical authority that itself ultimately relies on charisma for its legitimacy. Coakley, 24.

56. Bynum, 9–21, 247–62.

57. Ibid., 261.

58. Sigmund Freud, *Massenpsychologie und Ich-Analyse* (1921), in *Studienausgabe*, ed. Alexander Mitscherlich, Angela Richards, and James Strachey, 11 vols. (Frankfurt am Main: S. Fischer, 1969), 9:65.

59. Peter Bürger, "Der Ort der Frau," in *Das Verschwinden des Subjekts: Eine Geschichte der Subjektivität von Montaigne bis Barthes* (Frankfurt am Main: Suhrkamp, 1998), 238–48. The approaches of the Bürgers and of Charles Taylor to the history of modern forms of identity are discussed in greater detail above, in chapter 4.

60. Philipp Strauch, ed., *Margaretha Ebner und Heinrich Von Nördlingen: Ein Beitrag zur Geschichte der deutschen Mystik* (Freiburg i.B. / Tübingen: J. C. B. Mohr, 1882), 270–71 (letter 57).

61. For further biographical information on both Heinrich and Margaretha, see the relevant entries of Wolfgang Stammler, Karl Langosch, and Kurt Ruh, eds., *Die deutsche Literatur des Mittelalters: Verfasserlexikon*, 2 ed. (Berlin: Walter de Gruyter, 1977–).

62. Strauch, ed., 237–38 (letter 40).

63. Elizabeth Alvilda Petroff, "Male Confessors and Female Penitents: Possibilities for Dialogue," in *Body and Soul: Essays on Medieval Women and Mysticism* (Oxford: Oxford University Press, 1994), 139–40.

64. Strauch, ed., 16.

65. Ibid., 84–91.

66. Ibid., 84.

67. Ibid., 25.

68. Ibid., 31.

69. Ibid., 9.

70. Oskar Pfister, "Hysterie und Mystik bei Margaretha Ebner (1291–1351)," *Zentralblatt für Psychoanalyse* 1, no. 10/11 (1911): 476–80.

71. Hadewijch, *Brieven*, ed. J. van Mierlo, 2 vols. (Antwerp: Standaard, 1947), 1:37–41 (letter 4).

72. Niklaus Largier and Josef Quint, eds., *Meister Eckhart Werke*, 2 vols., vols. 20–21 of *Bibliothek des Mittelalters* (Frankfurt am Main: Deutscher Klassiker Verlag, 1993), 1, 26–28 (sermon 2).

73. Amy M. Hollywood, *The Soul as Virgin Wife: Mechthild of Magdeburg, Marguerite Porete, and Meister Eckhart*, vol. 1 of *Studies in Spirituality and Theology* (Notre Dame, Ind.: University of Notre Dame Press, 1995), 26–39.

74. Largier and Quint, eds., 2:208–29 (sermon 86).

75. Strauch, ed., 8.

76. Ibid., 87–91.

77. "Ich leg uf dich den schwerer tail mins lidens, wann so vil du mer minnen hast, so vil magtu mer tragen den ich." Strauch, ed., 228 (letter 35).

78. Ibid., 213 (letter 28), 248 (letter 44).

79. Ibid., 225–26 (letter 34), 260 (letter 59).

80. For a positive reading of the practices of ritualization evident from the correspondence between Margaretha and Heinrich, see Patricia Zimmerman Beckman, "The Power of Books and the Practice of Mysticism in the Fourteenth Century: Heinrich of Nördlingen and Margaret Ebner on Mechthild's *Flowing Light of the Godhead,*" *Church History: Studies in Christianity and Culture* 76, no. 1 (2007): 61–83.

81. Strauch, ed., 131–34.

82. Ibid., 84.

83. Ibid., 114.

84. Eckhart, "Acta Echardiana," in *Die lateinischen Werke*, ed. Josef Koch, et al., 6 vols., *Die deutschen und lateinischen Werke* (Stuttgart: Kohlhammer, 1936–), 5:188 (§42).

85. Ruth Meyer, ed., *Das "St. Katherinentaler Schwesternbuch": Unterschung—Edition—Kommentar* (Tübingen: Niemeyer, 1995), 131–33.

86. Eckhart, "Acta Echardiana," 5:188 (§42).

87. Hollywood, 122–27.

88. Grace M. Jantzen, *Power, Gender, and Christian Mysticism* (Cambridge: Cambridge University Press, 1995), 121–22.

89. Ruth Anthony El Saffar, *Rapture Encaged: The Suppression of the Feminine in Western Culture* (London: Routledge, 1994), 97–99.

90. Eckhart, *German Sermons and Treatises*, trans. Maurice O'C Walshe, 3 vols. (Shaftesbury: Element Books, 1979), 2: 272; Largier and Quint, eds., 1:556 (sermon 52).

91. Marie-Luise Ehrenschwendtner "*Puellae Litteratae*: The Use of the Vernacular in the Dominican Convents of Southern Germany," in *Medieval Women in Their Communities*, ed. Diane Watt (Cardiff: University of Wales Press, 1997), 49–71, 58–59.

92. Strauch, ed., 158.

93. Hollywood, 26–39.

94. Quint, ed., 528.

95. Winfried Trusen, *Der Prozeß gegen Meister Eckhart: Vorgeschichte, Verlauf und Folgen* (Paderborn: Ferdinand Schöningh, 1988), 52.

96. Martina Wehrli-Jons, "Mystik und Inquisition: Die Dominikaner und die sogenannte Häresie des Freien Geistes," in *Deutsche Mystik im abendländischen Zusammenhang: Neu erschlossene Texte, neue methodische Ansätze, neue theoretische Konzepte: Kolloquium Kloster Fischingen, 1998*, ed. Walter Haug and Wolfram Schneider-Lastin (Tübingen: Niemeyer, 2000), 243.

97. Trusen, 19.

98. Eckhart, "Acta Echardiana," *Die lateinischen Werke*, 5:184–86 (§39).

99. Eckhart, "Acta Echardiana," *Die lateinischen Werke*, 5:186–87 (§40).

100. Freimut Löser, *Meister Eckhart in Melk* (Tübingen: Niemeyer, 1999), 273–302.

101. "The 'Sister Catherine' Treatise," trans. by Elvira Borgstädt, *Meister Eckhart: Teacher and Preacher*, ed. in Bernard McGinn (New York: Paulist Press, 1986), 347–87; Franz-Josef Schweitzer, *Der Freiheitsbegriff der deutschen Mystik: Seine Beziehung zur Ketzerei der "Brüder und Schwestern vom Freien Geist," mit besonderer Rücksicht auf den pseudoeckartischen Traktat "Schwester Katrei" (Edition)*, vol. 378 of *Europäische Hochschulschriften. Reihe I, Deutsche Sprache und Literatur* (Frankfurt am Main: Peter Lang, 1981), 322–70. Further references will be given parenthetically, with the page number for the English addition followed by that for the German edition (e.g., 351/324).

102. "Sol ich alle ding laussen, so muos ich uch och laussen" (351/324).

103. Eckhart, *German Sermons & Treatises*, 1:72–73; Largier and Quint, eds., 1:26–28 (Sermon 2).

104. The element of genuine exchange in the dialogue is noted by Bernard McGinn, *The Harvest of Mysticism in Medieval Germany (1300–1500)*, vol. 4 of *The Presence of God: A History of Western Christian Mysticism* (New York: Herder and Herder, 2005), 344.

105. "Mir ist von herczen leide, das ich menschen ratt ie als lang gevolget vnd dem ratte des heilgen geist[es] widerstanden han" (352/326).

106. "Dich mag nieman hindren denn du dich selbs" (351/326).

107. "Ich han einen menschen gehört, ich enweis vnd zwifel dar an, ob er ein mensch oder ein engel si" (356/331–32).

108. "[F]röwent uch mitt mir, ich bin gott geworden!" (358/334).

109. "Die tochter seit jm also vil von der grössen gottes und von der vermügenheit gottes und von der fürsichtikeit gottes, das er von allen sinen vssern sinnen kam" (383/369).

110. Franz-Josef Schweitzer, ' "Schwester Katrei," ' in Stammler, Langosch, and Ruh, eds., vol. 8, col. 949.

111. Allusions are listed and commented on by Schweitzer, *Der Freiheitsbegriff der deutschen Mystik*, 669–84.

112. "Item quod homo magis tenetur sequi instinctum interiorum quam veritaten ewangelii, que cottidie predicatur." Alexander Patschovsky, "Straßburger Beginenverfolgungen Im 14. Jahrhundert," *Deutsches Archiv für Erforschung des Mittelalters* 30 (1974): 137; quoted in Schweitzer, 557. For a more detailed discussion of the Strasbourg heretics, see Ben Morgan, "Eckhart and the Incarnation: Some Practical Details," *Eckhart Review* 13 (2004): 37–50.

113. John D. Caputo and Gianni Vattimo, *After the Death of God*, ed. Jeffrey W. Robbins (New York: Columbia University Press, 2007), 81–82.

114. Emmanuel Levinas, *Time and the Other*, trans. Richard A. Cohen (Pittsburgh: Duquesne University Press, 1987), 80.

115. "Alle menschen möchten nitt gebesseren einen gebresten, got wölt jn denne von minnen vergeben" (354/328–29).

116. "Das ist war. Es ist aber nitt, als die lütt verstond" (363/341).

117. Barbara Newman, *From Virile Woman to WomanChrist: Studies in Medieval Religion and Literature* (Philadelphia: University of Pennsylvania Press,

1995), 180. The orthodoxy of the text is emphasized also by McGinn, *The Harvest of Mysticism*, 348.

7. The Makings of the Modern Self

1. Kari Elisabeth Børresen, *Subordination and Equivalence: The Nature and Role of Woman in Augustine and Thomas Aquinas*, trans. Charles H. Talbot (Washington, D.C.: University Press of America, 1981), 166; *Summa theologiæ*, ed. Robertus Busa, in *Thomas Aquinas Opera Omnia*, 7 vols. (Stuttgart-Bad Cannstatt: Frommann-Holzboog, 1980), 2:322 (I qu. 93, art. 4).

2. The *vita apostolica* is discussed at greater length above, in chapter 6.

3. Herbert Grundmann, *Religious Movements in the Middle Ages: The Historical Links between Heresy, the Mendicant Orders, and the Women's Religious Movement in the Twelfth and Thirteenth Century, with the Historical Foundations of German Mysticism*, trans. Steven Rowan (Notre Dame, Ind.: University of Notre Dame Press, 1995), 25–27.

4. Robert E. Lerner, *The Heresy of the Free Spirit in the Later Middle Ages* (Berkeley: University of California Press, 1972), 82–83.

5. This is a point made over and over by Lerner in *Heresy of the Free Spirit*, e.g., 90.

6. Ibid.

7. "Item habent congregaciones et conventicula et modos singulares loquendi, vivendi, et conversandi." Alexander Patschovsky, "Straßburger Beginenverfolgungen Im 14. Jahrhundert," *Deutsches Archiv für Erforschung des Mittelalters* 30 (1974): 147; quoted in Franz-Josef Schweitzer, *Der Freiheitsbegriff der deutschen Mystik: Seine Beziehung zur Ketzerei der "Brüder und Schwestern vom Freien Geist," Mit besonderer Rücksicht auf den pseudoeckartischen Traktat "Schwester Katrei" (Edition)*, vol. 378 of *Europäische Hochschulschriften: Reihe I: Deutsche Sprache und Literatur* (Frankfurt am Main: Peter Lang, 1981), 562. For a fuller discussion of the Strasbourg heretics, see Ben Morgan, "Eckhart and the Incarnation: Some Practical Details," *Eckhart Review* 13 (2004): 39–48.

8. Charles-Joseph Hefele, *Histoires des C\conciles d'après les documents originaux*, trans. H. Leclercq, (Paris: Librairie Letouzey et Ané, 1915), 6.2:681.

9. Grundmann, 12.

10. The Latin text of the bull is published in M.-H. Laurent, "Autour Du Procès De Maître Eckhart: Les Documents Des Archives Vaticanes," *Divus Thomas* 3, no. 13 (1936): 435–44. (The notes of this edition helpfully indicate which texts the articles were originally extracted from.) A translation of the bull is published in James M. Clark, *Meister Eckhart: An Introduction to the Study of His Works with an Anthology of His Sermons* (London: Thomas Nelson, 1957), 253–58; also in *Meister Eckhart: The Essential Sermons, Commentaries, Treatises, and Defense*, ed. Edmund Colledge and Bernard McGinn (London: SPCK, 1981), 77–81. For discussions of Eckhart's condemnation, see Oliver Davies, "Why Were Eckhart's Propositions Condemned?" *New Blackfriars* 71 (1990): 433–45; Bernard McGinn, "Eckhart's Condemnation Reconsidered," *Thomist* 44 (1980): 390–414; Heinrich Stirnimann

and Ruedi Imbach, eds., *Eckardus Theutonicus, Homo Doctus et Sanctus: Nachweise und Berichte zum Prozeß gegen Meister Eckhart* (Freiburg, CH: Universitätsverlag, 1992); Winfried Trusen, *Der Prozeß gegen Meister Eckhart: Vorgeschichte, Verlauf und Folgen* (Paderborn: Ferdinand Schöningh, 1988); Bernhard Welte, *Meister Eckhart: Gedanken zu seinen Gedanken* (Freiburg: Herder, 1979), 249–61; Richard Woods, *Eckhart's Way* (London: Darton, Longman and Todd, 1986).

11. Robert E. Lerner, "New Evidence for the Condemnation of Meister Eckhart," *Speculum—A Journal of Medieval Studies* 72, no. 2 (1997): 347–66.

12. Article 10: Clark, 255; Laurent, 438. Also Article 11.

13. "Item, Deum ipsum quis blasphemando Deum laudat." Article 6: Clark, 255; Laurent, 437.

14. "Deus animas amat, non opus extra." Article 19: Clark, 256; Laurent, 440.

15. "Quicquid proprium est divine nature, hoc totum proprium est homini iusto et divino. Propter hoc iste homo operatur, quicquid Deus operatur, et creavit una cum Deo celum et terram, et est generator verbi eterni, et Deus sine tali homine nesciret quicquam facere." Article 13: Clark, 255; Laurent, 439.

16. Eckhart, *Selected Writings*, trans. Oliver Davies (Harmondsworth: Penguin, 1994), 8, Niklaus Largier and Josef Quint, eds., *Meister Eckhart Werke*, 2 vols., vol. 20–21, *Bibliothek des Mittelalters* (Frankfurt am Main: Deutscher Klassiker Verlag, 1993), 2:344.

17. Eckhart, 9–10; Largier and Quint, eds., 2:346.

18. Eckhart, 191; Largier and Quint, eds., 2:64 (sermon 5A).

19. For differing views of the role played by Henry of Virneburg, compare Davies and Trusen. Trusen sees the two Dominican friars as mainly responsible; Davies defends the more usual position that it is the archbishop himself who is the main force behind the inquisitorial tribune.

20. F. Pelster, "Ein Gutachten aus dem Eckehart-Prozeß in Avignon," *Beiträge zur Geschichte der Philosophie des Mittelalters*, suppl. 3.2 (1935): 1099–124.

21. Trusen, 118. The same interpretative techniques that were used to condemn Eckhart are in evidence in the trial of Marguerite Porete in 1309–1310, from whose mystical treatise *The Mirror of Simple Souls* fifteen statements were extracted, regardless of context or authorial intention, for examination by a commission of twenty-one masters. Paul Verdeyen, "Le procès contre Marguerite Porete et Guiard de Cressonessart (1309–1310)," *Revue d'histoire ecclésiastique* 81 (1986): 54.

22. Joseph Koch, "Philosophische und Theologische Irrtumslisten von 1270–1329," in *Kleine Schriften*, 2 vols. (Rome: Edizioni di Storia e Letteratura, 1973), 2:423–50; Koch, "Der Kardinal Jacques Fournier (Benedikt XII) als Gutachter in theologischen Prozessen," 2:367–86.

23. Bernard Hamilton, *The Medieval Inquisition* (London: Edward Arnold, 1981); Winfried Trusen, "Der Inquisitionsprozeß: Seine Historischen Grundlagen und Frühen Formen," *Zeitschrift der Savigny-Stiftung für Rechtsgeschichte* 105 (1988): 168–230.

24. Winfried Trusen, “Von den Anfängen des Inquisitionsprozesses zum Verfahren bei der *inquisitio haereticae pravitatis*,” in *Die Anfänge der Inquisition im Mittelalter*, ed. Peter Segl (Cologne: Böhlau, 1993), 46–47.

25. Ibid., 51–52.

26. Koch, “Philosophische und Theologische Irrtumslisten von 1270–1329,” 2:423–50.

27. “Maiestatis crimen illud est, quod adversus populum romanum et adversus securitatem ejus committitur”; quoted in Segl, ed., 62.

28. Richard Kieckhefer, *The Repression of Heresy in Medieval Germany* (Liverpool: Liverpool University Press, 1979), 82.

29. Segl, ed., 67.

30. Ibid., 64–65.

31. Ibid., 70–73.

32. Bernard Gui, *Manuel de l'inquisiteur*, ed. Guillaume Mollat, trans. Guillaume Mollat, 2 vols. (Paris: Honoré Champion, 1926–27). English selections are given in *Heresies of the High Middle Ages*, ed. Walter L. Wakefield and Austin P. Evans (New York: Columbia University Press, 1969), 373–445. To the modern reader, Gui might be familiar as the ruthless embodiment of ecclesiastical power in Umberto Eco's *The Name of the Rose.*

33. Gui, 1:178; Wakefield and Evans, eds., 436.

34. Gui, 1:176; Wakefield and Evans, eds., 435.

35. “Et in hoc et super hoc standum est non eorum false opinioni set judicio inquirentis.” Gui, 1:178; Wakefield and Evans, eds., 436.

36. “Prout qualitas negocii et persone conditio exegerit.” Gui, 1:182; Wakefield and Evans, eds., 437.

37. The same accusation—of calling evil good and making darkness light—that we find in Gui's text returns in the report by the commission in Avignon. See: Pelster, 1113, l. 32.

38. For two discussions of Eckhart's trial that focus on this issue, see McGinn, “Eckhart's Condemnation Reconsidered”; Welte, 249–61.

39. For a translation of the public statement, see Clark, 252. For a presentation of this phase of the trial, see Trusen, *Der Prozeß gegen Meister Eckhart*, 91–95. For a clear account of the medieval concept of heresy, see Trusen, *Der Prozeß gegen Meister Eckhart*, chap. 6, “Zum Häresiebegriff im Spätmittelalter.”

40. P. Augustin Daniels, “Eine lateinische Rechtfertigungsschrift des Meister Eckhart,” *Beiträge zur Geschichte der Philosophie des Mittelalters* 23, no. 5 (1923): 34, ll. 22–24. Selections from the defense are given in Colledge and McGinn, eds., 71–77 (here 76).

41. Raymond Blakney, ed., *Meister Eckhart: A Modern Translation* (New York: Harper and Row, 1941), 286; Daniels, 39, ll. 1–14.

42. Pelster, 1115–16 (article 15).

43. Laurent, 443; Verdeyen, 78. See also the Clementine decree against beguines discussed in this chapter. For an account of Eckhart's trial that takes this concern for the uneducated to be the main issue, see: Georg Steer, “Der Prozess

Meister Eckharts und die Folgen," *Literaturwissenschaftliches Jahrbuch* 27 (1986): 47–64.

44. Robert E. Lerner, "A Case of Religious Counter-Culture: The German Waldensians," *American Scholar* 55 (1986): 234–47.

45. Heinrich Seuse, *Das Buch der Wahrheit*, ed. Loris Sturlese and Rüdiger Blumrich (Hamburg: Felix Meiner, 1993), xv–xvii.

46. Ibid., lxvi.

47. "Du solt wissen, daz inrlichú gelazenheit bringet den menschen zů der nehsten warheit." Ibid., 2.

48. Ibid., 4.

49. "Wan swem underscheides gebristet, dem gebristet ordenunge, und waz ane reht ordenunge ist, daz ist beose und gebreste." Ibid., 58.

50. For example, Ibid., 16–26, §5.

51. For the genuinely dialogic aspect of the *Sister Catherine* treatise, see Bernard McGinn, *The Harvest of Mysticism in Medieval Germany (1300–1500)*, vol. 4 of *The Presence of God: A History of Western Christian Mysticism* (New York: Herder and Herder, 2005), 344.

52. Seuse, 24–26.

53. Compare Eckhart, 142, and Largier and Quint, eds., 1;442–44; Seuse, 18.

54. Seuse, 26.

55. Ibid., 38.

56. "Der mensch wirt niemer so gar vernihtet in disem nihte, sinen sinnen blibe dennoch underscheit ir eigennes ursprunges und der vernunft dez selben ir eigen kiesen, wie daz alles in sinem | ersten grunde unangesehen blibet." Ibid., 58–60.

57. This element of control is not considered in the otherwise very informative article by Heinrich Stirnimann, "Mystik und Metaphorik: Zu Seuses Dialog," in *Das "Einig Ein": Studien zu Theorie und Sprache der deutschen Mystik*, ed. Alois M. Haas and Heinrich Stirnimann (Freiburg, CH: Universitätsverlag, 1980), 209–80.

58. Seuse, lxv.

59. Ibid., xx.

60. "Aber daz er nit bandes enhat, daz ist da von, wan er daz selb wúrket usser gelazsenheit, daz dü gemeinde würket usser bezwungenheit." Ibid., 66–68.

61. The terminology that Meister Eckhart uses in place of the modern noun *the self* is discussed in greater detail above, in chapter 5..

62. Seuse, 18–22.

63. Ibid., 20.

64. "Swas wir verstant oder sprechent von der ersten sachen, das sin wir me selber, dan es die erste sache si, wan si ist vber allis sprechen vnd verstan." Eckhart, 236; Largier and Quint, eds., 2:190.

65. Eckhart, 237; Largier and Quint, eds., 2:192.

66. "Got mvos vil bi ich werden vnd ich vil bi got, alse gar ein, das dis 'er' vnd dis 'ich' Ein 'ist' werdent." Eckhart, 238; Largier and Quint, eds., 2:194.

67. "Ein ieklicher mensch hat fúnfley Sich." Seuse, 20.

68. Jacques le Goff, *Medieval Civilization, 400–1500*, trans. Julia Barrow (Oxford: Blackwell, 1988), 327.

69. See the discussion above, in chapter 6.

70. For more details, see the discussion below, in chapter 8.

71. See below, chapter 8.

72. Seuse, 56.

73. For a fuller discussion of being-with-others being the background against which personal identity emerges, see above, chapter 3.

74. "Si trat zů ime und zogte ime, wie adellich si in die blossen gotheit vergangen were." Karl Bihlmeyer, ed., *Heinrich Seuse: Deutsche Schriften im Auftrag der württembergischen Kommission für Landesgeschichte* (Frankfurt am Main: Minerva, 1961), 194.

75. Walter Blank, "Heinrich Seuse's 'Vita': Literarische Gestaltung und Pastorale Funktion Seines Schriftums," *Zeitschrift für deutsches Altertum und deutsche Literatur,* 122 (1993): 310–11.

76. Bihlmeyer, ed., 7.

77. Ursula Peters, *Religiöse Erfahrung als literarisches Faktum: Zur Vorgeschichte und Genese frauenmystischer Texte des 13. und 14. Jahrhunderts* (Tübingen: Niemeyer, 1988), 141. Kurt Ruh, *Die Mystik des deutschen Predigerordens und ihre Grundlegung durch die Hochscholastik*, vol. 3 of *Geschichte der Abendländischen Mystik* (Munich: Beck, 1996), 445.

78. "Etwaz gutter lere wart och na ir tode in ir person von im [Seuse] dur zů geleit." Bihlmeyer, ed., 8.

79. Ibid., 4.

80. Ibid., 3. For an account that examines how the text creates Seuse as an exemplary figure and that pays particular attention to the images transmitted in the manuscripts, see "Medieval Self-Fashioning: Authorship, Authority, and Autobiography in Suso's Exemplar," Jeffrey F. Hamburger, *The Visual and the Visionary: Art and Female Spirituality in Late Medieval Germany* (New York: Zone Books, 1998), 233–79.

81. Bihlmeyer, ed., 4–6.

82. Ibid., 97–98.

83. The text speaks of "ein lindes wehsli bi dem fúre, daz der forme dez insigels enpfenklich ist worden." Bihlmeyer, 155.

84. "Hie von sprichet diu sêle in *der minne buoche*: 'drücke mich in dich als ein wahs in ein ingesigel'." Eckhart, *German Sermons and Treatises*, trans. Maurice O'C Walshe, 3 vols. (Shaftesbury: Element Books, 1979), 2:216–17; Largier and Quint, eds., 1:650–52.

85. The *Sister Catherine* treatise is discussed in more detail above, in chapter 6.

86. Bihlmeyer, ed., 156, 157–59.

87. Ibid., 162–63.

88. "Dú tohter sprach: 'gelopt sie got dez gůten underscheides!' " Ibid., 158.

89. "Du schinest noh ein jungú ungeuͤptú swoͤster, dar umbe dir und dinen glichen ist núzzer ze wússene von dem ersten begin, wie man súl an vahen, und von uͤbigem lebene und gůten heiligen bilden, wie diser und der gotesfrúnd, die och einen goͤtlichen anvang haten, wie sich die des ersten mit Cristus leben und lidene ůptin, waz sú eblich erlidden und wie sú sich von innen und von ussnan hieltin, ob sú got dur suͤssekeit ald dur hertikeit zugi, und wenn ald wie in dú bild ab vielin." Ibid., 98.

90. Ferdinand Vetter, ed., *Das Leben der Schwestern zu Töß beschrieben von Elsbet Stagel samt der Vorrede von Johannes Meier und dem Leben der Prinzessin Elisabet von Ungarn* (Berlin: Weidmannsche Buchhandlung, 1906). Stagel's authorship of the text has been called into question, with Klaus Grubmüller concluding that she wrote only the prologue, the life of Elsbeth Bechlin, and a few additions to the lives of other nuns. Klaus Grubmüller, "Die Viten Der Schwestern Von Töss Und Elsbeth Stagel," *Zeitschrift für deutsches Altertum und Literatur* 98 (1969): 171–204.

91. Dewey Weiss Kramer, "'Arise and Give the Convent Bread': Christine Ebner, the Convent Chronicle of Engelthal, and the Call to Ministry among Fourteenth-Century Religious Women," in *Women as Protagonists and Poets in the German Middle Ages: An Anthology of Feminist Approaches to Middle High German Literature*, ed. by Albrecht Classen (Göppingen: Kümmerle, 1991), 187–207.

92. Vetter, ed., 54–55.

93. "Female Visionary Experience," Ruth Anthony El Saffar, *Rapture Encaged: The Suppression of the Feminine in Western Culture* (London: Routledge, 1994), 81–103.

94. Blank: 310.

95. Georg Misch, *Geschichte der Autobiographie* (Frankfurt am Main: Schulte-Bulmke, 1967), 4.1:115.

96. Ruh, 446; Blank, 286–94.

97. "[Daz erste bůch] seit úberal mit bildgebender wise von eim anvahenden lebene und git togenlich ze erkennen, in weler ordenhafti ein reht anvahender mensch sol den ussern und den inren menschen rihten nah gotes aller liepsten willen." Bihlmeyer, ed., 3.

98. Ibid.

99. See the discussion above, in chapter 5.

100. Hamburger, 277.

101. Heinrich Stirnimann, "Mystik und Metaphorik. Zu Seuses Dialog," in Haas and Stirnimann, eds., 226.

102. "Dú tohter sprach: 'gelopt sie got dez gůten underscheides!'" Bihlmeyer, ed., 158.

103. Ibid., 107.

104. See the discussion above, in chapter 1.

105. "Dú trůg ein wúlfin herz under einem gůtigen wandel und barg daz als genote, daz es der brůder in vil langer zit nie kond gemerken." Bihlmeyer, ed., 119.

106. Ibid., 135.

107. See the discussion above, in chapter 1.

8. Taking Leave of Sigmund Freud

1. The historical and personal background to the case history is reconstructed in Hannah S. Decker, *Freud, Dora, and Vienna 1900* (New York: Free Press, 1991).

2. Sigmund Freud, *Bruchstück einer Hysterie-Analyse* (Frankfurt am Main.: Fischer, 1993), 120.

3. "The 'Sister Catherine' Treatise," trans. by Elvira Borgstädt in *Meister Eckhart: Teacher and Preacher*, ed. Bernard McGinn (New York: Paulist Press, 1986), 347–87, 51; Franz-Josef Schweitzer, *Der Freiheitsbegriff der deutschen Mystik: Seine Beziehung zur Ketzerei der "Brüder und Schwestern vom Freien Geist," mit besonderer Rücksicht auf den Pseudoeckartischen Traktat "Schwester Katrei" (Edition)*, vol. 378 of *Europäische Hochschulschriften: Reihe I, Deutsche Sprache und Literatur* (Frankfurt am Main: Peter Lang, 1981), 322–70, 24.

4. Freud, *Bruchstück einer Hysterie-Analyse*, 95.

5. Freud quotes Rumi in his analysis of Daniel Paul Schreber's *Denkwürdigkeiten eines Nervenkranken*: Sigmund Freud, *Studienausgabe*, ed. Alexander Mitscherlich, Angela Richards, and James Strachey, vol. 7 of *Conditio Humana* (Frankfurt am Main: S. Fischer, 1969), 188. The note on mysticism is to be found in Sigmund Freud, "Ergebnisse, Ideen, Probleme (London, Juni 1938)," in *Gesammelte Werke, chronologisch Geordnet: Siebzehnter Band: Schriften aus dem Nachlaß* (Frankfurt am Main: Fischer, 1991), 149–52, here 152 (22.6.1938).

6. Henri F. Ellenberger, *The Discovery of the Unconscious: The History and Evolution of Dynamic Psychiatry* (New York: Basic Books, 1970).

7. Ibid., 53–60.

8. Rosa Mayreder, *Das Haus in der Landskrongasse: Jugenderinnerungen* (Vienna: Mandelbaum, 1998); Ulrike Döcker, *Die Ordnung der bürgerlichen Welt: Verhaltensideale und soziale Praktiken im 19. Jahrhundert* (Frankfurt am Main: Campus, 1994).

9. William M. Johnston, *The Austrian Mind: An Intellectual and Social History, 1848–1938* (Berkeley: University of California Press, 1972), 156.

10. Frank J. Sulloway, *Freud: Biologist of the Mind*, 2nd ed. (Cambridge, Mass.: Harvard Uuniversity Press, 1991); Carl E. Schorske, "Politics and Parricide in Freud's *Interpretation of Dreams*," in *Fin-de-Siècle Vienna: Politics and Culture* (Cambridge: Cambridge University Press, 1981), 181–207; William J. McGrath, *Freud's Discovery of Psychoanalysis: The Politics of Hysteria* (Ithaca, N.Y.: Cornell University Press, 1986).

11. Bruno Bettelheim, *Freud and Man's Soul* (London: Chatto and Windus, 1983), 5.

12. Mayreder, 36–37.

13. Bruce Thompson, *Schnitzler's Vienna: Image of a Society* (London: Routledge, 1990), 3.

14. Jacques Le Rider, *Modernity and Crises of Identity: Culture and Society in Fin-de-Siècle Vienna*, trans. Rosemary Morris (Cambridge: Polity, 1993), 20, 27.

15. Mayreder, 33.

16. Döcker, 194.

17. Ibid., 166.

18. Ibid., 197.

19. Ibid., 203.

20. Ibid., 206: "Kunstwissen, Kleidung, rhetorische Kompetenz, Reisen, Musikalität."

21. Ibid., 251: "Ein kleiner Anstrich von weiblicher Sanftmut."

22. "Dem Gentleman macht vieles, was in der Welt rechts und links von ihm vorgeht wahren Schmerz. Er wehrt sich aber kräftig gegen jeden Hang zur Schwermut. Er verschließt was ihm weh thut und er nicht ändern kann in seine tiefste Brust. Solche Wunden hie und da im Umgang mit Weibern hervorzukehren, um ihr Mitleid und was etwa daran hängen möchte zu gewinnen, ist ein Vorgehen ähnlich dem des Bettlers, der ein offenes Gebreste den Vorübergehenden unter die Augen streckt, um eine Gabe zu erpressen, eines Gentleman's ist es völlig unwürdig." Emil Wallberg, *Wie der Wiener ein Gentleman wird. Zwölf Lectionen* (Vienna: 1860), 46. Quoted in Döcker, 251.

23. "Die Höflichkeit . . . ist ein trefflicher und erlaubter Mantel, unsere unangenehmen Empfindugen anderen Leuten gegenüber zu verbergen, und je mehr der Mensch sich selbst in der Gewalt hat, je mehr ihm die Formen des guten Tons zu eigene geworden sind, desto sicherer wird auch er in der höflichen Form unangenehme Dinge von sich abzuwehren verstehen, ohne Anderen zu verletzen." Johann Edler von K——ski, *Der Gute Ton: Oder Anleitung, um sich in den verschiedensten Verhältnissen des Lebens und der Gesellschaft als feiner, gebildeter Mann zu benehmen* (Pesth, 1865), 262; quoted in Döcker, 197.

24. Thomas Mann, *Buddenbrooks* (Frankfurt am Main: Fischer, 1960), 400.

25. Max Weber, *The Protestant Ethic and the Spirit of Capitalism*, trans. Talcott Parsons (New York: Scribner, 1958), 181.

26. Claudia Honneger, "Die Stellung der Frau im modernen Leben," in *Die Ordnung der Geschlechter: Die Wissenschaft vom Menschen und das Weib 1750–1850* (Frankfurt am Main: Campus, 1991), 264.

27. Ibid., 209.

28. Ibid., 210 (quoted): "Alles, was wir an dem wahren Weibe weibliches bewundern und verehren, ist nur eine Dependenz des Eierstockes."

29. Ibid., 244–50.

30. Ibid., 242–59.

31. Rosa Mayreder, *Zur Kritik der Weiblichkeit—Essays* (Vienna: Mandelbaum, 1998), 12–17.

32. "Wenn ein innerlich so wohl erzogenes junges Mädchen die Merkmale [von Bescheidenheit] auch auf die äußere Person überträgt, ein unschuldiges Lachen dem reizenden Munde entströmt, während die Haltung des Rückgrates eine aufrechte und doch sittsam bescheidene bleibt, nur das Köpfchen mit den lustigen

Augen ein wenig emporgerichtet ist, kann sich Niemand des Zaubers eines solchen Anblickes erwehren." *Damen-Chic* (1891), 61, quoted in Döcker, 245.

33. Mayreder, *Das Haus in der Landskrongasse: Jugenderinnerungen*, 26–29.

34. "Wohin sollte ein Sportsman spazieren gehen, wenn nicht in den Prater?" (10 May 1868). Daniel Spitzer, *Wiener Spaziergänge*, ed. Walter Obermaier (Vienna: Edition Wien, 1987), 2:202.

35. Mayreder, *Das Haus in der Landskrongasse: Jugenderinnerungen*, 40.

36. Ibid., 129–30.

37. Ibid., 131: "Die Verleugnung der eigenen Persönlichkeit."

38. Ibid., 61.

39. Ibid., 43.

40. Ibid., 146.

41. Ibid., 148: "[Ein] Mangel an Sittsamkeit."

42. Rosa Mayreder, *Tagebücher 1873–1937*, ed. Harriet Anderson (Frankfurt am Main: Insel, 1998).

43. Juliet Mitchell, *Psychoanalysis and Feminism: A Radical Reassessment of Freudian Psychoanalysis*, 2nd ed. (Harmondsworth: Penguin, 2000), xviii.

44. Wallberg, 46; quoted in Döcker, 251.

45. In the following analysis, I draw on Eva Klingstein, *Die Frau mit Eigenschaften: Literatur und Geschlecht in der Wiener Frauenpresse um 1900* (Cologne: Böhlau, 1997), 182–92.

46. "Aber die gnädige Frau vergass jede Höflichkeit und Selbstbeherrschung. Die gnädige Frau ging mit der Miene eines gescholtenen Kindes aus dem Zimmer. —'So eine hysterische Person!'—murmulte Professor Barth ihr nach. So etwas freut sich nun daran, minderwerthig zu sein und mag sich einfach nicht heilen lassen." Toni Schwabe, "Nervös: Geschichte einer Ehe," *Dokumente der Frauen* (15 June 1902), 177, quoted in Klingstein, 185–86.

47. Klingstein, 189.

48. "Psychiatry and its Unknown History," in *Beyond the Unconscious: Essays of Henri F. Ellenberger in the History of Psychiatry*, ed. Mark Micale (Princeton, N.J.: Princeton Universtiy Press, 1993), 240–41.

49. Ibid., 242.

50. Ellenberger, 890; *The Discovery of the Unconscious*, 890. For Jung's own account of this breakdown, see Carl Gustav Jung, *Memories, Dreams, Reflections*, ed. Aniela Jaffé, trans. Richard Winston and Clara Winston (London: Fontana, 1983), 194–225.

51. Ellenberger, 130–31.

52. Ibid., 20–22.

53. Ibid., 78–81.

54. Ibid., 98–99.

55. Ibid., 315–16.

56. I. M. Lewis, *Ecstatic Religion: A Study of Shamanism and Spirit Possession*, 2nd ed. (London: Routledge, 1989), 70–77.

57. Ellenberger, 484.

58. The standard, historical account of the case is Albrecht Hirschmüller, *Physiologie und Psychoanalyse in Leben und Werk Josef Breuers*, Jahrbuch der Psychoanalyse Beiheft 4 (Bern: Hans Huber, 1978). Hirschmüller gives all the surviving documentation of the case, 348–82. For a critical account of the case and a comparison of the different documents relating to it, see Mikkel Borch-Jacobsen, *Remembering Anna O.: A Century of Mystification*, trans. Kirby Olson in collaboration with Xavier Callahan and the author (New York: Routledge, 1996). The negative findings of Borch-Jacobsen have been disputed by Richard A. Skues, *Sigmund Freud and the History of Anna O.: Re-opening a Closed Case* (Basingstoke: Palgrave Macmillan, 2006). Skues puts the documents back in the context of medical discourse in the 1880s and 1890s to argue that Breuer did not overstate the efficacy of the talking cure and did not ignore physiological as opposed to psychological aspects of Pappenheim's condition.

59. Josef Breuer, "Case 1: Fräulein Anna O.," Sigmund Freud and Josef Breuer, *Studies in Hysteria*, ed. Angela Richards (Harmondsworth: Penguin, 1974), 3:75–76.

60. Ibid., 73.

61. Sigmund Freud, "Über Psychoanalyse," in *Abriß der Psychoanalyse* (Frankfurt am Main: Fischer, 1994), 107.

62. Ellenberger, 301. Breuer and Freud acknowledge the work of both Benedikt and Pierre Janet in a footnote to the theoretical introduction to Sigmund Freud and Josef Breuer, *Studien über Hysterie*, 3rd ed. (Leipzig: Franz Deuticke, 1916), 4–5.

63. "Nein, nein; etwas von der Seele heruntersprechen, das regt mich nicht auf, das macht still." Theodor Fontane, *Effi Briest*, ed. Walter Keitel and Helmuth Nürnberger (Munich: Carl Hanser, 1974), 293 (chap. 36).

64. Ellenberger summarises the report of 1882 in "The Story of 'Anna O.': A Critical Review with New Data," in Micale, ed., 265–69. The case notes are reprinted in Hirschmüller, 348–64.

65. Freud and Breuer, *Studies in Hysteria*, 95.

66. Ibid.

67. Micale, ed., 271; Richard Webster would agree with Micale. Richard Webster, *Why Freud Was Wrong: Sin, Science, and Psychoanalysis* (London: HarperCollins, 1995), 118: "What cannot be denied is that almost all the behavioural and physiological manifestations of Anna O.'s illness, including the most bizarre, *are* found in neurological disorders."

68. Webster, 125.

69. Ibid., 99.

70. Malcolm Macmillan, *Freud Evaluated: The Completed Arc*, 2nd ed. (Cambridge, Mass.: MIT Press, 1997), 631–32.

71. Skues, 40–52.

72. There is a reconstruction of the sequence of events: Skues, 168–73.

73. Freud and Breuer, *Studien über Hysterie*, 16; Freud and Breuer, *Studies in Hysteria*, 74.

74. "Während alle sie anwesend glaubten, lebte sie im Geiste Märchen durch, war aber, angerufen, immer präsent, so daß niemand davon wußte." Freud and Breuer, *Studien über Hysterie*, 16; Freud and Breuer, *Studies in Hysteria*, 74.

75. "Sie habe nichts gesagt, denn sie wolle höflich sein." Freud and Breuer, *Studien über Hysterie*, 27; Freud and Breuer, *Studies in Hysteria*, 88.

76. Macmillan, 632–33.

77. Fritz Schweighofer, *Das Privattheater der Anna O.: Ein Emanzipationsdrama* (Munich: Ernst Reinhardt Verlag, 1987); quoted in Borch-Jacobsen, 43.

78. "Eine Therapie, die darin bestand, das Bewußtsein in direkte Beziehung zum Unbewußten zu setzen—ohne Theorien, ohne Lehrgebäude, die sich dazwischenschieben. Bertha Pappenheim wurde durch diese Behandlung zu dem geboren, was sie war—zu ihrem *ich*." Christina von Braun, *Nicht Ich: Logik, Lüge, Libido* (Frankfurt am Main: Neue Kritik, 1988), 67.

79. "Bei Anna O . . . war besonders auffallend, wie sehr die Produkte des 'schlimmen Ichs,' wie die Kranke selbst es nannt, ihren moralischen Habitus beeinflußten. Wären sie nicht fortlaufend weggeschafft worden, so hätte man in ihr eine Hysterika von der bösartigen Sorte gehabt, widerspenstig, träge, unliebenswürdig, boshaft; während so, nach Entfernung dieser Reize, immer wieder sogleich ihr wahrer Charakter zum Vorschein kam, der von all dem das Gegenteil war." Freud and Breuer, *Studien über Hysterie*, 36; Freud and Breuer, *Studies in Hysteria*, 101.

80. For presentation of the relevant material see Borch-Jacobsen, 34–43. Borch-Jacobsen concludes that the suggestion that the treatment ended with a sexual crisis is Freud's retrospective interpretetation of events, and finds little corroboration in the letters and records that have survived from the early 1880s. Skues concurs, concluding that what lies behind Freud's account is Freud's view of the necessarily sexual etiology of hysteria and his concern with the question of transference. Skues, 76–79, 88–89.

81. Borch-Jacobsen, 40–41; Skues, 105.

82. Cranefield, "Josef Breuer's Evaluation of His Contribution to Psycho-Analysis," *International Journal of Psychoanalysis* 39, no. 5 (1958): 319–20; quoted in Borch-Jacobsen, 38.

83. Skues, 102.

84. Hirschmüller, 156.

85. Borch-Jacobsen, 25.

86. "Anna Ettlinger war nicht nur von Bedeutung, weil sie Bertha ermutigte, weiter zu schreiben. Die wichtigste Botschaft an Bertha Pappenheim zu diesem Zeitpunkt war vor allem ihre Art der eigenständigen Lebensbewältigung." Marianne Brentzel, *Anna O. Bertha Pappenheim: Biographie* (Göttingen: Wallstein, 2002), 65.

87. Paul Berthold, *In der Trödelbude: Geschichten* (Lahr: Moritz Schauenburg, 1890).

88. The note is reprinted Hirschmüller, 369–70. Meredith Kimball suggests that writing is an integral part of Pappenheim's recovery but does not discuss

texts in detail. Meredith M. Kimball, "From 'Anna O.' To Bertha Pappenheim: Transforming Private Pain into Public Action," *History of Psychology* 3, no. 1 (2000): 30. An earlier collection of reinterpretations of the case history incudes two brief mentions of the book but no extended analysis. Max Rosenbaum and Melvin Muroff, eds., *Anna O.: Fourteen Contemporary Reinterpretations* (New York: Free Press, 1984), 14, 109.

89. " 'Schilt mir meinen Kram nicht tot und häßlich,' sagte Franz, und ein leichtes Lächeln erhellte sein Gesicht. 'Der Kram ist nicht so tot, wie du meinst. Nachts, wenn alles Leben ringsum schläft, der Laden geschlossen und die Thüre zu meinem Zimmer offen ist, da geht ein Wispern und Flüstern durch die Regale, und mancher der Gegenstände, die unbedeutend und wertlos aussehen, erzählen von ihren Erfahrungen und Erlebnissen. Ich lausche, und wenn ich höre, wie viel Elend allenthalben in der Welt ist, wie wenig Heiteres es giebt, dann denke ich, daß mein Unglück nur ein kleiner Teil des großen Elends ist.' " *Trödelbude*, 18–19.

90. "Die beruhigenden erklärenden Worte, die in sanfter Stimme an des Mädchens Ohr klangen, übten auf den Sprecher selbst tröstliche Rückwirkung." *Trödelbude*, 101.

91. "Es ist kein angenehmes Gefühl, so von allen Seiten betrachtet und nach seinem Aussehen und Wert geprüft zu werden." *Trödelbude*, 31.

92. "Es ist schrecklich, an einem Krankenlager nichts als eine Puppe zu sein, vom besten Willen beseelt, nicht, gar nicht helfen zu können." *Trödelbude*, 34.

93. "Und es war mir ein unendlicher Kummer, meinen guten, lieben Herrn in düsten Gedanken vor mir stehen zu sehen, ohne ihm helfen zu können." *Trödelbude*, 44–45.

94. This could also be said of the story of the pince-nez. Here, Ina arranges things to ensure that Emma can meet the man she loves. The change is possible because the figure of authority, a middle-aged woman, can be called into question. Even the inanimate object has a more reliable view of the world than does the principal herself. "Durch ihre Kurzsichtigkeit gewann ich bald Einsicht in vieles, ja sogar mehr als die würdige Dame [Fräulein Marwitz] selbst, denn sie konnte nur sehen, wenn sie mich zu Hilfe nahm, während ich auch beobachtete, wenn ich unbenutzt an meinem Schnürchen hing." *Trödelbude*, 60.

95. "Als sie [die Spitze] schwieg, sagte eine alte Sandauer Dose, der die Vornehmheit der Spitze ein Dorn im Auge war, in hämischem Ton: 'Und wenn sie nicht gestorben sind, so leben sie heute noch, wie Prinz und Prinzessin im Märchen.' " *Trödelbude*, 28.

96. "Straßenlaternen können doch nicht weinen." *Trödelbude*, 87.

97. "Aber eine Kaffeemühle, die das Bedürfnis hat, sich auszusprechen, und dazu aufgefordert wird, überwindet solche Momente schwächlicher Sprachlosigkeit bald, und so hub sie denn mit etwas kreischender Stimme alsbald zu erzählen an." *Trödelbude*, 36–37.

98. Amy Colin, "Metamorphosen einer Frau: Von Anna O. zu Bertha Pappenheim," in *Von einer Welt in die Andere: Jüdinnen im 19. und 20. Jahrhundert*,

ed. Jutta Dick and Hahn Barbara (Vienna: Christian Brandstätter, 1993), 210–11.

99. The *Sister Catherine* treatise is discussed at greater length above in chapter 6.

100. The poem is given in Hirschmüller, 382. Amy Colin similarly reads the poem as evidence that the sequence of roles adopted by Pappenheim was not finally fulfilling. Colin, 210.

101. "Affektloses Erinnern ist fast immer völlig wirkunglos; der psychische Prozeß, der ursprünglich abgelaufen war, muß so lebhaft als möglich wiederholt, in statu nascendi gebracht und dann 'ausgesprochen' werden." Freud and Breuer, *Studien über Hysterie*, 4; Freud and Breuer, *Studies in Hysteria*, 57.

102. Borch-Jacobsen, 60.

103. The case history made Ida Bauer eighteen, a year older than she actually was at the time of the therapy. Decker, xi.

104. Freud, *Bruchstück einer Hysterie-Analyse*, 62.

105. Ibid., 15.

106. Webster, 220–21. Frank J. Sulloway reconstructs the scientific debate in the 1890s about connections between the nose and sex organs; Sulloway, 147–52.

107. Freud, *Bruchstück einer Hysterie-Analyse*, 101–02.

108. Webster, 198.

109. "Jede Person, bei welcher ein Anlaß zur sexuellen Erregung überwiegend oder ausschließlich Unlustgefühle hervorruft, würde ich unbedenklich für eine Hysterika halten." Freud, *Bruchstück einer Hysterie-Analyse*, 30.

110. Ibid., 83.

111. Ibid., 36–37.

112. John Forrester argues that psychoanalysis necessarily requires patients to give up their initial grasp of their situation and surrender to free association and the quasi-surgical interpretative interventions of the analyst. John Forrester, *Dispatches from the Freud Wars: Psychoanalysis and Its Passions* (Cambridge, Mass.: Harvard University Press, 1997), 225. This does not address the problem of Freud's interpretations being theory-led and not engaging with the patient's actual situation.

113. Many rereadings of the case history stay within the terms of reference defined by Freud rather than trying to step back and assess Bauer's situation independently of his interpretative framework, "Dora: An Exemplary Failure," in Lisa Appignanesi and John Forrester, *Freud's Women* (London: Virago, 1993), 146–67. It is also true of Hanna S. Decker, who reconstructs the historical background only to stay on Freudian territory of a narrowly defined sexual desire. Decker, 70–72.

114. Freud, *Bruchstück einer Hysterie-Analyse*, 64.

115. Ibid., 93, 99.

116. Ibid., 85.

117. Ibid., 98–99.

118. Ibid., 91–92.

119. Ibid., 116.

120. Jeffrey Masson, "Dora and Freud," in *Against Therapy* (London: Collins, 1989), 102–14. For a reading of the case from a psychoanalytic perspective that clear-sightedly reads the case history and its positive reception by the early psychoanalytic movement as "an example of continued sexual abuse," see Patrick J. Mahony, *Freud's Dora: A Psychoanalytic, Historical, and Textual Study* (New Haven, Conn.: Yale University Press, 1996), 148–49.

121. Sigmund Freud, *Case Histories 2*, ed. Angela Richards (Harmondsworth: Penguin, 1979), 9:259.

122. Ibid., 266.

123. Masson, 110–11; Stavros Mentzos, "Nachwort," in Freud, *Bruchstück einer Hysterie-Analyse*, 130.

124. Freud, *Bruchstück einer Hysterie-Analyse*, 95.

125. "Es war dieses Bild das Hauptaltarblatt des Klosters St. Sixti in Piacenza. Liebhaber und Kenner der Kunst gingen dahin, um diesen Raffael zu sehen, so wie man nur allein nach Thespiä reisete, den schönen Cupido von der Hand des Praxiteles daselbst zu betrachten." Johann Joachim Winckelmann, *Gedanken über die Nachahmung der griechischen Werke in der Malerei und Bildhauerkunst* (Stuttgart: Reclam, 1969), 24.

126. Brigid Doherty, "Between the Artwork and Its 'Actualization': A Footnote to Art History in Benjamin's 'Work of Art' Essay," *Paragraph* 32, no. 3 (2009): 331–58.

127. "Täglich habe ich die griechischen Ideale und die italienischen Meisterstücke besucht, und jedesmal, wenn ich in der Galerie trat, stundenlang vor dem einzigen Raphael dieser Sammlung, vor jener Mutter Gottes gestanden, mit dem hohen Ernste, mit der stillen Größe, ach Wilhelmine, und mit Umrissen, die mich zugleich an zwei geliebte Wesen erinnerten." Heinrich von Kleist, *Sämtliche Werke und Briefe*, ed. Helmut Sembder, 2 vols. (Munich: Carl Hanser, 1984), 2:650–61.

128. Gerhard Schulz, ed., *Novalis Werke*, 2nd ed. (Munich: Beck, 1981), 584.

129. "Die Gemälde—Gespräch," August Wilhelm Schlegel and Friedrich Schlegel, *Athenaeum: Eine Zeitschrift*, Photomechanical reprint, vols. 1–3 (Berlin / East: Rütten & Loening, 1960), vol. 2, no. 1 (1799), 124.

130. Friedrich Nietzsche, *Menschliches, Allzumenschliches*, ed. Giorgio Colli and Mazzino Montinari, *Kritische Gesamtausgabe* (Berlin: de Gruyter, 1968–), §73.

131. "Denn sagt, wer würde sich nicht gern neben diesen Knieenden vor der hohen Jungfrau niederwerfen?" Schlegel and Schlegel, vol. 2, no. 1 (1799), 126.

132. Ibid.

133. John Forrester discusses the image of the Sistine Madonna in "The Untold Pleasures of Psychoanalysis: Freud, Dora, and the Madonna," in John Forrester, *The Seductions of Psychoanalysis: Freud, Lacan, and Derrida* (Cambridge: Cambridge University Press, 1990), 49–61. But he uses the painting to explore Freudian aspects of the interaction between Bauer and her physician—Freud not

wanting to play the role of the seductive maternal analyst (60)—rather than as an index of the cultural situaton beyond the consulting room.

134. If Bauer was more active in relation to her family and to Freud, she was not able to be so after the therapy, going on to an unhappy marriage, whereas Pappenheim established a role for herself as writer and social reformer. Bauer's later life, from her marriage to her death, is presented in Decker, 151–89.

135. Freud, *Bruchstück einer Hysterie-Analyse*, 120.

136. Abraham de Swaan, "On the Sociogenesis of the Psychoanalytic Setting," in *Human Figurations: Essays for Norbert Elias*, ed. Peter R. Gleichmann, Johan Goudsblom, and Hermann Korte (Amsterdam: Amsterdams Sociologisch Tijdschrift, 1977), 381–413.

137. Ibid., 397.

138. Bettelheim, 4–5; D. W. Winnicott, *The Piggle: An Account of the Psychoanalytic Treatment of a Little Girl* (Harmondsworth: Penguin, 1991).

139. "Das Unbewußte," Sigmund Freud, *Das Ich und das Es* (Frankfurt am Main: Fischer, 1992), 124 (§1).

140. "Das Reale wird immer 'unerkennbar' bleiben": Freud, *Abriß Der Psychoanalyse*, 92.

141. Sigmund Freud, *Die Traumdeutung* (Frankfurt am Main: Fischer, 1991), 155–57 (§4).

142. Ibid., 596–97 (§7).

143. Freud, "Das Unbewußte," in *Das Ich und Das Es*, 137–39 (§5, "Die besonderen Eigenschaften des Systems *Ubw*"). In 1915, Freud presents this mode of operation as one that is radically distinct from that of the secondary processes. "Eine neue Bedeutung erhält die Unterscheidung der beiden psychischen Systeme, wenn wir darauf aufmerksam werden, daß die Vorgänge des einen Systems, des *Ubw*, Eigenschaften zeigen, die sich in dem nächst höheren nicht wiederfinden." (*Das Ich und Das Es*, 137). When he first presented the distinction in *Die Traumdeutung* in 1900, the distinction between the two levels was less clear. Indeed, he explicitly commented on a contradiction that appeared in his presentation of dreams. "Wir haben einerseits die Traumgedanken durch völlig normale geistige Arbeit entstehen lassen, andererseits aber eine Reihe von ganz abnormen Denkvorgängen unter den Traumgedanken, und von ihnen aus zum Trauminhalt aufgefunden, welche wir dann bei der Traumdeutung wiederholen" (§8E, 580). He then sought to explain the contradiction by saying that trains of thought that were started and then interrupted because they seemed inappropriate to consciousness continue in the preconscious and then are taken over by impulses from the unconscious. "Wir können sagen, der bisher vorbewußte Gedankengang *ist ins Unbewußte gezogen* worden" (§8E, 582). "So können wir uns also der Einsicht nicht erschließen, daß an der Traumbildung zweierlei wesensverschiedene psychische Vorgänge beteiligt sind; der eine schafft vollkommen korrekte, dem normalen Denken gleichwertige Traumgedanken; der andere vefährt mit demselben auf eine höchst befremdende, inkorrekte Weise" (§8E, 585).

144. John A. Bargh, "The Automaticity of Everyday Life," in *Advances in Social Cognition*, ed. Robert S. Wyer Jr. (Mahwah, N.J.: Lawrence Erlbaum, 1997), 17–18.

145. Ibid., 16.

146. Ibid., 23.

147. Lawrence E. Williams, Julie Y. Huang, and John A. Bargh, "The Scaffolded Mind: Higher Mental Processes Are Grounded in Early Experience of the Physical World," *European Journal of Social Psychology* 39 (2009): 1262–63.

148. Ibid., 1264.

149. Bargh, 23.

150. Ibid., 11–12; John Dewey, *Human Nature and Conduct* (Amherst, N.Y.: Prometheus, 2002), 14.

151. Paula M. Niedenthal and Martha W. Alibali, "Conceptualizing Scaffolding and Goals for a Full Account of Embodied Cognition," *European Journal of Social Psychology* 39 (2009): 1269–70.

152. Giacomo Rizzolatti et al., "Premotor Cortex and the Recognition of Motor Actions," *Cognitive Brain Research* 3, no. 2 (1996): 131–41.

153. Mirror neurons are discussed in more detail in chapter 3 above. For a general introduction to the area of research, see Marco Iacoboni, *Mirroring People: The New Science of How We Connect with Others* (New York: Farrar, Straus and Giroux, 2008).

154. Slavoj Žižek, *How to Read Lacan* (London: Granta, 2006), 51–55.

155. J. Allan Hobson, *Dreaming: A Very Short Introduction* (Oxford: Oxford University Press, 2005), 78.

156. Ibid., 62.

157. Ibid., 130.

158. Ibid., 140.

159. Ibid., 134.

160. Ibid., 118.

161. J. Allan Hobson, "REM Sleep and Dreaming: Towards a Theory of Protoconsciousness," *Nature Reviews Neuroscience* 10, no. 11 (2009): 808.

162. Daniel C. Dennett, *Consciousness Explained* (Bostson: Little, Brown, 1991), 259.

163. Ibid., 242.

164. "Ich wußte es ja nicht oder besser, ich wollte es nicht wissen, wollte es mir aus dem Kopfe schlagen, nie mehr daran denken, ich glaube, es ist mir auch in der letzten Zeit gelungen." Freud and Breuer, *Studien über Hysterie*, 100; Freud and Breuer, *Studies in Hysteria*, 181.

165. Freud and Breuer, *Studien über Hysterie*, 100–1; Freud and Breuer, *Studies in Hysteria*, 181.

166. Jean-Paul Sartre, *Being and Nothingess: An Essay on Phenomenological Ontology*, trans. Hazel E. Barnes (London: Routledge, 1969), 47–54.

167. For a positive reading of Sartre's consciousness-centred approach to identity, see Manfred Frank, ed., *Selbstbewußtseinstheorien von Fichte bis Sartre*

(Frankfurt am Main: Suhrkamp, 1991). For a brief critique, see chapter 3 above.

168. Martin Heidegger, *Being and Time*, trans. John Macquarrie and Edward Robinson (Oxford: Basil Blackwell, 1962), §27.

169. Ludwig Wittgenstein, *Lectures and Conversations on Aesthetics, Psychology, and Religious Belief* (Oxford: Blackwell, 1966), 43.

170. "Psychoanalyse ist jene Geisteskrankheit, für deren Therapie sie sich hält." Karl Kraus, "Nachts," *Die Fackel* 15, no. 376–77 (1913): 22.

171. Skues, 80–89.

172. For an account of the constraints to which young women from the background of a Pappenheim or a Bauer were subject, see Marion A. Kaplan, "Anna O. and Bertha Pappenheim: An Historical Perspective," in Rosenbaum and Muroff, eds., 101–17.

173. Frank J. Sulloway, "Reassessing Freud's Case Histories: The Social Construction of Psychoanalysis," *Isis* 82, no. 2 (1991): 275.

174. Michel Foucault, "What Is Enlightenment?" *The Foucault Reader*, ed. Paul Rabinow and Hubert L. Dreyfus (Harmondsworth: Penguin, 1984), 48.

175. Freud, *Das Unbehagen in der Kultur*, in *Studienausgabe*, 9:191–270.

176. Carl Gustav Jung, *Die Beziehungen zwischen dem Ich und dem Unbewußten* (Munich: dtv, 1990), 116.

177. Carl Gustav Jung, *Psychologie und Religion* (Munich: dtv, 1991), 31.

178. Carl Gustav Jung, "Die praktische Verwendbarkeit der Traumanalyse," in *Traum und Traumdeutung* (Munich: dtv, 1990); 156. Anthony Storr, ed., *The Jung Reader* (London: Fontana, 1983), 176.

179. Jung, *Die Beziehungen zwischen dem Ich und dem Unbewußten*, 106.

180. Jung, *Psychologie und Religion*, 9.

181. Jung, "Die praktische Verwendbarkeit der Traumanalyse," in *Traum und Traumdeutung*, 158.

182. "Psychoanalysis and Neurosis" (1916), Storr, ed., 52.

183. Jung, "Vererbte Kategorien," in *Die Beziehungen zwischen dem Ich und dem Unbewußten*, 21.

184. Ibid., 91–95.

185. Sonu Shamdasani, *Jung and the Making of Modern Psychology: The Dream of a Science* (Cambridge: Cambridge University Press, 2003), 6–8.

9. Everyday Acknowledgments

1. On urine and the marking of territory in male humans, see Andrew R. Gustavson, Michael E. Dawson, and Douglas G. Bonett, "Androstenol, a Putative Human Pheromone, Affects Human (Homo Sapiens) Male Choice Performance," *Journal of Comparative Psychology* 101, no. 2 (1987): 210–12.

2. "Three Ways of Spilling Ink," in J. L. Austin, *Philosophical Papers*, 3rd ed. (Oxford: Oxford University Press, 1979), 273.

3. Sidney Halpern, "The First Exploration of a Slip of the Tongue," *Classical Journal* 57, no. 8 (1962): 355–58.

4. For a recent discussion of Lucian's treatment of identity and its tensions, see Simon Goldhill, *Who Needs Greek: Contests in the Cultural History of Hellenism* (Cambridge: Cambridge University Press, 2002), 60–93.

5. Tim Whitmarsh, *Greek Literature and the Roman Empire: The Politics of Imitation* (Oxford: Oxford University Press, 2001), 127.

6. Lucian, *Drei Satiren des Lucian: Für die deutsche Bühne bearbeitet von Paul Lindau* (Breslau: Schlesiche Buckdruckerei, Kunst- und Verlagsanstalt, 1902).

7. Karl Kraus, "Gebildeter," *Die Fackel*, no. 199 (1906): 23–24.

8. Graham Frankland, *Freud's Literary Culture* (Cambridge: Cambridge University Press, 2000), 43–46, 30–31. For a discussion of Bernays's dismissal of Lucian, see Manuel Baumbach, *Lukian in Deutschland: Eine forschungs- und rezeptionsgeschichtliche Analyse vom Humanismus bis zur Gegenwart* (Munich: Wilhelm Fink, 2002), 188–93.

9. Sigmund Freud, *Die Traumdeutung* (Frankfurt am Main: Fischer, 1991), 268–73.

10. Halpern, 358.

11. The background cultural details are presented in Sidney Halpern, "The First Exploration of a Slip of the Tongue," *The Classical Journal* 57, no. 8 (1962): 355.

12. Lucian, "A Slip of the Tongue in Greeting," in *Lucian*, vol. 6, trans. K Kilburn (Cambridge, Mass.: Harvard University Press, 1959), 173. Further references to Lucian's essays from this volume of the Loeb edition will be given parenthetically in the text, with abbreviations for the relevant text—e.g. "A Slip of the Tongue," "Apology," "Hermotimus."

13. On Lucian's frequent treatment of blunders committed in front of an audience, see Graham Anderson, "Metrical Howlers in Lucian," *Hermes* 104, no. 2 (1976): 254–56.

14. On the paucity of biographical information in Lucian's texts, and its significance for his reflection on cultural identity, see Goldhill, 63–67. For a contrasting reading of the "Apology" as "part of an ongoing process of subversion and re-establishment of the authority of Lucian's own literary voice" (293), see Whitmarsh, 291–93.

15. Goldhill (82) extracts as the motto from "Hermotimus" the saying of Epicharmus that Lycinus quotes: "Keep sober, and remember to disbelieve [*nēphe kai memnēso apistein*]" ("Hermotimus," 350–51). This fits Goldhill's postmodern emphasis on the slipperiness of cultural positions. But the motto expresses an attitude that is only one stage of Lucian's argument. If it were possible to try out all the different philosophies, we could try them out without falling for them in the spirit of Epicharmus's motto. But there isn't time to try them out, and we don't know what it is we should be trying out anyway. So the skeptical investigation that Lycinus briefly proposes is finally replaced by the affirmation of everyday life and the importance of acting wisely, justly, and bravely.

16. Angela Richards, introduction to *The Psychopathology of Everyday Life*, by Sigmund Freud, ed. Angela Richards (Harmondsworth: Penguin, 1975), 31.

Further references will be given parenthetically in the text, giving the page number of the English edition but also that of the German. Sigmund Freud, *Zur Psychopathologie des Alltagslebens: Über Vergessen, Versprechen, Vergreifen, Aberglauben und Irrtum* (Frankfurt am Main: Fischer, 1954).

17. Karl Kraus, "Tagebuch," *Die Fackel* 10, no. 256 (1908): 22.

18. The details of the trip are given in Freud's letter to Wilhelm Fließ (22 September 1898) where he first discusses the slip. Sigmund Freud, *Briefe an Wilhelm Fliess, 1887–1904*, ed. Jeffrey Masson and Michael Schröter (Frankfurt am Main: Fischer, 1986), 357–58. The account in the *Psychopathology* doesn't give so much detail. For a discussion of the different versions of Freud's analysis of the slip, see Michael Billig, "Freud's Different Versions of Forgetting 'Signorelli': Rhetoric and Repression," *International Journal of Psycho-Analysis* 81 (2000): 483–98.

19. "[D]as Größte, was ich bisher gesehen." Freud, *Briefe an Wilhelm Fliess 1887–1904*, 357.

20. Joseph Kalinowski and Tim Saltuklaroglu, "Choral Speech: The Amelioration of Stuttering via Imitation and the Mirror Neuronal System," *Neuroscience & Biobehavioral Reviews* 27, no. 4 (2003): 339–47.

21. Frankland, 235.

22. Kraus, "Tagebuch," 22. Bernard Gui's *Manual of an Inquisitor* is discussed in more detail above, in chapter 7.

23. Freud, *Briefe an Wilhelm Fliess 1887–1904*, 354–55 (letters of 26 and 31 August 1898).

24. John A. Bargh and Ezequiel Morsella, "The Unconscious Mind," *Perspectives on Psychological Science* 3, no. 1 (2008): 73–79.

25. For the account of what makes a speech act felicitous see J. L. Austin, *How to Do Things with Words*, ed. J. O. Urmson and Marina Sbisà, 2nd ed. (Oxford: Clarendon Press, 1975), 24–52.

26. Arthur Schnitzler, *Der Wegs ins Freie* (Frankfurt am Main: Fischer, 1990), 117.

27. Ibid., 153.

28. "Never Done, Never to Return: Hysteria and After," Rachel Bowlby, *Freudian Mythologies: Greek Tragedy and Modern Identities* (Oxford; New York: Oxford University Press, 2007), 47–74.

29. Richard A. Skues, *Sigmund Freud and the History of Anna O.: Re-opening a Closed Case* (Basingstoke: Palgrave Macmillan, 2006). For a more detailed discussion of the *Studies*, see above, chapter 8.

30. Adolf Strümpell, "Dr. Jos. Breuer und Sigm. Freud, 'Studien Über Hysterie,'" *Deutsche Zeitschrift für Nervenheilkunde* 8, no. 1–2 (1895): 159–61.

31. Bruno Bettelheim, *Freud and Man's Soul* (London: Chatto and Windus, 1983).

32. Frank J. Sulloway, "Reassessing Freud's Case Histories: The Social Construction of Psychoanalysis," *Isis* 82, no. 2 (1991): 245–75.

33. "A Plea for Excuses," Austin, *Philosophical Papers*, 182.

34. Michel de Certeau, *The Practice of Everyday Life*, trans. Steven Rendall (Berkeley: University of California Press, 1984), 8–10.

35. Carl Gustav Jung, *Die Beziehungen Zwischen Dem Ich und dem Unbewußten* (Munich: dtv, 1990), 106.

36. Martin Heidegger, *Being and Time*, trans. John Macquarrie and Edward Robinson (Oxford: Basil Blackwell, 1962), 345–47 (§60).

37. Eckhart, *German Sermons and Treatises*, trans. Maurice O'C Walshe, 3 vols. (Shaftesbury: Element Books, 1979), 1:81; Niklaus Largier and Josef Quint, eds., *Meister Eckhart Werke*, 2 vols., vol. 20–21 of *Bibliothek des Mittelalters* (Frankfurt am Main: Deutscher Klassiker Verlag, 1993), 2:212 (sermon 86).

38. Sigmund Freud and Josef Breuer, *Studien über Hysterie*, 3rd ed. (Leipzig: Franz Deuticke, 1916), 100; Sigmund Freud and Josef Breuer, *Studies in Hysteria*, ed. Angela Richards (Harmondsworth: Penguin, 1974), 181.

39. Austin, *Philosophical Papers*, 271.

40. John Dewey, *Human Nature and Conduct* (Amherst, N.Y.: Prometheus, 2002), 281–82.

41. Ibid., 282.

42. Ben Morgan, "The Limits of Human Togetherness," *Limbus: Australian Yearbook of German Literary and Cultural Studies* 3 (2010): 159–76.

43. For replacing *God* with *life* in the idioms of everyday speech, see Don Cupitt, *Life, Life* (Santa Rosa, Calif.: Polebridge Press, 2003).

Bibliography

Abbey, Ruth, ed. *Charles Taylor, Contemporary Philosophy in Focus*. Cambridge: Cambridge University Press, 2004.

Adorno, Theodor W. *Gesammelte Schriften*. Edited by Rolf Tiedemann. 20 vols. Frankfurt am Main: Suhrkamp, 1970–.

Adorno, Theodor W., and Max Horkheimer. *Dialectic of Enlightenment*. Translated by John Cumming. London: Verso, 1979.

Allen, Prudence. *The Early Humanist Reformation, 1250–1500*. Vol. 2 of *The Concept of Woman*. Grand Rapids, Mich.: William B. Eerdmans, 2002.

Anderson, Graham. "Metrical Howlers in Lucian." *Hermes* 104, no. 2 (1976): 254–56.

Anderson, Pamela Sue. "Life, Death, and (Inter)Subjectivity: Realism and Recognition in Continental Feminism." *International Journal for Philosophy of Religion* 60, nos. 1–3 (2006): 41–59.

Anderson, Pamela Sue, ed. *New Topics in Feminist Philosophy of Religion: Contestations and Transcendence Incarnate*. Dordrecht: Springer Netherlands, 2010.

Appignanesi, Lisa, and John Forrester. *Freud's Women*. London: Virago, 1993.

Aquinas, Thomas. *Supplementum Tertiæ Partis Summæ Theologiæ, Opera Omnia*. Rome: Typographia Polyglotta, 1888–.

Asmuth, Christoph, ed. *Sein—Reflexion—Freiheit: Aspekte der Philosophie Johann Gottlieb Fichtes*. Vol. 25 of *Bochumer Studien zur Philosophie*. Amsterdam: Grüner, 1997.

Auerbach, Erich. *Mimesis: The Representation of Reality in Western Literature*. Translated by Willard R. Trask. Princeton, N.J.: Princeton University Press, 1968.

Austin, J. L. *How to Do Things with Words*. Edited by J. O. Urmson and Marina Sbisà. 2nd ed. Oxford: Clarendon Press, 1975.
———. *Philosophical Papers*. 3rd ed. Oxford: Oxford University Press, 1979.
Baest, Marieke J. E. H. T. van, ed. *Poetry of Hadewijch, Studies in Spirituality Supplement 3*. Leuven: Peters, 1998.
Bargh, John A. "The Automaticity of Everyday Life." In *Advances in Social Cognition*, edited by Robert S. Wyer Jr., 1–61. Mahwah, N.J.: Lawrence Erlbaum, 1997.
Bargh, John A., and Ezequiel Morsella. "The Unconscious Mind." *Perspectives on Psychological Science* 3, no. 1 (2008): 73–79.
Bataille, Georges. *L'expérience intérieure*. Paris: Gallimard, 1954.
———. *La Somme athéologique*. Vols. 5–6, *Œuvres complètes*. Paris: Gallimard, 1970.
Baumbach, Manuel. *Lukian in Deutschland: Eine forschungs- und rezeptionsgeschichtliche Analyse vom Humanismus bis zur Gegenwart*. Munich: Wilhelm Fink, 2002.
Beauvoir, Simone de. *Journal de guerre: Septembre 1939–janvier 1941*. Edited by Sylvie Le Bon de Beauvoir. Paris: Gallimard, 1990.
———. *Le deuxième sexe*. 2 vols. Paris: Gallimard, 2006.
———. *The Second Sex*. Translated by H. M. Parshley. London: Vintage, 1997.
Beckett, Samuel. *Worstward Ho*. London: John Calder, 1983.
Beckman, Patricia Zimmerman. "The Power of Books and the Practice of Mysticism in the Fourteenth Century: Heinrich of Nördlingen and Margaret Ebner on Mechthild's *Flowing Light of the Godhead*." *Church History: Studies in Christianity and Culture* 76, no. 1 (2007): 61–83.
Benjamin, Andrew E., ed. *The Lyotard Reader*. Oxford: Basil Blackwell, 1989.
Berthier, Joseph Joachim, ed. *B. Humberti de Romanis Quinti Praedicatorum Magistri Generalis, Opera de Vita Regulari*. 2 vols. Rome: A. Befani, 1888/89.
Berthold, Paul. *In der Trödelbude: Geschichten*. Lahr: Moritz Schauenburg, 1890.
Bettelheim, Bruno. *Freud and Man's Soul*. London: Chatto and Windus, 1983.
Bihlmeyer, Karl, ed. *Heinrich Seuse: Deutsche Schriften im Auftrag der württembergischen Kommission für Landesgeschichte*. Frankfurt am Main: Minerva, 1961.
Billig, Michael. "Freud's Different Versions of Forgetting 'Signorelli': Rhetoric and Repression." *International Journal of Psycho-Analysis* 81 (2000): 483–98.
Blakney, Raymond, ed. *Meister Eckhart: A Modern Translation*. New York: Harper and Row, 1941.
Blank, Walter. "Heinrich Seuse's 'Vita': Literarische Gestaltung und Pastorale Funktion seines Schriftums." *Zeitschrift für deutsches Altertum und deutsche Literatur*, 122 (1993): 285–311.
Blumenfeld-Kosinski, Renate, and Timea Szell, eds. *Images of Sainthood in Medieval Europe*. Ithaca, N.Y.: Cornell University Press, 1991.
Blumrich, Rüdiger, and Philipp Kaiser, eds. *Heinrich Seuses Philosophia Spiritualis: Quellen, Konzept, Formen, und Rezeption: Tagung Eichstätt 2.–4. Oktober 1991*. Wiesbaden: Dr. Ludwig Reichert, 1994.

Borch-Jacobsen, Mikkel. *Remembering Anna O.: A Century of Mystification.* Translated by Kirby Olson in collaboration with Xavier Callahan and the author. New York: Routledge, 1996.

Børresen, Kari Elisabeth. *Subordination and Equivalence: The Nature and Role of Woman in Augustine and Thomas Aquinas.* Translated by Charles H. Talbot. Washington, D.C.: University Press of America, 1981.

Bourdieu, Pierre. *The Logic of Practice.* Translated by Richard Nice. Cambridge: Polity, 1990.

Bowie, Malcolm. *Lacan.* London: Fontana, 1991.

Bowlby, Rachel. *Freudian Mythologies: Greek Tragedy and Modern Identities.* Oxford: Oxford University Press, 2007.

Bråten, Stein, ed. *Intersubjective Communication and Emotion in Early Ontogeny.* Cambridge: Cambridge University Press, 1998.

Braun, Christina von. *Nicht Ich: Logik, Lüge, Libido.* Frankfurt am Main: Neue Kritik, 1988.

Breckman, William. "The Idea of the Self Thought and Experience in Western Europe since the Seventeenth Century." *Journal of British Studies* 46, no. 1 (2007): 158–61.

Breger, Claudia. "The Leader's Two Bodies—Slavoj Žižek's Postmodern Political Theology." *Diacritics* 31, no. 1 (2001): 73–90.

Brentzel, Marianne. *Anna O. Bertha Pappenheim: Biographie.* Göttingen: Wallstein, 2002.

Brinker, Claudia, Urs Herzog, Niklaus Largier, and Paul Michel, eds. *Contemplata Aliis Tradere: Studien zum Verhältnis zon Literatur und Spiritualität.* Bern: Peter Lang, 1995.

Bronfen, Elisabeth. "Femme Fatale—Negotiations of Tragic Desire." *New Literary History: A Journal of Theory and Interpretation* 35, no. 1 (2004): 103–16.

Brooke, Rosalind B., ed. *Scripta Leonis, Rufini et Angeli, Sociorum S. Francisci.* Oxford: Clarendon Press, 1970.

Bruner, Jerome S. *Child's Talk: Learning to Use Language.* Oxford: Oxford University Press, 1983.

Bubner, Rüdiger, ed. *Deutscher Idealismus.* Vol. 6 of *Geschichte der Philosophie in Text und Darstellung.* Stuttgart: Reclam, 1978.

Bullowa, Margaret, ed. *Before Speech: The Beginning of Interpersonal Communication.* Cambridge: Cambridge University Press, 1979.

Bürger, Christa. *"Diese Hoffnung, eines Tages nicht mehr allein zu denken": Lebensentwürfe von Frauen aus vier Jahrhunderten.* Stuttgart: J. B. Metzler, 1996.

Bürger, Peter. *Das Verschwinden des Subjekts: Eine Geschichte der Subjektivität von Montaigne bis Barthes.* Frankfurt am Main: Suhrkamp, 1998.

Busa, Robertus, ed. *Thomas Aquinas Opera Omnia.* 7 vols. Stuttgart-Bad Cannstatt: Frommann-Holzboog, 1980.

Butler, Judith. *Antigone's Claim: Kinship between Life and Death.* New York: Columbia University Press, 2000.

———. *Bodies That Matter: On the Discursive Limits of "Sex"*. New York: Routledge, 1993.
———. *Gender Trouble: Feminism and the Subversion of Identity*. New York: Routledge, 1990.
———. "Giving an Account of Oneself." *Diacritics* 31, no. 4 (2001): 22–40.
———. *The Psychic Life of Power: Theories in Subjection*. Stanford, Calif.: Stanford University Press, 1997.
———. *Undoing Gender*. New York: Routledge, 2004.
Bynum, Caroline Walker. *Holy Feast and Holy Fast: The Religious Significance of Food to Medieval Women*. Berkeley: University of California Press, 1987.
———. *Jesus as Mother: Studies in the Spirituality of the High Middle Ages*. Berkeley: University of California Press, 1982.
Cadava, Eduardo, Peter Connor, and Jean-Luc Nancy. *Who Comes after the Subject?* London: Routledge, 1991.
Cadden, Joan. *Meanings of Sex Difference in the Middle Ages: Medicine, Science, and Culture*. Cambridge: Cambridge University Press, 1993.
Canfield, John V. "The Living Language: Wittgenstein and the Empirical Study of Communication." *Language Sciences* 15, no. 3 (1993): 165–93.
Caputo, John D. *Radical Hermeneutics: Repetition, Deconstruction, and the Hermeneutic Project*. Bloomington: Indiana University Press, 1987.
———. *The Mystical Element in Heidegger's Thought*. Rev. reprint. ed. New York: Fordham University Press, 1986.
———. *The Prayers and Tears of Jacques Derrida: Religion without Religion*. Bloomington: Indiana University Press, 1997.
Caputo, John D., and Gianni Vattimo. *After the Death of God*. Edited by Jeffrey W. Robbins. New York: Columbia University Press, 2007.
Card, Claudia, ed. *The Cambridge Companion to Simone de Beauvoir*. Cambridge: Cambridge University Press, 2003.
Carpendale, J. I. M., C. Lewis, N. Susswein, and J. Lunn. "Talking and Thinking: The Role of Speech in Social Understanding." In *Private Speech, Executive Functioning, and the Development of Verbal Self-Regulation*, edited by A. Winsler, C. Fernyhough, and N. Montero. Cambridge: Cambridge University Press, 2008.
Carpendale, Jeremy I. M., and Charlie Lewis. "Constructing an Understanding of Mind: The Development of Children's Social Understanding within Social Interaction." *Behavioral and Brain Sciences* 27 (2004): 79–151.
———. *How Children Develop Social Understanding*. Oxford: Basil Blackwell, 2006.
Carruthers, Peter, and Peter K. Smith, eds. *Theories of Theories of Mind*. Cambridge: Cambridge University Press, 1996.
Cave, Terence. *Pré-Histoires. Textes troublés au seuil de la modernité*. Geneva: Droz, 1999.
Cavell, Stanley. *Contesting Tears: The Hollywood Melodrama of the Unknown Woman*. Chicago: University of Chicago Press, 1996.

———. *Must We Mean What We Say? A Book of Essays*. Updated ed. Cambridge: Cambridge University Press, 2002.
Certeau, Michel de. *The Practice of Everyday Life*. Translated by Steven Rendall. Berkeley: University of California Press, 1984.
Chanter, Tina. *Time, Death, and the Feminine: Levinas with Heidegger*. Stanford, Calif.: Stanford University Press, 2001.
Cheng, Yawei, Andrew N. Meltzoff, and Jean Decety. "Motivation Modulates the Activity of the Human Mirror-Neuron System." *Cerebral Cortex* 17, no. 8 (2007): 1979–86.
Chenu, Marie-Dominique. *Nature, Man, and Society in the Twelfth Century: Essays on New Theological Perspectives in the Latin West*. Translated by Jerome Taylor and Lester K. Little. Chicago: University of Chicago Press, 1986.
Clark, James M. *Meister Eckhart: An Introduction to the Study of His Works with an Anthology of His Sermons*. London: Thomas Nelson, 1957.
Classen, Albrecht, ed. *Women as Protagonists and Poets in the German Middle Ages: An Anthology of Feminist Approaches to Middle High German Literature*. Göppingen: Kümmerle, 1991.
Coakley, John Wayland. *Women, Men, and Spiritual Power: Female Saints and Their Male Collaborators*. New York: Columbia University Press, 2006.
Cohen, Anthony. *Self Consciousness: An Alternative Anthropology of Identity*. London: Routledge, 1994.
Colin, Amy. "Metamorphosen einer Frau: Von Anna O. zu Bertha Pappenheim." In *Von einer Welt in die andere: Jüdinnen im 19. und 20. Jahrhundert*, edited by Jutta Dick and Hahn Barbara, 197–215. Vienna: Christian Brandstätter, 1993.
Colledge, Edmund, and Bernard McGinn, eds. *Meister Eckhart: The Essential Sermons, Commentaries, Treatises, and Defense*. London: SPCK, 1981.
Constable, Giles. *The Reformation of the Twelfth Century*. Cambridge: Cambridge University Press, 1996.
———. *Three Studies in Medieval Religious and Social Thought*. Cambridge: Cambridge University Press, 1995.
Coward, Harold G., and Toby Foshay, eds. *Derrida and Negative Theology*. Albany: State University of New York Press, 1992.
Cranefield. "Josef Breuer's Evaluation of His Contribution to Psycho-Analysis." *International Journal of Psychoanalysis* 39, no. 5 (1958): 319–22.
Crary, Alice, and Rupert Read. *The New Wittgenstein*. London: Routledge, 2000.
Cupitt, Don. *Life, Life*. Santa Rosa, Calif.: Polebridge Press, 2003.
Daniels, P. Augustin. "Eine lateinische Rechtfertigungsschrift des Meister Eckhart." *Beiträge zur Geschichte der Philosophie des Mittelalters* 23, no. 5 (1923): 1–66.
Davies, Oliver. "Why Were Eckhart's Propositions Condemned?" *New Blackfriars* 71 (1990): 433–45.
Dawkins, Richard. *The God Delusion*. London: Bantam, 2006.
Decker, Hannah S. *Freud, Dora, and Vienna 1900*. New York: Free Press, 1991.

Dennett, Daniel C. *Breaking the Spell: Religion as a Natural Phenomenon*. London: Allen Lane, 2006.

———. *Consciousness Explained*. Boston: Little, Brown, 1991.

Derrida, Jacques. *Margins of Philosophy*. Translated by Alan Bass. Brighton: Harvester, 1982.

———. *The Politics of Friendship*. Translated by George Collins. London: Verso, 1997.

Derrida, Jacques, and John D. Caputo. *Deconstruction in a Nutshell: A Conversation with Jacques Derrida*. New York: Fordham University Press, 1997.

Deutscher, Penelope. *A Politics of Impossible Difference: The Later Work of Luce Irigaray*. Ithaca, N.Y.: Cornell University Press, 2002.

Deutsches Wörterbuch. Edited by Berlin-Brandenburgische Akademie der Wissenschaften and Akademie der Wissenschaften zu Göttingen. Stuttgart: S. Hirzel, 1993.

Dewey, John. *Human Nature and Conduct*. Amherst, N.Y.: Prometheus, 2002.

Dinzelbacher, Peter. "Zur Interpretation erlebnismysticher Texte des Mittelalters." *Zeitschrift für deutsches Altertum und deutsche Literatur* 117 (1988): 1–23.

Döcker, Ulrike. *Die Ordnung der bürgerlichen Welt: Verhaltensideale und soziale Praktiken im 19. Jahrhundert*. Frankfurt am Main: Campus, 1994.

Doherty, Brigid. "Between the Artwork and Its 'Actualization': A Footnote to Art History in Benjamin's 'Work of Art' Essay." *Paragraph* 32, no. 3 (2009): 331–58.

Dreyfus, Hubert L. *Being-in-the-World: A Commentary on Heidegger's Being and Time, Division I*. Cambridge, Mass: MIT Press, 1991.

———. *On the Internet*. London: Routledge, 2001.

Eckhart. *Die lateinischen Werke*. Edited by Josef Koch, Heribert Fischer, Konrad Weiß, Karl Christ, Bruno Decker, Albert Zimmermann, Bernhard Geyer, Ernst Benz, Erich Seeberg, and Loris Sturlese. 6 vols, *Die deutschen und lateinischen Werke*. Stuttgart: Kohlhammer, 1936–.

———. *German Sermons and Treatises*. Translated by Maurice O'C Walshe. 3 vols. Shaftesbury: Element Books, 1979.

———. *Selected Writings*. Translated by Oliver Davies. Harmondsworth: Penguin, 1994.

El Saffar, Ruth Anthony. *Rapture Encaged: The Suppression of the Feminine in Western Culture*. London: Routledge, 1994.

Ellenberger, Henri F. *The Discovery of the Unconscious: The History and Evolution of Dynamic Psychiatry*. New York: Basic Books, 1970.

Elms, Alan C. "Jung's Lives." *Journal of the History of the Behavioral Sciences* 41, no. 4 (2005): 331–46.

Ennen, Edith. *Frauen im Mittelalter*. 5th ed. Munich: Beck, 1994.

Flasch, Kurt. *Das Philosophische Denken im Mittelalter* Stuttgart: Reclam, 1986.

Fontane, Theodor. *Effi Briest*. Edited by Walter Keitel and Helmuth Nürnberger. Munich: Carl Hanser, 1974.

Forrester, John. *Dispatches from the Freud Wars: Psychoanalysis and Its Passions.* Cambridge, Mass.: Harvard University Press, 1997.

———. *The Seductions of Psychoanalysis: Freud, Lacan, and Derrida* Cambridge: Cambridge University Press, 1990.

Foucault, Michel. *Discipline and Punish: The Birth of the Prison.* Translated by Alan Sheridan. Harmondsworth: Penguin, 1977.

———. *Ethics: Subjectivity and Truth.* Edited by Paul Rabinow. London: Penguin, 2000.

———. *The Care of the Self.* Vol. 3 of *The History of Sexuality.* Translated by Robert Hurley. Harmondsworth: Penguin, 1988.

———. *The Foucault Reader.* Edited by Paul Rabinow and Hubert L. Dreyfus. Harmondsworth: Penguin, 1984.

———. *The History of Sexuality: An Introduction.* Translated by Robert Hurley. Harmondsworth: Penguin, 1979.

———. *The Order of Things: An Archaeology of the Human Sciences.* Translated by Alan Sheridan. London: Tavistock, 1971.

———. *The Use of Pleasure.* Vol. 2 of *The History of Sexuality.* Translated by Robert Hurley. Harmondsworth: Viking, 1986.

Frank, Manfred. *Selbstbewußtsein und Selbsterkenntnis: Essays zur Analytischen Philosophie der Subjektivität.* Stuttgart: Reclam, 1991.

Frank, Manfred, ed. *Selbstbewußtseinstheorien von Fichte Bis Sartre.* Frankfurt am Main: Suhrkamp, 1991.

Frankland, Graham. *Freud's Literary Culture.* Cambridge: Cambridge University Press, 2000.

Frazer, Elizabeth, and Nicola Lacey. *The Politics of Community: A Feminist Critique of the Liberal–Communitarian Debate.* New York; London: Harvester Wheatsheaf, 1993.

Freed, John B. "Urban Development and the 'Cura Monialium' in Thirteenth-Century Germany." *Viator* 3 (1972): 311–27.

Freud, Sigmund. *Abriß der Psychoanalyse.* Frankfurt am Main: S. Fischer, 1994.

———. *Briefe an Wilhelm Fliess, 1887–1904.* Edited by Jeffrey Masson and Michael Schröter. Frankfurt am Main: S. Fischer, 1986.

———. *Bruchstück einer Hysterie-Analyse.* Frankfurt am Main: S. Fischer, 1993.

———. *Case Histories 2.* Edited by Angela Richards. Harmondsworth: Penguin, 1979.

———. *Das Ich und das Es.* Frankfurt am Main: S. Fischer, 1992.

———. *Die Traumdeutung.* Frankfurt am Main: S. Fischer, 1991.

———. *Gesammelte Werke, chronologisch geordnet: Siebzehnter Band: Schriften aus dem Nachlaß.* Frankfurt am Main: S. Fischer, 1991.

———. *Studienausgabe.* Edited by Alexander Mitscherlich, Angela Richards, and James Strachey. 11 vols. Frankfurt am Main: S. Fischer, 1969.

———. *The Psychopathology of Everyday Life.* Edited by Angela Richards. Harmondsworth: Penguin, 1975.

———. *Zur Psychopathologie des Alltagslebens: Über Vergessen, Versprechen, Vergreifen, Aberglauben und Irrtum*. Frankfurt am Main: S. Fischer, 1954.

Freud, Sigmund, and Josef Breuer. *Studien über Hysterie*. 3rd ed. Leipzig: Franz Deuticke, 1916.

———. *Studies in Hysteria*. Edited by Angela Richards. Harmondsworth: Penguin, 1974.

Fries, Albert, ed. *Albertus Magnus Ausgewählte Texte*. Darmstadt: Wissenschaftliche Buchgesellschaft, 1981.

Fromm, Erich. *To Have or to Be?* London: Abacus, 1979.

Gallagher, Shaun. *How the Body Shapes the Mind*. Oxford: Clarendon Press, 2005.

———. "Direct Perception in the Intersubjective Context." *Consciousness and Cognition* 17 (2008): 535–43.

Gallese, V. "The Roots of Empathy: The Shared Manifold Hypothesis and the Neural Basis of Intersubjectivity." *Psychopathology* 36, no. 4 (2003): 171–80.

Gallese, Vittorio. "Intentional Attunement: A Neurophysiological Perspective on Social Cognition and Its Disruption in Autism." *Brain Research* 1079 (2006): 15–24.

Gatens, Moira. *Imaginary Bodies: Ethics, Power, and Corporeality*. London: Routledge, 1995.

Gazzola, V., G. Rizzolatti, B. Wicker, and C. Keysers. "The Anthropomorphic Brain: The Mirror Neuron System Responds to Human and Robotic Actions." *NeuroImage* 35, no. 4 (2007): 1674–84.

Gazzola, Valeria, Henk van der Worp, Theo Mulder, Bruno Wicker, Giacomo Rizzolatti, and Christian Keysers. "Aplasics Born without Hands Mirror the Goal of Hand Actions with Their Feet." *Current Biology* 17, no. 14 (2007): 1235–40.

Gilman, Sander L. *Franz Kafka, the Jewish Patient*. New York: Routledge, 1995.

Goff, Jacques le. *Medieval Civilization, 400–1500*. Translated by Julia Barrow. Oxford: Blackwell, 1988.

Goldhill, Simon. *Who Needs Greek? Contests in the Cultural History of Hellenism*. Cambridge: Cambridge University Press, 2002.

Grosholz, Emily, ed. *The Legacy of Simone de Beauvoir*. Oxford: Clarendon Press, 2004.

Grubmüller, Klaus. "Die Viten der Schwestern von Töss und Elsbeth Stagel." *Zeitschrift für deutsches Altertum und deutsche Literatur* 98 (1969): 171–204.

Grundmann, Herbert. *Religious Movements in the Middle Ages: The Historical Links between Heresy, the Mendicant Orders, and the Women's Religious Movement in the Twelfth and Thirteenth Century, with the Historical Foundations of German Mysticism*. Translated by Steven Rowan. Notre Dame, Ind.: University of Notre Dame Press, 1995.

Gui, Bernard. *Manuel de l'inquisiteur*. Translated by Guillaume Mollat. Edited by Guillaume Mollat. 2 vols., Paris: Honoré Champion, 1926–27.

Guignon, Charles B., ed. *The Cambridge Companion to Heidegger*. 2nd ed. Cambridge: Cambridge University Press, 2006.

Gustavson, Andrew R., Michael E. Dawson, and Douglas G. Bonett. "Androstenol, a Putative Human Pheromone, Affects Human (Homo Sapiens) Male Choice Performance." *Journal of Comparative Psychology* 101, no. 2 (1987): 210–12.
Gutting, Gary, ed. *The Cambridge Companion to Foucault*. 2nd ed. Cambridge: Cambridge University Press, 2005.
Haas, Alois M., and Heinrich Stirnimann, eds. *Das "Einig Ein": Studien zu Theorie und Sprache der deutschen Mystik*. Freiburg, CH: Universitätsverlag, 1980.
Habermas, Jürgen. *The Philosophical Discourse of Modernity: Twelve Lectures*. Translated by Frederick Lawrence. Cambridge, Mass: MIT Press, 1987.
Hadewijch. *Brieven*. Edited by J. van Mierlo. 2 vols. Antwerp: Standaard, 1947.
Halpern, Sidney. "The First Exploration of a Slip of the Tongue." *Classical Journal* 57, no. 8 (1962): 355–58.
———. "The First Exploration of a Slip of the Tongue." *Classical Journal* 57, no. 8 (1962): 355–58.
Hamburger, Jeffrey F. *The Visual and the Visionary: Art and Female Spirituality in Late Medieval Germany* New York: Zone Books, 1998.
Hamilton, Bernard. *The Medieval Inquisition*. London: Edward Arnold, 1981.
Haug, Walter, and Wolfram Schneider-Lastin. *Deutsche Mystik im abendländischen Zusammenhang: Neu erschlossene Texte, neue methodische Ansätze, neue theoretische Konzepte: Kolloquium Kloster Fischingen 1998*. Tübingen: Niemeyer, 2000.
Hefele, Charles-Joseph. *Histoires des conciles d'après les documents originaux*. Translated by H. Leclercq. Vol. 6, pt. 2. Paris: Librairie Letouzey et Ané, 1915.
Heidegger, Martin. *Being and Time*. Translated by John Macquarrie and Edward Robinson. Oxford: Basil Blackwell, 1962.
———. *Die Grundbegriffe der Metaphysik: Welt—Endlichtkeit—Einsamkeit*. Edited by Friedrich Wilhelm von Hermann. Frankfurt am Main: Klostermann, 1983.
———. *Die Grundprobleme der Phänomenologie*. Vol. 24 of *Gesamtausgabe*. Frankfurt am Main: Klostermann, 1975.
———. *Phänomenologische Interpretationen zu Aristoteles*. Stuttgart: Reclam, 2002.
Heinkle, Fritz. *Humbert von Romans, der fünfte Ordensmeister der Dominikaner, historische Studien*. Berlin: Dr. Emil Ebering, 1933.
Herrmann, Friedrich-Wilhelm von. "'Gelassenheit' bei Heidegger und Meister Eckhart." In *From Phenomenology to Thought, Errancy, and Desire: Essays in Honor of William J. Richardson, S.J.*, edited by Babette E. Babich. Dordrecht: Kluwer, 1995.
Hines, Melissa. *Brain Gender*. Oxford; New York: Oxford University Press, 2004.
Hirschmüller, Albrecht. *Physiologie und Psychoanalyse in Leben und Werk Josef Breuers, Jahrbuch der Psychoanalyse Beiheft 4*. Bern: Hans Huber, 1978.

Hobson, J. Allan. *Dreaming: A Very Short Introduction*. Oxford; New York: Oxford University Press, 2005.
———. "Rem Sleep and Dreaming: Towards a Theory of Protoconsciousness." *Nature Reviews Neuroscience* 10, no. 11 (2009): 803–13.
Hobson, R. Peter. *The Cradle of Thought*. London: Macmillan, 2002.
Holland, Anna, and Richard Scholar, eds. *Pre-histories and Afterlives: Studies in Critical Method*. London: Legenda, 2009.
Hollywood, Amy M. *The Soul as Virgin Wife: Mechthild of Magdeburg, Marguerite Porete, and Meister Eckhart*. Vol. 1 of *Studies in Spirituality and Theology*. Notre Dame, Ind.: University of Notre Dame Press, 1995.
———. *Sensible Ecstasy: Mysticism, Sexual Difference, and the Demands of History, Religion, and Postmodernism*. Chicago: University of Chicago Press, 2002.
———. "Gender, Agency, and the Divine in Religious Historiography." *Journal of Religion* 84, no. 4 (2004): 514–28.
Honneger, Claudia. *Die Ordnung der Geschlechter: Die Wissenschaft vom Menschen und das Weib 1750–1850*. Frankfurt am Main: Campus, 1991.
Howell, Martha C. *Women, Production, and Patriarchy in Late Medieval Cities*. Chicago: University of Chicago Press, 1986.
Huntington, Patricia J. *Ecstatic Subjects, Utopia, and Recognition: Kristeva, Heidegger, Irigaray*. Albany, N.Y.: State University of New York Press, 1998.
Iacoboni, Marco. *Mirroring People: The New Science of How We Connect with Others*. New York: Farrar, Straus and Giroux, 2008.
———. "The Quiet Revolution of Existential Neuroscience." In *Social Neuroscience: Integrating Biological and Psychological Explanations of Social Behavior*. Edited by Eddie Harmon-Jones and Piotr Winkielman. New York: Guilford Press, 2007.
Irigaray, Luce. *I Love to You: Sketch for a Felicity within History*. Translated by Alison Martin. London: Routledge, 1996.
———. *Sexes and Genealogies*. Translated by Gillian C. Gill. New York: Columbia University Press, 1993.
———. *Speculum of the Other Woman*. Translated by Gillian C. Gill. Ithaca, N.Y.: Cornell University Press, 1985.
Jacob, Pierre, and Marc Jeannerod. "The Motor Theory of Social Cognition: A Critique." *Trends in Cognitive Sciences* 9, no. 1 (2005): 21–25.
Jantzen, Grace M. *Power, Gender, and Christian Mysticism*. Cambridge: Cambridge University Press, 1995.
Jay, Martin. *Downcast Eyes: The Denigration of Vision in Twentieth-Century French Thought*. Berkeley: University of California Press, 1993.
Jerome, Carroll. "The Limits of the Sublime, the Sublime of Limits: Hermeneutics as a Critique of the Postmodern Sublime." *Journal of Aesthetics and Art Criticism* 66, no. 2 (2008): 171–81.
Johnston, William M. *The Austrian Mind: An Intellectual and Social History, 1848–1938*. Berkeley: University of California Press, 1972.

Joy, Morny, Kathleen O'Grady, and Judith L. Poxon, eds. *Religion in French Feminist Thought: Critical Perspectives.* London: Routledge, 2003.

Jung, C. G. *Psychological Types, or, the Psychology of Individuation.* Translated by H. Godwin Baynes. London: Routledge and Kegan Paul, 1923.

Jung, Carl Gustav. *Die Beziehungen zwischen dem Ich und dem Unbewußten.* Munich: dtv, 1990.

———. *Memories, Dreams, Reflections.* Translated by Richard Winston and Clara Winston. Edited by Aniela Jaffé. London: Fontana, 1983.

———. *Psychologie und Religion.* Munich: dtv, 1991.

———. *Traum und Traumdeutung.* Munich: dtv, 1990.

K——ski, Johann Edler von. *Der Gute Ton. Oder Anleitung, um sich in den verschiedensten Verhältnissen des Lebens und der Gesellschaft als feiner, gebildeter Mann zu benehmen.* Pesth, 1865.

Kafka, Franz. *Drucke zu Lebzeiten.* Edited by Wolf Kittler, Hans-Gerd Koch, and Gerhard Neumann. Frankfurt am Main: S. Fischer, 1994.

———. *Drucke zu Lebzeiten: Apparatband,* Edited by Wolf Kittler, Hans-Gerd Koch, and Gerhard Neumann. Frankfurt am Main: S. Fischer, 1996.

Kakar, Sudhir. *The Analyst and the Mystic: Psychoanalytic Reflections on Religion and Mysticism.* Chicago: University of Chicago Press, 1990.

Kalinowski, Joseph, and Tim Saltuklaroglu. "Choral Speech: The Amelioration of Stuttering via Imitation and the Mirror Neuronal System." *Neuroscience and Biobehavioral Reviews* 27, no. 4 (2003): 339–47.

Kant, Immanuel. *Critique of Pure Reason.* Translated by J. M. D. Meiklejohn and Vasilis Politis. Edited by Vasilis Politis. London: Dent, 1993.

Karamustafa, Ahmet T. *Sufism: The Formative Period.* Edited by Carole Hillenbrand. Edinburgh: Edinburgh University Press, 2007.

Kaye, Joel. *Economy and Nature in the Fourteenth Century: Money, Market Exchange, and the Emergence of Scientific Thought.* Cambridge: Cambridge University Press, 1998.

Kieckhefer, Richard. *The Repression of Heresy in Medieval Germany.* Liverpool: Liverpool UP, 1979.

Kilner, James M., Karl J. Friston, and Chris D. Frith. "The Mirror Neuron System: A Bayesian Perspetctive." *NeuroReport* 18, no. 6 (2007): 619–23.

Kimball, Meredith M. "From 'Anna O.' To Bertha Pappenheim: Transforming Private Pain into Public Action." *History of Psychology* 3, no. 1 (2000): 20–43.

Klapisch-Zuber, Christiane, ed. *Silences of the Middle Ages.* Vol. 2 of *A History of Women in the West.* Cambridge, Mass.: Harvard University Press, 1992.

Kleist, Heinrich von. *Sämtliche Werke und Briefe.* Edited by Helmut Sembder. 2 vols. Munich: Carl Hanser, 1984.

Klingstein, Eva. *Die Frau mit Eigenschaften: Literatur und Geschlecht in der Wiener Frauenpresse um 1900.* Cologne: Böhlau, 1997.

Köbele, Susanne. *Bilder der Unbegriffenen Wahrheit: Zur Struktur mystischer Rede im Spannungsfeld von Latein und Volkssprache.* Tübingen: Francke, 1993.

Koch, Hans-Gerd, ed. *"Als Kafka mir Entgegenkam . . .": Erinnerungen an Franz Kafka*. Berlin: Wagenbach, 1995.
Koch, Joseph. *Kleine Schriften*. 2 vols. Rome: Edizioni di Storia e Letteratura, 1973.
Kraus, Karl. "Gebildeter." *Die Fackel*, no. 199 (1906): 23–24.
———. "Nachts." *Die Fackel* 15, no. 376–77 (1913): 18–25.
———. "Tagebuch." *Die Fackel* 10, no. 256 (1908): 16–32.
Kretzmann, Norman, Anthony Kenny, and Jan Pinborg, eds. *The Cambridge History of Later Medieval Philosophy*. Cambridge: Cambridge University Press, 1982.
Kuhn, Annette, and Bea Lundt, eds. *Lustgarten und Dämonenpein: Konzepte von Weiblichkeit in Mittelalter und Früher Neuzeit*. Dortmund: edition ebersbach, 1997.
Lacan, Jacques. *Écrits: A Selection*. Translated by Alan Sheridan. London: Routledge, 1977.
———. *On Feminine Sexuality: The Limits of Love and Knowledge*. Translated by Bruce Fink. New York: Norton, 1998.
Langer, Otto. *Mystische Erfahrung und spirituelle Theologie: Zu Meister Eckharts Auseinandersetzung mit der Frauenfrömmigkeit seiner Zeit* Munich: Artemis Verlag, 1987.
Largier, Niklaus. "Meister Eckhart: Perspektiven der Forschung, 1980–1993." *Zeitschrift für deutsche Philologie* 114, no. 1 (1995): 29–98.
Largier, Niklaus, and Josef Quint, eds. *Meister Eckhart Werke*. 2 vols. Vol. 20–21 of *Bibliothek des Mittelalters*. Frankfurt am Main: Deutscher Klassiker Verlag, 1993.
Laurent, M.-H. "Autour du procès de Maître Eckhart: Les documents ses archives vaticanes." *Divus Thomas* 3, no. 13 (1936): 331–48, 430–47
Le Rider, Jacques. *Modernity and Crises of Identity: Culture and Society in Fin-de-Siècle Vienna*. Translated by Rosemary Morris. Cambridge: Polity, 1993.
Lerner, Robert E. "A Case of Religious Counter-Culture: The German Waldensians." *American Scholar* 55 (1986): 234–47.
———. "New Evidence for the Condemnation of Meister Eckhart." *Speculum* 72, no. 2 (1997): 347–66.
———. *The Heresy of the Free Spirit in the Later Middle Ages*. Berkeley: University of California Press, 1972.
Levinas, Emmanuel. *Autrement qu'être ou au-delà de l'essence*. The Hague: Nijhoff, 1978.
———. *Carnets de captivité et autres inédits*. Edited by Rodolphe Calin and Catherine Chalier. Paris: Bernard Grasset / IMEC, 2009.
———. *Le temps et l'autre*. Paris: Quadrige/PUF, 1983.
———. *Time and the Other*. Translated by Richard A. Cohen. Pittsburgh: Duquesne University Press, 1987.
Lewis, I. M. *Ecstatic Religion: A Study of Shamanism and Spirit Possession*. 2nd ed. London: Routledge, 1989.

Lewis, Michael. *Heidegger and the Place of Ethics: Being-with in the Crossing of Heidegger's Thought*. London: Continuum, 2005.
Liskar, Elisabeth, ed. *Europäische Kunst um 1300 (Akten der XXV. Internationalen Kongress für Kunstgeschichte, Wien 4–10.9.1983)*. Vienna: Hermann Böhlhaus, 1986.
Little, Lester K. *Religious Poverty and the Profit Economy in Medieval Europe*. London: Paul Elek, 1978.
Lochner, Georg Wolfgang Karl, ed. *Leben und Gesichte der Christina Ebnerin, Klosterfrau zu Engelthal*. Nuremberg: Aug. Recknagel's Buchandlung, 1872.
Löser, Freimut. *Meister Eckhart in Melk*. Tübingen: Niemeyer, 1999.
Lucian. Vol. 6. Translated by K. Kilburn. Cambridge, Mass: Harvard University Press, 1959.
———. *Drei Satiren des Lucian. Für die deutsche Bühne Bearbeitet von Paul Lindau*. Breslau: Schlesiche Buckdruckerei, Kunst-und Verlagsanstalt, 1902.
Lutz, Eckart Conrad, ed. *Mittelalterliche Literatur im Lebenszusammenhang*. Vol. 8 of *Scrinium Friburgense*. Freiburg, CH: Universitätsverlag, 1997.
MacIntyre, Alasdair. "Critical Remarks on *Sources of the Self* by Charles Taylor." *Philosophy and Phenomenological Research* 54, no. 1 (1994): 187–90.
Mack, Phyllis. "Religion, Feminism, and the Problem of Agency: Reflections on Eighteenth-Century Quakerism." *Signs* 29, no. 1 (2003): 149–77.
Macmillan, Malcolm. *Freud Evaluated: The Completed Arc*. 2nd ed. Cambridge, Mass: MIT Press, 1997.
Magdeburg, Mechthild von. *The Flowing Light of the Godhead*. Translated by Frank Tobin. New York: Paulist Press, 1998.
Mahony, Patrick J. *Freud's Dora: A Psychoanalytic, Historical, and Textual Study*. New Haven, Conn.: Yale University Press, 1996.
Mandler, Peter. "The Idea of the Self: Thought and Experience in Western Europe since the Seventeenth Century." *American Historical Review* 112, no. 2 (2007): 575–76.
Mann, Thomas. *Buddenbrooks*. Frankfurt am Main: S. Fischer, 1960.
Marso, Lori Jo, and Patricia Moynagh, eds. *Simone de Beauvoir's Political Thinking*. Urbana: University of Illinois Press, 2006.
Martin, Raymond, and John Barresi. *The Rise and Fall of Soul and Self: An Intellectual History of Personal Identity*. New York: Columbia University Press, 2006.
Mason, Herbert, ed. *Testimonies and Reflections: Essays of Louis Massignon*. Notre Dame, Ind.: University of Notre Dame Press, 1989.
Massignon, Louis. *The Passion of Al-Hallaj: Mystic and Martyr of Islam*. 4 vols. Princeton, N.J.: Princeton University Press, 1982.
Masson, Jeffrey. *Against Therapy*. London: Collins, 1989.
Mayreder, Rosa. *Das Haus in der Landskrongasse: Jugenderinnerungen*. Vienna: Mandelbaum, 1998.
———. *Tagebücher 1873–1937*. Edited by Harriet Anderson. Frankfurt am Main: Insel, 1998.
———. *Zur Kritik der Weiblichkeit—Essays*. Vienna: Mandelbaum, 1998.

McGinn, Bernard. "Eckhart's Condemnation Reconsidered." *Thomist* 44 (1980): 390–414.

———. *The Harvest of Mysticism in Medieval Germany (1300–1500).* Vol. 4 of *The Presence of God: A History of Western Christian Mysticism.* New York: Herder and Herder, 2005.

McGinn, Bernard, ed. *Meister Eckhart: Teacher and Preacher.* New York: Paulist Press, 1986.

McGrath, William J. *Freud's Discovery of Psychoanalysis: The Politics of Hysteria* Ithaca, N.Y.: Cornell University Press, 1986.

McNay, Lois. *Foucault and Feminism: Power, Gender, and the Self.* Cambridge: Polity Press, 1992.

Meeks, Wayne A., and John T. Fitzgerald, eds. *The Writings of St Paul: Annotated Texts, Reception and Criticism.* 2nd ed. New York: Norton, 2007.

Meyer, Ruth, ed. *Das "St. Katherinentaler Schwesternbuch": Unterschung—Edition—Kommentar* Tübingen: Niemeyer, 1995.

Micale, Mark, ed. *Beyond the Unconscious: Essays of Henri F. Ellenberger in the History of Psychiatry.* Princeton, N.J.: Princeton University Press, 1993.

Misch, Georg. *Geschichte der Autobiographie.* Frankfurt am Main: Schulte-Bulmke, 1967.

Mitchell, Juliet. *Psychoanalysis and Feminism: A Radical Reassessment of Freudian Psychoanalysis.* 2nd ed. Harmondsworth: Penguin, 2000.

Moi, Toril. "From Femininity to Finitude: Freud, Lacan, and Feminism, Again." *Signs* 29, no. 3 (2004): 841–78.

———. *What Is a Woman? And Other Essays.* Oxford; New York: Oxford University Press, 1999.

Montgomery, Kimberly J., Nancy Isenberg, and James V. Haxby. "Communicative Hand Gestures and Object-Directed Hand Movements Activated the Mirror Neuron System." *Social Cognitive and Affective Neuroscience* 2, no. 2 (2007): 114–22.

Mooney, Catherine M., ed. *Gendered Voices: Medieval Saints and Their Interpreters.* Philadelphia: University of Pennsylvania Press, 1999.

Moran, Dermot, Lester E. Embree, Tanja Staehler, and Elizabeth A. Behnke, eds. *Phenomenology: Critical Concepts in Philosophy.* Vol. 2. Abingdon: Routledge, 2004.

Morgan, Ben. "Eckhart and the Incarnation: Some Practical Details." *Eckhart Review* 13 (2004): 37–50.

———. "The Limits of Human Togetherness." *Limbus: Australian Yearbook of German Literary and Cultural Studies* 3 (2010): 159–76.

———. "The Project of the Frankfurt School." *Telos*, no. 119 (2001): 75–98.

Morris, Colin. *The Discovery of the Individual, 1050–1200.* Toronto: University of Toronto Press, 1987.

Mulchahey, M. Michèle. *"First the Bow Is Bent in Study . . .": Dominican Education before 1350.* Toronto: Pontifical Institute of Medieval Studies, 1998.

Nancy, Jean-Luc. *Being Singular Plural.* Translated by Robert D. Richardson and Anne E. O'Byrne. Stanford, Calif.: Stanford University Press, 2000.
Neumann, Hans, ed. *Das fließende Licht der Gottheit.* Vol. 100 of *Münchener Texte und Untersuchungen zur deutschen Literatur des Mittelalters.* Munich: Artemis, 1990.
Newman, Barbara. *From Virile Woman to Womanchrist: Studies in Medieval Religion and Literature.* Philadelphia: University of Pennsylvania Press, 1995.
Niedenthal, Paula M., and Martha W. Alibali. "Conceptualizing Scaffolding and Goals for a Full Account of Embodied Cognition." *European Journal of Social Psychology* 39 (2009): 1268–71.
Nietzsche, Friedrich. *Kritische Gesamtausgabe.* Edited by Giorgio Colli and Mazzino Montinari. Berlin: de Gruyter, 1968–.
O'Neill, John. "The Specular Body: Merleau-Ponty and Lacan on Infant Self and Other." *Synthese* 66, no. 2 (1986): 201–17.
Olafson, Frederick A. *Heidegger and the Ground of Ethics: A Study of Mitsein.* Cambridge: Cambridge University Press, 1998.
Pascal, Roy. *Kafka's Narrators: A Study of His Stories and Sketches.* Cambridge: Cambridge University Press, 1982.
Patschovsky, Alexander. "Straßburger Beginenverfolgungen im 14. Jahrhundert." *Deutsches Archiv für Erforschung des Mittelalters* 30 (1974): 56–198.
Pellegrino, G., L. Fadiga, L. Fogassi, V. Gallese, and G. Rizzolatti. "Understanding Motor Events: A Neurophysiological Study." *Experimental Brain Research* 91, no. 1 (1992): 176–80.
Pelster, F. "Ein Gutachten aus dem Eckehart-Prozeß in Avignon." *Beiträge zur Geschichte der Philosophie des Mittelalters,* suppl. 3.2 (1935): 1099–124.
Peters, Ursula. *Religiöse Erfahrung als Literarisches Faktum: Zur Vorgeschichte und Genese frauenmystischer Texte des 13. und 14. Jahrhunderts.* Tübingen: Niemeyer, 1988.
Petroff, Elizabeth Alvilda. *Body and Soul: Essays on Medieval Women and Mysticism.* Oxford; New York: Oxford University Press, 1994.
Pfeiffer, Franz. *Meister Eckhart.* Vol. 2 of *Deutsche Mystiker des vierzehnten Jahrhunderts.* Leipzig: G. J. Göschen'sche Verlagsbuchhandlung, 1857.
Pfister, Oskar. "Hysterie und Mystik Bei Margaretha Ebner (1291–1351)." *Zentralblatt für Psychoanalyse* 1, no. 10/11 (1911): 468–85.
Philipse, Herman. "Heidegger and Ethics." *Inquiry* 42 (1999): 439–74.
Phillips, Dayton. "Beguines in Medieval Strasbourg: A Study of the Social Aspect of Beguine Life." PhD diss., Stanford University, 1941.
Porete, Marguerite. *The Mirror of Simple Souls.* Translated by Ellen L. Babinsky. New York: Paulist Press, 1993.
Preece, Julian, ed. *The Cambridge Companion to Kafka.* Cambridge: Cambridge University Press, 2002.
Priest, Ann-Marie. "Woman as God, God as Woman: Mysticism, Negative Theology, and Luce Irigaray." *Journal of Religion* 83, no. 1 (2003): 1–23.

Quint, Josef, ed. *Meister Eckehart. Deutsche Predigten und Traktate*. Munich: Carl Hanser, 1963.
Rabaté, Jean-Michel, ed. *Lacan in America*. New York: Other Press, 2000.
———. *The Cambridge Companion to Lacan*. Cambridge: Cambridge University Press, 2003.
Racine, Timothy P., and Jeremy I. M. Carpendale. "The Role of Shared Practice in Joint Attention." *British Journal of Developmental Psychology* 25 (2007): 3–25.
Reddy, Vasudevi, and Paul Morris. "Participants Don't Need Theories: Knowing Minds in Engagement." *Theory and Psychology* 14 (2004): 647–65.
Ringler, Siegfried. *Viten- und Offenbarungsliteratur in Frauenklöstern des Mittelalters: Quellen und Studien*. Vol. 72 of *Münchener Texte und Untersuchungen zur deutschen Literatur des Mittelalters*. Munich: Artemis Verlag, 1980.
Rizzolatti, Giacomo, and Laila Craighero. "The Mirror-Neuron System." *Annual Review of Neuroscience* 27, no. 1 (2004): 169–92.
Rizzolatti, Giacomo, Luciano Fadiga, Vittorio Gallese, and Leonardo Fogassi. "Premotor Cortex and the Recognition of Motor Actions." *Cognitive Brain Research* 3, no. 2 (1996): 131–41.
Rorty, Richard. *Contingency, Irony, and Solidarity*. Cambridge: Cambridge University Press, 1989.
Rosenbaum, Max, and Melvin Muroff, eds. *Anna O.: Fourteen Contemporary Reinterpretations*. New York: The Free Press, 1984.
Roudinesco, Elisabeth. *Jacques Lacan: Outline of a Life, History of a System of Thought*. Translated by Barbara Bray. New York: Columbia University Press, 1997.
Ruffing, Janet K., ed. *Mysticism and Social Transformation*. Syracuse, N.Y.: Syracuse University Press, 2001.
Ruh, Kurt. *Die Mystik des deutschen Predigerordens und ihre Grundlegung durch die Hochscholastik*. Vol. 3 of *Geschichte der abendländischen Mystik*. Munich: Beck, 1996.
———. *Meister Eckhart: Theologe, Prediger, Mystiker*. Munich: Beck, 1985.
Salih, Sara, and Judith Butler, eds. *The Judith Butler Reader*. Oxford: Basil Blackwell, 2004.
Sartre, Jean-Paul. *Being and Nothingess: An Essay on Phenomenological Ontology*. Translated by Hazel E. Barnes. London: Routledge, 1969.
Saxe, Rebecca. "Against Simulation: The Argument from Error." *Trends in Cognitive Sciences* 9, no. 4 (2005): 174–79.
Sayers, Janet. *Divine Therapy: Love, Mysticism, and Psychoanalysis*. Oxford; New York: Oxford University Press, 2003.
Schatzki, Theodore R. "Early Heidegger on Sociality." In *A Companion to Heidegger*, edited by Mark A. Wrathall and Hubert L. Dreyfus, 233–47. Oxford: Basil Blackwell, 2005.
Schlegel, August Wilhelm, and Friedrich Schlegel. *Athenaeum: Eine Zeitschrift, Photomechanical*. Reprint, vols. 1–3. Berlin / East: Rütten & Loening, 1960.
Schnitzler, Arthur. *Der Wegs ins Freie*. Frankfurt am Main: S. Fischer, 1990.

Schorske, Carl E. *Fin-de-Siècle Vienna: Politics and Culture.* Cambridge: Cambridge University Press, 1981.

Schroeder, H. J., ed. *Disciplinary Decrees of the General Councils.* London: Herder, 1937.

Schulz, Gerhard, ed. *Novalis Werke.* 2nd ed. Munich: Beck, 1981.

Schürmann, Reiner. "Heidegger and Meister Eckhart on Releasement." *Research in Phenomenology* 3 (1973): 95–119.

Schweighofer, Fritz. *Das Privattheater der Anna O.: Ein Emanzipationsdrama.* Munich: Ernst Reinhardt Verlag, 1987.

Schweitzer, Franz-Josef. *Der Freiheitsbegriff der deutschen Mystik: Seine Beziehung zur Ketzerei der "Brüder und Schwestern vom Freien Geist," mit besonderer Rücksicht auf den pseudoeckartischen Traktat "Schwester Katrei" (Edition).* Vol. 378 of *Europäische Hochschulschriften: Reihe I, Deutsche Sprache und Literatur.* Frankfurt am Main: Peter Lang, 1981.

Seemüller, Joseph, ed. *Ottokars Österreichische Reimchronik, nach den Abschriften Franz Liechtensteins.* 2 vols. Hanover: Hahnsche Buchhandlung, 1890–93.

Segl, Peter, ed. *Die Anfänge der Inquisition im Mittelalter.* Cologne: Böhlau, 1993.

Seigel, Jerrold E. *The Idea of the Self: Thought and Experience in Western Europe since the Seventeenth Century.* Cambridge: Cambridge University Press, 2005.

Seuse, Heinrich. *Das Buch der Wahrheit.* Edited by Loris Sturlese and Rüdiger Blumrich. Hamburg: Felix Meiner, 1993.

Shamdasani, Sonu. *Jung and the Making of Modern Psychology: The Dream of a Science.* Cambridge: Cambridge University Press, 2003.

———. "Misunderstanding Jung: The Afterlife of Legends." *Journal of Analytic Psychology* 45 (2000): 459–72.

Simons, Walter. *Cities of Ladies: Beguine Communities in the Medieval Low Countries, 1200–1565.* Philadelphia: University of Pennsylvania Press, 2002.

———. "The Beguine Movement in the Southern Low Countries: A Reassessment." *Bulletin de l'institut historique belge de Rom* 59 (1989): 63–105.

Singer, Tania. "The Neuronal Basis and Ontogeny of Empathy and Mind Reading: Review of Literature and Implications for Future Research." *Neuroscience and Biobehavioral Reviews* 30, no. 6 (2006): 855–63.

Skues, Richard A. *Sigmund Freud and the History of Anna O.: Re-opening a Closed Case.* Basingstoke: Palgrave Macmillan, 2006.

Smart, Barry, ed. *Michel Foucault: Critical Assessments.* 7 vols. London: Routledge, 1994.

Spitzer, Daniel. *Wiener Spaziergänge.* Edited by Walter Obermaier. Vol. 2. Vienna: Edition Wien, 1987.

Spörl, Uwe. "Mystisches Erleben, Leben und Schreiben um 1900: Überlegungen zu den Grenzen der Literaturwissenschaft." *KulturPoetik: Zeitschrift für Kulturgeschichtliche Literaturwissenschaft/Journal of Cultural Poetics* 1, no. 2 (2001): 214–30.

Stammler, Wolfgang, Karl Langosch, and Kurt Ruh, eds. *Die deutsche Literatur des Mittelalters: Verfasserlexikon.* 2 ed. Berlin: Walter de Gruyter, 1977–.

Steer, Georg. "Der Prozess Meister Eckharts und die Folgen." *Literaturwissenschaftliches Jahrbuch* 27 (1986): 47–64.

———. *Scholastische Gnadenlehre in mittelhochdeutscher Sprache.* Vol. 14 of *Münchener Texte und Untersuchungen zur deutschen Literatur des Mittelalters.* Munich: Beck, 1966.

Steer, Georg, and Loris Sturlese, eds. *Lectura Eckhardi: Predigten Meister Eckharts von Fachgelehrten gelesen und gedeutet.* Stuttgart: Kohlhammer, 1998–.

Stirnimann, Heinrich, and Ruedi Imbach, eds. *Eckardus theutonicus, homo doctus et sanctus: Nachweise und Berichte zum Prozeß gegen Meister Eckhart.* Freiburg, CH: Universitätsverlag, 1992.

Storr, Anthony, ed. *The Jung Reader.* London: Fontana, 1983.

Strauch, Philipp, ed. *Margaretha Ebner und Heinrich von Nördlingen: Ein Beitrag zur Geschichte der deutschen Mystik.* Freiburg i.B. / Tübingen: J. C. B. Mohr, 1882.

Strümpell, Adolf. "Dr. Jos. Breuer und Sigm. Freud, 'Studien über Hysterie.'" *Deutsche Zeitschrift für Nervenheilkunde* 8, nos. 1–2 (1895): 159–61.

Sturlese, Loris. *Die deutsche Philosophie im Mittelalter: Von Bonifacius bis zu Albert dem Großen.* Translated by Johanna Baumann. Munich: Beck, 1993.

Sulloway, Frank J. *Freud: Biologist of the Mind.* 2nd ed. Cambridge, Mass.: Harvard University Press, 1991.

———. "Reassessing Freud's Case Histories: The Social Construction of Psychoanalysis." *Isis* 82, no. 2 (1991): 245–75.

Swaan, Abraham de. "On the Sociogenesis of the Psychoanalytic Setting." In *Human Figurations: Essays for Norbert Elias*, edited by Peter R. Gleichmann, Johan Goudsblom, and Hermann Korte, 381–413. Amsterdam: Amsterdams Sociologisch Tijdschrift, 1977.

Taylor, Charles. *A Secular Age.* Cambridge, Mass.: Harvard University Press, 2007.

———. *Philosophy and the Human Sciences.* Cambridge: Cambridge University Press, 1985.

———. *Sources of the Self: The Making of the Modern Identity.* Cambridge: Cambridge University Press, 1989.

Taylor, Dianna, and Karen Vintges. *Feminism and the Final Foucault.* Urbana: University of Illinois Press, 2004.

Thompson, Bruce. *Schnitzler's Vienna: Image of a Society.* London: Routledge, 1990.

Trusen, Winfried. "Der Inquisitionsprozeß: Seine historischen Grundlagen und frühen Formen." *Zeitschrift der Savigny-Stiftung für Rechtsgeschichte* 105 (1988): 168–230.

———. *Der Prozeß gegen Meister Eckhart: Vorgeschichte, Verlauf und Folgen.* Paderborn: Ferdinand Schöningh, 1988.

Tully, James, and Daniel M. Weinstock, eds. *Philosophy in an Age of Pluralism: The Philosophy of Charles Taylor in Question.* Cambridge: Cambridge University Press, 1994.

Ueda, Shizuteru. *Die Gottesgeburt in der Seele und der Durchbruch zur Gottheit: Die Mystische Anthropologie Meister Eckharts und ihre Konfrontation mit der Mystik des Zen-Buddhismus*. Gütersloh: Mohn, 1965.

Verdeyen, Paul. "Le procès contre Marguerite Porete et Guiard de Cressonessart (1309–1310)." *Revue d'histoire ecclésiastique* 81 (1986): 47–94.

Vetter, Ferdinand, ed. *Das Leben der Schwestern zu Töß beschrieben von Elsbet Stagel samt der Vorrede von Johannes Meier und dem Leben der Prinzessin Elisabet von Ungarn*. Berlin: Weidmannsche Buchhandlung, 1906.

Vignemont, Frederique de, and Tania Singer. "The Empathic Brian: How, When, Why?" *Trends in Cognitive Sciences* 10, no. 10 (2006): 435–41.

Vries, Hent de, ed. *Religion: Beyond a Concept*. New York: Fordham University Press, 2008.

Wahrig, Gerhard. *Deutsches Wörterbuch*. Edited by Ursula Hermann, Renate Wahrig-Burfeind, Klaus Rüme, and Norbert Raum. 3rd ed. Munich: Mosaik Verlag, 1986.

Wakefield, Walter L., and Austin P. Evans, eds. *Heresies of the High Middle Ages*. New York: Columbia University Press, 1969.

Wallberg, Emil. *Wie der Wiener ein Gentleman wird: Zwölf Lectionen*. Vienna, 1860.

Watt, Diane, ed. *Medieval Women in Their Communities*. Cardiff: University of Wales Press, 1997.

Weber, Max. *The Protestant Ethic and the Spirit of Capitalism*. Translated by Talcott Parsons. New York: Scribner, 1958.

Webster, Richard. *Why Freud Was Wrong: Sin, Science, and Psychoanalysis*. London: HarperCollins, 1995.

Welte, Bernhard. *Meister Eckhart: Gedanken zu seinen Gedanken*. Freiburg: Herder, 1979.

Wenin, Christian, ed. *L'homme et son univers au moyen âge. Actes du septième congrès international de philosophie médiévale*. 2 vols. Louvain-la-Neuve: Éditions de l'institut supérieur de philosophie, 1986.

West, Candace, and Don H. Zimmerman. "Doing Gender." *Gender and Society* 1, no. 2 (1987): 125–51.

Whitmarsh, Tim. *Greek Literature and the Roman Empire: The Politics of Imitation*. Oxford; New York: Oxford University Press, 2001.

Williams, Lawrence E., Julie Y. Huang, and John A. Bargh. "The Scaffolded Mind: Higher Mental Processes Are Grounded in Early Experience of the Physical World." *European Journal of Social Psychology* 39 (2009): 1257–67.

Winckelmann, Johann Joachim. *Gedanken über die Nachahmung der griechischen Werke in der Malerei und Bildhauerkunst*. Stuttgart: Reclam, 1969.

Wingert, Lutz, and Klaus Günther. *Die Öffentlichkeit der Vernunft und die Vernunft der Öffentlichkeit: Festschrift für Jürgen Habermas*. Frankfurt am Main: Suhrkamp, 2001.

Winnicott, D. W. *Playing and Reality*. London: Routledge, 1989.

———. *The Child, the Family, and the Outside World.* Harmondsworth: Penguin Books, 1964.
———. *The Maturational Processes and the Facilitating Environment: Studies in the Theory of Emotional Development.* London: Karnac and the Institute of Psycho-Analysis, 1990.
———. *The Piggle: An Account of the Psychoanalytic Treatment of a Little Girl* Harmondsworth: Penguin, 1991.
Wittgenstein, Ludwig. *Lectures and Conversations on Aesthetics, Psychology, and Religious Belief.* Oxford: Basil Blackwell, 1966.
Woods, Richard. *Eckhart's Way.* London: Darton, Longman and Todd, 1986.
Wright, Georgia Sommers. "The Reinvention of the Portrait Likeness in the Fourteenth Century." *Gesta: International Center of Medieval Art* 39, no. 2 (2000): 117–34.
Young, Iris Marion. *On Female Body Experience: "Throwing Like a Girl" and Other Essays.* Oxford: Oxford University Press, 2005.
Zahavi, Dan. *Husserl and Transcendental Intersubjectivity: A Response to the Linguistic-Pragmatic Critique.* Translated by Elizabeth A. Behnke. Athens: Ohio University Press, 2001.
———. *Subjectivity and Selfhood: Investigating the First-Person Perspective.* Cambridge, Mass.: MIT Press, 2005.
Žižek, Slavoj. *How to Read Lacan.* London: Granta, 2006.
———. *Liebe deinen Nächsten? Nein, Danke: Die Sackgasse des Sozialen in der Postmoderne.* Berlin: Volk u. Welt, 1999.
———. "The Rhetorics of Power." *Diacritics* 31, no. 1 (2001): 91–104.
———. *The Sublime Object of Ideology.* London: Verso, 1989.
Žižek, Slavoj, ed. *Cogito and the Unconscious.* Durham, N.C.: Duke University Press, 1998.

Index

Perspectives in Continental Philosophy

John D. Caputo, series editor

John D. Caputo, ed., *Deconstruction in a Nutshell: A Conversation with Jacques Derrida.*

Michael Strawser, *Both/And: Reading Kierkegaard—From Irony to Edification.*

Michael D. Barber, *Ethical Hermeneutics: Rationality in Enrique Dussel's Philosophy of Liberation.*

James H. Olthuis, ed., *Knowing* Other-*wise: Philosophy at the Threshold of Spirituality.*

James Swindal, *Reflection Revisited: Jürgen Habermas's Discursive Theory of Truth.*

Richard Kearney, *Poetics of Imagining: Modern and Postmodern.* Second edition.

Thomas W. Busch, *Circulating Being: From Embodiment to Incorporation—Essays on Late Existentialism.*

Edith Wyschogrod, *Emmanuel Levinas: The Problem of Ethical Metaphysics.* Second edition.

Francis J. Ambrosio, ed., *The Question of Christian Philosophy Today.*

Jeffrey Bloechl, ed., *The Face of the Other and the Trace of God: Essays on the Philosophy of Emmanuel Levinas.*

Ilse N. Bulhof and Laurens ten Kate, eds., *Flight of the Gods: Philosophical Perspectives on Negative Theology.*

Trish Glazebrook, *Heidegger's Philosophy of Science.*

Kevin Hart, *The Trespass of the Sign: Deconstruction, Theology, and Philosophy.*

Mark C. Taylor, *Journeys to Selfhood: Hegel and Kierkegaard.* Second edition.

Dominique Janicaud, Jean-François Courtine, Jean-Louis Chrétien, Michel Henry, Jean-Luc Marion, and Paul Ricœur, *Phenomenology and the "Theological Turn": The French Debate.*

Karl Jaspers, *The Question of German Guilt.* Introduction by Joseph W. Koterski, S.J.
Jean-Luc Marion, *The Idol and Distance: Five Studies.* Translated with an introduction by Thomas A. Carlson.
Jeffrey Dudiak, *The Intrigue of Ethics: A Reading of the Idea of Discourse in the Thought of Emmanuel Levinas.*
Robyn Horner, *Rethinking God as Gift: Marion, Derrida, and the Limits of Phenomenology.*
Mark Dooley, *The Politics of Exodus: Søren Kierkegaard's Ethics of Responsibility.*
Merold Westphal, *Overcoming Onto-Theology: Toward a Postmodern Christian Faith.*
Edith Wyschogrod, Jean-Joseph Goux, and Eric Boynton, eds., *The Enigma of Gift and Sacrifice.*
Stanislas Breton, *The Word and the Cross.* Translated with an introduction by Jacquelyn Porter.
Jean-Luc Marion, *Prolegomena to Charity.* Translated by Stephen E. Lewis.
Peter H. Spader, *Scheler's Ethical Personalism: Its Logic, Development, and Promise.*
Jean-Louis Chrétien, *The Unforgettable and the Unhoped For.* Translated by Jeffrey Bloechl.
Don Cupitt, *Is Nothing Sacred? The Non-Realist Philosophy of Religion: Selected Essays.*
Jean-Luc Marion, *In Excess: Studies of Saturated Phenomena.* Translated by Robyn Horner and Vincent Berraud.
Phillip Goodchild, *Rethinking Philosophy of Religion: Approaches from Continental Philosophy.*
William J. Richardson, S.J., *Heidegger: Through Phenomenology to Thought.*
Jeffrey Andrew Barash, *Martin Heidegger and the Problem of Historical Meaning.*
Jean-Louis Chrétien, *Hand to Hand: Listening to the Work of Art.* Translated by Stephen E. Lewis.
Jean-Louis Chrétien, *The Call and the Response.* Translated with an introduction by Anne Davenport.
D. C. Schindler, *Han Urs von Balthasar and the Dramatic Structure of Truth: A Philosophical Investigation.*
Julian Wolfreys, ed., *Thinking Difference: Critics in Conversation.*
Allen Scult, *Being Jewish/Reading Heidegger: An Ontological Encounter.*
Richard Kearney, *Debates in Continental Philosophy: Conversations with Contemporary Thinkers.*
Jennifer Anna Gosetti-Ferencei, *Heidegger, Hölderlin, and the Subject of Poetic Language: Towards a New Poetics of Dasein.*
Jolita Pons, *Stealing a Gift: Kierkegaard's Pseudonyms and the Bible.*
Jean-Yves Lacoste, *Experience and the Absolute: Disputed Questions on the Humanity of Man.* Translated by Mark Raftery-Skehan.
Charles P. Bigger, *Between* Chora *and the Good: Metaphor's Metaphysical Neighborhood.*

Dominique Janicaud, *Phenomenology "Wide Open": After the French Debate.* Translated by Charles N. Cabral.

Ian Leask and Eoin Cassidy, eds., *Givenness and God: Questions of Jean-Luc Marion.*

Jacques Derrida, *Sovereignties in Question: The Poetics of Paul Celan.* Edited by Thomas Dutoit and Outi Pasanen.

William Desmond, *Is There a Sabbath for Thought? Between Religion and Philosophy.*

Bruce Ellis Benson and Norman Wirzba, eds., *The Phenomenology of Prayer.*

S. Clark Buckner and Matthew Statler, eds., *Styles of Piety: Practicing Philosophy after the Death of God.*

Kevin Hart and Barbara Wall, eds., *The Experience of God: A Postmodern Response.*

John Panteleimon Manoussakis, *After God: Richard Kearney and the Religious Turn in Continental Philosophy.*

John Martis, *Philippe Lacoue-Labarthe: Representation and the Loss of the Subject.*

Jean-Luc Nancy, *The Ground of the Image.*

Edith Wyschogrod, *Crossover Queries: Dwelling with Negatives, Embodying Philosophy's Others.*

Gerald Bruns, *On the Anarchy of Poetry and Philosophy: A Guide for the Unruly.*

Brian Treanor, *Aspects of Alterity: Levinas, Marcel, and the Contemporary Debate.*

Simon Morgan Wortham, *Counter-Institutions: Jacques Derrida and the Question of the University.*

Leonard Lawlor, *The Implications of Immanence: Toward a New Concept of Life.*

Clayton Crockett, *Interstices of the Sublime: Theology and Psychoanalytic Theory.*

Bettina Bergo, Joseph Cohen, and Raphael Zagury-Orly, eds., *Judeities: Questions for Jacques Derrida.* Translated by Bettina Bergo and Michael B. Smith.

Jean-Luc Marion, *On the Ego and on God: Further Cartesian Questions.* Translated by Christina M. Gschwandtner.

Jean-Luc Nancy, *Philosophical Chronicles.* Translated by Franson Manjali.

Jean-Luc Nancy, *Dis-Enclosure: The Deconstruction of Christianity.* Translated by Bettina Bergo, Gabriel Malenfant, and Michael B. Smith.

Andrea Hurst, *Derrida Vis-à-vis Lacan: Interweaving Deconstruction and Psychoanalysis.*

Jean-Luc Nancy, *Noli me tangere: On the Raising of the Body.* Translated by Sarah Clift, Pascale-Anne Brault, and Michael Naas.

Jacques Derrida, *The Animal That Therefore I Am.* Edited by Marie-Louise Mallet, translated by David Wills.

Jean-Luc Marion, *The Visible and the Revealed.* Translated by Christina M. Gschwandtner and others.

Michel Henry, *Material Phenomenology.* Translated by Scott Davidson.

Jean-Luc Nancy, *Corpus.* Translated by Richard A. Rand.

Joshua Kates, *Fielding Derrida.*

Michael Naas, *Derrida From Now On.*

Shannon Sullivan and Dennis J. Schmidt, eds., *Difficulties of Ethical Life.*

Catherine Malabou, *What Should We Do with Our Brain?* Translated by Sebastian Rand, Introduction by Marc Jeannerod.

Claude Romano, *Event and World*. Translated by Shane Mackinlay.

Vanessa Lemm, *Nietzsche's Animal Philosophy: Culture, Politics, and the Animality of the Human Being.*

B. Keith Putt, ed., *Gazing Through a Prism Darkly: Reflections on Merold Westphal's Hermeneutical Epistemology.*

Eric Boynton and Martin Kavka, eds., *Saintly Influence: Edith Wyschogrod and the Possibilities of Philosophy of Religion.*

Shane Mackinlay, *Interpreting Excess: Jean-Luc Marion, Saturated Phenomena, and Hermeneutics.*

Kevin Hart and Michael A. Signer, eds., *The Exorbitant: Emmanuel Levinas Between Jews and Christians.*

Bruce Ellis Benson and Norman Wirzba, eds., *Words of Life: New Theological Turns in French Phenomenology.*

William Robert, *Trials: Of Antigone and Jesus.*

Brian Treanor and Henry Isaac Venema, eds., *A Passion for the Possible: Thinking with Paul Ricoeur.*

Kas Saghafi, *Apparitions—Of Derrida's Other.*

Nick Mansfield, *The God Who Deconstructs Himself: Sovereignty and Subjectivity Between Freud, Bataille, and Derrida.*

Don Ihde, *Heidegger's Technologies: Postphenomenological Perspectives.*

Françoise Dastur, *Questioning Phenomenology*. Translated by Robert Vallier.

Suzi Adams, *Castoriadis's Ontology: Being and Creation.*

Richard Kearney and Kascha Semonovitch, eds., *Phenomenologies of the Stranger: Between Hostility and Hospitality.*

Michael Naas, *Miracle and Machine: Jacques Derrida and the Two Sources of Religion, Science, and the Media.*

Alena Alexandrova, Ignaas Devisch, Laurens ten Kate, and Aukje van Rooden, *Re-treating Religion: Deconstructing Christianity with Jean-Luc Nancy*. Preamble by Jean-Luc Nancy.

Emmanuel Falque, *The Metamorphosis of Finitude: An Essay on Birth and Resurrection*. Translated by George Hughes.

Scott M. Campbell, *The Early Heidegger's Philosophy of Life: Facticity, Being, and Language.*

Françoise Dastur, *How Are We to Confront Death? An Introduction to Philosophy.* Translated by Robert Vallier. Foreword by David Farrell Krell.

Christina M. Gschwandtner, *Postmodern Apologetics? Arguments for God in Contemporary Philosophy.*

Ben Morgan, *On Becoming God: Late Medieval Mysticism and the Modern Western Self.*